Edinburgh University Library

Books may be recalled for return earlier than du
if so you will be contacted by e-mail or letter.

D1758361

Due Date	Due Date	

30150 021405334

Collaboration and Resistance in Occupied France

Also by Christopher Lloyd

J.K. HUYSMANS AND THE FIN-DE-SIÈCLE NOVEL

MIRBEAU'S FICTIONS

Collaboration and Resistance in Occupied France

Representing Treason and Sacrifice

Christopher Lloyd

EDINBURGH UNIVERSITY LIBRARY

WITHDRAWN

palgrave
macmillan

© Christopher Lloyd 2003

All rights reserved. No reproduction, copy or transmission of this publication may be made without written permission.

No paragraph of this publication may be reproduced, copied or transmitted save with written permission or in accordance with the provisions of the Copyright, Designs and Patents Act 1988, or under the terms of any licence permitting limited copying issued by the Copyright Licensing Agency, 90 Tottenham Court Road, London W1T 4LP.

Any person who does any unauthorised act in relation to this publication may be liable to criminal prosecution and civil claims for damages.

The author has asserted his right to be identified as the author of this work in accordance with the Copyright, Designs and Patents Act 1988.

First published 2003 by
PALGRAVE MACMILLAN
Houndmills, Basingstoke, Hampshire RG21 6XS and
175 Fifth Avenue, New York, N. Y. 10010
Companies and representatives throughout the world

PALGRAVE MACMILLAN is the global academic imprint of the Palgrave Macmillan division of St. Martin's Press, LLC and of Palgrave Macmillan Ltd. Macmillan® is a registered trademark in the United States, United Kingdom and other countries. Palgrave is a registered trademark in the European Union and other countries.

ISBN 1–4039–2031–1

This book is printed on paper suitable for recycling and made from fully managed and sustained forest sources.

A catalogue record for this book is available from the British Library.

Library of Congress Cataloging-in-Publication Data
Lloyd, Christopher, 1953–
    Collaboration and Resistance in occupied France : representing treason and sacrifice / by Christopher Lloyd.
       p. cm.
    Includes filmography
    Includes bibliographical references and index.
    ISBN 1–4039–2031–1 (cloth)
       1. World War, 1939–1945—Underground movements—France.
    2. France—History—German occupation, 1940–1945—Collaborationists.
    I. Title.

    D802.F8L5725 2003
    940.53'44—dc21
                                                          2003050890

10   9   8   7   6   5   4   3   2   1
12   11   10   09   08   07   06   05   04   03

Printed and bound in Great Britain by
Antony Rowe Ltd, Chippenham and Eastbourne

Contents

Preface

Chapter six of Joseph Kessel's novel *L'Armée des ombres* (1943), entitled 'Une veillée de l'âge hitlérien' (a vigil in the age of Hitler) opens with a German sentry peering through the spyhole in a prison cell which contains seven members of the French resistance, whose sentence of execution is to be carried out the following morning. The sentry briefly notes their apparently fearless demeanour, wonders how he would behave in similar circumstances and what they have done to deserve such a fate, before dismissing such speculations and returning to his round. As we might well expect from a novel which sets out to celebrate the heroic struggle of those who resist totalitarian oppression, the remaining twelve pages of the chapter take us into the cell and show us its inmates, offering us the understanding and insight which the sentry failed to achieve. In the following chapter, we witness the execution of all but one of the prisoners; Gerbier, the central character in the novel, manages to escape from the German machine gunners thanks to an almost miraculous chain of events.

Such episodes and characters are of course fictional, yet since they also occurred to real people on innumerable occasions during the German occupation of France (as Kessel reminds us forcefully in the preface to his novel, even if few achieved Gerbier's last-minute escape from death), most readers will interpret them not only as a dramatic (perhaps melodramatic) re-enactment of actual historical events but as an attempt to recreate the psychology and mentality of resistance, to offer us the vicarious experience of others' emotions and motives which we generally expect from novelists. Historians of the resistance also recount such incidents, but usually from a perspective closer to that of Kessel's sentry: violent drama and subjective experience are normally excluded from accounts which read like laconic statements of risks and casualties noted by a sort of historical loss adjuster. The twenty-two pages that Kessel devotes to his fictional execution are typically reduced in historical narratives to a few paragraphs or indeed a few lines. Thus François-Georges Dreyfus writes, in his *Histoire de la résistance* (1996: 59): 'As early as January 1941, M. Nordmann was arrested, then in February Levitsky, Boris Vildé ... On 23 February 1942, they were executed at Mont-Valérien.'

F.-G. Dreyfus notes that Vildé's prison diary was published posthumously, but apparently feels no obligation to quote from it; Vildé's thoughts and feelings play no part in his broader and more distanced chronicle of resistance, although we might wonder whether such exclusion of the personal and the tragic does not in practice severely impede a meaningful comprehension of resistance. We might contrast the dispassionate neutrality characteristic of the post-war historian, who simply records the betrayal, trial and death of the resisters associated with the Musée de l'Homme as a series of factual events showing the dangers of resistance, with the version of their execution recorded a few days after it occurred by a contemporary observer like the diarist Jean Guéhenno:

> They were warned on the Monday morning that they would be shot. Vildé saw his wife in the morning and had the strength to tell her nothing. In the afternoon, they were taken from Fresnes prison to Mont-Valérien. They drove across Paris crowded in a lorry with their guards. They were singing. Each man had a piece of white paper pinned over his heart and they were killed almost at point blank range. Vildé, as he had requested, was executed last. (Guéhenno, 1973: 243)

Guéhenno's account is also second-hand and emotionally distanced, but each act and gesture that he describes is clearly invested with a significance that stresses the tragic, moral grandeur of resistance. Death seems to be a certain outcome, but at least it can be faced with dignity and patriotic solidarity, so that it acquires a certain exemplary value rather than seeming a futile sacrifice. Such examples show how the immediacy and symbolic force achieved by the diarist and novelist offer an insight into historical experience which are denied to most historians by the generic boundaries they respect.[1]

The general purpose of this book is to study the ways in which people who lived through the occupation of France by the Germans from 1940 to 1944 recorded and represented their experiences. More specifically, the intention is to investigate the concepts of treason and sacrifice, since these are closely related to the three choices which were effectively available to most of the French population: active resistance against the Germans and eventually against the French government based in Vichy which supported the Germans; active collaboration with the Germans and the Vichy government; or a more passive acceptance of the evolving social and political circumstances brought about by the war and occupation, a form of behaviour known in French as *attentisme*, a term which effectively encapsulates a reluctance to commit oneself to any cause or course of action which does not offer immediate personal advantage. Resistance, collaboration and *attentisme* are of course familiar historical phenomena, even if the third category usually attracts far less attention than the first two (the inglorious norm of selfish opportunism is no doubt less appealing and less influential than the more exceptional and far more dangerous commitment to oppose or serve the occupying forces and their puppet government). It is less commonly realised that these phenomena are almost invariably perceived and judged in terms of betrayal and sacrifice, that is in terms of the willingness and ability of individuals and groups to adopt forms of behaviour which either destroy or reinforce the key values which are deemed to be essential to the nation's survival, unity and identity, if necessary at the cost of their own liberty or existence.

Both resisters and collaborators were and continue to be judged, during and after the occupation, either literally by their political adversaries in a legal forum, or in a more abstract moral fashion by historians and other commentators. When they are prosecuted, the usual accusation is some form of betrayal in the case of those deemed to have transgressed against accepted codes (whether the hierarchy of military discipline, the integrity of the nation, or the sanctity of humanity). Those held up for admiration as models of heroic virtues, on the other hand, usually sacrificed their fortune, reputation, liberty, or frequently their existence, on behalf of a greater, collective good (at least in the view of their supporters; for their adversaries, they are fanatics, terrorists or dupes). In fact, there is no simple dichotomy between heroic resisters and treasonable collaborators; nor for that matter is it merely a question of opposing sides levelling similar charges against each other. Admittedly, General de Gaulle was condemned to death by a military tribunal operating under the Vichy regime in August 1940, while with appropriate ironic symmetry the High Court of Justice set up by de Gaulle's provisional government sentenced Marshal Pétain to death in August 1945.[2] But Pétain, who famously offered the sacrifice of his person to the nation on adopting the role of head of state in 1940, can be perceived as either hero or traitor (as the subtitle of Lottman's 1985 biography reminds us). At the same time, many members of the resistance were accused and sometimes convicted of criminal or treasonable acts, not just by their ideological opponents but also by their own side; betrayal is in fact one of the constant defining features of resistance, whether through dissidence, venality, duplicity or desperation. Nor, for that matter, is the identification and separation of resisters and collaborators necessarily straightforward, as three famous examples demonstrate: President François Mitterrand worked as a junior administrator for Vichy in 1942–43 and was rewarded for his efforts with the *Francisque*, a decoration reserved for Marshal Pétain's favourites, although by the time he received it he had already switched his allegiance to active resistance (at great personal risk, since those of his associates who were captured faced deportation and death). The Vichy police chief René Bousquet (a post-war friend of Mitterrand's) was directly responsible during the same period for implementing the arrest and internment of thousands of Jews, the first stages in deportation and genocide.[3] Yet at his trial in June 1949, he was acquitted after a hearing lasting only three days on charges relating to treason and intelligence with the enemy, his contacts with the resistance and assistance to individual victims of persecution counting in his defence; he was charged with crimes against humanity only in March 1991 and assassinated in June 1993 before the case had come to trial. Maurice Papon, on the other hand, who, like Bousquet, as a senior administrative official was directly involved in anti-Semitic persecution on a large scale in the Bordeaux region, was finally sentenced to ten years' imprisonment for complicity in crimes against humanity after a trial prolonged over many months in 1997–98, despite the support of some members of the resistance whom he too had assisted.[4]

The aim of historical enquiry is to discover essential facts about past events and interpret them in a coherent narrative form so that they can be understood and judged by the present. Yet such cases show how problematic this can be in practice: the overlapping boundaries between resistance and collaboration mean that it was quite possible to move from one activity to the other, or even combine both to a greater or lesser extent. And however much the historian may strive for objectivity, moral judgements remain inseparable from the investigation of acts that could cause hundreds or thousands of deaths. The belated trial of Papon (and his subsequent release in 2002 on compassionate grounds), half a century after his crimes and at the end of his brilliant post-war career as police chief and government minister, seems a bizarre history lesson which reveals the continuing obsession with the national shame and guilt of collaboration and urge to rewrite the story and history of the occupation years in a more honourable fashion. Does the nation seek to make heroes or traitors out of figures whose virtues and vices are mainly retrospective fictional and ideological projections? Is this because heroism and treason are equally a mythified construction of the collective imagination? How do literary and cultural representations of resistance, collaboration and occupation determine our historical understanding of the period? My aim is to explore these and related questions by studying a corpus of material relating to significant cultural and literary manifestations: novels, memoirs, speeches and films. The book takes the form of an introductory overview of historical and methodological issues, followed by contextualised case studies in the areas of politics, civil administration, military action, literature and cinema.[5] The figures studied are chosen not only because of their representative or even iconic nature but also because most of them left a record expressing their own vision of the occupation.

References to sources used are normally given in abbreviated form in the text, with full details provided in the bibliography in the case of works which are central to this study. To save space and avoid unnecessary duplication, material of a more peripheral nature cited in the endnotes or briefly mentioned in the text does not usually figure in the bibliography. The publication dates of primary sources given in the notes and bibliography are those of the edition actually cited or consulted; original dates of publication are indicated in the text when this is helpful. Individual contributions to collective works are normally referenced is the bibliography under the name of the main editor of the volume in question. English translations are my own, unless indicated otherwise. Readers should note that initial capital letters are reserved for proper names, ranks, titles and organisations (for example, General de Gaulle, Communist Party), whereas historical events and phenomena are spelt in lower case (for example, liberation, resistance). Finally, heartfelt thanks are due to the British Academy and Durham University for providing financial support and research leave, as well as to colleagues and students with whom I have fruitfully discussed the ideas contained in this book over a period of years.

1
Understanding and Representing the Occupation

Representations

In the first instance, it is important to clarify more fully the facts, concepts and judgements which determine the context of this study and our understanding of the occupation and its consequences. There is no intention of providing a broad factual survey of the sort already to be found in excellent books such as Julian Jackson's *France: the Dark Years* (2001), Azéma's *De Munich à la Libération* (1979) and Ousby's *Occupation* (1999). It is however necessary to highlight certain key events and acts which effectively influence any form of reflection on the period, in other words to outline the spaces, places, dates, conflicts, groups, organisms and figures which make up the history of resistance and collaboration, as well as the choices, attitudes and opinions which drive judgements about the veracity or rightness of particular acts and decisions. Before turning to specific topics related to resistance, collaboration and liberation, it is useful to examine some broader issues of a methodological sort, which are partly formal (relating to historiography and the historical acceptability of certain genres) and partly ethical and moral (most books on the Second World War usually rest on assumptions about good and evil, right and wrong, even if their authors do not always make their views explicit).

If one is writing about memoirs, novels and films because of the fascinating things they have to tell us about war and occupation, perceiving them as social documents as much as aesthetic forms, one needs to determine what their status and value are as representations of historical events. There is no simple answer to this question, although there are several unsatisfactory solutions which vary in subtlety and persuasiveness: the crudest or most naive would no doubt

1

be to treat literary and artistically created texts as one would other historical documents, rather in the fashion of a medieval chronicler, making little or no distinction between fact or fiction, myth and reality, or their intended purpose or audience. It is in fact likely that most people's grasp of history is precisely just such an odd blend of fact and fancy, legend and propaganda, as conveyed in most Hollywood movies that purport to deal, say, with the Middle Ages, and the pedagogic variety of which is amusingly parodied in such classic works as Sellar and Yeatman's *1066 and All That* (1930).[1] The purpose of the serious study of history (whether in the classroom, cinema or books) is to disentangle such nonsense and achieve some verifiably objective and consensual knowledge within the constraints of the chosen medium. The obvious need to distinguish between genres and purposes does not mean of course that a novel is necessarily any less informative or veracious than, say, a work of history or diplomatic memorandum (there are plenty of tendentious and duplicitous history books about the occupation and most other subjects).

A variant but not dissimilar approach, which is however rather more disingenuous and possibly beguiling, might be called extreme postmodernism, that is the denial that there is any such thing as historical truth and the consequent assertion that all genres are equally valid or invalid.[2] Neither statement is true, in my opinion, however elusive or partial any version of the truth may be in practice. In fact, the most satisfactory answer is likely to be obtained by widening the question to refer to all forms of historical writing. Here two statements by Hayden White (1999: 1, 4) usefully delineate the goal and limitations of the method: 'historical discourse is possible only on the presumption of the existence of the past as something about which it is possible to speak meaningfully', and 'every history is first and foremost a verbal artifact'. Or as Conan and Rousso put it, in their book on France's failure to come to terms with Vichy, historians 'cannot describe "what happened", but only reconstitute by means of the evidence available a plausible order of events which has some meaning for their contemporaries' (1994: 159). Truth is discursively constructed, but some reconstructions are more truthful and useful than others. Useful, in an ethical and civic sense. As these two authors suggest, the citizen needs truth and certainty about the past, however subject to revision such notions may be. In his study of the modes of production of historical works, *L'Histoire sous surveillance*, Marc Ferro sums up the diverse and possibly conflicting aims of historical enquiry as consolidating the unity of the nation and the legitimacy of the state, seeking the 'truth' about the past, restoring the identity of particular communities, or helping citizens understand the mechanisms of economic and political life (1985: 11). Given the political and ideological constraints which such goals imply, he notes that literary writing or imaginary productions can often get round topics which remain forbidden to 'the discourses on the real' practised by historians (p. 67).[3]

In fact, one could argue that many novels that deal with social and political issues set out to fulfil very similar ideological goals to those outlined by Ferro (for example, Joseph Kessel's *L'Armée des ombres* was written in 1943 to promote and legitimise the struggle of the resistance). What most obviously distinguishes fictional production from historical reconstruction is its ability to recreate the immediacy of first-hand, lived experience through imaginary narrative. Historians who view the imaginary as being in opposition to the real are understandably reluctant to accept novels and feature films as legitimate sources. Yet novels and films about World War Two or any other historical event are obviously produced within the same general framework of historical reflection, even if they are not apparently subject to the same criteria of verifiability as historical writing. In practice, while historical fictions may not have to rely explicitly on documented and verifiable sources in the fashion of academic history books, their success is usually perceived in terms of criteria such as plausibility, authenticity, honesty; the invention of a story does not automatically remove any obligation to respect the events of history or legitimise mendacious or tendentious interpretations of the past. Success in this context means their ability to fulfil the didactic intention implicit in the choice of subject, that is to contribute to historical understanding, rather than merely achieve popularity with a wide public. Such success may be limited, since most feature films are obviously driven more by commercial imperatives than disinterested scientific enquiry and tend to rehearse familiar myths and conventional stereotypes. The same observation can be applied to the profusion of mediocre novels about the war, which are often clichéd adventure stories, violent entertainments offering the vicarious consolation of past triumphs to readers who live in more mundane times.[4] But whatever the limitations of such works, the myths and clichés that they endlessly recycle themselves merit examination, since our perceptions of the past, of national identity and virtues, are often unwittingly shaped by them.

While factual distortion and biased interpretations should always be pointed out and condemned, whether in academic histories or popular novels, and the excellent distinguished from the mediocre, it seems misguided simply because of its problematic nature to ignore or dismiss the vast production of cultural material stimulated by World War Two. Its very quantity makes it a phenomenon both remarkable and often unexplored. In the literary sphere, between novels and history books lies the intermediate genre of memoirs, journals and autobiography, which supposedly combine the personal immediacy of fiction with the obligations to objectivity of history writing. In practice, the distinction between all three genres is often blurred: novels sometimes prove to be disguised autobiographies, while Thibaudet famously summed up autobiography as 'the novel for those who can't be novelists' (quoted by Lejeune, 1971: 9). The self-justifying memoir which judiciously reinterprets the facts in the author's favour is a frequent phenomenon in writing on the war, the most notorious example being Albert's Speer's *Inside the Third Reich* (lesser-known examples relevant to the occupation of France could be cited by Heller, 1981; Guitry, 1947; and Jamet, 1947).[5] Since the author's persuasiveness may be a measure of his or her literary success rather than his honesty, the reader has to approach such works far more sceptically as historical documents.

However, a similar warning has to be sounded about works which purport to be objective historical studies, particularly those written by protagonists in the drama of resistance or by defenders of collaboration. Many of the early histories of the resistance were personal testimonies written by survivors who sought to glorify their activities 'in epic mode', as Azéma and Bédarida observe in an essay on 'L'Historisation de la Résistance' (*Esprit*, 1994: 19); their patriotic authority initially made it difficult to challenge their failings as historians. Much the same can be said of early studies of collaboration, as practised by Pétain and Vichy, which tend to elaborate on the defence enunciated at Pétain's trial, namely that the Marshal and his régime sought to shield most of their citizens, perhaps by sacrificing a few outsiders, and that their war of attrition against German demands was itself a form of resistance. To sustain this thesis, inconvenient facts showing the immense scale of sacrifices entailed by collaboration have to be toned down or omitted. In the case of actively pro-German collaborationists, systematic denial of knowledge (or sometimes the reality) of Nazi atrocities is usually linked with virulent anti-communism (the Soviet Union and its acolytes are seen as the most dangerous foe). Authors like Christian de La Mazière and Marc Augier, who wrote enthusiastic accounts of their engagement in the French division of the Waffen SS, create their own form of epic, celebrating the bloody virtues of the warrior caste, scornful of politicians and their double-dealing, courageously ready for any sacrifice, while skirting over the fact that their 'sacrifice' frequently involved the mass murder of defenceless civilians. Augier (1908–90) produced a stream of books under the pseudonym 'Saint-Loup', such as *Les Hérétiques* (1965), which he claims to be a work of history dressed in the more readable garb of fiction: over 500 pages, much of them cast in dialogue form, he celebrates the final struggle of the Waffen SS, whose adventures are skilfully limited to the immediate heroism of combat against overwhelming odds and whose ethics are limited to loyalty to comrades.

Yet such works are of immense interest, provided one does not accept them at face value and takes due account of factual error, omission and bias. Personal testimony and fictional reconstruction are indispensable to historical understanding; indeed, there are many aspects of war and occupation that can be understood *only* through works that attempt to convey subjective experience. Writing about the First World War, J. Norton Cru (1967) observed that the strategic and political history written by most professional historians completely failed to convey the daily horrors of front-line combat which countless memorialists and novelists had recounted far more effectively. Official history writing, with its preference for abstract general categories and reliance on official documents derived from states and governments, too often produces a bloodless reality, even when dealing with a bloody business like war.[6] Academic historians in particular often show an impressive mastery of technical details in a relatively narrow area, such as, say, the history of a particular resistance movement or the civil service under Vichy; but their works rarely if ever attempt to evoke the material and psychological reality that faced the individual resister or civil servant, although, as Daniel Cordier remarks, such personal elements 'are invaluable in evoking the affective nature of an event or the poetic aura of a period' (1989: 299). If one wants to learn in any detail about the experience of torture, the motivation of collaborators, the callousness of bureaucrats, the survival skills needed to be a clandestine agent, the attractiveness or brutality of Germans, one needs to turn to autobiographical writing and fiction, though all these examples are obviously central to any understanding of the effects of occupation.

The conventional distinction between genres, which effectively contrasts and separates fact and fiction, the literary and the literal, the imaginary and the scientific, tends to imply a scale of historical relevance and informativeness (as opposed to, say, entertainment value or aesthetic merit) which breaks down in practice, insofar as a good novel on the resistance may tell us a great deal more than a timorously narrow monograph. As has already been suggested, our knowledge of the past hardly breaks down into discrete categories. The vast range of cultural productions related to the Second World War (from books and films to museums and monuments) perpetuates a version of the past which depends as much on myth-making, folk memory, and ideological projections as it does on scientific historical enquiry limited to objectively verifiable facts. Myth, memory and ideology are sometimes placed in opposition to history, in that they are seen to involve wilful distortion of past events for the benefit of particular individuals or groups who place their own interests in the centre of their version of the past. The opponents of such groups usually claim a monopoly on historical truth which seems equally partial. Thus René Fallas writes in his preface to Gérard Chauvy's book *Aubrac Lyon 1943* that 'Resistance is not a myth, but mythomaniacs of resistance and their sycophantic supporters are legion' (Chauvy, 1997: iii). In fact, Chauvy's attempt to cast doubts on the authenticity of the Aubracs' resistance activities cost him large sums in libel damages (despite the belated admission on page 267 that there was no real evidence to justify his innuendoes against them).

As Angus Calder argues more convincingly in *The Myth of the Blitz*, it is misleading to use myth pejoratively or dismissively, as a synonym for historical untruth, when it is itself a historical phenomenon, an inevitable part of the process of historical interpretation and revision, which usually produces a simplified account involving the exaggeration of some events and the omission of others (thus the genocide of the Jews can be either excluded from the history of Vichy or alternatively made into the central crime committed by the regime).[7] Myths contain 'parahistory', to use K.K. Ruthven's (1976) term, that is, what people believe happened in the past as part of their effort to find order in the present. In the political domain, myths are narratives which serve the eminently practical purpose of explaining past events in order to reinforce the authority of present holders of power (such as the October Revolution for Stalin, Aryanism for the Nazis or resistance for de Gaulle's provisional government).[8] Memory too is a central element in what John Keegan dubs *The Battle for History* (1997), a study of the major controversies in the historiography of World War Two. Those who are forgotten tend to disappear entirely from history; hence Hitler's notorious observation 'No one remembers the Armenians', whose fate offered a grim rehearsal for the final solution of the Jewish problem.[9]

Memory is indispensable but also subjective and selective, as most honest memorialists admit. Thus Raymond Aubrac (1996: 34) prefaces his memoirs with the warning statement:

> I have probably forgotten painful incidents, for individual memory – like collective memory, where examples also come to mind – is organised so as to suppress events whose memory would be difficult to tolerate. In fact, this is a condition of survival.

Robert Frank defines group memory as 'collective subjectivity and ... its relationship to the past' (in Azéma and Bédarida, 1993: 485–6) and, like many historians, offers examples of its tendency to observe the past through a selective filter which removes unwanted elements (thus official histories tone down the discreditable acts committed by the Vichy regime and exaggerate the extent of support for the resistance).[10] An alternative tendency, usually found in the works of anti-establishment journalists and other writers, involves addition rather than subtraction, that is overstating the complicity or villainy of political leaders and state-controlled organisms in abetting or committing atrocities and war crimes; here the individual seeks the moral superiority of denying his or her membership of a group that claims to act on his behalf, while simultaneously attributing a level of foresight and responsibility to those whose actions are criticised that is out of all proportion to the facts as they were understood at the time when decisions were made. Thus the British government has been criticised both for admitting large numbers of Ukrainian SS members to the UK after the end of the war (and thereby sparing them prosecution and persecution in the USSR), yet also for handing back large numbers of Cossacks and other Nazi collaborators to the Soviet authorities. The journalist Christopher Booker has produced a compelling account of the controversy surrounding the case of these enforced repatriations, noting that, although the accusations of complicity in crimes against humanity made against Harold Macmillan and other British officials are not substantiated by close factual investigation and have been rejected in a notorious libel trial, nevertheless the interpretation which discredits the British establishment continues to be cited not only in the media but also by reputable historians like Norman Davies.[11]

The facts of such tragic incidents fall outside the scope of this book, although the urge of commentators to present the events so as to create culprits for moral retribution, with the ensuing drama being enacted as much in the courtroom and media as in the archive or monograph, is clearly paralleled by the twists and turns of the 'Vichy syndrome' in France.[12] Booker's conclusion is however directly relevant to the study of history and fiction, since his argument is that a complex episode has been reduced to sensationalist semi-fiction, and that this is an unavoidable temptation:

> The real problem with history is precisely the fact that it is telling a story. Stories deal in conflict, with heroes and villains, seeing the world in terms of light and dark. When we come to write history, it is this power of the storyteller's imagination which inevitably to some extent takes over, as we pick out from all the complex and confused accumulation of data those pieces of evidence which allow the story to be told in a clear, manageable and meaningful fashion. (1997: 439–40)

The history of the Second World War in particular has long been subject to fictional manipulation: indeed, myth-making was an essential part of the propaganda war, with deception and illusion forming much of the public appearance of things. Hence Paul Fussell's assertion in his book on understanding and behaviour in the war that 'Living in wartime thus resembled living in a play, with nothing real or certain' (1989: 47). His central argument is that 'For the past fifty years the Allied war has been sanitized and romanticized almost beyond recognition' (p. ix) and that this failure of representation makes it not merely a political catastrophe but also 'a perceptual and rhetorical scandal' (p. 115). The reality conveyed during wartime was largely a 'heroic fiction'; while the public remained unaware of the horrors of death and injuries suffered by combatants, the media and war correspondents nevertheless had considerable power in sustaining a 'plausible public narrative' which did not invariably involve censoring negative elements (thus Patton's notorious soldier-slapping was revealed by the press because Eisenhower refused to dismiss him). Fiction itself, in Fussell's opinion, rarely deals adequately with the 'drab culture of anonymity and uniformity' typical of wartime (p. 70) or the random nature of death and survival, since novels normally present exceptional individualists and need to exhibit plot and pace and fulfil moral expectations. A better source is found in the clandestine diaries (forbidden in theatres of war) which 'offer one of the most promising accesses to actuality' (p. 291). He cites E.B. Sledge's *With the Old Breed* (1981) as an outstanding example dealing with front-line combat in the Pacific.

While historians have rightly praised the honesty and authenticity of Sledge's memoir, such virtues really have little to do with Fussell's somewhat ingenuous argument that the diary is somehow a non-literary form free of the inventions and adornments that distort fictionalised accounts of warfare. Indeed, despite expressing his mistrust of 'literature', Fussell invests this book with the very literary and philosophic qualities that elsewhere he derides, claiming for instance that it presents the mystique of killing and torturing in the 'passion and madness of combat' (introduction to Sledge, 1990: xvi). In fact, torture features nowhere in Sledge's journal, which is generally a carefully neutral description of the horrors inflicted on and by decent men in a situation where civilised values are irrelevant. His flatness of tone also makes for some monotony and repetition; it is far from evident that his record is in any way superior either factually or formally to classic fictional accounts of the war in the Pacific by other combatants, such as Mailer's *The Naked and the Dead* and James Jones's *The Thin Red Line*.

Nevertheless, this reassertion of the pervasiveness of myth-making in all genres dealing with warfare, and of the value of the personal memoir, is worth retaining if we return to the context of occupied Europe. As far as I am aware, nobody has attempted to apply Fussell's broad cultural and historical analysis to France in particular. The corpus of material on which one can draw is vast and in many areas largely uncharted. In the case of the cinema, one can at least cite the detailed filmographies and comprehensive analytic surveys provided by Henry Rousso in his justly celebrated study of post-war reactions to occupation, *Le Syndrome de Vichy* (1990), and more recently by Sylvie Lindeperg in *Les Écrans de l'ombre* (1997), which covers the period from 1944 to 1969. In the literary domain, the sheer quantity of novels and memoirs dealing with the war and occupation published in France seems to have deterred anyone from attempting to establish a systematic, analytic bibliography of the total output of imaginative works. In addition, specialised libraries like the Institut d'Histoire du Temps Présent and the Bibliothèque de Documentation Internationale Contemporaine possess a large number of unpublished memoirs which mostly remain forgotten and unread.

Much of this material is, of course, mediocre (in other words, obscure works remain obscure because they tell the reader nothing new about the period in a historical sense and fail to create interesting stories, characters or forms if judged as literature), but it is still regrettable that the quantity and range· of the phenomenon have not received more attention, given its significant role in the creation of our imagined and historical memory of the war. Critics and historians who study the literature about the occupation of France almost invariably focus on a small corpus of works by famous writers.[13] Thus David Boal has produced one of the very few substantial studies of autobiographical writing, *Journaux intimes sous l'occupation* (1993), and quite understandably limits his analysis to major works by nine authors, all of them professional writers and male. Margaret Atack's *Literature and the French Resistance* (1989) draws on a rather wider corpus of just under 100 novels, mostly produced in the decade between 1940 and 1950, which allows for a much more representative discussion (at the cost of dealing with individual works fairly summarily). Were one to extend her account to the end of the twentieth century rather than 1950, the corpus of fiction would undoubtedly expand from hundreds to a thousand or more items, a quantity difficult for one commentator to encompass in any meaningful discussion.[14] Atack's analysis is broadly ideological, in that novelists are seen as taking a stance in the political and social debate about the dilemmas of collaboration, resistance and liberation, joining in the 'battle for meaning' (p. 235), the verbal (and legal) drama of justification and interpretation that follows (or actually is concomitant with) the physical conflict. In fact, from the outset she makes the crucial point that resistance was as much an ideological and discursive phenomenon as a military one, highly dependent on written texts for its effort of persuasion and propaganda (tracts, journals, even clandestine literature), as well as its espionage and intelligence gathering activities (recording, encoding, transmitting, receiving, decoding information: a clerical, almost bureaucratic process that was both laborious and highly dangerous, as many resistance workers insist in their autobiographical and fictional accounts).

Atack uses the general analytic categories of persuasion, unity and ambiguity in her discussion, which inevitably perhaps do not always fit particular works. For example, while writers like Vercors and Vailland may ostensibly set out to promote the unity of resistance, fictions like *Le Silence de la mer* (1942) and *Drôle de jeu* (1945) actually reveal the disunity and problematic nature of resistance (which also reflects a far more interesting and historically relevant approach): in the first text, supposedly written as a call for patriotic unity in 1941, the protagonists' only act of resistance is to snub a German officer who is hostile to Nazism and who goes off to his death on the eastern front, rather than face the dilemma of becoming a traitor; in Vailland's novel, produced after the liberation, the plot hinges on the pursuit of a traitor, the betrayal of other members of the network, and the main character's sceptical views about resistance (what the leader of Libération-Sud, Emmanuel d'Astier, called a 'childish and deadly game', a phrase echoed in Vailland's title). Further discussion is better reserved for the chapter on literary writers, where my intention is to complement the approaches outlined here by deliberately concentrating on a few individuals in reasonable detail, chosen both for the intrinsic interest of their works and their striking diversity (defending resistance or collaboration, writing fictionalised autobiography or adopting more popular genres like science fiction and the thriller). In the other chapters, the criteria for selection are that the figures chosen were first-hand witnesses of the period and left an interesting and valuable record of what they did or saw (whether in written or audio-visual form); the aim is to set their insights about an important activity into a broader historical context, rather than to survey memoirs, films and songs generated by the occupation.

To conclude this discussion of problems of representation, the most satisfactory answer to the question concerning the status of different narrative genres as forms of historical enquiry is surely to draw attention to the fluidity of the boundaries between them. All are useful, provided they are approached with caution and open-mindedness. To assess their value, one can in fact apply broadly similar criteria, even if different works evidently function better according to some criteria than others. I would suggest these might be: authenticity and authority (that is, the author's status as a witness or investigator); didacticism (his or her manifest or implicit intentions); veracity (whether the account respects the factual evidence as known); narrative skills (the readability and plausibility of the account); characterisation (the ability to evoke individual, subjective experience). Further discussion is again better deferred to subsequent chapters. Before sketching in the historical context, it is useful to return in a little more detail to the notions of heroism and treason and the moral choices and judgements behind them which, as has already been noted, determine most interpretations of France during the occupation.

Moral issues

It is virtually impossible to think or write about the Second World War without making explicit or implicit moral judgements. This is hardly surprising, given the massive loss of life, devastation and enormous political, social and economic upheavals brought about by the war, which was the most momentous event of the twentieth century. We are all the children or grandchildren of wartime generations, and the war continues to possess our collective memory and imagination. Were one to summarise the moral positions from which most people living in countries that formed the western alliance observe the war and its outcome, one might discern two conflicting views, one triumphalist and optimistic, the other relativistic and pessimistic. In the first scenario, good triumphs against evil, as the allies under their heroic warlords overcome the forces of fascism (which crush the rights of the individual citizen and nation, practise massive repression and systematic pillage, and institutionalise slave labour in the name of a racist ethic that leads to mass murder on an unparalleled scale) and restore democratic legality and eventually economic prosperity. (According to one version of this scenario, World War Two ended only in 1989, with the collapse of communism in eastern Europe.) The second scenario offers a more cynical version, based on realpolitik: here the allies belatedly confront the forces of fascism only after betraying the small countries of central and eastern Europe to the twin monstrosities of Nazi Germany and Stalin's Soviet Union. Their eventual success has nothing to do with the rightness of their cause, or the skills of their military leaders, and everything to do with vastly superior economic resources and firepower, achieved by the unholy pact between western capitalism and communist totalitarianism. Admittedly, Nazi Germany is crushed (but the Federal Republic rapidly replaces it as an economic power that dominates western Europe), though at the price of leaving the countries of eastern Europe enslaved to communism for another half century, and of the destruction of Britain and France as imperial powers. And all the horrors perpetrated by the Axis powers can be matched by an equal level of atrocity achieved by their adversaries: systematic bombing of civilians, ending in the use of atomic weapons, and, less visibly, complicity in sustaining the Soviet Empire with its millions of political detainees and slave labourers. Indeed, the closer one focuses on the war in eastern Europe, the harder it seems to extract any sense of moral rightness from the conflict.

Any interpretation which in the face of such atrocities and complexities either abandons moral judgements or grossly simplifies them is however inadequate, if not futile.[15] Are the fundamental moral concepts of right and wrong, good and evil, heroism and treason, simply makeshift products manufactured by victors' justice, or are they essential to make sense of any historical event? In the narrower context of occupied Europe and France, for instance, the primary justification of resistance against German oppression was precisely its rightness (whereas judged in purely material, pragmatic terms, it seemed at first a hopeless cause). The fact that so many people belatedly or retrospectively aspired to the badge of resistance, despite the flimsiness of many claims, reveals more than opportunistic realignment for social and political advantage. This demonstrates an urge to belong to the side of right, which can be defined either in positive, humanitarian terms (defence of the integrity of the individual and nation, of a liberty and legality based on equity) or by what it opposes: systematic and institutionalised violation of persons and groups. There is no need to have recourse to metaphysical absolutes to see that good and evil are fundamental, instrumental notions for understanding acts that seek either to avoid or perpetuate unnecessary human suffering. The historian or commentator needs to clarify his or her awareness of such moral concepts and also of the related ethical responsibilities which fall on those who pursue and reconstruct history: such as a basic respect of the facts, the honest pursuit of truth and fair interpretations (or the avoidance of tendentious selectivity, of facile judgements and inequitable parallels).

In practice, of course, such simple, convenient distinctions between good and evil, justified and specious interpretations, may be impossible to achieve. Most discussions of resistance and collaboration insist on the moral and political ambiguities of both positions, sometimes to the point of suggesting that they are virtually interchangeable, that the hero and traitor are merely two sides of the same coin. It is therefore helpful briefly to review what is normally understood by the terms heroism and treason, before moving on to a discussion of the historical and historiographical problems of the occupation relevant to our study of images of collaboration and resistance. Although it is not uncommon to talk of unknown heroes (indeed, the French resistance counted thousands) and hidden traitors (and again, the occupation was a breeding ground for all forms of betrayal), the heroes and traitors who feature in historical or fictional discourse normally are explicitly identified and recognised by some external authority (whether by a historian, epic poet, court of law, political supporter or adversary). While the hero (or heroine) usually achieves glory (that is positive recognition and success) by sacrificing his or her individual security for a collective good, the traitor is branded as a failure, since the traitor normally sacrifices both personal integrity (through cowardice, venality, duplicity) and a wider group (resistance movement, party, nation). The traitor's defence (apart from straightforward denial of committing the treasonable act at all) is usually to redefine the crime as a virtuous act in terms of different loyalties, sometimes allowing the traitor to become a heroic figure if the new cause is recognised as succeeding (such as betraying communism or fascism for democracy). The usual critique of the hero, on the other hand, is that the hero's sacrifice is on closer examination futile, either because it serves only self-aggrandisement or because the cause itself is ill-chosen (such as French volunteers in the Waffen SS defending Hitler's bunker in the closing weeks of the war).

Treason in particular is a ubiquitous and slippery notion in the context of state conflict and warfare, all the more unavoidable when war becomes civil war as it so often does in occupied Europe. In the loosest sense, everyone who is disapproved of by someone else is betraying something. Words like 'collabo' and 'traître' were thus all-purpose insults in the disorderly months and years immediately following the occupation in France. A slightly comical example is offered by the adolescent diarist Micheline Bood, when she records that her schoolmate Huguette has her face slapped by her father for kissing an American soldier and retaliates by calling him a traitor (25 August 1944, 1974: 336). This conflict between personal inclination, paternalistic authority and patriotic exigency is not so different, however, from the deliberate blurring of categories practised by those accused of treason who reduce it to a matter of political and ideological expediency. Milovan Djilas observed that 'In a divided nation the traitor is simply the person who betrays one's own side' (1977: 99). Adolf Hitler served nine months of a five-year prison sentence for treason in 1923 after the failed Munich putsch, and drew the lesson that it was better to gain power by preserving a façade of legality without instigating a civil war; the enabling act voted in 1933 allowed him to dispense with democratic process in a quasi-legal fashion, and Nazi People's Courts subsequently convicted thousands of opponents for treason. Thousands of Russian prisoners of war who survived German captivity were likewise consigned to Soviet camps for alleged treason on their return to the USSR.

Such examples could be multiplied endlessly, as indeed they are in André Thérive's polemical *Essai sur les trahisons*, in order to demonstrate that 'treason is another name for opposition', as Raymond Aron notes in his preface (Thérive, 1951: xxxi). As an intellectual collaborator, it was obviously in Thérive's interest to vindicate his position by seeking to relativise the concept of treason. He does however add an important new dimension, that of mendacity: 'it is through negation, lying, fraud and ruse that genuine treason can be defined. An ostentatious traitor breaks the essential rule of deception' (p. 51). To duplicity and hypocrisy one has to add some evaluation of the traitor's cause, its ends and means, and of his personal responsibility as an agent for this cause. Roger Casement was executed by the British in Pentonville Prison in August 1916 for his part in the abortive Easter uprising in Dublin (and more specifically for the eighteen months he spent in Germany unsuccessfully inducing Irish prisoners of war to join an Irish Brigade armed by the Germans to liberate Ireland). He had concluded ruefully of Irish patriotism: 'It is the lost cause of history! Men can save Ireland only by sacrificing themselves' (quoted by Hyde, 1964: 48). Whereas Casement's honesty and sincerity seem genuine, and the cause of Irish independence was certainly politically and morally defensible (however misguided the means), it seems difficult to say the same of traitors like William Joyce, executed in January 1946 for broadcasting pro-Nazi propaganda from Germany during the war, under the celebrated nickname 'Lord Haw-Haw', after a long and inglorious career as a fascist activist. Not surprisingly, Joyce's defenders stressed not the worthiness of his cause but rather the legality of the charges, since he was not technically a British subject. However, as Rebecca West (whose husband was one of the prisoners that Casement failed to convert in Germany) rightly observes in her study of wartime traitors, *The Meaning of Treason*, having masqueraded for thirty years as a British citizen and held a British passport under false pretences, Joyce was hardly in a position to switch nationality.

Arguments about legality are in fact just as crucial as those about political allegiance in the debate about treason, and apply in practice as much to resistance as collaboration. Just as Pétain's government displaced the discredited parliamentary democracy of the Third Republic which had led the nation to humiliation and defeat in 1940, so in turn the internal resistance and ultimately the Free French provisional government rejected and eventually replaced the discredited authoritarian and collaborationist French State, as the Vichy regime was officially known. And if one adds that both Pétain's and de Gaulle's regimes effectively put their predecessors on trial, until they too gave way to the equally discredited Fourth Republic, it may seem again that justice and law are purely political concepts, the arbitrary tools of power. Was there any real source of legal and moral authority during the occupation? A comment about the basically illegal nature of resistance made by the historian M.C. Weitz, prefacing Lucie Aubrac's memoirs, places this in doubt: 'Conventional morality was overturned during the occupation in the face of the suppression of traditional liberties. In the course of resistance work respectable citizens became counterfeitors and thieves, even killers' (Aubrac, 1993: xvii).

Lucie Aubrac reiterates this point, that morality and legality were effectively suspended for the duration of resistance activity: 'We all entered the universe of lying with the most perfect serenity ... We considered that our action as resisters forced us to modify the hierarchy of certain moral values. At the end of the war, we had to learn once more to respect legality' (Aubrac, 1997: 77). For their adversaries, of course, resistance activists were indeed dissidents, terrorists or criminals.

In fact, it is a common stratagem of collaborators and their apologists to equate the excesses and atrocities committed by the resistance and their allies with those of the Germans and their collaborators, thereby denying any objective moral responsibility. The fascist sympathiser Maurice Bardèche criticised the allies' self-righteous prosecution of German war crimes on the grounds that they had committed equally appalling crimes ('Having been killers, they promoted themselves to policemen ... Phosphorous bombs are just as bad as concentration camps', 1948: 17, 30). To rebut this argument, one has to return to ends and means, and also questions of scale and degrees of responsibility. The basic goal of resistance is a creditable one: to restore individual and national liberty. Collaboration, on the other hand, was at best an awkward and increasingly unsuccessful compromise with a superior power whose aims seem entirely evil. That said, it is perfectly true that resistance partisan groups committed acts that seem to have little justification either in terms of achieving the final goal or shorter-term tactical advantage (notably, the random assassination of German soldiers, or the premature 'liberation' of isolated towns and regions, both of which invariably led to massive reprisals against hostages and defenceless civilians). As for the controversial subject of bombings of civilian centres of population (for which the allies were much criticised by the resistance as well as by their adversaries), the figures lend some support to Bardèche: 40,000 civilians died in the London Blitz of 1940–41, whereas nearly 600,000 German civilians were killed by later allied bombing and there is scant evidence that these deaths hastened the end of the war. But if the means were unjustifiable, the end was certainly not the systematic extermination of Germany; and the scale of deaths is 10 per cent of those caused by the Nazis' pursuit of the final solution. Bardèche's equation is spurious because it exploits genuine weaknesses and errors in the allied cause to divert attention from the far greater crimes of the Third Reich.[16]

Nonetheless, if we cherish heroes, is it perhaps because they are supposedly untarnished by any such suspicion of guilt and complicity? It is all too easy to point out that such figures do not exist in the real world. Thus Kevin Foster argues in his book on myths of national identity, *Fighting Fictions* (1999), that heroism has more to do with the self-promotion of charismatic individuals than altruistic sacrifice for the collective good. The maquisard leader Georges Guingouin suggested that, on the contrary, such denigratory and cynical judgements reflected the revenge taken by the weak and cowardly after the event to excuse their own inadequacy (cited by Ruffin, 1980: 17). One can apparently further subvert the concept of heroic sacrifice by noting that it appears to be a central tenet of fascism.[17] However, the 'heroism' of the SS warrior or camp guard is based not on altruistic self-sacrifice, but on ruthless inhumanity, willingness to commit mass murder and to subject others to systematic degradation.[18]

A particularly constructive discussion of heroic sacrifice and related issues is to be found in several books about the morality of war and ethics of history written in the 1990s by Tzvetan Todorov. It is not my intention to summarise them here in any detail, but rather to end this section by drawing out some key points which allow one to establish a positive morality.[19] The fact that concepts like heroism, legality and morality can be perverted to evil ends does not invalidate what they stand for, which is an essential defence of humane values. Killing others or having them killed are pseudo-heroic acts, although unfortunately few monuments are raised to those who save others' lives. Social and political evil is encapsulated in totalitarian regimes, whose emblems are ghettos and concentration camps and whose laws are criminal (thus those who obey such laws may be more dangerous than those who break them). Denial of responsibility by those who implement such laws may be a facile defence: the compartmentalisation and secrecy surrounding the camps allowed even Eichmann to deny ever killing anyone or ordering their death (often detainees were put in charge of the gas chambers, but they too were victims acting under compulsion). In any case, justice as a historical enterprise is not about punishment or forgiveness, but rather re-establishing the truth about the past and maintaining its presence in the collective memory. Totalitarian regimes wage war on memory to conceal their criminality; hence Himmler's comment on the final solution as 'a glorious page in our history that was never written and never will be' (quoted in Todorov, 1995: 11). Moral judgements should not be confused with facile moralising. When Yves Durand states that '*Morality* is the basis of Vichy's whole political conception. The issue is to moralise politics' (1972: 64), one has therefore to gloss this comment by noting that Vichy exemplifies the hypocritical double standards of the moraliser who imposes moral constraints on others while himself abusing them (in this case, persecuting supposed corrupters of the nation while tolerating the corrupting presence of the Germans). The same warning can be addressed to historians and other commentators who confuse careful evaluation of actions and responsibilities in the past with anachronistic condemnation.[20]

Occupation and collaboration

The political, social and economic conditions of the occupation of France were largely determined by the armistice convention signed on 22 June 1940 in the forest of Compiègne by General Keitel and the French government's plenipotentiaries. Its twenty-four articles established the zones of occupation, invited the collaboration of the French authorities, and guaranteed the neutrality of the French fleet. In theory, the French government was free to return to Paris; in practice, this never occurred, for the 'collaboration' envisaged was not a matter of cooperation between equals but rather a relationship of master and servant. Thus article eighteen imposed on the French government the upkeep costs of German troops stationed in France, while subsequent articles demanded the release of German prisoners of war and the handing-over on demand of all German nationals who had sought refuge in France, but forbade the release of French prisoners (who numbered nearly two million in 1940) until a formal peace agreement was concluded. Article ten explicitly outlawed all forms of resistance:

> The French government will forbid French nationals from fighting against Germany in the service of states with which Germany is still at war. French nationals who disobey this ban will be treated by German troops as illegal combatants.

Not surprisingly, General de Gaulle, who famously appealed for a continuation of hostilities from abroad a few days earlier on 18 June, rejected the armistice as treasonable surrender of French sovereignty. Yet there is little doubt that most of the French population welcomed Pétain's success, as last prime minister of the Third Republic, in bringing a rapid end to a conflict which over a period of only six weeks had led to the total collapse of the French armed forces, the ignominious flight of the government to Bordeaux, and widespread panic as millions of refugees fled before the German invaders. The history of the occupation could be summed up as a gradual but inexorable shift from relief at the restoration of relative stability and admiration for Marshal Pétain's apparent success in imposing order on the chaos caused by his predecessors, to disillusionment, fear and suffering, as the longer-term consequences of the armistice emerged: namely, increasing privations and threats to the security of more and more citizens, as the Germans' systematic exploitation of the country's resources took effect. The Vichy government's fragile political auton-omy virtually disappeared after the Germans invaded the unoccupied southern zone in November 1942, principally in order to defend the Mediterranean coastline against an allied invasion from North Africa. With hindsight, the fact that Vichy was bound to fail in its aims of defending French interests is evident from the concessions granted from the beginning.

The territorial division into occupied and unoccupied zones, for example, effectively deprived the French government of access to es-sential resources (while allowing the Germans the benefit of French administrative structures across the country). Some 55 per cent of French territory, 67 per cent of the population and 80 per cent of the economy came under direct German control; sections of the occupied zone in the north-east of the country were made virtually inaccessible either to French officials or to civilians who had taken refuge else-where during the fighting (thus the provinces of Alsace and Lorraine were annexed to the Reich, the departments of the Nord and Pas-de-Calais placed under German military control in Brussels, with depart-ments in adjoining areas being declared reserved or forbidden; from October 1941, a defensive zone extending thirty kilometres inland along the entirety of the Atlantic coast was placed off-limits). In add-ition, the Italians occupied the border departments of the south-east, with a significant extension of their zone after November 1942. The demarcation line extending for almost 1000 kilometres between north and south zones was relaxed only from March 1943, until when it made communication of people or goods difficult or impossible. Clocks in the occupied zone were advanced by two hours to match German time (they remained one hour ahead of those in the unoccu-pied zone until uniformity was imposed in May 1941). The extortion-ate payment of a daily indemnity and the living costs of the occupying forces to which the French government had agreed effectively turned the country into an indentured supplier of Germany, while creating massive shortages among the ordinary civilian population and encouraging the growth of black-marketeering on a huge scale, much of it surreptitiously controlled by German agents. The occupation costs levied have been estimated as fifty times greater than the actual sum needed to support German forces stationed in France, and equivalent to fifteen months of national revenue over the four years of the occupation (as opposed to the two months' national revenue paid by the Germans in reparations after 1918: Rochebrune and Hazera, 1997).

Rationing of food was introduced nationally from September 1940 (having been started in February) and lasted for a decade (by way of comparison, rationing continued on some products in the UK until 1954); the official adult food ration was set at about half the actual pre-war level of consumption. Those most affected in practice lived in urban centres of population, whereas the 36 per cent of the population employed in agriculture and the 50 per cent resident in rural communes remained largely self-sufficient in food; a far greater negative impact was caused on rural people by the forced labour laws imposed in the last two years of the occupation. The Parisian diarist Flora Groult recalls the rare pleasure of eating eggs and the disappearance of basic products and services (gas and electricity supplies were frequently cut off), themes endlessly repeated in memoirs of the period. Deprivation and poverty became the norm for many, when an average daily wage in 1943 might be at most 100 francs, the price of one meal in a black-market restaurant or five kilos of potatoes. By 1944, when the franc had more than halved in value from the beginning of the occupation, the journalist Claude Jamet estimated that his large family needed 10,000 francs a month to live adequately. Those who continued to enjoy the pleasures of life usually obtained their privileges by offering services to the Germans. As part of its campaign for moral regeneration, the Vichy government banned dance halls and casinos (though not, curiously, brothels, which remained centres of attraction for occupying troops and their associates and thrived until they were closed down by the post-war government in 1946).

Daily life was thus conditioned for many by the struggle to surmount material hardship, which left them indifferent to the fate of the Jews or the cause of resistance, at least until the final months of the occupation. Collaboration in its widest sense might indeed be defined as self-centred indifference or as a willingness to abrogate personal responsibility to the authority of Marshal Pétain, whose role was to act as self-declared saviour of the French. His ostensible goal was to protect them from the worst of German demands, at the price of imposing an authoritarian political regime, with a dubious programme of national renewal; this meant in practice penalising and purging undesirable elements in the community. By the end of 1942, however, Pétain's political authority was stripped away, and the persecution of foreigners, Jews and political adversaries began to extend far beyond the pretext of upholding public order; from 1943, the introduction of conscripted labour in Germany for French workers and the use of Vichy paramilitary police forces to combat resistance activities meant that the French government was actively supporting the Nazi war effort and engaging in civil war against large numbers of its own citizens. Pétain of course had received his mandate not from a direct vote of the people, but from the 590 parliamentarians who on 10 July 1940 consented to suspend their authority and make the Marshal head of state (80 deputies and senators famously voted against; 237 others were absent). Although the Gaullist provisional government of the liberation would deny the legality and legitimacy of the transfer of power and cast Pétain as a usurper, the size of the majority in his favour and his undoubted widespread popularity make this argument nugatory. In 1940, he seemed the only credible alternative to direct German rule, particularly as he enjoyed the prestige of having successfully held the Germans at bay in 1916 at Verdun, unlike his successors in 1940. Vichy's collaboration is thus a story of success turning to failure, of the failure of Pétain (and of the political and establishment élites which eagerly supported the suspension of democratic rights) to offer the protection on which they founded their pretensions to rule and reform.

The constitutional act of 11 July 1940 gave all judicial, executive and legislative power to Pétain, apart from the right to declare war. (It is worth noting that the armistice effectively amounted to an uneasy cessation of hostilities, making occupied France a temporarily neutral or neutralised power trapped between the Germans and the allies.) An act of 30 July 1940 promised the trial of those deemed responsible for the nation's defeat, while as head of state Pétain had the power to imprison ministers and administrators for treason. He had no hesitation in using this power: his immediate predecessor as Prime Minister, Reynaud, was arrested, imprisoned and eventually deported to Germany, while even after the trial of other senior government figures of the Third Republic like Daladier, Blum and Mandel had been suspended in April 1942, they too remained in detention and suffered deportation. Pétain might indeed be reproached primarily for vindictive score-settling and failing to use his progressively declining political and moral authority to impede and condemn the inhumane acts perpetrated under his regime. Collaboration was announced as official government policy after his meeting with Hitler in October 1940, although the Marshal never intended that France should become a military ally of Germany and on 13 December 1940 he dismissed the deputy head of government Laval, who was far more actively sympathetic to the Nazi cause. He refused to sign the agreement negotiated by Laval's successor Darlan in May 1941, which would have put France back into the war on the German side (although Vichy forces opposed attempts by the Free French to seize control of the territories within the vast French empire, with less and less success, when the Germans invaded the occupied zone in November 1942, they were prevented from entering Toulon until the large French fleet harboured there had been scuttled). Within eighteen months of Laval's dismissal, however, the Marshal had been marginalised and reduced to the status of symbolic figurehead. An act of April 1942 made Laval head of government and by November 1942 he was effectively head of state, sporting the title 'President', much to the Marshal's irritation; although he remained a prestigious symbolic figure, during the last six months of the occupation, Pétain was under virtual house arrest until he was taken forcibly to Sigmaringen when the Germans retreated from France.

Pétain ultimately became a victim of his fondness for the trappings of power, the prisoner first of the more active collaborationists whom he helped bring to power, then of his adversaries; he escaped execution, unlike Laval, but at the price of life imprisonment for his legitimisation of a political regime that abetted Nazism. Vichy's project of moral regeneration, announced as part of a so-called national revolution, seems equally spurious in retrospect, in that its few positive aspects are outweighed by many negative features. It was antidemocratic and authoritarian in nature, rather than totalitarian (as much for practical as ideological reasons: a defeated country could hardly create a one-party state with a programme of imperial expansion to rival Germany's), its counter-revolutionary values being summed up in the famous slogan 'travail, famille, patrie', adopted from the pre-war extreme right Croix de feu (the slogan appeared on the masthead of their leader La Rocque's *Le Petit Journal* in 1936). It was all too easy to deride this pious trinity by observing that work meant forced labour, families were separated when thousands of men remained prisoners of war, and the fatherland was being pillaged by Germans. A mocking variant invented by Léon-Paul Fargue was 'tracas, famine, patrouilles' ('trouble, famine, patrols'). The Jewish politician

Georges Mandel (who was assassinated by the Milice – the Vichy government's paramilitary police force – at the end of the occupation) summed up Vichy's project more accurately as 'terreur blanche, bibliothèque rose, marché noir'.[21]

The Vichy government in fact continued and expanded the practice adopted in the final years of the Third Republic of detaining without due legal process thousands of refugees and political undesirables. While the central issue at the trials of Vichy politicians and other collaborators held immediately after the liberation was usually treason in the sense of betraying the state, delivering the nation, its resources and citizens, to the Germans (rather than acting as a buffer, as the defence claimed), nowadays we are much more inclined to accuse the Vichy government and its servants of betrayal in a humanitarian sense, of callous complicity in crimes against humanity. Since detention without trial and mass deportation were such defining features of occupied France, it is essential to review the facts and judgements regarding these grim phenomena. In the immediate aftermath of the war, the term deportation was used as an all-embracing one, encapsulating all those removed from French territory at German demand during the occupation. Thus volunteer and conscripted workers, whose chances of survival were high, were sometimes conflated with political deportees (mostly members of the resistance, with at best a 50 per cent chance of survival), or even the racial victims of the Nazi policy of genocide (whose purpose was to ensure their extermination). Even though Vichy's contribution to the final solution is no longer concealed by such blurring of categories, it remains difficult to obtain accurate figures and statistics for many aspects related to deportations, deaths and atrocities which occurred during the occupation and its immediate aftermath; many figures cited by historians are in fact rough estimates, sometimes minimised or exaggerated for polemical purposes. Two notorious examples are the numbers of resistance activists summarily executed by the Germans and the numbers of collaborators summarily executed by the resistance: while the communist resistance claimed to have '75 000 fusillés' among its ranks, inflating its martyrs at least threefold in order to boost its importance, defenders of collaboration have claimed on occasion that as many as 100,000 collaborators were murdered in the spring and summer of 1944 (minimising their own guilt by exaggerating at least fivefold the atrocities of their opponents).

As far as racial deportation is concerned, however, there is general acceptance that 75,721 Jews were deported from France to death camps in Poland; only 2567 survived. This figure was established from Serge Klarsfeld's study of the records kept at the internment camp at Drancy, the first staging post on the route to extermination. The first convoy took 1100 Jews from Drancy to Auschwitz on 27 March 1942; it was followed by eighty-four others right until the final weeks of occupation (no attempt was made by the resistance or allies to sabotage any of the trains). As has already been noted, the majority of Jews were arrested by the French police (one of the great advantages of collaboration was that it allowed the Germans to maintain only about 3000 police agents of their own in France, and make full use of the 100,000 or so police employed by the French government). Thousands of Jews and other foreigners were detained in squalid internment camps run by the French authorities in both occupied and unoccupied zones or conscripted to forced labour battalions. It is now well known that Vichy's early policy of identifying Jews and excluding them from many professional and economic activities was undertaken voluntarily rather than in response to German demands, even if Nazi anti-Semitic persecution offered an obvious model. Censuses were undertaken in the occupied zone in September 1940 and in June 1941 in the unoccupied zone; decrees of October 1940 and June 1941 were the first French laws to identify individuals on racial grounds and ban them from professions such as teaching, the law, the civil service, the press and the cinema (and a law of July 1941 allowed the expropriation of Jewish businesses). That Pétain was a prime mover in the outlawing of Jews is also now generally agreed, even if the Marshal never made any public anti-Semitic statement.

There is far less agreement concerning the exact numbers of volunteer workers sent to Germany or members of the resistance executed or deported by the occupation authorities (estimates of resisters and hostages executed are about 30,000, and political deportations 65,000). Volunteering for work in Germany could bring more favourable conditions (but after the war seemed discreditable, if not a form of collaboration: this is why the Communist Party leader George Marchais consistently lied about his past as a factory worker in Germany). A maximum figure for voluntary workers in Germany between 1940 and 1942 is 180,000 (although most returned quickly to France, so that only 75,000 were away at any given time), whereas the 'relève', created in mid-1942 in order to attract 250,000 further volunteers, actually supplied only 50,000. What is clear is the increasing German need for a massive, conscripted labour force, and Vichy's compliance with German demands by its creation of the 'Service du travail obligatoire'.

The STO law of September 1942 introduced compulsory national labour for men aged eighteen to fifty and single women aged twenty-one to thirty-five, while a further law of February 1943 compelled younger men to work in Germany (exemptions were progressively removed, so that by February 1944, married women without children and men aged sixteen to sixty were all liable to work in Germany). The 7.6 million foreign workers in Germany in 1944 (most of them from Poland and the USSR) included some 1.3 million Frenchmen (half of them prisoners of war, and half conscripted labourers); there were also 44,000 French women.

The Vichy government's justification for abetting Nazi racial persecution and forced labour demands was that it was able to mitigate their worst excesses. Here again, a grim debate can be waged over comparative statistics. It is perfectly true that only 25 per cent of the Jewish population was deported from France during the occupation; 40,000 Jews remained in Paris even in 1943–44 without being arrested, and the majority of Jews with French nationality survived the occupation. In the Netherlands, on the other hand, 110,000 Dutch Jews out of 140,000 were deported and only 6000 of them survived; overall chances of survival, either absolutely or comparatively, were therefore much higher in France. If one looks at overall deaths in France during World War Two, one finds a figure estimated at between 500,000 and 600,000 (and divided roughly equally between soldiers killed in combat, civilians killed in combat and bombing, and victims of racial and political persecution). In comparison, at least 1.5 million French soldiers were killed in the First World War and Poland lost six million of its citizens in the Second World War. One might therefore conclude, on a very crude quantitative basis, that the French suffered ten times less than the Poles during the war, and attribute some credit to the Vichy government for this. Yet this is at best a purely negative achievement, and judgements made on a profit and loss basis can be very skewed. Peter Novick argues that this was a fundamental flaw in the prosecution case against Pétain at his trial in 1945, which he describes as 'an elaborate ceremonial aimed at symbolically condemning a policy', which 'played into the hands of the defense by placing the indictment on a material rather than a moral plane' (1968: 173, 176). Judged on such a purely material basis, he asserts somewhat provocatively, 'the very limited military contribution of the resistance seems doubly insignificant when weighed against the deportations and massacres which it provoked' (p. 20). Apart from a dubious causal link between resistance action and German excesses, this comparison

wilfully overlooks the fact that most deportations were not even provoked by resistance activity; however, the wider issue of comparative
judgements will be discussed in more detail in the concluding section
of this chapter.

Before turning to resistance and the aftermath of the liberation, we
need to widen the discussion of collaboration beyond the political and
administrative responsibilities of the Vichy regime to consider its
social and psychological dimensions. How extensive was collaboration,
and what motivated collaborators? The answer to both questions
depends to a large extent on how widely one chooses to define collaboration. The limits range between accusing the entire population of
collaboration, as 'quarante millions de pétainistes', and acquitting the
entire population by blaming a few thousand fanatics who seized the
reins of power (here resistance in the most notional sense becomes
the mass phenomenon). The two extremes actually meet, in the sense
that 'we are all guilty' effectively means everyone has to be acquitted.
Nonetheless, the idea of mass support for Pétain seems well founded,
and the notion of an enduring national shame or culpability for the
humiliations and crimes perpetrated by his state helps explain the
continuing obsession with the occupation in contemporary France.[22]
But as was suggested at the beginning of this chapter, a meaningful
analysis of collaboration has to be based on actual choices and acts,
and passive complicity distinguished from active commitment. If
taken to mean behaviour and attitudes which supported and sustained
either the German cause or the Vichy government's commitment to
cooperate with the occupying forces, collaboration extended to a wide
range of domains, from the industrial, political and economic, to the
military, paramilitary, judicial and intellectual. Does one include the
750,000 civil servants employed by Vichy (whose numbers rose to
nearly one million by 1944), the 300,000 French workers building the
coastal fortifications known as the Atlantic wall, not to mention all
the other volunteer and conscripted labourers whose work contributed
to German war production? Since the majority of these employees and
workers had very little alternative choice, they are generally seen as
passive collaborators whose personal responsibility was strictly limited.
Active commitment is taken to mean either more conscious ideological choices (such as producing pro-German propaganda or joining
organisations whose goal was to prevent resistance or pursue racial
persecution) or at least deriving personal benefit from association
with the occupying authorities (such as career advancement or
profiteering).

The figure of 1 per cent of the population is sometimes given for active collaborators (for example, Defrasne, 1982). This author notes that 160,000 legal cases of alleged collaboration went before the post-war courts (and also estimates that perhaps 80,000 babies were born from Franco–German unions during the occupation, which if correct would be spectacular evidence of the extent of so-called horizontal collaboration).[23] If the percentage refers to the adult population, it gives a figure of 250,000 collaborators, which is curiously close to that estimated for active resisters: by this convenient symmetry, both collaboration and resistance are shown to be minority, albeit significant activities. A further, important distinction (especially for supporters of Vichy) separates those who were unreservedly pro-German from those who took a supposedly more neutral position, claiming like Pétain to be defending French interests from hostile forces which could include the Germans. The term 'collaborationniste' (which Marcel Déat may have coined in November 1940), as opposed to 'collaborateur', is often used to characterise the most extreme ideological collaborators, most of whom were avowed fascists prepared to pay direct allegiance to Germany and criticise Vichy for its reluctance to join the Nazi camp. The best-known collaborationists headed fascistic political parties or analogous organisations, often linked to newspapers which printed virulent propaganda; they were usually based in Paris and received subsidies from the Germans. Despite their frequent quarrels, they were united in their anti-Semitism, anti-communism, and enthusiasm for German pan-Europeanism (which meant in effect turning much of Europe into vassal states).

They were, in other words, traitors, whether judged on political, moral or humanitarian grounds; their cult of violent invective or violent action did however require a certain physical courage and often brought them to a premature and violent end. Though some were kept at a distance by Vichy, others eventually achieved influence (thus Déat, Darnand and Henriot all entered the government in the last six months of the occupation). Darquier de Pellepoix headed the Rassemblement antijuif before becoming the commissioner for Jewish questions; Jacques Doriot, head of the Parti populaire français and a member of the LVF (Legion of French Volunteers against Bolshevism) who fought in German uniform, wrote in the journal *Au pilori* in 1941, 'The Jew is not a man. He's a stinking beast' (quoted by Defrasne, 1982: 50); the more intellectual Robert Brasillach likewise urged the wholesale deportation of Jewish children in *Je suis partout*, the collaborationist weekly; Eugène Deloncle, long associated with the 'Cagoule' and MSR (the Mouvement Social Révolutionnaire, which had plotted the overthrow of the Third Republic through a pre-war terrorist campaign) was himself assassinated by Gestapo agents in January 1944. Déat survived several assassination attempts (one of which he suspected Deloncle of instigating) and finally fled abroad, as did Darquier (who re-emerged in the 1970s to deny the existence of the Holocaust). Darnand, Henriot, Doriot and Brasillach were all killed or executed in 1944 or 1945.

The question of whether the infamous collaborationists and their henchmen had specific psychological traits in common is often raised, though discussion tends to resort to caricatural stereotypes.[24] What motivated them to join, for instance, any of the four most notorious organisations associated with extremist collaboration: namely, the Milice and Gestapo, which were engaged in police activities in mainland France, or the LVF and Waffen SS, which recruited French military volunteers to operate on the eastern front? Sartre's essay 'Qu'est-ce qu'un collaborateur?', published in August 1945 (reprinted in Sartre, 1949), is one of the earliest attempts to offer a general portrait and to insist on the marginal nature of most collaborators (both socially and ideologically, it appears). Since marginality is however sometimes cited as a characteristic of resisters as well, it perhaps denotes at best a sign of a potential outlaw. Nor can members of the political, administrative or military elites who rose to power under Vichy (for example, Laval, Bousquet, Darlan) be called marginal in any meaningful sense. On the other hand, Philippe Aziz's (1970) biography of the two French Gestapo agents Bonny and Lafont certainly emphasises the importance of exclusion in their careers. While Lafont was a semi-literate petty criminal who graduated from prison to become head of the notorious gang of killers and extortionists based in the rue Lauriston in Paris (nominally run by two German NCOs answerable to Colonel Knochen of the SD), his associate Pierre Bonny was a disgraced former police inspector who turned his professional skills to pursuit of the resistance.

Calculating that as many as 30,000 Frenchmen served in German military units in the course of the war (though the majority were not active combatants), Pierre Giolitto observes that an organisation like the LVF, created at the instigation of the Parisian collaborationists in July 1941 and reluctantly accepted by Vichy, is something of an enigma:

> Who are these men, heroes for some, traitors or misguided patriots for others, who chose to face suffering and death, in the heart of an

icy continent, wearing a uniform not their own, with the goal of defending a cause to which most French people were indifferent? (1999: 61)

Most in fact were manual workers, some former soldiers, others fascists, others eager for adventure. To understand their intentions and experience, one needs again to turn to the more personal records given in autobiographical or fictional accounts (which will be studied in the chapter on combatants). As for the Milice, it remains one of the most hated organisations created under the aegis of the Vichy regime, 'une sorte de Gestapo française' (Defrasne, 1982: 95).[25] It was not, however, an agency of the German security services, but created under the authority of Laval from January 1943, under the leadership of Darnand, as a paramilitary police force. That said, although it numbered up to 30,000 members of both sexes, it is normally remembered on account of the 5000 members of its uniformed branch, the Franc-Garde, which was armed by the Germans and engaged with German forces in combating the resistance, as well as practising extortion, torture and murder. That Darnand eventually became head of all police services for the French government (having gained the rank of Sturmbannführer in the SS in August 1943) shows how spurious Vichy's claim of upholding legality and public order had become by the end of the occupation.

Resistance and liberation

Resistance can be defined, in the widest sense, as the struggle for personal and political liberty against an oppressive, external force. Henri Noguères asserts the essential moral justification that drove resisters: 'We were free, in our deepest core, because our fight was a fight for human dignity and for freedom' (1984: 256). And in his essay on collaboration, Sartre contrasted the defeatism of collaborators like Drieu, who by embracing fascism accepted the 'suicide of humanity', with the defiance of those prepared to confront overwhelming odds: 'resistance, which finally triumphed, shows that the role of man is to be able to say *no* to events, even when it seems one must submit to them' (1949: 60, 61). It is worth asserting (and if necessary reasserting) the rightness of these goals, because they separate resistance radically from the authoritarian movements and ideologies which it opposed; this distinction between the ultimate intentions and ends of humanitarian and totalitarian systems also allows one to question the tendentious parallels between resistance and collaboration that invariably appear when the discussion focuses on means and outcomes in a more pragmatic fashion.

In the more specific context of occupied France, the historians Azéma and Bédarida observe in their essay on 'L'Historisation de la Résistance' that writing on the resistance reflects 'the hybridisation of science and myth', since resistance relates to a triple paradigm' for the French, which is as much moral and psychological as political (it aspires to the recovery of national honour and identity as well as the restoration of republican government) (*Esprit*, 1994: 20–1). They offer a definition of resistance which echoes Noguères's but which is nonetheless more concrete and which intentionally extends beyond the purely military domain, as:

Clandestine action undertaken, in the name of the freedom of the nation and the dignity of humankind, by volunteers organising to struggle against the domination (and most often the occupation) of their country by a Nazi or fascist regime, or by their satellites and allies. (pp. 22–3)

This definition clearly only applies to occupied western Europe in World War Two (as does most of my subsequent discussion). In other words, resistance against colonising forces or communist regimes is not encompassed, although one of the grim paradoxes of French post-war history was precisely the failure of many influential resistance figures to apply the aims and lessons of their past struggle against Nazi and Vichy tyranny to that of nationalists for independence in Indochina and Algeria or of dissidents and satellite states against Soviet tyranny in eastern Europe (as a consequence, some celebrated members of the resistance became apologists for the worst atrocities committed in the name of colonialism or communism).[26]

More positively, the definition emphasises two important but problematic aspects of resistance: its clandestinity and its voluntary but organised nature. Given the overwhelming material superiority of the Germans and the French state which supported them, resistance could only be undertaken in secrecy within mainland France or more publicly from the safer distance of exile abroad. However, secrecy can amount to virtual invisibility, either in terms of being seen to achieve useful practical results or of obtaining public support by broadcasting one's cause, or for that matter of leaving evidence which allows historians to evaluate what has been done and by whom. It also facilitates spurious claims, not to mention the infiltration of double agents and traitors. Although the initial choice to resist depends on individual decision (unlike, say, conscription into the military) and willingness to defy unjust laws, resistance thereafter is only really meaningful and legitimate if undertaken as part of a credible organisation whose aims and acts are (or at least become) acceptable to the larger population. Resistance which does not fulfil these last criteria can be hard to distinguish either from futile and ineffectual protesting and boasting (as shown by certain celebrated intellectuals like Sartre and Malraux, whose resistance seems mainly to amount to self-promotion)[27] or from outright banditry (an accusation frequently made against some maquis groups, especially in the south-west).

The overall history of the French resistance is indeed a success story, a hard-won battle for legitimacy and popular support which reverses the trajectory of Vichy from success to failure. Many commentators suggest, however, that its ultimate success was to enter the domain of legend, as founding myth or civic religion, and that in historical terms this was a sort of failure, insofar as the harsh reality of resistance activity and above all the courage, suffering and sacrifice of the small minority of genuine resisters, were largely forgotten and eclipsed by a myth of national struggle that may be sentimentally comforting but also reveals the most cynical form of expediency and manipulation.[28] As has already been argued, myth itself is a historical phenomenon and therefore has its place in any enquiry, provided that every effort is made to disentangle fact from fancy. Because we view the past retrospectively, our perception of resistance and collaboration is inevitably distorted by our knowledge of the final outcome; whereas in 1940, German defeat seemed all but impossible and resistance was therefore a desperate gamble taken by a few hundred people mostly regarded as misguided or undisciplined eccentrics and trouble-makers. De Gaulle was an unknown junior general and politician, who in August 1940 had rallied only 2000 Frenchmen to his cause in London and whose supporters controlled only a small fraction of the empire in Cameroon and Chad.

De Gaulle's conquest of influence and power was achieved with tortuous slowness and despite much opposition, not only from Vichy but also from rivals who belatedly espoused the cause of resistance yet found greater favour with the allied leaders who sponsored the Free French. Senior political and military figures in France were unwilling at first to offer any support either to the Comité National Français in London (constituted in September 1941 as an embryonic government in exile, its first major supporter from France was the ex-prefect Jean Moulin) or to the internal resistance; the latter comprised 'a handful of individuals striving to raise the awareness of their fellow citizens', in Lucie Aubrac's words (1997: 60). For the first eighteen months of the occupation, external and internal resistance evolved in virtual isolation from each other. The gradual shift in favour of resistance was progressively triggered as events began to reveal that German invincibility was far from assured. The invasion of the USSR in June 1941 finally legitimised communist resistance, since till that point Germany and the Soviet Union were officially allied (although the communist-based French resistance movement the Front National was established from May 1941, its paramilitary wing, the Francs-Tireurs et Partisans Français (FTPF/FTP), came into existence in March 1942). Until the spring of 1942, Vichy took a relatively soft line towards non-communist resistance activity in the unoccupied zone (its counter-intelligence service even occasionally arrested German agents), but with Laval's return to power in April 1942 and the allied landings in North Africa in November 1942, rapidly followed by the German occupation of the south zone, a far more repressive policy was adopted; such factors had a major positive impact on potential resisters, just as the creation of STO encouraged large numbers of French draft-dodgers to join maquis units from 1943 (although most of those who avoided compulsory labour did not participate in resistance).

This increasing acceptance of resistance is illustrated by the change in attitudes of some of the senior officers who had originally been members of the court martial that condemned de Gaulle to death on 2 August 1940. Its president, General Frère, set up the Organisation de Résistance de l'Armée in early 1943, following the disbandment of the armistice army, and was eventually deported to Struthof where he died. General de la Laurencie became pro-resistance from December 1941, until he too was interned. General de la Porte du Theil became head of the Chantiers de jeunesse, a youth labour scheme which replaced military service but formed a recruiting base for some resisters and was eventually stopped by the Germans; he too was deported in January 1944. Yet this did not necessarily imply support for Gaullist resistance. In fact, when the allies took the French colonies of Algeria and Morocco in November 1942, they did their best to find a more compliant French leader than the notoriously belligerent de Gaulle (who Roosevelt suggested in May 1943 might be sidelined by being made governor of Madagascar). Laval's predecessor Admiral Darlan conveniently changed sides, claiming to have Pétain's secret authorisation to make a pact with the allies. When Darlan was assassinated in December 1942, General Giraud, who had spectacularly escaped from a German fortress and nonetheless remained loyal to Marshal Pétain, was selected as a promising rival to de Gaulle. The two generals met in Algiers on 30 May 1943 and became co-presidents of the Comité Français de Libération Nationale (CFLN); by November, however, de Gaulle had outmanoeuvred his politically naive partner and was in sole charge of what was in effect a provisional government based in Algiers and rivalling Vichy in credibility; the Free French now at last controlled most of the overseas empire and an army of 400,000 men, equipped by the US and drawn in large part from French colonial troops.

The political history of the internal resistance in mainland France similarly reveals de Gaulle's progressive imposition of his authority, although the Communist Party remained a strong competitor. Top-down histories of the resistance invariably insist, in fact, on such competitive struggle, sometimes creating the impression that resistance leaders devoted as much energy to combating their rivals as the Germans. It is certainly true that the hostility expressed towards de Gaulle's delegate, Jean Moulin, by early resistance leaders like Henri Frenay, was largely motivated by resentment at having been marginalised by latecomers. When Moulin presided over the first meeting of the Conseil National de la Résistance in Paris on 27 May 1943 (less than a month before his arrest), he had effectively created a body that united the major resistance movements, left-wing political parties and trades unions under de Gaulle's leadership. By the end of the occupation, admittedly, the senior military leadership of the internal resistance was dominated by communists; in practice, however, the feared communist revolution never occurred. In any case, by its very nature much resistance activity depended on guerrilla actions undertaken at a local level and even the FTPF had only a minority of communists in their ranks, according to their leader Charles Tillon (cited by Kedward, 1978: 236).

This rapid sketch of the evolution of resistance as an important political force leaves unanswered some of the most interesting questions concerning resistance, if it is examined from a more specific psychological and military angle: such as the actual extent, achievements and motivations of its movements, networks, maquis groups and their members. Like collaboration, active resistance was undoubtedly a minority activity, the crucial difference being that membership of this minority generally brought moral and material benefits rather than disgrace in the post-war reckoning. Consequently, claims regarding membership of resistance organisations tend to be inflated and disputed. This is shown by examining, for example, numbers of decorations awarded. The most prestigious resisters were appointed Compagnons de la Libération: but of the 1061 Compagnons, 238 were honoured posthumously, only six were women, and only twelve communists, while 783 were from the Free French, 107 from networks and 157 from the metropolitan resistance: the unjust bias in favour of de Gaulle's men is striking. Some 49,000 resistance medals were awarded to lower ranks, and about 250,000 cards granting the status of 'combattant volontaire de la Résistance' (CVR) distributed, although there were 500,000 claimants. While this last figure indicates that by the most generous estimate, resistance membership never exceeded 2 per cent of the adult population, 80 per cent of the members of the constituent assemblies elected in 1945 and 1946 were active resisters. This prestige was however relatively short lived: de Gaulle resigned as head of the provisional government in January 1946, as the party clans reasserted their influence, while the communists were expelled from the government in May 1947. Resistance never became a viable and durable political movement, and while its two main branches, Gaullism and communism, went into opposition under the Fourth Republic, by the elections of June 1951 right-wingers sympathetic to collaboration were returning to power as successive amnesties released former collaborators from imprisonment or ineligibility.

Discussing the sociology of resistance, François Marcot (in Prost, 1997) observes that overall numbers count less than relations with the population at large; resistance can only survive and become effective if it achieves significant public support. Although the British and Gaullist intelligence services kept lists of agents, these have never been released. The use of post-facto dossiers to reconstitute membership data is thus inevitable, but is vitiated by serious discrepancies: for example, the acceptance rate of applications for CVR cards varied between different departments from 4 per cent to 85 per cent (and many genuine resisters may never have bothered to apply in the first place). Another controversial issue concerns motivation. The leader of Libération-Sud, Emmanuel d'Astier, caused a stir by describing most resisters as socially marginal figures when interviewed by Marcel Ophuls for his documentary film *Le Chagrin et la pitié* (1971). Less provocative historians suggest that in fact most resistance leaders (apart from the communists) belonged to intellectual and political elites; thus according to Laurent Douzou, 'their marginality was due to the state of opinion and not to their social situation' (Prost, 1997: 15). Rebelliousness and the willingness to take risks are obviously key factors; I have never seen convincing estimates for the survival rates of active resisters, but it is a tragic fact that many of the early resisters ended up dead.

Most resisters were relatively young and male (70 per cent under forty and 85 per cent male according to Rousso, 1985), although with significant variations. The maquis was composed almost entirely of men aged between sixteen and twenty-five, as might be expected of often untrained and relatively mobile partisan units; the 'groupes francs', armed action units attached to movements and networks, similarly drew recruits from this age group, whereas intelligence networks normally used agents aged thirty to fifty because of the skills and experience they needed. Since nearly all internal resistance activity was effectively based either on maquis groups or networks and movements, brief clarification about these organisations is useful. In the post-war era, some 45 movements and 270 networks were officially recognised via their 'liquidateurs' (that is, resisters given the task of retrospectively identifying genuine claims).[29] The BCRA (the London-based Gaullist intelligence service) defined the essential criteria for a resistance movement as publication of a journal for propaganda purposes, together with an efficient intelligence network and paramilitary group. Over 1000 clandestine periodicals were published during the occupation; the most important usually took the name of their movement (the best known including *Combat*, *Libération* and *Franc-Tireur*). Many networks were however directly linked to overseas intelligence agencies (such as the BCRA or the British SOE, Special Operations Executive), without being allied to movements in mainland France.

The Mouvements Unis de la Résistance, formed by the fusion of the main movements in the unoccupied zone, claimed that their military wing, the Armée secrète, numbered 75,000 men in June 1943, but this is probably a gross overestimate. By autumn 1943, there were perhaps 30,000 maquisards, only 10,000 of whom had light arms. In any case, the resistance had little impact on German troops before the closing months of the occupation; given the overwhelming superiority of German forces in numbers, arms and training, this is hardly surprising (in the first two years of occupation, at least 350,000 German troops were stationed in the occupied zone; by early 1944, there were 54 Wehrmacht divisions in France comprising 1.4 million men mostly based in coastal areas in order to repel the expected allied invasion). It should be stressed that resistance functioned more as a form of political opposition, and in specific clandestine activities such as sabotage, information-gathering and escape networks, than as an organised military force. When maquis units engaged in large-scale, direct conflict (rather than surreptitious guerrilla actions) with German troops, usually following a premature attempt to 'liberate' territory, they were invariably wiped out, with vicious reprisals being visited on civilians assumed to have supported them. The most notorious case was the battle for the Vercors in June and July 1944, which led to bitter recriminations and accusations of betrayal against the CFLN and allies for failing adequately to support the premature uprising.[30] The maquis, in fact, remains one of the most contested elements of the French resistance, as regards both its political goals and tactical efficacy. As H.R. Kedward observes, in a thoroughly researched study, 'the maquis were born outside the initiative of the national leaders of the resistance' (1993: 35), and consequently viewed with hostility not merely by the occupying forces but also by allied and resistance leaders whose authority they contested. In consequence:

> The maquis in retrospect has been assigned to a largely inferior canon of history, transmitted by methods seen as lightweight, or even dubious, such as stories, anecdotes and polemic. The maquis, ostensibly due to its association with requisitions and retributive justice, was allotted this lower historical status almost immediately after the liberation. (Kedward, 1993: 230)

Both the political legitimacy and military effectiveness of the maquis have been called into question.

Accusations of extortion and banditry against maquis groups and leaders were not necessarily limited to their avowed adversaries. One of the less explored aspects of post-war justice is the prosecution of resistance activists for criminal offences committed under the occupation. In 1952, for instance, at least one hundred former resistance fighters were still imprisoned, having been convicted despite their membership of recognised groups; Henry Rousso suggests in his article 'L'Épuration en France' (1992) that as many as 1000 individuals were tried between 1944 and 1953 for crimes allegedly committed under the guise of resistance. There is no doubt that many profiteers, collaborators and extortionists attempted to masquerade as resisters; the 'faux résistant' is a figure of legend. Sonia Combes cites several notorious cases, including a Vichy *sous-chef de cabinet* responsible for arrests of Jews who subsequently became a well-known historian of the resistance, having been deported as a resister in 1944 (1994: 35–6). What is more disturbing is the persecution of genuine resisters, most of them low-ranking members of the communist FTP lacking influential protection. Noting in 'Destins de maquisards dans l'après-guerre' (in Boursier, 1997) that several hundred legitimate resisters were in prison in 1947, Robert Chantin observes 'genuine cases of police and judicial harassment of resisters, with investigations being pursued into their property and actions during the occupation'; in his view, this shows 'a terrible political defeat for resisters' (pp. 127, 129), since many of them were the victims of policemen, prosecutors and judges who had served Vichy and then continued their careers under the Republic. He cites the telling case of a Polish resister condemned to death for executing an anti-resistance police inspector, whose sentence was eventually commuted to three years' imprisonment and expulsion from France.

As for the military efficacy of the resistance, General Eisenhower famously compared the contribution of the Forces Françaises de l'Intérieur (FFIs) to the liberation of France to that of fifteen regular army divisions. In his speech celebrating the liberation of Paris in August 1944, de Gaulle triumphantly declared, 'we have expelled the enemy from our land with the aid of our dear and admirable allies' (quoted by Daninos, 1979: 78), while the communist leader Rol-Tanguy went so far as to assert that 'the resistance alone liberated three quarters of metropolitan France' (in Guérin, 2000: 21). None of these statements can be taken at face value. From thirty-nine allied divisions, only one French division under General Leclerc actually participated in the Normandy landings, which were the direct cause of liberation; it was this division which liberated Paris. Leclerc himself estimated that only 10 per cent of the FFI (the combined military units of the internal resistance) were 'genuine combatants' (cited by Dreyfus, 1996: 508). The historian F.-G. Dreyfus suggests that Eisenhower's diplomatic compliment is no more than a reference to the total numbers of FFIs (about 125,000 joined the regular French army of 550,000 men which fought in the final months of the war in Europe). And Philippe Buton similarly argues that the FFI played no more than a nominal role in the liberation of 85 per cent of French towns (they were most active in the north-west and south-west), although the symbolic importance of the liberation of Paris did play a vital part in restoring France to the victors' camp and building Gaullist legitimacy (in Azéma and Bédarida, 1993). The allies' preference for saturation bombing of strategic targets in France, which caused large-scale civilian casualties, has often been questioned by resistance supporters, on the grounds that sabotage could have been more widely exploited; but as far as the allies were concerned, resistance was peripheral as a military force, to be used for espionage purposes or small-scale guerrilla action.

The fact that individual resistance agents were likely to be captured and to betray secret information under duress was at times exploited quite cynically by their masters in London. Special Operations Executive agents, for example, were sometimes given false information (without their knowledge) in the expectation that eventually they would betray it to the Germans. Though some agents heroically refused to reveal anything, others found themselves playing a double game, in effect offering their services to both sides, sometimes with the consent of their superiors. Their dilemma was arguably worse than the situation of those who had the courage to endure torture in silence, as Cathelin and Gray argue:

> Such agents, who were manipulated by those who held real power in intelligence and police matters, whether French or German, were sacrificial victims who could be disavowed at any moment; they ran as much risk of being executed by resisters, unaware of their real role and assuming them to be collaborators, as by the Germans, who had discovered or simply suspected their game. (1972: II, 26)

This may be one reason why certain double agents were treated fairly leniently if they survived the occupation, since it was barely possible to achieve any certainty about where their loyalties finally lay. The SOE agent Henri Déricourt, and René Hardy, a senior figure in Combat (a resistance movement in the south zone), for example, were acquitted of treason in post-war trials, despite the existence of considerable evidence against them.

Such ambiguities and complexities, when multiplied across hundreds and thousands of cases involving both collaborators and resisters, explain why post-war judgements were bound to be controversial and contested, as issues such as ideological or opportunistic commitment, moral responsibility and individual or collective guilt were increasingly difficult if not impossible to disentangle.[31] What is most surprising, however, is not the somewhat arbitrary nature of the justice delivered in the name of the re-established Republic in the years immediately following the liberation, but rather the protraction until the very end of the twentieth century of judgements and punishments delivered in the courtroom for crimes committed during the occupation. The inquisition of prosecutor and judge has not always given way to the more dispassionate enquiry of the historian, as might have been expected; instead, courts rather bizarrely have called upon historians to act as expert witnesses on events of which few of the protagonists have first-hand knowledge. To conclude this discussion, we need briefly to review the legal and moral questions raised by the liberation purges, and their continuation well beyond the normal statute of limitations in certain notorious cases, since treason against the state or betrayal of humane values are central to the accusations levelled against those under judgement.

Two essential points worth emphasising from the outset are that some of the facts regarding the 'épuration', the purging or purification of the nation of the evils of occupation, remain contested or obscure, and that such obscurity has often become a pretext for defenders of collaboration to establish spurious parallels between the excesses of resistance or liberation justice and those committed by the Vichy government, its agents and the occupying forces. The Conseil National de la Résistance (CNR) included the punishment of traitors and collaborators in its programme of post-war reforms; the supposed illegality of the Vichy regime was a key issue in prosecuting collaborators. Article 75 of the existing penal code, relating to treason defined as intelligence with an enemy power, was deemed broad enough to include collaboration, although the CFLN also enacted legislation to facilitate the extension of article 83 to include attacking resisters and allied forces in the category of acts harmful to national defence. Moreover, the lesser offence of 'national indignity' was created in August 1944, which meant in effect offering services to Vichy and collaboration. Three special courts were set up to try collaborators and traitors: the Haute Cour de justice to judge senior political figures (which sat until 1949, tried 108 cases and delivered eight death sentences, only three of which were executed); and local courts of justice and civic chambers, the first to deal with other serious charges and the second with lesser forms of 'national indignity'. These latter courts dealt with 124,751 cases up to 1951, sentencing 40,000 people to 'dégradation nationale' (which meant loss of civic rights and financial penalties), 39,000 to imprisonment, and 7000 to death (though in practice only 767 death sentences were carried out). In addition, military tribunals dealt with other cases, and delivered some 800 death sentences which were executed. Although prison sentences were often severe, progressively broader amnesties voted by parliament in 1947, 1951 and 1953 led to the release of most collaborators and the restoration of their lost rights; the amnesty of August 1953, justifiable in the spirit of national reconciliation, in fact made the naming of collaborators illegal and also offered exemption for crimes committed as acts of war on behalf of the resistance.

Apart from the justification of such punishments or the final equation between crimes of collaboration or resistance, what has been most bitterly contested, however, are the acts of retribution committed against collaborators in the closing months of the occupation outside the legal framework eventually set up by de Gaulle's provisional government. While the figure of some 1567 executions carried out following the verdicts of duly constituted courts is generally accepted, there is no consensus about the actual numbers of French people killed in more summary fashion either in combat with the resistance or by improvised resistance tribunals. Robert Aron, who devoted several books to the 'épuration', noted that quasi-legal purges of supposedly undesirable elements in society began with Daladier's banning of the Communist Party in September 1939, and were eagerly pursued by the Vichy regime's exclusions for 'crimes of opinion or belonging to the wrong organisation' (1967: 16). The resistance and liberation government, in other words, were driven to follow the practice of their adversaries by pursuing justice that was both political and retroactive; the armistice agreement and Pétain's government were deemed to be illegal partly in order to legitimise their opponents' claims to power, and thus collaboration was belatedly turned into a crime, for all that it was arguably an obligation for most citizens during the occupation. From an understandable insistence on imitation, Aron moves to a more dubious equation, however, when he compares the atrocities of the liberation with those of the Gestapo (1967: 571) and asserts that about 40,000 summary executions were carried out in the spring and summer of 1944, a figure five times higher than the one usually computed from semi-official sources (see for example, Rousso, 'L'Épuration en France', 1992). Other historians suggest that this lower figure of 8000 deaths may be a gross underestimate and that estimates conflated from gendarmerie reports produce a higher figure of about 17,000 summary killings (see for example, Dreyfus, 1996: 565).

There is little doubt that appalling atrocities were committed by both sides in the state of civil war that marked the closing months of the occupation. What distinguishes collaboration from resistance, however, is not merely the enormous discrepancy in numbers of deaths, which only the most prejudiced commentator can ignore (that is, some 200,000 executions and deportations carried out by the occupying forces over four years, as opposed to the likely maximum of 20,000 executions carried out by the forces of resistance), but also the fact that de Gaulle's government and its successors rapidly restored the acceptable legal processes which the Vichy government had subverted by its policies of mass internment and deportation. Reconciliation and acceptance of responsibility have been harder to achieve; the very notion of justice, at least as pursued through courts of law which inflict sanctions, may make the dispassionate acceptance of individual and collective guilt impossible. Fifty years after the war ended, Jacques Chirac became the first head of state to acknowledge publicly the crimes committed by the French government during the occupation, setting aside the pettifogging legal niceties which had allowed his predecessors to deny any moral responsibility on the part of the French state for acts committed by the Vichy regime. On the other hand, the trials of Barbie, Touvier and Papon for crimes against humanity forty or fifty years after they were committed can be seen at best as offering younger generations an exemplary history lesson and belated, somewhat nominal recompense to their victims; at worst, they are grotesque media spectacles which raise far more questions than they ever answer (such as why prosecution was delayed for three or more decades and why other torturers and desk-murderers escaped similar retribution). The accused do not accept any guilt; indeed, Papon has presented himself as a victim of injustice and is appealing to the European Court of Human Rights for redress.[32] When both former resisters and alleged collaborators do not hesitate to use the courts to impede historical investigation, and access to potentially incriminating archival records remains very restricted, any attempt to reconstruct the history of the occupation must remain partial.

2
Leaders and the People

Prefacing a book enticingly entitled *Le Rire en guerre*, Mina and André Guillois make an interesting observation about the shortcomings of most historical studies: 'One thing struck us in reading the hundreds of books and articles devoted to the Second World War. Most describe the business of war like an accountant drawing up a balance sheet' (1969: 9).

The studied neutrality which most historians regard as a prerequisite of their discipline, their respect for objectively verifiable facts, can in other words lead them to undervalue or ignore the emotional, psychological and material aspects of human experience which remain buried in their material. Horrific events are reduced to the level of statistics or strategic conundrums; the historian features as a sort of arbiter whose judgements are uncontaminated by any admission of feelings or direct involvement.[1] This reluctance to confront the personal, either in the event or its retelling, creates a curious ethical and emotional void in many historical accounts. The fact that warfare involves mass killing, and more specifically the large-scale and usually pointless slaughter of young men and unprotected civilians, initiated and directed by small groups of powerful old men, whether statesmen or generals, who also take every step to protect their own security, remains oddly invisible. War, one might say, is the betrayal and sacrifice of the people by their leaders, leaders whose virtues nonetheless continue to be extolled to subsequent generations, even when their principal achievement is as perpetrators of mass murder.[2] The contrasting experiences and judgements of ordinary citizens and those who aspired to lead them through the rigours of defeat, occupation and liberation in wartime France form the subject of this chapter (while subsequent chapters will look more closely at those who served the state in a humbler, bureaucratic capacity, those who committed themselves directly to violent action for or against the German occupiers, and finally those who turned their experience of occupation into cultural products like novels and films).

That sense of disconnection which we often have between the chaotic reality of daily events, especially at a time of crisis, and the self-serving gloss put upon them by politicians or the historians who too often become their uncritical spokesmen, can find emotional expression in despair, rage or humour. Hence the well-known joke summing up the French infantryman's perception of the national fiasco which took phoney war to resounding defeat in the period from September 1939 to June 1940: 'Eight months' card-playing and one month's running'. This quip is recycled in the Guillois's anthology, a book which illustrates a different methodological problem from the ethical dilemma confronting the historian whose neutralised account lapses into neutered accountancy: one joke may offer a witty and telling insight into ordinary people's perceptions, whereas an interminable enumeration of jokes, good and bad, offers no more than the most anecdotal, superficial insight into humour, mass psychology or cultural modes. Unfortunately, nearly all the works like *Le Rire en guerre* which purport to study aspects of daily and cultural life under the occupation turn out to be such uncritical, repetitive compilations which make little attempt to relate individual events and experiences to wider issues.[3]

Until quite recently, academic historians have preferred to leave what could be called the texture of daily life with its material and moral exigencies to more journalistic chroniclers, novelists and diarists. Hence Jean-Pierre Rioux's comment, in an essay bemoaning 'Le Clair-obscur du quotidien', that 'the weight of daily living, of day-to-day survival, the terrible, crushing patience needed as time seemed suspended, have been rarely taken into consideration or account in the historiography of the period 1940–44' (in Azéma and Bédarida, 1992: 622). Pierre Laborie's *L'Opinion française sous Vichy* (1990) had in fact attempted to take account of the symbolic and imaginary in the shaping of social and political attitudes and, as its title suggests, Dominique Veillon's *Vivre et survivre en France 1939–1947* (1995) represents a further, equally rigorous attempt to fill the gap in the social and sociological understanding of the period. Such books do tell us a great deal about the widespread material misery that surrounded pockets of privilege or how *attentisme* was a subtle, shifting phenomenon, as much a necessary survival strategy as a sign of abject abnegation or crass opportunism. But how individuals reflected on events, were shaped by them or tried to shape them, how they related their personal experiences to collective goals, patriotic loyalties and national identities, how they judged their fellow citizens and leaders: such issues are central to any understanding of the occupation, yet still remain half forgotten and disconnected in the countless journals and memoirs of the period.

Opinion and daily life

Before we examine a representative sample of such material and what it tells us about the social, political and ethical issues that determined the course of the occupation (such as material deprivation, personal and national identity, power relations, authority and legitimacy), some general comments about the conditions of daily life will provide a useful context. The relationship between the private and political domains during the occupation is oddly paradoxical: on the one hand, one can see an obvious, increasing separation between the ruling elite and the people, in that Pétain, unlike other dictators such as Napoleon III or indeed Hitler, never sought a popular, plebiscitary mandate beyond that given by the demoralised National Assembly in July 1940, while his unelected government progressively curtailed civil rights and abetted the persecution of large groups of citizens. The social reforms promised by the so-called National Revolution had relatively little impact in practice, particularly compared with the all too visible negative effects created by the demands and depredations of the German occupying forces. Ultimately, the Vichy government became little more than a repressive agency reluctantly acting on behalf of the Germans, rather than a body directing and unifying the nation, as the gap between official discourse and social reality grew ever wider. Hence Célia Bertin's observation, in a study of women during the occupation, that 'There was an astonishing inconsistency between Vichy's decisions or Pétain's declarations, and life as it really was' (1993: 58). Yet this political and moral bankruptcy, which vainly sought to justify the suppression of republican political liberties under the guise of national regeneration, actually had the effect of politicising daily life to a far greater extent than is the case under a stable, consensual regime, in that such routine acts as purchasing food, travelling, sending letters or even listening to the radio and expressing an opinion became subject to totalitarian controls which indicated the increasingly intrusive nature of the government and occupying forces.

RC

The Jewish writer Léon Werth perceived the totalitarian tendencies implicit in the notorious pre-printed inter-zone postcards, which for a long period restricted communication to a few standardised phrases, noting sarcastically in his journal (13 November 1940):

> A strong government ought to authorise only this sort of correspondence, even after peace was signed. It would thus avoid its subjects experiencing the dangerous aberrations of intimate feelings and its subjects would be constantly reminded that all feelings and thoughts are under the control of the state. (1992: 90–1)

Real power, in the material and economic sense, lay with the Germans, who with their control of prisoners of war, the demarcation line and the movement of supplies, were constantly able to exert pressure on the government and demand compliance while conceding nothing. The Vichy regime's political impotence is one reason why Marshal Pétain functioned on a sort of spiritual plane, appealing to values and ideals that exceeded practical realities. Twelve million photographs of the Marshal were sold in 1941, but his pervasive image was as much that of a quavering saviour as of a stern dictator: omnipresent perhaps as an icon whose efficacy seemed increasingly dubious, but from November 1942 largely absent from the domain of meaningful political action. The same might be said of de Gaulle, a rival saviour offering an eternal vision of French grandeur equally at odds with the apparent turn of events, except that the General moved in a trajectory that reversed Pétain's, from the absent obscurity of exile to glorious restoration as liberator and unifier. While the territorial battle for French soil was largely fought between the allies and the Germans, Vichy and its Gaullist opponents engaged in 'a formidable struggle for the soul of the nation' (Bédarida, in Azéma and Bédarida, 1992: 82).

Vichy, however, lost this spiritual or psychological battle not merely because of the changing course of the war but primarily because it had already lost the battle with the Germans for the body of the French nation and its citizens. Pétain promised unity and cohesion at the cost of material sacrifices, when in fact the armistice brought material hardship as well as division, repression and pillage, and the path of collaboration led to servile abasement. Apart from the disruption caused by territorial fragmentation and the exclusion of prisoners, deportees and racial outsiders, economic constraints such as rationing further weakened national solidarity: even the division of citizens into a dozen different rationing categories, from infants to the aged, reveals how inequitable separation became a systematised feature of everyday existence. Despite some palliative measures to control goods and prices, the shortages created mainly by the draconian armistice terms led to wide-scale hoarding and black-marketeering. In practice, small-scale dealing by individuals was generally tolerated. While 7000 people were employed by 1944 ostensibly to stop contraband dealing and profiteering, many of these agents were themselves active black-marketeers, as were the Germans who had access to the huge surplus funds available through the 'frais d'occupation' and who set up semi-official purchasing bureaux to buy up enormous quantities of goods. The bypassing of official controls was thus 'raised to the level of an institution, with the general complicity of the whole nation' (Sédillot, 1985: 145). At the same time, the Germans exploited the parallel market through a constellation of French intermediaries who operated on an industrial level and amassed vast fortunes.[4]

Crime rates rose significantly during the occupation: imprisonment for petty offences doubled between 1938 and 1942, with around 100,000 convictions annually in 1942 and 1943 for offences related to rationing (see Aubusson de Cavarlay, 1993 for details). Most of these offenders received fines. Crimes of opinion often attracted more severe punishment. Although no official statistics recorded their frequency, diarists opposed to Vichy often note newspaper reports which show how hostile opinion expressed too visibly was quashed. Pétain's predecessor as prime minister, Paul Reynaud, who spent over four years in detention thanks to the callous malice of the Marshal, notes the case of a man who derisively referred to Pétain in public as 'the old monkey' being sentenced to three months' imprisonment in 1940 for insulting the head of state, the sentence being increased to six months on appeal. Léon Werth also records a number of similar cases, such as a six months' sentence given to five individuals in July 1941 for singing 'seditious songs'. By way of comparison, it is worth noting that recorded crime and convictions also rose by over 50 per cent in war-time Britain, where new offences relating for example to 'disrupting morale' were created and courts were used for political purposes: thus an elderly American woman was given one month's hard labour and fined in March 1942 for abusing Churchill and Roosevelt in writing (see Smithies, 1982). Churchill himself remarked that 'In time of war the machinery of government is so strong it can afford largely to ignore popular feeling' (quoted by Ponting, 1990: 171).

In the last years of the occupation, however, the machinery of government at Vichy was far from strong, as it lost its territorial autonomy, fleet and empire, as Laval supplanted Pétain, and as Laval in turn was threatened with replacement by pro-German collaborationists, three of whom took over the key functions of propaganda, the maintenance of order and the labour force in the final months of his government (that is, Henriot, Darnand and Déat). Perhaps because of this vulnerability and the precariousness of collaboration, the Vichy regime was surprisingly attentive to public opinion, even if it took no steps to restore its initial popularity. Although an institute for sampling opinion (IFOP) had been established in 1939, the occupation government's authoritarian, counter-revolutionary ideology opposed any official democratic form of consultation, whether through polls or elections. Nonetheless, Jacques Doriot's comment in the early months of the regime, 'if there were just a handful of us surrounding the Marshal, it would be treason; but there are millions of us, so it's opinion!' (quoted by Chaix, 1985: 41), shows how mass support did legitimise Pétain's efforts as peace-broker.

Had Pétain sought public approval for his constitutional role through a plebiscite in the first six months of the occupation, there is little doubt that he would have won a majority as large as that given him by the National Assembly (and de Gaulle's attack on Vichy's legitimacy would have been considerably weakened). Within eighteen months, however, such popular support had rapidly dwindled. Accounts of public attitudes and feelings, whether undertaken during the occupation or subsequently by historians, are inevitably approximate and selective samples. Some investigators overstate the range of their knowledge: thus a work by Marcel Baudot entitled *L'Opinion publique sous l'occupation* (1960) proves to be based on archival material held in one single department, the Eure (where, if we are to believe this author, there was hardly a single collaborator in the ranks of the police and civil service). Summaries of opinion during the occupation, whether by officials like prefects or resistance activists, were even more subject to distortion, since they were undertaken clandestinely and slanted according to their audience. Nevertheless, following on from Laborie, Jean-Marie Flonneau has outlined persuasively some six phases in 'L'Évolution de l'opinion publique de 1940 à 1944' (in Azéma and Bédarida, 1992), based on information contained in reports provided by prefects, mayors and postal censors and Vichy, German and allied intelligence agents. From initial acceptance of the armistice and the regime across the country in 1940, by spring 1941 there was a noticeable divergence between the zones, with growing hostility towards the policy of collaboration in the occupied zone, especially in the 'zone interdite'. By the end of 1941, though Pétain retained his prestige, there were increasing doubts about his regime in the south zone (as his notorious 'vent mauvais' speech of August 1941, to be discussed below, testifies). This divorce between the population and Vichy was fully consummated in 1942; by the end of the year, there was more support for de Gaulle than Pétain. The invasion of the unoccupied zone in November 1942 and the forced labour laws led to more open hostility; in the last nine months of occupation, most people wanted only liberation, while fearing the return of full-scale war which it entailed.

There are four other important points worth stressing about general attitudes. Hostility towards the Germans and sympathy towards the British were constants; the British attack on the French fleet at Mers-el-Kebir in July 1940, or subsequent clashes between British/Free French troops and Vichy forces at Dakar or in Syria had surprisingly little negative impact. Second, opinion tended to misjudge Pétain's own position, assuming him to be hostile to collaboration or at least playing a double game (hence his dismissal of Laval in December 1940 was perceived as the courageous removal of a collaborator rather than the vindictive elimination of a rival which it actually was). Third, the October 1940 statute excluding Jews from many professions had little effect on the majority of the population, whereas the more visible persecution of Jews with the mass round-ups begun in 1942 did arouse hostility towards Vichy's anti-Semitism. Nevertheless, and finally, as the sub-prefect of Pithiviers noted in January 1944, 'the sensitive points on the barometer of opinion are indisputably stomachs and wallets' (quoted by Flonneau, in Azéma and Bédarida, 1992: 520). Opinions were largely determined by fear and self-interest; as Roger Grenier observed, writing a few years after the occupation, 'As for the collective consciousness, it was deadened by an inertia that inclined it towards hostility towards the disturbing presence of the occupier, but you cannot call this feeling resistance' (1948: 109). Passive hostility towards Vichy shifted towards passive complicity with resistance.

There were a few acts of public protest against the government or occupying forces, which were rapidly repressed. A miners' strike in the Nord/Pas-de-Calais region in May and June 1941, for instance, ended with 450 arrests and 244 deportations. Consequently, most statements and acts of opposition were made privately. Some of these were recorded by the Service du contrôle technique (SCT), an official but secret organisation which employed thousands of civil servants to intercept letters and telephone calls; its records were largely un-

explored until they were finally made available to the historian Antoine Lefébure, whose book *Les Conversations secrètes des Français sous
l'occupation* (1993) offers a fascinating account of the interaction between citizens and government authorities. Spying on letters (known
as 'perlustration') dates back to Louis XIII and the early postal service;
it continues today, albeit in a more limited form targeted at specific
individuals. During the occupation, about 10 per cent of letters were
opened and copied (before being sent on to their addressee), while
some telephone calls were transcribed or recorded on 78 rpm records.
The objective was both to canvas opinion and to uncover potential
crimes. The Service was under German control in the north zone (and
the whole SCT system was taken over by the Germans from March
1944); at the same time, some resisters within the postal system tapped
German calls or forwarded some SCT reports to London. Each *département* produced a regular regional synthesis sent to the prefect and
higher authority; some two million letters were examined monthly
in 1942.

While wartime censorship of mail was overt, the SCT functioned
secretly, although most people were aware vaguely that the post was
insecure. The hypocritical morality that characterises Vichy's authoritarian attitude towards its citizens (and is inseparable from its craven
servility towards the Germans) is well demonstrated by a missive circulated by the Minister for Communications Di Pace in August 1942,
reprimanding staff for violating professional ethics: their offence was
not to open private mail, but to reveal that the practice occurred.
Lefébure notes that although the organism offered only a crude estimate of public opinion, 'on the other hand, its policing role was important. It also permitted the authoritarian Vichy state to maintain a
climate of anxiety and delation which discouraged any movement of
open revolt' (1993: 45). Thus the *chef de la sûreté* had no hesitation in
recommending in April 1941 that two Jewish women living in Nice
who were Dutch refugees, and whose supposedly subversive telephone
conversation was intercepted, should be arrested and sent to Drancy.
Lefébure says that of the 100,000 letters which he read during his
research, few showed any sympathy for the Jews; on the other hand,
he cites letters sent by Jews denouncing other Jewish business rivals to
the authorities, which reveal a depressing lack of solidarity even
among the victims of Vichy.

Delation (that is, such vindictive acts of denunciation, often taking
the form of anonymous letters) was a common practice; as
André Halimi (1983) observes in his study of the phenomenon, it is an

inherent feature of coercive regimes which violate the privacy of their citizens. Most of Marshal Pétain's voluminous postbag consisted of letters from his admirers denouncing their colleagues and neighbours, with envy and malice masquerading as public-spiritedness (Ferro, 1987: 150). Halimi estimates that as many as five million letters of denunciation may have been sent during the occupation (and the practice continued after the liberation), leading Pétain to criticise their excesses in January 1942, although 'Denunciation was to all intents and purposes a civic act incited by legislative texts and encouraged by leaders' (Halimi, 1983: 8). Such betrayal of trust was indeed institution-alised by Pétain's regime: by identifying his enemies not as the Germans, but as ideological or racial opponents to be denounced as terrorists and dissidents or arrested and deported, he fractured national unity and solidarity, while hypocritically distancing himself from those whose zeal in persecuting their fellow citizens he had initially encouraged (as his belated criticism of the criminal behaviour of the Milice demonstrates). Ultimately, Vichy's attempts to control and con-ciliate public opinion failed: repression replaced the quest for approval. The Vichy government was far more successful in upholding public order and excluding undesirable elements than it was in offering pro-tection to its citizens, in sustaining its credibility or even in ensuring its own integrity and autonomy. Yet while Pétain's political leadership evidently faltered, his power as a symbol remained much more vital. While in one sense Pétain was the victim of the propaganda that at-tributed qualities to him as a statesman which manifestly he did not possess, as a misguided heroic martyr whose ultimate sacrifice was disgrace and life imprisonment he remains a compelling figure. These contrasting forms of leadership (put simply, between the pragmatic and the symbolic), and changing perceptions of them, demand fuller investigation.

Pétain and de Gaulle

The parallels and similarities between the two military and political adversaries who both claimed to incarnate a certain idea of France and to lead the nation from the chaos of defeat to unity and salvation have often struck their biographers (J.R. Tournoux produced a long book on the subject in 1964),[5] even if history offers a more brutal contrast between the loser and the winner: in 1940, Pétain committed the in-defensible act of betraying his country to the Nazis, while in 1944, de Gaulle restored France to democratic government and political independence (and withdrew into private life when his role had been fulfilled). Both pursued relatively undistinguished military careers until late middle age, in part because both took a belligerently critical stance towards the outmoded military doctrines favoured by the army high command: in Pétain's case, a recognition of the devastating effect of firepower and the consequent folly of unprotected frontal attacks by infantry; in de Gaulle's, an understanding of the importance of mechanised warfare driven by strong armoured divisions (although he underestimated the part to be played by aircraft). The outbreak of war in 1914 and 1939 proved both of them to be right in their predictions and took them with astonishing rapidity from the obscurity of the middle ranks to power and notoriety. Aged fifty-eight in 1914, Pétain's only immediate prospect was retirement, but within four years he rose from colonel to Marshal of France. De Gaulle was promoted from colonel to acting brigadier-general at the age of forty-nine in May 1940 to command an armoured division, and then called into Reynaud's government as under-secretary of state for war on 6 June, a ministerial position which he held for eleven days, until his rejection of the armistice and Pétain's government in the celebrated speech broadcast from London on 18 June.

From this point onwards, de Gaulle ceased to be a conventional military or political figure: within a few weeks, he was stripped of his rank by Vichy and finally sentenced to death for 'desertion' by a military court. From being a mutineer without an army, an exile without a country, a leader without a people, within three years he achieved the almost miraculous feat of becoming the head of a French government in exile which controlled most of the overseas empire and had greater credibility with the nation than the rival puppet government in Vichy. He refused promotion to full general, understanding that he operated outside hierarchical ranks. Pétain, on the other hand, sought and acquired honours and ranks even when they fell outside his real achievements and competence. This is not the place to review his career in detail, but to understand how his conception of leadership and his relationship with the people were manufactured and practised it is worth recalling that as the general who saved Verdun and quelled the mutinies in the French army in 1917, Pétain acquired a reputation as a military strategist and humane leader which in the inter-war years brought him positions of influence and immense popularity. He was commander-in-chief of the French armies until February 1920, and then vice-president of the supreme war council (a body chaired by the minister of war, but dominated by aged generals and marshals), as well

EDINBURGH UNIVERSITY LIBRARY

WITHDRAWN

as inspector general of the army from 1922, in effect controlling military policy until his retirement in 1931, when Weygand replaced him as vice-president and Gamelin became chief of general staff. His influence continued well into the 1930s, for example with his appointment as minister of war for nine months in Doumergue's government in February 1934. From this period, he became a favourite of the right as a possible extra-parliamentary head of state; at this stage the Marshal himself, however, though disillusioned by his first-hand experience of the parliamentary intrigues that led to the fall of most Third Republic governments within months, or even days, 'wanted, not dictatorship, but a strong Republic under a President who would at the same time be head of the executive' (Griffiths, 1994: 195), a position close to that adopted unsuccessfully by de Gaulle at the beginning of the Fourth Republic and successfully with the creation of the Fifth Republic twelve years later.

Yet this was the period when France's failure to re-arm and adopt new strategies set in train the defeat of 1940; as a military planner, Pétain proved unable to adapt to the demands of mechanised and aerial warfare. Nonetheless, his authority, for all that it derived from achievements that were seriously outmoded, extended to the intellectual and literary domains: he was made a member of the Académie des sciences morales et politiques in 1919 and elected to the French Academy in 1931. In September 1920, at the age of sixty-four, he married a divorcee Eugénie Hardon to whom he had unsuccessfully proposed nineteen years earlier. His first encounter with Charles de Gaulle occurred in 1912, when the latter began his career in the 33rd Infantry Regiment under Pétain's command. In the 1920s, de Gaulle benefited from Pétain's protection and patronage: his undistinguished grades at the École de Guerre were raised at the Marshal's insistence in 1922 and he joined his protector's staff. But they quarrelled 'over a literary matter', as one biographer quaintly puts it (Atkin, 1998: 46), when de Gaulle drafted a book on behalf of the Marshal but subsequently published it under his own name. In fact, this act of insubordination or misappropriation (according to whose argument one accepts) triggered by literary ambitions reveals how both understood the importance of controlling the written record, of inscribing their identity into the national destiny through the manipulation of symbols and discourse.

De Gaulle emerged victorious from his literary encounter with Pétain as he did from their political conflict. While the General's memoirs were republished on the thirtieth anniversary of his death in 2000 in Gallimard's prestigious Pléiade collection (thereby entering

EDINBURGH UNIVERSITY LIBRARY

WITHDRAWN

what one reviewer called 'the symbolic temple of the great works of universal literature'; Lepape, 2000: ii), the Marshal's writings have survived only because of the efforts of his enthusiastic defenders, and notably his lawyer Jacques Isorni. De Gaulle's best works bear the unmistakable stamp of personal and national grandeur, even if his rhetorical and historical archaisms seem to pastiche literary greatness rather than actually achieve it. On the other hand, Pétain's texts from the Vichy period are too often sanctimonious sermons and pathetic apologies for mediocrity and betrayal of humane and national values; his more glorious deeds from the Great War are recorded in the cautious fashion of campaign reports. Hence de Gaulle's caustic observation that 'The Marshal could never recognise the difference between a book and a general staff report' (quoted by Rey-Herme, 1978: 7). The most obvious difference is that books are written by individuals and reports by committees, a distinction which explains another trenchant observation made by de Gaulle about his former benefactor: 'He wanted to be an academician, he who had scarcely written anything in his life' (quoted by Lacouture, 1990: 80). Pétain was a writer whose books and speeches were written by other people.

Richard Griffiths notes that Pétain's fellow Marshals Joffre and Foch likewise had their memoirs written by subordinates: 'Alone among such military men, Pétain corrected the style of his collaborators' (1994: 127).[6] The use of ghost-writers by statesmen and celebrities is of course a routine procedure, driven by commercial imperatives but also part of the mythic construction of heroic figures whose greatness supposedly extends beyond their professional genius to the intellectual and artistic domains (Winston's Churchill's prodigious output of books notoriously owed much to teams of researchers).[7] Petain's pretensions as a writer are tragi-comical as much as duplicitous, mainly because of the grotesque disparity between the injunctions and judgements which emerge from his texts and broadcasts and the historical reality which they purport to convey. In practice, he was an editor rather than a writer, who attended pedantically to stylistic details while overlooking, or unquestioningly accepting, the tendentious and mendacious message which his words communicated. Gérard Miller, in a incisive polemical essay on the discourse of *pétainisme*, observes that 'It is impossible to measure the part played by Pétain in the composition of his texts, but one can get an idea of the way in which he wielded his pen: he pruned' (1988: 77–8). He famously stated his preference for the plainest style and syntax by banishing adjectives and asserting that 'The semicolon is a bastard' (p. 78).

To study the texts attributed to Pétain is in other words to study a figure who was in large part constructed and controlled by the propaganda efforts of his entourage.[8] Henri Amouroux states that every aspect of Pétain's existence at Vichy was subject to scrutiny and thus is known to historians (1982: 440), overlooking the fact that very little is known about the Marshal's inner life or thoughts, since the biographical record owes so much to intermediaries whose good faith and veracity are extremely doubtful. Some doubted whether Pétain retained any inner life: hence the cruel joke that circulated about him, that he had expired but that his courtiers had neglected to tell him he was dead. De Gaulle said that Pétain had indeed died in 1925, meaning that the last twenty-five years of the Marshal's existence were no more than a discreditable afterlife, ruining the glory of Verdun. The deafness and inattentiveness which increasingly characterised Pétain's behaviour in his last years as head of state and at his trial are obviously attributable to advanced old age (he was eighty-nine in 1945), even if they were also a convenient defensive posture. Since the man had become myth, the distinction is, in practice, of little importance. It is more interesting to look at the construction of the image and the cult of the Marshal, known as *maréchalisme*, before examining the ideology and influence of *pétainisme* expressed in his speeches and discourse and returning to our comparison with de Gaulle.

In his well-known study of political myths, Raoul Girardet argues that the saviour figure who makes a frequent appearance in the history of post-revolutionary France normally belongs to one or more of four categories: the aged hero called back from retirement; the young warrior; the legislator; the prophet who possesses 'the specific power of the Word' (1990: 79) and seeks to embody the collective identity. (Hitler is a more convincing example of this last model than Pétain, although the Marshal clearly conforms to a great extent to three of the types, as does de Gaulle.)[9] The idolisation to which Pétain was subject during the occupation rather defies belief nowadays, given our entirely negative perception of collaboration and its consequences. But although, as Amouroux dryly observes, by August 1944 most French people also found this idolatry 'inexplicable and inexpiable' (1982: 483), it demonstrates how the relationship between people and leader functions as much on the imaginary and emotional level as in the domain of practical action. How much credence individuals and groups really gave to this myth-making is another matter; the proliferation of propaganda and lack of officially sanctioned alternative sources of information, together with the muzzling of opposition, do not demonstrate either its plausibility or popularity.

In Louis Malle's film *Lacombe Lucien* (1974), a group of French Gestapo agents use a photograph of Pétain for target practice and call him 'the old bum'. A feature film set in June 1944 can offer no more than a hypothetical reconstruction of social attitudes, although such cynical contempt does match the evolution of opinion outlined above. It is certainly hard to believe that anyone except the most simple-minded took seriously the more extreme examples of propaganda offered by some of the Marshal's proselytisers. A bizarre illustration is offered by the works of René Benjamin (1885–1948), such as *Le Maréchal et son peuple*, published in 1941, when the author was a member of the Académie Goncourt. Benjamin announces from the outset that the Marshal's destiny goes beyond history to enter the realm of legend, and therefore demands a poet rather than a historian, although he also emphasises the positive, political rewards offered by acceptance of Pétain's benign dictatorship: 'To all he restores above all what they have forgotten, the visible image of power, of real power, which defends its subjects and grants them the blessed opportunity for respect' (1941: 93). But from this implicit justification of the armistice and constitutional reform, which shows a rational desire to persuade, the writer moves to what can only be called a mystical level, attributing outright supernatural powers to his leader: the purity of his physical being ('His moustache has the impeccable whiteness of virtue', p. 6[10]) is an incarnation of goodness which irradiates his people ('It is the destiny of the Marshal to spread happiness', p. 78) and banishes evil ('Merely by appearing, he expels demons', p. 92).

The bathetic hyperbole with which Benjamin celebrates the Marshal's encounter with his people now reads like an absurdist parody worthy of Ionesco (the novelist Jean Dutourd offered an accurate imitation of it in his satirical novel *Au bon beurre*, published in 1952). It aroused scorn and scepticism during the occupation, even if they were perforce expressed confidentially. Writing in his private journal (published in 1946), Léon Werth questions the motivation of those who purvey such puerile propaganda: ideological conviction or the basest opportunism? The latter seems more probable, in his view. Thus of Benjamin, who won the Goncourt prize in 1915 for the jingoistic *Gaspard*, Werth writes in May 1943: 'The shirking jingoist of 1914–1918 has become by 1940 the man of the Marshal and of Nazism' (1992: 479). Such individuals are consistent only in their extremism and self-serving insincerity. (Benjamin was imprisoned after the liberation, released in 1946 and died in 1948.) Thus Werth notes how Philippe Henriot's vitriolic denunciations of the allies broadcast during the last six months of the occupation exactly match the vitriolic attacks on the Germans which he published in the first six months of the war.

Countless other examples of such short-lived pro-Vichy propaganda could be cited. Historians of the subject like Gilles Ragache (1997) and Judith Proud (1995) have shown how many producers of children's literature hastily switched from promotion of Vichy to the resistance after the liberation, as Pétain vanished from textbooks and street names to be replaced by de Gaulle and Leclerc. Thus the artist Victor Dancette managed to produce for the same publisher one comic book, *Il était une fois un pays heureux*, extolling Vichy in 1943, and to collaborate on another in 1945 vilifying Nazism, *La Bête est morte*, where the war is fought out among animals which reflect some unflattering stereotypes (the French are rabbits, the Germans wolves, the Japanese yellow monkeys, and the Italians hyenas, while the British at least are bulldogs). The folkloric celebrations of the Marshal's stalwart longevity and vitality which strove to cast him as an unshakeable force of nature also verge on the farcical, at least when viewed from the safe distance of this century. On 8 November 1940, in the forest of Tronçais a 270-year-old oak measuring 42 metres was ceremoniously dedicated to the head of state; the unfortunate tree was chopped down by the maquis in the last months of the occupation in a symbolic act of reprisal.

Judith Proud concludes that it is difficult to know whether such propaganda 'did indeed reach its target audience and make any impression' (1995: 69). What is most striking in retrospect is how unconvincing the Pétain of the 1940s appears as a heroic figure. As Lindenberg says, the French nation found in the Marshal 'a "hero" fitting their lassitude and collective renunciation' (1990: 13). The rhetoric and delivery of his speeches convey a pathetic fatalism, wearily stressing the tribulations and suffering which must be endured like so many natural disasters. Whatever his physical vitality, he still sounds like a scolding old man burdened with an office beyond his capacities: 'In his authoritarian but quavering voice, Pétain knows how to whine' (Gervereau and Peschanski, 1990: 130). The political and ideological defence of collaboration presented by his speeches (the transcript of which fills a substantial volume) merits attention, particularly since the essential argument is that honour, unity and authentic national values can be restored only at the price of necessary sacrifices. However, there is a strange denial at the heart of Vichyist discourse: the unstated but glaringly obvious fact that France's misfortunes are due to the Germans and cannot be put right while they are pillaging the country. In an admonitory letter sent to Pétain by his predecessor,

Paul Reynaud, who was arrested in September 1940 and eventually handed over to the Germans in November 1942 to serve as a convenient hostage, along with many other senior figures from the Third Republic, the former prime minister wrote: 'it is not possible to stand tall and to bow down at the same time' (Reynaud, 1997: 58). He also observed in his journal that: 'All the government's efforts are aimed at diverting towards the former regime the hatred which normally would be directed at the enemy' (1997: 106). This substitution of confrontation of the real enemy by harassment of political adversaries leads Vichy ultimately to the treasonable position of openly pursuing those of its citizens courageous enough to fight against the Germans.

The sorry tale of broken promises, evasion of responsibility and malicious willingness to blame others unfolds over four years in the Marshal's addresses to the nation, which if scrutinised critically prove to be damning documents. What is most odd about many of his most celebrated utterances is that they offer at best hollow moralising, at worst blatant falsehoods. On 17 June 1940, the day he became the last head of government of the Third Republic, Pétain famously asserted 'I am making France the gift of my person in order to lessen her misfortune' (1989: 57), casting himself as reluctant martyr rather than incipient dictator. A week later, on 25 June, he was offering his diagnosis of the ills that had brought the defeat and armistice:

> At least honour has been saved...I do not intend to deceive you with lying words. I hate the lies which have done you so much harm...Our defeat is due to our laxness. The spirit of pleasure-seeking destroys what the spirit of sacrifice has created. In the first instance, I would urge you of the need for intellectual and moral recovery. (p. 66)

There is a double irony in these words: first of all that significant parts of the speech (especially the phrase about the hateful lies) were actually composed by the Jewish writer Emmanuel Berl, who was eventually forced to quit Vichy and go into hiding as the anti-Semitic persecution instigated by the government to which he lent his talents took effect. Second, deceitfulness and mendacity are an integral part of Pétain's discourse. References to honour almost invariably seek to cloak dishonourable capitulation. This is shown in June 1940, for example, by the clauses of the armistice (the exact details of which remained a state secret until 1945) outlawing all forms of resistance against the Germans and surrendering German nationals who had sought refuge in France from Nazi persecution. Entering 'the path of collaboration' after his meeting with Hitler at Montoire in October 1940, Pétain again assures his listeners that this is 'with honour and to maintain French unity' (p. 95), promising them in return (albeit in the form of verbs cast in the hypothetical form of the conditional passive) improvement of prisoners' conditions and reduction in the occupation levy, fewer restrictions on movement and better supplies. As we know, he failed to achieve any of these goals. Again, the Marshal protests that 'we have saved our honour' in July 1941 (p. 163) when Vichy forces were beaten into submission and obliged to withdraw from Syria within a few weeks by a combined British and Free French onslaught.

Pétain's attribution of the debacle of 1940 to moral laxity and hedonism reflects the authoritarian elitism behind the National Revolution, and more generally the right's suspicion of the social reforms and disruption brought about by the Popular Front government of 1936; such blanket condemnation of the previous political and moral climate conveniently evades the more immediate causes of defeat, such as gross tactical incompetence on the part of the military high command and its generals during the ten months before the armistice, compounded by two decades of inadequate planning and strategic and political blindness. His statements about the military situation, claiming that the German forces grossly outnumbered the allies in manpower and weaponry, are meant to make defeat seem inevitable; in fact, while the Germans did enjoy vast superiority in air power, they had fewer armoured vehicles and no more men. Pétain's references to the maintenance of French unity are rapidly subverted by his need to blame and punish the groups that contest his legitimacy and authority. In August 1940, he is promising that 'These failings and betrayals will be sought out and punished' (p. 73), especially through a 'purging of our administrative bodies, into which too many recently naturalised Frenchmen have been infiltrated' (p. 72). Paradoxically, unity can be achieved only by a policy of exclusion and limitation of national identity; the problem is that exclusion extends beyond foreigners and Jews to so many other groups that the purge of the body politic effectively finishes off the patient altogether. Unsurprisingly, the Marshal makes no overt reference to the most brutal exclusionary measures of his government at its early or later stages, such as the anti-Semitic legislation and forced labour laws.

As collaboration failed to produce any substantial political or economic benefits, Pétain was increasingly reduced to denouncing his opponents and preaching resignation. He cautioned against 'the deceitful promises of dissidence' in April 1941 (p. 122), a tacit admission that Gaullism was becoming a plausible alternative. Four months later, on 12 August 1941, he delivered his longest broadcast speech, which he began with the notorious reference to the 'vent mauvais' ('ill wind') of doubt and subversion which he detected blowing across the country. The consensus of 1940 has been lost, yet 'France can only be governed with the assent of opinion, assent which is still more necessary in a regime based on authority. Today opinion is divided' (p. 169). The solution offered, however, is unlikely to counteract this alienation since it mainly involves a series of repressive measures: for example, a reinforcement of Darlan's powers (although only three months earlier Pétain and Weygand had forestalled his efforts to allow military collaboration with the Germans); or the creation of a Conseil de justice to judge those held responsible for the disaster (as a consequence, Daladier, Blum, Gamelin, Reynaud and Mandel were all condemned to life imprisonment in October 1941, that is before the abortive Riom trial held in 1942). Recalling his success in putting down the mutinies of 1917 and the rout of 1940, the Marshal assures his listeners that 'Today I wish to save you from yourselves' (p. 172), an effective acknowledgement that the salvation he offers finds little enthusiasm among the nation.

Later speeches insist forlornly on France's dubious neutrality; in January 1942, the whole world is aflame but France at least 'remains outside the conflict' (p. 211). By May 1943, however, France is 'a defeated country, which is no longer in the war but which remains under conditions of war' (p. 307). In a speech given to heads of the Legion of Veterans in August 1943, the Marshal admits openly that events overwhelm him: 'I suffer more than I lead' (p. 310). But Pétain indiscriminately classifies as 'deserters' and 'adversaries' all those who practise dissidence, delation and profiteering. General Giraud's dealings with the Americans after the landings of November 1942 in North Africa are denounced as treason, as is Admiral Darlan's agreement of a cease-fire. In a broadcast on 19 November, Pétain orders continuing resistance against 'Anglo-American aggression' and confirms that he has surrendered his legislative powers to Laval as head of government (both actions making later undocumented claims of secret complicity with Darlan's switch of allegiance seem highly implausible). While in April 1943, Pétain praises the Milice as an 'indispensable force for carrying out the struggle against all sorts of hidden forces' (a barely coded reference to resistance), in a broadcast made on 28 April 1944 (only five weeks before the allied landings in Normandy), the Marshal reiterates his denunciation of communism, terrorism, dissidence and indiscipline, stating: 'Frenchmen, any of you, whether public servants, soldiers or ordinary citizens, who join resistance groups are compromising the future of the country. It is in your interest to maintain a correct and loyal attitude towards the occupying troops' (p. 325).

His own words (or the words that he chose to pronounce), with their demand for 'loyalty' towards the Germans and rejection of resistance as damaging the national interest, suffice to convict him of treason, in its customary sense of intelligence with the enemy, and to invalidate later claims that he was himself a proponent of resistance. In June 1945, for instance, he asserted 'I have always resisted the Germans. Thus I could only be in favour of resistance' (Pétain, 1974: 629). The problem is that his few authenticated acts of resistance were private and ineffectual, while all the statements quoted above were made publicly and correspond to the material support offered by his government and administration to the Germans. In October 1941, he proposed offering himself as a hostage to the Germans to deter them from carrying out the mass execution of French hostages as reprisals for resistance assassinations, but was deterred by his entourage. In October 1943, he failed to obtain Laval's resignation in a bid to restore the authority of the National Assembly. He wrote letters to Hitler protesting about German atrocities in July 1944 and to Laval disavowing the Milice in August 1944, when the damage was done. In a message composed on 20 August which he was unable to broadcast, he offered his famous defence of collaboration: 'if I could no longer be your sword, I wished to be your shield' (Pétain, 1989: 341); five days later he was forcibly removed from Vichy and ceased to play any significant role in French affairs until his trial one year later, after the end of the war in Europe.

The Marshal's most energetic defender, the lawyer Jacques Isorni, sought to defend his policy of collaboration on the grounds that moral concessions were made to acquire material benefits, whereas the resistance was willing to make immediate sacrifices in order to gain longer-term moral advantages. The problem with this argument is that in reality the 'shield' policy made certain categories of people expendable, while offering no real possibility of obstructing German demands. (As Julian Jackson observes (2001: 234), 'Pétain's shield was more like a sieve'.) Laval was prepared to sacrifice foreign Jews (children included) in order to protect French nationals, but it remains doubtful whether the survival of 75 per cent of Jews resident in France was actually due to such cynical manoeuvres, as opposed to the increasing reluctance of most of the population to support the government. Pétain's biographer Marc Ferro reasserts Isorni's defence: 'If between 1940 and 1944 the logic of sacrifice saved material goods and human lives, the price was often the honour of the nation. This was a tragic fate for the man who wished to be the moral leader of the French' (1987: 721).

Perhaps the most convincing defence of Vichy is the strategic argument put forward at Pétain's trial: the armistice not only saved France from full-scale devastation but also denied the Germans immediate access to the Mediterranean by allowing the French government to retain control over the south zone and its African colonies, thereby aiding the allied victory in North Africa in 1942–43 (the fact that Vichy officially opposed the landings in November 1942 rather weakens the case, however).

That Pétain failed as both a political and moral leader can hardly be disputed. Had he resigned in 1942, he might well be remembered as a pragmatic defeatist who, by negotiating the armistice, minimised the negative consequences of a defeat brought about by an incompetent military and political class to which he had ceased to belong. By remaining in power even when powerless, by refusing to support resistance, by callously supporting the adversaries of resistance and demanding sacrifices from the population which actually amounted to victimisation and exploitation, he lost all credibility. But while his political impotence after the return of Laval in April 1942 and the reinforcement of Laval's powers in November is rarely contested, his responsibility thereafter as a symbolic figurehead still remains ambiguous. Although the High Court of Justice sentenced him to death for treason in August 1945, the three judges had in fact recommended a far more lenient sentence of five years' banishment; the jury made up of parliamentarians and resisters who had opposed Vichy voted for the harsher punishment by the narrowest of margins (fourteen votes to thirteen), and de Gaulle commuted their sentence to life imprisonment.[11]

That Pétain retained a high level of symbolic credit was partly due to the enduring legend of the victor of Verdun and to a reluctance to subject the acts of the Vichy government to dispassionate scrutiny. Pétain's abandonment of executive power to Laval as head of government also counted in his favour; the latter was executed after a trial in October 1945, where the judgement and execution were despatched in a particularly brutal fashion. Like the Marshal, his prime minister had little time for autobiography. As a consequence, the defence of Laval is often left to highly prejudiced witnesses. His lawyer Jaffré recorded his final words in a book where his disgraced client is cast as the victim of 'a regime based on latent terror' (1953: 13), that is the judicial expediency of the liberation authorities, despite his efforts to protect all the French, as 'the official receiver of a bankruptcy' (p. 117) attempting to salvage some benefits from the ruins of the Third Republic. By remaining in power, Laval claims, he saved Blum and Reynaud from execution (on the other hand, the murder of other ministers like Zay and Mandel and his sanctioning of summary courts martial run by the Milice, which obviously subvert this line of defence, are passed over in silence). When he was originally dismissed by Pétain in December 1940, Laval notoriously abused the head of state as 'a puppet, a windbag, a weathercock blowing with every wind' (quoted by Kupferman, 1988: 280). But he underestimated Pétain's survival skills and ability to shift responsibility on to others. As Fred Kupferman remarks, it was Laval, not Pétain, who publicly stated his wish for German victory in June 1942, who took on what he himself called the thankless task of 'sewage cleaner', and who finished his career in front of a firing squad (just as his turncoat predecessor Admiral Darlan was gunned down by an assassin), while the despised puppet survived and retained much of his heroic allure. Julian Jackson notes that 'Laval took sombre comfort in his unpopularity, as if it conferred the nobility of sacrifice upon him' (2001: 227), though the consolation was illusory.

Laval's defenders argue that he was executed with such indecent haste, just a week before the first legislative elections held on 21 October 1945, because the provisional government needed to demonstrate its willingness to liquidate collaboration. His trial was essentially political: 'His trial, like Pétain's, establishes the legitimacy of the provisional government' (Kupferman, 1988: 506). It is perfectly true that both the Vichy government under Pétain and Laval and its provisional successor under de Gaulle existed in a legal vacuum, since in both cases they operated without a direct democratic mandate or a formally agreed constitution. Vichy's plans to turn the parliamentary regime of the Third Republic into a quasi-dictatorial presidential regime never came to fruition (other than in the version that, ironically, was imposed two decades later by de Gaulle for the Fifth Republic); the curious diarchy of Pétain and Laval in any case soon diverged significantly from this model and their ambiguous regime was known officially only as the 'French State'. Nevertheless, while it is certainly true that de Gaulle's greatest achievement during the occupation was to create from nothing a legitimate government in exile, which was able progressively to take over the running of the empire, rebuild the armed forces, and restore France as a fighting force and respected power on the allied side, it is misleading to imply that the two rival governments and their leaders in Vichy and Algiers can be equated in their arbitrary claims to legitimacy and unity. By 1944, Vichy had degenerated into a police state dominated by pro-German collaborationists (Laval admitted that he had little control over the Milice[12]), whereas popularity, authority and effective action were to be found only in Algiers.

If we return to our comparison of Pétain and de Gaulle, the differences between them are far more important than the similarities, whether in terms of political leadership, personality or literary talents and historical vision. Like Pétain (and no doubt many senior military figures born in the nineteenth century), de Gaulle possessed a domineering character which many found abrasive and authoritarian, though more submissive associates were prepared to act as fawning courtiers. Illuminating anecdotes abound about de Gaulle's ungraciousness towards subordinates who had sacrificed everything to join him in London. When André Dewavrin (who became famous as Colonel Passy, head of the BCRA, the Free French intelligence service) ventured to suggest that a less dictatorial manner might win more friends, the General retorted 'I don't need lessons from a whippersnapper like you!'[13] De Gaulle himself records in his memoirs that he was known, familiarly but regally, as 'le grand Charles'; he does not record less flattering nicknames such as 'Malikoko' (after a fictitious black despot) or 'Charlie Wormwood' (after wormwood and gall).

Unlike Pétain, a childless womaniser and gourmand who hypocritically denounced the perils of such sensuous pleasures when pursued by others, de Gaulle was an austere family man (one of his children was mentally handicapped), largely indifferent to personal comfort or the trappings of power. While both Marshal and General had a quasi-mystical sense of their own importance for the nation's destiny, de Gaulle had a far better grasp of the strategic and political circumstances which would permit him to operate effectively. He therefore understood the necessity to retreat voluntarily from public life when his authority ceased to work. Pétain clung to a regime that survived for four years, deprived him of moral and political authority, and made his claims to be a national saviour look like the self-serving and egotistical delusions of an old man too vain to perceive his limitations. During these four years, spent in exile in England and Algeria, de Gaulle made himself into a competing and more convincing symbol of unity; but less than eighteen months after returning to France as head of the government that replaced Pétain, from August 1944 to January 1946, he abandoned public office, recognising the futility of battling against the parliamentary forces that he had restored to power. Like Pétain, he was called back from retirement as a saviour to resolve a political and military crisis which had defeated his successors (the war for independence in Algeria); but the crisis was resolved and the political regime which he created to solve it has lasted for over forty years and survived de Gaulle's departure.

De Gaulle's rebelliousness made him an exceptional character among senior military figures (whereas Pétain was especially celebrated for quelling mutiny and his hierarchical prestige as the highest-ranking officer in the army was mistakenly thought to endow him with statesmanlike qualities). De Gaulle exemplified the spirit of resistance, not merely in his defiance of authority and disregard of the elite groups which hastened to accept the armistice regime, but in his presumption to embody an alternative form of authority and to claim that his authority was a more authentic representation of the national interest. Members of the internal resistance noted with some bitterness how most army officers were opportunistic *attentistes* who professed loyalty to the Marshal and who often deliberately obstructed resistance, at least during the first three years of the occupation. General Weygand refused to join the resistance in late 1941, after he had been dismissed first as minister of defence and then as governor general in North Africa for his anti-German sentiments (he was deported the following year). When General de Lattre was arrested after a derisory attempt to resist the German invasion of the south zone in November 1942, he refused an offer from the resistance to help him escape (although he changed his mind after some months in prison). General Giraud, whom the Americans unsuccessfully manipulated in order to supplant the intransigent de Gaulle, shared Pétain's reactionary political views and faith in hierarchical authority.

De Gaulle's views on leadership and national grandeur were elaborated in his lectures and written works long before he had the opportunity to put them into practice. *Le Fil de l'épée*, first published in 1932, creates a sententious portrait of the military chief which at times seems comically close to its author's own acerbic temperament and the setbacks which this had caused him. Thus we learn:

> Strong characters are habitually abrasive, awkward, not so say inflexible. If the majority secretly admit to their superiority and vaguely acknowledge their rightness, they are rarely liked or in con-

sequence favoured. The choices which shape careers fall more will-ingly on those who please than on those who merit. (1973: 37)

He discerns a crisis of authority, due to post-war lassitude and the conflicts of rival interest groups. Nevertheless, 'At bottom men cannot do without being led, any more than they can without eating, drink-ing or sleeping. These political animals need organisation, that is order and leaders' (1973: 64). Although de Gaulle was fond of emphasising the inherently divisive nature of the parliamentary regime of the Third (and Fourth) Republic (which he encapsulated trenchantly in the ob-servation that the right despised the nation, while the left opposed the state), he tempered the authoritarian nostalgia of this early book with more forward-looking republican principles when he became leader of the Free French. Marshal Pétain accepted 'the collapse of France' (de Gaulle, 1999: 79), its abasement to the Nazi order, whereas the role of the truly great man was to restore French grandeur, which meant to ensure the sovereignty of the nation, the liberation of the people and territory, and the empowerment of the state through legally represen-tative bodies.

The *Mémoires de guerre* recount this quest for national salvation by a hero who invests himself with an authority 'which fell outside hier-archies' (de Gaulle, 1999: 143). The first two volumes, running up to the liberation in August 1944, were published in 1954 and 1956, when the General's retirement from public life seemed definite. This gave him the advantage (and leisure) to reconstruct the glorious legacy of *La France combattante* from a position of dispassionate neutrality, while of course reminding his readers that the saviour could be summoned back for further service. Like most political memoirs, the work is an act of skilful self-justification, although few statesmen achieve the epic grandeur of de Gaulle's protagonist, his soaring trajec-tory in shaping history, his stirring persuasiveness. This is in part due to considerable literary skill, or as Robert Pickering puts it, in an essay on de Gaulle's rhetoric of action, 'Far more than simply repre-senting events, the writing enacts them, and substantiates their pro-gression' (in Gough and Horne, 1994: 53). It would be more accurate to see the writing as *re-enacting* events, since the memoirs are also a historical chronicle as well as an exercise in persuasion. While most diarists of the occupation adopt the role of witnesses and observers (as we shall see), de Gaulle is an actor who drives people and events and who on occasion records his actions in the third person, as if the writer and character he records were different people. Pickering interprets this distancing of author and actor as a form of modesty, asserting that these references to the protagonist as 'de Gaulle' are 'an act of self-effacement' and 'certainly not pretentious or manipulative' (p. 59). But the self-effacement is a pose, or rather a deliberate stratagem to construct his grandeur as an historic figure who casts aside personal preoccupations and a demotic style. This is shown from the beginning when he asserts the overweening nature of his enterprise.[14]

Reviewing the Pléiade edition of the *Mémoires*, Pierre Lepape sums up the General's aim as to 'offer to history the marble of legend', which necessitates eschewing routine and mundane concerns:

> No place for shadows, for doubt, for fiction or for farce. No Shakespeare in de Gaulle. And no Charles either, who is the great missing figure in these memoirs: the Charles who feels, struggles, suffers, thinks is completely devoured by the persona of de Gaulle. (2000: ii)

Although this edition reveals that the General wrote as many as five versions of his text, frequently eliminating more sensitive personal elements (unsurprisingly, the fact that he considered suicide after the humiliating failure of the joint British and Free French venture to liberate Dakar and French West Africa in September 1941 does not appear), his tone and perceptions are more varied and nuanced than the marmoreal indifference to lowly matters of the holder of a sacred mission and high office. Indeed, he asserts that the bond between himself and the people is essentially an emotional one; in August 1942, inspecting the Free French troops who held off superior German forces at Bir-Hakeim despite heavy losses, he discerns 'between them and me a contact, a harmony of souls, which sent a wave of joy flowing through us and made our steps spring more lightly over the sand' (1980: 22). National unity and salvation depend on such a 'tide of wills and feelings' (p. 148). His greatest epiphany is recorded by the justly celebrated account of the triumphal descent of the Champs-Élysées on 26 August 1944, when leader and people unite to reclaim the capital (the allies are significantly absent from the event). For that matter, we do learn about the confiscation of his property by Vichy, his domestic arrangements, and the arrest and deportation of several members of his family.[15] He is also capable of humour, particularly when depicting the antics of his rivals and the endless subterfuges of the 'Anglo-Saxons' who strive in vain to demean the dignity of France as incarnated in General de Gaulle (thus his conflict with Giraud, a puppet manipulated by the Americans as a substitute for Pétain, is a 'lamentable vaudeville', p. 138).

History has treated de Gaulle well, partly because of his skill in shaping it as a memorialist who erects his own monument as an heroic leader, and partly because his rivals lacked his stature and integrity. As president of the Fifth Republic, he was for many a divisive figure (whether for the rebellious officers and colonialists who failed to over-throw his government and assassinate him in the early 1960s, when Algeria finally gained independence, or for the revolting students and striking workers in May 1968 whose protests finally undermined his authority). But as Pierre Nora says, thirty years after his death, and after both colonialism and communism have been discredited, de Gaulle remains as 'the indubitable champion of French national mem-ory...the ultimate symbol of unity and cohesion' (1996: 205). Whereas Pétain's failure to achieve national renewal and unity can be attributed to the external pressures of occupation and his own conser-vative fatalism, moral blindness and political ineptitude, de Gaulle does fulfil the positive characteristics of the heroic leader, as defined by Todorov in *Face à l'extrême*: 'the hero revolts against appearances and through an act of an extraordinary nature succeeds in overturning destiny. The hero is the opposite of the fatalist; he is on the side of revolutionaries' (1994a: 13).

Diarists and autobiographers

De Gaulle's lofty authoritarianism and containment of the personal have already been mentioned. This apparent lack of human warmth was incorporated in his theory of leadership. Thus he wrote: 'My nature warns me, my experience has taught me, that at the height of affairs one can protect one's time and person only by adopting meth-odically a somewhat lofty and distant bearing' (1980: 206). The heroic leader can be an unsympathetic figure, condemned to solitary grand-eur: 'on the one hand, he fights for abstractions rather than for indi-viduals; on the other, the existence of beings close to him would make him vulnerable' (Todorov, 1994a: 17). De Gaulle's family did indeed suffer for his rebellion (although his wife and children escaped to England in June 1940, several other relatives were deported), while Pétain's readiness to dispose of associates and rivals has also been men-tioned. General Weygand, who was one of them, commented: 'The Marshal likes collective categories: the people, the soldier, and espe-cially the peasant, but not individuals. And that is why he is a hard master to serve' (quoted by Ferro, 1987: 648). De Gaulle's patriotism depends above all on a militaristic conception of French national grandeur which may seem brutally archaic; hence his argument that, since a conquered nation ceases to exist, the sacrifice of countless individual civilian hostages and armed combatants is justified and necessary in order to restore national sovereignty.

For most of us, on the contrary, individuals count far more than abstract collectivities. Unsurprisingly, de Gaulle's epic account of the war years bears little immediate resemblance to the events and feelings chronicled by ordinary citizens who experienced occupation directly, rather than from self-imposed exile. The contrast between such apparently conflicting grandiose and mundane perceptions merits some exploration, since it is highly revealing about loyalties, identities and daily realities. Other political figures, who found themselves effectively demoted to the role of hostages during the occupation, experienced and therefore recorded more tellingly than de Gaulle the discrepancy between the concrete indignity of private concerns and the abstract and sometimes unreal ideals of public affairs. A good example is provided by Paul Reynaud's *Carnets de captivité*, a private journal published only in 1997 by his daughter Évelyne Demey, thirty-one years after his death (the notebooks would have formed the basis for the third volume of his memoirs). Reynaud, we recall, replaced Daladier as prime minister on 21 March 1940 and resigned in favour of Marshal Pétain on 16 June when he was outmanoeuvred by the defeatists in his government. Pétain had him arrested in September 1940 (though he was never formally charged with any crime) and handed over to the Germans in November 1942. As his daughter says, he was thus condemned to spend most of the war as an 'impotent spectator observing France in the thrall of the Nazis and the Vichy regime' (Reynaud, 1997: 7).

As a consequence, his notebooks (even in the tactfully edited version made public) offer an odd mixture of sardonic jibes against the Marshal and his entourage and less appealing brooding about his own personal humiliation and material deprivations. Thus he remarks of the instability of the Vichy regime, on 15 January 1941 'The present government is like the metro: people get on and off at every station. Only the driver never changes' (p. 25). (One could extend the comparison by wondering if the driver actually knew how to operate the controls of the train and understood the direction in which it was heading.) Eventually, he was detained in the Austrian castle of Itter, near Dachau, along with other senior political and military figures (such as Gamelin, Daladier, Weygand, Michel Clemenceau, La Rocque and the Confédération générale du travail (CGT) trade union leader Jouhaux).[16] This elite group enjoyed material conditions far superior to those of ordinary political detainees, better in fact than those provided by Vichy ('Les maîtres se conduisent mieux que leurs valets', Reynaud observes, p. 305). Léon Blum was detained for two years in Buchenwald, along with Georges Mandel (who was to be murdered by the Milice, rather than the Nazis), but kept isolated from the main camp (about whose atrocious conditions he learned belatedly), well treated and even allowed to marry his third wife Jeanne, who shared his captivity.[17] Reynaud himself had an operation for a detached retina performed in Innsbruck in September 1944.

He notes the complaints and squabbles of his group with a certain self-mockery ('Our Punch and Judy show continues', as he puts it, p. 366). Reynaud's band of quarrelsome puppets included two former prime ministers and commanders-in-chief, who managed to unite only when complaining about the curtailment of such privileges as heated bedrooms and two baths a week (otherwise, Reynaud and Weygand were not on speaking terms). The principal butt of Reynaud's ridicule, however, is the unfortunate Colonel de La Rocque, whom he refers to derisively as 'Casimir' (after a slow-witted donkey) and a 'mythomane' (p. 350). While Reynaud survived his ordeal and returned to political life (he was minister of finance in 1948 and remained a deputy until his opposition to the election of the president by universal suffrage in 1962 cost him his seat, at the age of eighty-three), La Rocque has been one of the more neglected victims of the period. Historians too often dismiss him as a half-hearted fascist (Robert Paxton notes that his movement the Croix de Feu was 'contemptuously spoonerized as "Froides Queues"'; 1982: 23[18]), although its appeal was strong enough to draw such members as François Mitterrand, who joined the youth movement in 1934. La Rocque's biographer Jacques Nobécourt (1996) argues that he had the misfortune to be hated by left and right since he was a conservative nationalist who rejected both Marxism and Nazism. Although Vichy adopted the slogan 'Travail, famille, patrie' from the Parti social français, which he created in 1936, he was offered only a junior administrative post by the regime and opposed both its collaboration and anti-Semitism. He was involved in two resistance networks (Klan and Alibi) linked to British Intelligence and arrested in March 1943. On returning to France, he was interned again and died in April 1946, mortified that his resistance activities had not been recognised (his widow was offered posthumous recognition in 1961).

These cases of public figures reduced to the condition of expendable hostages remind us that success, chance and the opportunity to control the historical record, as much as character, beliefs and the actual course of events, all play a vital part in the construction of the heroic leader. Resistance memoirs are full of cases of heroic sacrifices made by extraordinarily courageous men and women, known to and recognised by only their immediate comrades. Most are condemned to the obscurity of anonymous martyrs and thus possess only the most limited symbolic capital. One of the great virtues of the diaries kept by ordinary citizens, beyond their usefulness as chronicles of material conditions and changing attitudes, is that they allow us to widen our understanding of the symbolic domain beyond the official record controlled by politicians and administrators. We have already remarked that such journals often receive scant attention from historians (although a prefect's private diary can be far more revealing than his official reports, as the next chapter will show). In David Boal's *Journaux intimes sous l'occupation* (1993), the only extended study of the topic to my knowledge, we find, despite the promises of his title, essentially an analysis of the problematic nature of autobiographical writing which focuses on a small group of major literary figures and makes only passing reference to the wider historical context of occupation. Thus he tells us a great deal about Ernst Jünger's ontological and metaphysical musings, but virtually nothing about what this German officer actually did in Paris (or for that matter why he should be the central figure in a book about French writers).

As Boal observes, the intimate journal differs in its immediacy, spontaneity and private nature from memoirs reconstructed at leisure and published long after the event, often as the final justification of a public career. In theory at least, the diary offers greater reliability and authenticity as an ongoing record of attitudes and behaviour. Indeed, while the reader of a diary enjoys the benefit of historical hindsight, the writer 'does not have the means to undertake a retrospective construction of the self in his text; his main character must appear half-naked before a public which knows some of his present secrets and some of his future dilemmas' (Boal, 1993: 74). In practice, such confessional innocence is a rarity, since most authors in a position to publish a journal submit it to some form of editing process, which involves stylistic and ideological alterations (such as omissions of unduly revealing material, the improvement of narrative coherence or the addition of post facto political judgements). In any event, the reconstruction of the self as a narrated other which preoccupies Boal is of less importance to this discussion than how diarists who did not belong to the governing elites endured the hardships of occupation, reflected on their experiences, and related their individual material circumstances to the collective and symbolic plane of national identity and loyalty.

As Boal admits, a journal like Galtier-Boissière's was in large part written for the historical record, 'for a posterity which would have partly forgotten the daily facts of the occupation' (1993: 149). To my mind, he underestimates the importance of such contingent factors (probably because most of the writers on whom he focuses did not suffer great hardships). Perhaps because he chooses to concentrate on figures like Benoist-Méchin, Jünger, Léautaud and Jouhandeau, none of whom had any connection with resistance (at least in France) and indeed opposed or despised it, Boal generally understates the moral issues and dilemmas which are central to understanding people's motivation and behaviour during the occupation. As a result, his perception of the context in which writers along with their fellow citizens existed suggests a curious ethical innocence. Thus he accuses Galtier-Boissière of being excessively partisan and losing no opportunity to ridicule the occupying forces (p. 141) and Guéhenno of overstating his condemnation of Vichy and collaboration at the expense of factual accuracy (p. 156), as though dispassionate neutrality were a virtue to be expected from people who had to face totalitarian oppression on a daily basis.

Regarding Léon Werth, Boal observes dismissively that 'Werth's journal leads one to think that talent as an observer is of little use if one has nothing to observe', for this writer 'reproduces very well the powerless situation of ordinary people in wartime' (pp. 162–3), a judgement one might be tempted to apply equally to Paul Léautaud (about whom he writes many interesting pages) were it not simply wrong. Boal overlooks the fact that Werth did not spend the entire occupation living as a hermit in the Jura; he spent the crucial eight months of 1944 before the eviction of the Germans in Paris, had many influential friends and associates, and his wife was involved in the resistance. The general point, however, is a valid one: what makes a journal an interesting or readable document? To produce a document of historical interest, the diarist needs to communicate effectively, to provide a convincing record of events and reactions to them, and to link personal or parochial feelings and reflections to a wider social and political context. In other words, literary talent has to be combined with perceptiveness as a witness and judgements that are not merely egocentric or partial. Unfortunately, most private chroniclers of the occupation usually fail on one or more of these counts, in varying degrees; the more successful accounts invariably prove to be written by individuals who are professional writers. While it would be otiose to enumerate journals and memoirs which add little to our knowledge of the period, it is worth offering a couple of examples, if only to provide a comparison to enhance our appreciation of the more effective accounts which will then be sampled.

Léon Gaultier's *Siegfried et le Berrichon: parcours d'un collabo* (1991) recounts its author's itinerary as a fascist and collaborator, from service in Paul Marion's cabinet in Vichy, membership of the Milice and Waffen SS, to a sentence of ten years' imprisonment and national indignity. But his fractured narrative simply presents a succession of disconnected incidents, devoid of any serious ideological reflection or personal introspection; we are left none the wiser as to why he chose collaborationism or how the choice might be justified. (Christian de La Mazière's (1972) memoirs, which cover similar ground, are far more informative, as we shall see in a subsequent chapter.) The espousal of collaboration or resistance is not in itself relevant to the interest of an autobiographical statement. Unlike Gaultier, the schoolgirl diarist Micheline Bood, whose occupation journal was published in abridged form in 1974, affirms her Gaullist loyalties from June 1940 (her older half-brother was in the RAF). Her diary was begun in 1940 when she was fourteen and does offer an engaging account of adolescence under the occupation. But its author's preoccupations are always personal and frequently trivial (more harrowing entries, detailing an emotional crisis possibly leading to a suicide attempt in 1942, have apparently been suppressed). This is not surprising, given her age and protected bourgeois environment, but hardly makes her an illuminating chronicler.

In comparison, the Groult sisters' occupation diary, *Journal à quatre mains* (1974), first published in 1962, reveals a far wider perspective. The Groults had the advantage of being older than Micheline Bood (Benoîte was born in 1921 and Flora in 1925), and of growing up to become professional writers and feminists (one does not know how far their journal was doctored between 1945 and 1962). Benoîte in particular is aware of the apparent gulf between her privileged intellectual existence as a student and the murderous material reality of war, noting on 8 June 1940: 'I'm translating Petronius while other people are getting killed or fleeing' (1974: 43). Within a few weeks, however, the Germans had arrived in Paris and the conventional gap between combatant and civilian ceased to exist. This at least allows Benoîte to add a patriotic dimension to her proto-feminist complaints about her disenfranchised state: 'I envy the boys who are now in England. If I was not a girl, I would surely have left. In the first place, the last bit of Free France is over there; and then for personal reasons: I too am an occupied country, by my parents, by habits, my place in society' (1 July 1940, p. 61). Her own marginality leads her to wonder, 'Who really makes history?', and to draw a parallel between individual impotence and national destiny which prefigures Marshal Pétain's later laments, already cited, about his own inability to influence events: 'The whole of France seems to be marginalised from what is currently happening in the country' (12 July 1940, p. 64).

The first years of the Groults' diary retrace Vichy's collapse into a mere simulacrum of a government, the apparent invincibility of the German war machine, and the privations and humiliations heaped on those who subsist in this state of occupation. As part of its campaign to place family values before equality, Vichy bans the employment of married women in public administration, causing Benoîte to observe: 'We are the Jews of the sexes' (17 October 1940, p. 141).[19] A year later, however, an entry shows how this parallel is overstated, when the curfew in Paris is lifted and a hundred Jews are shot instead: 'A terrible thing to say: thanks to those hundred Jews who were shot, I was able to go to the concert on Sunday' (15 December 1941, p. 291). Daily life is increasingly governed by the curtailment of ordinary needs and the consequent urge to sustain the few remaining pleasures, whether hygienic or culinary. Thus Flora is driven to record 'Saturday: public bath day' (23 January 1941, p. 198), and 'an egg tastes so good and one sees so few of them that my respect for these little spheres is infinite' (3 February 1941, p. 207). Such deprivations may seem trivial (especially to those readers who have not suffered them and are unable to imagine them), but cumulatively they amount to an erosion of civilisation. Hence Benoîte's observation, noting the closure of thirty metro stations: 'We are like a people shedding civilisation: from the age of electricity and the internal combustion engine, we have returned to the age of candles and bicycles' (11 January 1943, p. 378).

The sisters' transition from adolescence to adulthood in the later years of the occupation is marked by a shift back from the margins to the centre, at the cost of considerable personal suffering. Within eleven months, from June 1943 to May 1944, Benoîte has an abortion, marries, and sees her husband Blaise Landon die of wounds inflicted in a maquis skirmish. Liberation allows the shedding of restraints and inhibitions, although such compensations may seem sour and vengeful. Having studiously avoided all contact with German soldiers throughout the occupation, the sisters pursue their sexual liberation by frequenting and sleeping with US officers, recording their adventures with a sort of guilty indulgence ('She calls me a slut!', Benoîte complains of Flora, p. 569). The restoration of male authority is viewed with some scepticism. Flora witnesses the ritual public humiliation of women who 'sinned' with the Germans, adorned with swastikas and paraded half-naked, noting that the neighbourhood hairdresser has been conscripted for head-shaving and that 'he came home yesterday evening, proud as a hero' (25 August 1944, p. 512). While de Gaulle excites their admiration from June 1940, his troops parading through liberated Paris are 'unkempt, bandy-legged...a sort of beggars' army' (p. 512).

This blending of personal and public observations skilfully evokes an evolving, broader community of experience, largely united in its opposition to the Germans, but also revealing a suspicion of all forms of authority which claim a monopoly on patriotic values and demand allegiance while offering little but repression in return. Léon Werth's journal, published as *Déposition* in 1946, further elaborates such reflections on the citizen and the polity, from the perspective of a Jewish intellectual and literary journalist who spent most of the period in small villages and towns of the Jura, in the south zone. As Jean-Pierre Azéma points out, prefacing a new edition in 1992, perhaps because he was neither a politician nor a celebrated literary figure, Werth's diary has been ignored by most historians, although his marginal position actually makes him rather more typical and revealing of ordinary citizens deprived of influence and power. This impotence (which Boal decried) can be counteracted to a degree by offering at least tacit support to resistance activities or by practising a more private form of resistance in maintaining a written record. In Werth's case, his journal is no mere tale of woe and frustration; it abounds with satirical observations about the state of the nation and a humane indignation about the connivance of the governing classes. Like other Gaullist sympathisers (for whom the real source of national influence and honour has emigrated to London: hence, 'the fate of France is being played out by the Thames', 6 September 1940, p. 42), Werth doubts in any case whether the Vichy government enjoys much more power than its disenfranchised citizens. He compares Marshal Pétain to a mad concierge guarding the ruins of a factory of which he deludedly imagines himself to be the real owner; in fact he could be replaced by 'any village policeman' (p. 43, p. 57). By April 1943, he notes of a radio speech by Pétain:

> The text is so limp that one can surmise it was composed by the Marshal himself. It contains no allusion to current events. You might think that the Marshal was already dead and that his ghost was speaking at a spiritualist meeting. (p. 453)

Clichés 'parade like a phantom army', as vacuous discourse has to stand in for any effective impact on circumstances.

While Pétain's symbolic pontifications are seen to degenerate into self-deluding escapism, Werth also understands that many people have little awareness of patriotic obligations and the function of the state, let alone the wider development of the war, as three entries demonstrate. Thus 'The peasants here, when it is not a question of restrictions and requisitions, are absolutely indifferent to everything the government says and does' (5 December 1940, p. 123). Similarly, for food hoarders, 'Their supplies have taken on the special, sacred character which money does for a miser' (p. 80). And a year later: 'Background: Syria. Foreground: belly and tobacco' (30 June 1941, p. 223). Werth himself is unable to display such complacent and egotistical disregard for the wider world, since he is in effect a refugee highly dependent on others both within and outside the local community for his subsistence and survival. Just what he lives off, or how he passes his days without the support of family or employment, is never made very clear (apart from occasional visitors like Saint-Exupéry or the historian Lucien Febvre, his immediate companions appear to be a maidservant and a Siamese cat). What is clear, however, is his precarious status as a Jew, obliged by the law of June 1941 to declare his membership of this stigmatised category 'like having a contagious disease' (p. 216). For all his contemptuous suspicion of Vichy, Werth conforms to its laws by going to Lons to make his declaration in July 1941: 'I feel humiliated, it's the first time society has humiliated me. I feel humiliated, not at being a Jew, but at being assumed as a Jew to be of inferior quality' (p. 225). It has to be said that Werth (who spent fifteen months in the trenches in 1914–15, published an anti-militarist novel, *Clavel soldat*, in 1919, and was aged fifty-six in 1941), shows no inclination to practise active resistance, other than vicariously. His wife Suzanne finds her way unaided across the demarcation line in March 1942, at the risk of being shot by a patrol; in fact she belongs to a resistance network whose activities are recorded rather summarily: 'Suzanne, for four years. She has aided, hidden, saved people on the run. Dozens of them. She has crossed the demarcation line clandestinely thirteen times' (9 May 1944, p. 636).

One could argue, then, that Werth's anxieties are typical, even if his experiences are exceptional. Certainly, a writer like Pierre Andreu, in memoirs published in 1977, states bluntly that films or other accounts of the occupation that focus on 'the misfortune of the Jews or the exploits of the resistance – not that the fate of Jews was not appalling – completely ignore daily reality in occupied France. In 1943, resisters and Jews were of little importance' (p. 189). Reality is of course compartmentalised and solidarity fractured by the divisive effects of occupation, as Werth's analysis shows. In that sense, generalisations about behaviour are always provisional and precarious, and samples of autobiographical writing which purport to establish broader trends may be as arbitrary as opinion polls which reveal what the pollsters want to hear. Nevertheless, one noticeable distinction between accounts sympathetic to resistance and those which favour collaboration is what might be called the principle of affirmation as opposed to that of denial. In other words, those whose views and behaviour eventually placed them on the winning side tend to follow the rising trajectory set by de Gaulle's memoirs, discerning a movement from defeat and division to unity and salvation, or at the very least from disunity and repression to relative autonomy and fulfilment. Collaborators, on the other hand, adopt a more cynical posture, which often involves defending their position by denying both their own complicity and the moral and tactical superiority of those who supported resistance. The journalist Pierre Andreu, just cited, flirted briefly with fascism in the 1930s, was a friend of the Vichy propaganda minister Paul Marion, and found himself on a CNE (communist-dominated Comité National des Écrivains) blacklist for six months at the liberation (eventually his case was dropped without coming to court). Nevertheless, he notes sarcastically: 'Like many Frenchmen, I took part in resistance without knowing it. Unfortunately for me, I only found this out, much to my astonishment, long afterwards' (1977: 194). By this he means occasional gestures of aid and support offered to friends and acquaintances. Resistance, in other words, is diluted to become no more than a fancy term for what is routine social behaviour.

One of the most notorious examples of such denial of responsibility is provided by Sacha Guitry, who is commonly perceived as a leading figure among artistic collaborators in Paris.[20] He certainly did not follow the injunction which he claims he was given by Octave

Mirbeau on his death bed: 'Ne collaborez jamais!' (Guitry, 1947: 189). Guitry is at pains to point out, however, that while he was arrested in August 1944 and charged with intelligence with an enemy power, he was released after a few months and the case against him was quietly dropped three years later, once his reputation had been sufficiently blackened. His memoir, *Quatre ans d'occupations*, is a massive exercise in self-exculpation and self-promotion, although the vehemence and multiplicity of his denials actually undermine his defence. His adversaries are accused of cowardice and envy. Guitry is the target chosen 'to spare the truly guilty' and 'what they wanted to make me pay for were forty years of success and happiness' (p. 413, p. 556). Both statements are arguably true, in that he enjoyed no political or economic power during the occupation and that he was guilty only of exploiting his association with the cultural emissaries of the Third Reich in order to sustain his theatrical ventures and luxurious lifestyle. However, his claim to have fulfilled a patriotic mission by pursuing his career and performing plays in defence of French culture 'against the adversary' (p. 215) evokes a sham and rather comical form of resistance, where the protagonist confronts the enemy whom he encounters sitting on the front row of his theatre or at a cocktail party. Patriotism in the face of adversity, as previous memorialists have demonstrated but Guitry fails to realise, means sacrificing personal interest and security and offering service to a cause that places collective interests before the vanity of individuals.

Guitry illustrates the betrayal of social elites who shamelessly confused their privileges with national values and displayed a callous indifference to the misfortunes endured by many citizens (although he did help some of his acquaintances escape persecution). For collaborators and their associates, catastrophe too often means their own humiliation and stigmatisation after the war ended. While their justifications take the form of tendentious denials and make them suspect witnesses, they possess a certain exemplary status insofar as they bear the nation's collective shame, sometimes even down to subsequent generations. Pierre Rigoulot's book, *Les Enfants de l'épuration* (1993), based on interviews with some forty children of collaborators, explores the question of generational guilt, without however discerning a consistent pattern in the reactions of his subjects. Thus Philippe Alibert, son of the Justice Minister who was the principal author of Vichy's anti-Semitic decrees in 1940, practises evasive denial, claiming that Marcel Peyrouton, as Minister of the Interior, carried more responsibility than his father. The historian Emmanuel Le Roy Ladurie, whose

father was minister of agriculture in 1942, espouses a more confrontational, compensatory position, saying, 'I made my father pay for his
services to Vichy by joining the Communist Party' (Rigoulot, 1993:
83), whereas the historian Jean-Pierre Azéma prefers total silence, refusing to discuss the career of his father, an avowed fascist who was a
contributor to collaborationist newspapers and a member of the PPF
(the collaborationist Parti Populaire Français) and Waffen SS. One is
left to speculate whether his son's choice of career is a different form
of compensation. Marie Chaix, on the other hand, prefers an indirect,
confessional mode, in the shape of a fictionalised and somewhat lugu-
brious biography of her father Albert Beugras, another senior figure
in Doriot's PPF. Doriot considered him a 'Naive idiot' and warned
him 'Your family's crime will be to bear your name!' (Chaix, 1985:
112). In fact the unmentionable name Beugras is shortened to 'B'
throughout *Les Lauriers du lac de Constance* and the book remains suspended between lament and expiation, historical memoir and fictional
meditation.

Rigoulot (1993: 502) concludes that his lengthy study draws on 'a
disparate and unduly restricted sample'. Any attempt to sample opinions and analyse behaviour is liable to similar objections of selectivity
or bias. On the other hand, the material contained in personal
memoirs and journals is endlessly fascinating, with its dramas of heroism and suffering, its admissions and denials, its countless informative
glimpses of existence under extreme circumstances. This relatively
brief discussion has shown, moreover, how there is a recurrent dia-
lectic between the individual citizen and collective authority, between
the fragmented nature of personal experience and the symbolic plane
of national goals and values. Thus authority seeks to impose itself, at
the cost of derision, failure and rejection, but ultimately the cycle
demands it be replaced, while individuals invariably explain the par-
ticularities of their own experiences and choices by appeals to general,
more abstract notions that offer justification, if not salvation. State
authority in practice is represented by the officials who impose it on
their fellow citizens (from senior administrators and governors to primary school teachers and policemen). From issues of leadership and
daily survival, therefore, we turn next to the administration of the
country, to the dilemmas of those who continued to serve the state as
their political masters returned and departed.

3
Servants of the State

Collaboration, resistance and the dilemmas of administration

The dilemmas faced by those who chose to serve either Vichy and its German masters or their adversaries in the internal resistance or Free French were partly ethical and partly practical. To what authority does one offer one's loyalty when conflicting forces claim to represent the state and people? Should one sacrifice personal and material interest for some greater but rather nebulous cause? Is one in a position to make conscious and informed choices about possible courses of action whose consequences may be largely unpredictable? Is it really possible to play the double game of serving an authoritarian state while surreptitiously aiding its adversaries, as the influence and moral credit of the latter grow? How much damage or good can any particular servant of an organism do? To answer these questions, it is necessary to reconsider some of the problems of occupation in general terms, and to review the working of the administrative machinery of the French state in some detail. The most illuminating answers, however, come as always from individual experience, as one moves from the objective anonymity of the statistical record to the subjective immediacy of personal narrative. Here some of the diaries left by servants or opponents of the Vichy regime (administrators, teachers, policemen) are invaluable documents, even if their inevitable, self-justifying distortions demand that we read them with sceptical caution. There were few who, however compromised their position seemed, did not claim to have practised some form of resistance, at least after the event.

Until the closing months of the occupation, the French state efficiently served the economic and strategic needs of its German masters.[1]

While the *Militärbefehlshaber in Frankreich*, the supreme German command in the occupied zone, controlled 49 out of 87 metropolitan departments, 28 million people (70 per cent of the population) and 80 per cent of the French economy, to exploit these resources effectively the Germans needed the willing collaboration and practical experience of Vichy's governors, administrators and their staff. Each department in the occupied zone had a *Feldkommandatur* in its *chef-lieu* (principal town), under whose orders the local prefect and mayors were obliged to operate; disobedience led to dismissal. For most of the time, at least until it became clear in 1943 that Germany was likely to be defeated, this administrative support was enthusiastically provided, albeit at the expense of depriving ordinary French citizens of the basic necessities of existence, imposing forced labour on thousands of workers, and ruthlessly pursuing the ideological and racial opponents of the regime. When the Comité Français de Libération Nationale (CFLN), established in Algiers under the joint authority of Generals de Gaulle and Giraud, decided in September 1943 to prosecute Vichy ministers and officials for treason after the liberation, these eager servants of the state were given a stronger incentive to switch their allegiance to the resistance, particularly when they saw the former Minister of the Interior Pierre Pucheu (who was directly implicated in the mass shooting of communist hostages by the Germans) condemned to death in May 1943 at his trial in North Africa and executed the following year, after a belated attempt to defect to the Free French. Most administrators thus had at some point to decide to whom they owed most loyalty and to measure the risks and benefits which any change of allegiance or double game might entail.

Historians generally agree that the Vichy regime governed through administrative structures rather than political consensus: citizens and employees were disenfranchised as national and local elected bodies were suspended and replaced by appointed committees and powerful officials answerable only to the government and its German masters.[2] Senior civil servants, whether the secretaries general who headed ministries or the prefects who were regional and departmental governors, greatly increased their power and could be appointed only with German approval. Thus prefects, who were compelled to swear an oath of loyalty to the head of state (an obligation previously imposed under the dictatorial regime of Napoleon III), were put in control of all political, administrative and police matters, becoming 'veritable satraps in their *département*' (Baruch, 1997: 5). They were able to impose internment without trial upon those deemed subversive (60,000 people were held in detention camps by late 1940). Under the direction of René Bousquet, centralised control of the police (who numbered about 130,000 in total and belonged to a diverse range of sometimes competing organisms across the country) was tightened, in exchange for their active cooperation with the Germans in tracking down Jews and resisters. Following Bousquet's notorious encounter in spring 1942 with Heydrich and Oberg, the SS general newly responsible for the German security forces in France, 9000 members of the Parisian police played an active part in rounding up 13,000 Jews for deportation in the infamous raids of 16–17 July 1942.

The precarious autonomy and authority of the French state were thus bought at a high price, which meant in general making countless individuals expendable and in particular sacrificing moral scruples in favour of professional obedience and personal career benefits. Officials who eventually opted either to challenge or obstruct orders (which might at worst involve providing lists of hostages, arranging arrests, or tolerating torture and summary executions) or to resist more actively by joining a resistance network were themselves liable to summary dismissal, detention or deportation. Thus although Bousquet was involved in the arrest and deportation of some 59,000 French and foreign Jews as part of his effort to retain control over police services, his rivalry with the Milice (which was implicated in the assassination of his long-standing patron Sarraut in December 1943) finally led to his dismissal and replacement by Joseph Darnand, the head of the Milice, and an out-and-out collaborationist who committed himself and his organisation to the Nazi cause by joining the SS. While the excesses which Darnand openly encouraged (extortion, torture, summary executions) brought him before a firing squad in October 1945, Bousquet's dismissal and detention by the Germans in the final months of the occupation allowed him to argue that he had already paid the price for resisting German demands. He was imprisoned for a few years after the liberation, but at his trial, which was conveniently delayed until 1949, his supposed resistance activities led to his acquittal. Thirty years would pass before the issue of his complicity in crimes against humanity through mass deportations would become a legal and public issue, and with it the motivation, responsibility and dilemmas of those who chose to serve the Vichy state.

As secretary general for public order, Bousquet's successor Darnand was also technically a senior administrator answerable to the government and prime minister; in practice, he was more powerful than the minister to whom he was nominally accountable, the secretary of state

Lemoine (Darnand was officially promoted to ministerial level as *Secré-taire d'État à l'Intérieur* in June 1944). Neither Laval nor Pétain were able to impede the atrocities committed by *miliciens* (which included the murder of the two former Jewish ministers Mandel and Zay). By April 1944, local control of policing matters had been largely wrested away from civilian prefects and taken over by Darnand's paramilitary underlings in the Milice, who behaved like a French version of the Gestapo. Several of his immediate subordinates followed him into the SS (which Darnand allegedly joined when his overtures to the Free French were spurned). At government level, many ministers were themselves subject to summary dismissal (the most notorious example being the sacking and arrest of Laval in December 1940). Ministers were to all intents and purposes no longer professional polit-icians but civil servants and technocrats, serving the interests of the state and its leader rather than the nation, electors, or a political party and ideology. Thus Jean Bichelonne, Laval's Minister of Production, was a key planner, with his Nazi counterpart Albert Speer, of Franco–German industrial collaboration (in some ways a predecessor of the post-war common market, for all that it amounted to systematic pil-lage of the French economy).[3]

Collaboration, in other words, meant not merely active repression of opposition and dissidence, but compliance and complicity with new forms of authority in a regime which insisted on hierarchical order and imposed increasingly repellent demands on its servants. Although Vichy propaganda denounced the evils of bureaucracy, the number of public officials employed by the state rose by at least 30 per cent during the occupation, to over a million individuals, as decrees and laws which categorised and controlled citizens proliferated and the meagre resources left to the French state by the Germans demanded careful husbanding. These proliferating functionaries were the people who ran public services and who made collaboration work whenever they implemented government policy, whether unquestioningly or re-luctantly: policemen arresting Jews and resisters, teachers promoting the propaganda of the National Revolution, minor officials organising surveillance of the post or the rationing of supplies. Most of this very large group remain invisible to history, other than as statistics. The Vichy regime sacked about 35,000 officials in its initial purge of ideo-logical and racial opponents; the law of October 1940 excluded Jews from acting as civil servants and teachers. After the liberation, a very similar number of functionaries were sentenced by courts for crimes of collaboration, with about 15,000 losing their jobs (about 1 per cent of those who fell into the broad category of public servants); a further 2000 members of the police were dismissed (some 1.5 per cent of the national force).

For all the vehement protests about injustice made by individuals who lost their livelihood or liberty, many were reinstated or released within a few years, while the relatively low numbers of those punished (compared, say, with casualties caused by executions, deportations or bombing during the occupation) show the difficulty or impossibility of inflicting more than minor sanctions on a group of citizens who were essential for the efficient running of the state, whatever the political regime under which it operated. At the most senior level, of the 108 Vichy ministers and administrators judged by the high court, only three were actually executed (compared with four writers executed after their conviction by the lower courts of justice for publishing pro-German propaganda). And no fewer than 51 out of the 108 were eventually rehabilitated for purported 'resistance actions' (see Boulanger, 1997: 186). Many senior officials escaped prosecution entirely: for example, only 12 out of the 61 members of the cabinet of the minister of education found themselves in court after the liberation. The individuals who were prosecuted were quite frequently very minor officials, who occupied public positions in their local community, which they were accused of having compromised through indiscreet or indecent behaviour. In his well-documented study of *L'Épuration dans l'administration française*, François Rouquet cites cases of provincial schoolmistresses and postmistresses charged on the flimsiest of evidence with consorting with German soldiers, while stressing that their hierarchical superiors usually remained unscathed (1993: 232–5).

Perhaps because the bureaucrat is an unglamorous, mundane individual, whose power is often wielded indirectly through a system which makes its agents virtually invisible, only the most notorious figures tend to be remembered, whether as examples of personal integrity and heroic commitment to resistance, or of cynical opportunism and manipulation of the judicial and historical record.[4] They tend to be perceived as exemplary cases, when their behaviour actually deviates markedly from a norm which rarely ranges beyond obedient compliance with or cautious obstruction of the more excessive demands of collaboration, a norm which is primarily governed by opportunistic self-preservation. High-ranking civil servants like the former prefects Jean Moulin and Émile Bollaert, who sacrificed their careers and lives by becoming senior figures in the resistance, are exceptional both in their heroic stature and moral integrity. So too is a figure like Darnand, a patriotic, decorated war hero who paradoxically joined his country's enemies and thereby invalidated his past glory (such active combatants are considered at greater length in the following chapter). Survivors like the Vichy police chief Bousquet and Leguay, his delegate in the occupied zone (both of whom again held prefectoral rank) seem more typical of the complexities which allowed powerful officials to practise collaboration while also dabbling in resistance: Leguay was rehabilitated for supposed 'resistance actions' in 1955 and although eventually charged with crimes against humanity in 1979, died in 1989 before his case came to trial.

Hannah Arendt (1994) famously coined the expression 'the banality of evil' in her account of the trial of Adolf Eichmann, no doubt the most infamous bureaucrat to be judged and condemned for implementing Nazi genocide. Far from being a sadistic monster, Eichmann struck this observer as frighteningly normal. His organisational zeal and efficiency were unfortunately linked to mindless diligence and moral blindness, perhaps an inevitable consequence of the dehumanising effect of totalitarian bureaucracy. Eichmann, who rose from the ranks to head section B4 of Bureau IV of the Reich Security Service (responsible for Jewish matters), never killed anybody himself but oversaw the transportation of thousands of Jews to the death camps: for example, within two months of his arrival in Hungary in March 1944, 434,351 Jews were deported in 147 convoys to Auschwitz.[5] Eichmann defended himself as a loyal servant of the Third Reich, dutifully pursuing its leaders' policies (and resenting the fact that his achievements failed to win him promotion beyond the grade of *Obersturmbannführer* or lieutenant colonel). He went to the gallows without remorse. Arendt notes caustically that much sentimental nonsense was talked about collective German guilt for war crimes: this was a hypocritical diversion from the fact that many individual Germans occupying important positions in the post-war republic were extremely guilty, but clearly felt nothing of the sort (1994: 251). The Federal Republic belatedly founded an agency for investigating Nazi crimes in 1958; those who were prosecuted usually received extraordinarily lenient sentences (for example, a sentence of ten years' imprisonment given to Bradfisch of the *Einsatzgruppen* for killing 15,000 Jews). Since 40 per cent of German judges had also worked under Hitler, this was unsurprising. Practical necessity overrode the quest for just retribution: 'if the Adenauer administration had been too sensitive about employing officials with a compromising Nazi past, there might have been no administration at all' (Arendt, 1994: 17–18).

In comparison, of course, few Vichy officials were desk-murderers on such a massive scale, so actively complicit in implementing the initial stages of the final solution in France at national level. Arguably more typical of the crimes of collaboration is a lower-ranking official like Maurice Papon, who was actually promoted by the liberation government to full prefect for alleged resistance activities in Bordeaux; only in 1981 was his active role in organising hundreds of arrests and deportations in the region exposed, and only in 1998 was he belatedly convicted of complicity in crimes against humanity, after a brilliant post-war career as administrator, police chief, politician and government minister. Apart from Paul Touvier, a junior officer in the Milice, who was in fact sentenced to death after the liberation and spent the following decades in hiding until finally being convicted in 1994, Papon was the only important servant of the Vichy regime to be prosecuted and convicted of crimes against humanity (those convicted in the post-war trials were charged with treason, intelligence with an enemy power). Juridically, then, Papon was certainly an exception. Yet the suspicion remains that his career during and after the occupation (a career mainly distinguished by the ruthless imposition of brutal orders, administrative efficiency and self-advancement overriding any respect for human rights, professional ethics or veracity) followed much the same path as that of other powerful individuals who were more successful in concealing their iniquities and did not enjoy Papon's longevity (which ultimately defeated attempts to delay his trial until his death).

The suspicion that Papon's unscrupulous self-promotion and shameless mendacity were typical of much of the governing class during and after the occupation depends, however, on assertions which lack or suppression of evidence makes it impossible to substantiate. Rouquet notes, after studying thousands of occupation personnel files in the ministries of education and communications, that some had clearly been tampered with in order to remove incriminating material (1993: 240, n. 12). In her polemical study of French archives, *Archives interdites*, Sonia Combes observes that the law which supposedly liberalised access in 1979 actually extended the minimum delay for access to political files to sixty years, claiming that 'For the benefit of Papons large and small, the law was made to measure to guarantee the protection of the files of Vichy's civil servants' (1994: 145). Even employees of the Archives Nationales are forbidden access to Gestapo documents held for the period 1942–44 (pp. 57, 193). Other historians suggest that Combes greatly overstates her case and that access can in practice be obtained to files that are technically closed. Marc Olivier Baruch, for instance, was allowed to consult 99 per cent of the dossiers which he requested for his study of the Ministries of Education, Finance and the Interior, *Servir l'État français* (1997: 18n). Nevertheless, Combes also asserts that such 'dérogations', which allow exceptional consultation of embargoed material, are granted only to a few privileged historians, who are often closely associated with the political establishment. Baruch is himself just such an insider, as a civil servant employed by the ministry of culture.

Inevitably, other cases which support the accusation that the administrative elite betrayed the nation look rather anecdotal. The key questions are how far officials were prepared to go down the path of collaboration (to use Pétain's own metaphor), given that mass murder was the final destination, and whether any parallel resistance activity they engaged in actually has any redeeming value. However, unless they became public figures, the subject of court cases, or chose to publish memoirs defending their wartime activities, it is extremely difficult to offer reliable answers to such questions of motivation, guilt or redemption. Invisibility was of course a highly desirable defensive stratagem. A good example is afforded by Jean Jardin, a grey eminence who, after working for the French railways (SNCF) and for the Minister of Finance Yves Bouthillier, served as Laval's *directeur de cabinet* from May 1942 until November 1943, at which time he withdrew discreetly to Switzerland where he remained until he was reinstated as a senior civil servant in the mid-1950s (he was never threatened with prosecution by post-war governments). Jardin is known to the public only because, much to his irritation, his son Pascal published a series of comic memoirs about him in the 1970s (to be discussed in a subsequent chapter). The ebullient, heroic figure immortalised in these books probably bears little actual resemblance to Laval's chief of staff. His biographer Pierre Assouline more convincingly discerns in Jardin senior the personality traits one might expect to find in a senior administrator or executive running a government department or large commercial enterprise: energy and ambition, a fondness for order and dislike of democratic accountability, subservience to powerful figures in industry and politics, unscrupulousness. Jardin undoubtedly helped some resistance groups and victims of persecution (such as the Jewish historian Robert Aron, who published books sympathetic to the Vichy regime after the war), but he concealed his traces so effectively that few conclusions can be drawn about his career.

In comparison with Jardin's consistent discretion, the more blatant transformations achieved by some individuals are astonishing, not merely in their cunning evasion of retribution but also in their shameless manipulation of the judicial system and historiographical record. Sonia Combes quotes the example of an unnamed *sous-chef de cabinet de préfet* who organised the round-up of Jews in his community, was subsequently deported as a resister in 1944, and finally became a historian and local correspondent of the Comité d'histoire de la seconde guerre mondiale, the scholarly body created in 1951 under the auspices of the prime minister to pursue research on the occupation.[6] A more striking illustration of such adaptability is provided by the head of the regional police in Toulouse, Antoine Poggioli, who was charged with carrying out purges of collaborators at the liberation, when he himself had been an 'organiser of deportation convoys' in 1942 (Combes, 1994: 285). He ended his career as a prefect, which again raises the question: 'Does Poggioli represent a unique case or is he an emblematic figure, typifying those men in the Vichy administration who switched to resistance, double agents who were allegedly implicated in abetting genocide?' (p. 286). Similarly, Robert Gildea (2002: 343) cites analogous cases of senior police officers like Moracchini and Maurice being promoted to senior ranks after the liberation despite having cooperated blatantly with the Gestapo in pursuing resistance activists.

Since most senior civil servants were astute enough to offer some support to resistance and Free French organisms before the end of the occupation, the gradual transfer of allegiance away from Vichy and the Germans towards the allied cause, whether motivated by opportunism or patriotism, is by itself no vindication of compromises or crimes committed on behalf of collaboration (any more than resistance necessarily justifies criminal behaviour). Nevertheless, because resistance and collaboration have often been conveniently presented in exculpatory mythifying terms as radically opposed forces, the first somehow redeeming the second, this more complex perception of a progressive shift in attitudes and actions (often accompanied by denial or omission of blameworthy earlier episodes in individuals' careers) still does not find common acceptance, for all its greater plausibility. Part of Maurice Papon's defence was to cite testimony from reputable members of the resistance, who were genuinely convinced of the value of his support for their cause and therefore outraged at the accusations made against him (though completely unaware of his ruthless enforcement of anti-Semitic persecution). But as Jean Galtier-Boissière observed in his journal entry for 8 October 1944, 'Any collaborationist worth his salt saved at least one Jew, subsidised a resistance movement or underground newspaper. A simple insurance policy' (1992: 247–8).

Unsurprisingly, it is virtually impossible to assess just how extensive spurious claims of resistance activity were, particularly since from mid-1943 the 'noyautage de l'administration publique' (NAP), or infiltration of public bodies, became an important resistance stratagem. Civil servants were thus obliged to play a double game by concealing their transfer of loyalties, which ultimately made deciding which side they really favoured rather difficult. As Daniel Cordier remarks, the NAP had the disadvantage 'of providing prefects, sub-prefects, secretaries general and policemen with the means of redeeming at little cost the errors, faults or crimes which they might have committed' (1989: I, 75). Baruch estimates, however, that out of nearly one million Vichy functionaries, there were only 1500 active agents in the NAP. Fourteen prefects were arrested for NAP activities in May 1944, although Baruch estimates that most prefects dabbled in resistance (1997: 508).

The 'faux résistant' (whether masquerading as public official, maquisard, or secret agent) is a figure of legend who has been evoked more persuasively by authors of fiction than by historical researchers (Marcel Aymé included 'Le Faux Policier' in his collection of stories *Le Vin de Paris* in 1947, while more recently the retrospective manufacturing of a daring career as a Free French secret agent is described with engaging documentary verisimilitude in Jean-François Deniau's (1991) novel *Un héros très discret*, a work which gained wider currency through the film adaptation directed by Jacques Audiard in 1996).[7] André Devigny, whose heroic escape from Montluc prison in 1943 (Devigny, 1956) was the inspiration for Robert Bresson's masterly film *Un condamné à mort s'est échappé*, complains with some bitterness in his memoirs that the post-war period was the 'paradis des imposteurs' (1978: 329), without identifying any of them. At the same time, however, he recounts the murder of his uncle by phoney resisters, against whom he failed to obtain any legal redress, concluding: 'Robbery, pillage and crime: that was resistance for them' (p. 192).

As amnesty laws allowed former collaborators to return to positions of influence from the early 1950s, genuine members of the resistance who had resumed their ordinary existence (and who usually lacked the protection of a political party or influential organism) sometimes became the victims of vendettas instigated by Vichy officials who had retained or regained their power. A striking example is provided by the case of the erstwhile 'préfet du maquis' in the Limousin, Georges Guingouin, a communist primary school teacher who (along with many other French Communist Party (PCF) resistance leaders judged to be too rebellious and independent) was rapidly evicted from the Party, and then thrown into prison in 1953–54 on trumped-up charges. His biographer, the journalist Michel Taubmann (1994), identifies one of Guingouin's pursuers as an 'inspecteur C...', a member of the *police judiciaire* in Limoges actively involved in combating the resistance in 1943, who was promoted to *commissaire* in 1972. The case against Guingouin, which involved accusations of murder committed under his authority, was finally dropped in 1959.

The war between the agents of collaboration and resistance has thus continued until the present time, even if nowadays it is fought out in the form of self-justifying memoirs or in the courtroom, more often through libel cases than trials for crimes against humanity (Papon systematically instigated proceedings for defamation in an attempt to gag his accusers). Those who served Vichy in some official capacity nonetheless claim that they practised a more subtle form of resistance than their ostensible adversaries, who are accused of being bandits masquerading as patriots in the case of maquisards like Guingouin or émigrés comfortably ensconced in London and Algiers in the case of Gaullists (witness the memoirs of the prefects Trouillé and Lecornu, discussed below). Sometimes these claims are justifiable, just as the transferral of allegiance away from Vichy may be genuine. In this sense, the case of the late President François Mitterrand is quite typical, as Bloch-Lainé and Gruson observe in *Hauts Fonctionnaires sous l'occupation*: 'There are innumerable ambiguous career paths like his, revealing simultaneously close association with Vichy and courageous commitment to resistance' (1996: 12). It is worth noting that both these authors were officials in the *Inspection des Finances* during the occupation, itself a notorious bastion of support for Vichy (see Messmer, quoted in Benamou, 1999: 58); their judgement of their fellow functionaries is therefore, one suspects, relatively moderate. That said, Mitterrand's career in the resistance seems to have involved genuine risks (several fellow members of his network were arrested and deported).

Critical scrutiny falls, in any case, less on the eighteen months he spent as a junior official working for Vichy in the offices of the veterans' legion and prisoners of war than on the subsequent convenient omissions in his biographical record, and above all on his post-war association with René Bousquet. In a televised interview broadcast in the final months of his presidency in 1994, Mitterrand pleaded ignorance of Vichy's anti-Semitic policies and argued that national reconciliation was more important than the relentless pursuit of war criminals. However, his links with Bousquet date back as far as 1954, when several members of Bousquet's Vichy team joined Mitterrand's staff at the Ministry of the Interior. According to Gérard Boulanger, Bousquet (who became a successful banker after his acquittal) funded Mitterrand's presidential election campaign against de Gaulle in 1965 (1997: 289). De Gaulle himself was equally tolerant of former collaborators: by this time, Maurice Papon had finally acquired accredited status as a former resistance member, and within a few years had been elected as a Gaullist deputy and made party treasurer of the Gaullist party (UNR).

Structures of administration

That the two major statesmen of both left and right in post-war France should have surreptitiously supported the promotion of former collaborators may suggest a scandalous connivance between the political and administrative classes in concealing serious war crimes, or at best a cynical and expedient acceptance that peacetime retribution could take only a limited form. For de Gaulle, reconstructing the apparatus of the state counted more than chastising or rewarding individuals; hence he remarked gnomically that 'sentiment cannot count before reasons of state' (1980: 374). This respect for the machinery of the state and preferment of its loyal servants meant in practice that wherever possible he appointed high-ranking state officials to senior posts within the Free French hierarchy (such as Moulin, Bollaert, Parodi and Chaban-Delmas). On the other hand, members of the internal resistance and maquis, who had enjoyed considerable local, tactical autonomy as Vichy's authority crumbled in the last months of the occupation, often found themselves marginalised or demoted when the cadres of the liberation government and armed forces returned to restore the order of the state. Yet those who represented the French state at regional and local level, either during the occupation or in the turmoil of liberation, often had the unenviable, intolerable task of attempting to maintain order and ensure the distribution of limited resources to communities which were sometimes virtual or literal war zones, whether through the devastating impact of allied bombing, sabotage and executions carried out by resistance groups, or reprisals inflicted on hostages and civilians by German military forces and collaborationist agencies like the Milice. Before examining the revealing and dramatic case histories recorded by some servants of the state, it is useful to review in a little more detail some of the administrative structures of the occupation period, in order to understand the wider conditions in which they operated.

As has been already suggested, the centralising nature of the French state (before and after as well as during the occupation) is encapsulated in the prefectoral system, that is the use of powerful officials appointed by government to administer public affairs in regions and departments (they have no real equivalent in either the UK or the US). While the concept and term derive from the *praefecti* who administered the Roman republic and the *intendants* who headed the thirty-five *générali-tés* under Louis XVI, the prefectoral corps in France was created in 1800 as part of Napoleon's post-revolutionary reorganisation of the state. The imperial prefects enjoyed considerable wealth and status: a decree of 1804 placed them above bishops and brigadier-generals in the state hierarchy, and in 1810 all were given the title of count or baron. Under succeeding republican regimes, prefects continued to wear an ornate braided uniform, rather akin to an admiral's; their quasi-military appearance and rank (equivalent to a major-general) gave them an authority and prestige greater than that of an ordinary civilian administrator, a factor that could be important when dealing with military occupiers like the Germans.

The appointment of prefects was always determined by political factors in that they had to support the government and prevailing political parties and also to obtain the support of local deputies in their *département*. Consequently, most changes of political regime brought a purge of the prefectoral corps; thus 83 per cent of them were dismissed by Guizot after the July Revolution in 1830. In fact, the mobility of prefects has always corresponded closely to the degree of political stability in France: for example, between 1870 and 1877, when the durability of the Third Republic was far from assured, pre-fects remained in post on average for thirteen months, while under Vichy between 1940 and 1944 they survived for seventeen months, compared with an average of thirty-two months for the whole period from 1870 to 1958.[8]

Full prefects were always a minority of their corps, most of whose members were unlikely to rise beyond the rank of sub-prefect in a provincial backwater. In addition, by the 1920s, there were far more individuals of the rank of prefect than actual posts in *préfectures*. Com-petition for advancement and the influence and favour of patrons were thus determining elements in careers. The symbiotic link be-tween the administrative and political class, which was a marked characteristic of Vichy and subsists in contemporary France (where in 2001, for example, both the socialist Prime Minister Jospin and President Chirac were graduates of the prestigions École Nationale d'Administration – ENA), was established in the nineteenth century. From the Restoration until 1875, members of the prefectoral corps were allowed to combine an administrative post with an elected office; 25 per cent of prefects at this period had also been parliamentary deputies. Under the Third Republic, nearly all prefects rose through the ranks of sub-prefects, most of whom in turn were trained in university law faculties and began their careers as junior officials in prefectoral or ministerial cabinets. Until 1933, prefects were able to choose personally their *chefs de cabinet* (a position which meant acting as 'the prefect's private secretary and general fixer, without holding official rank'; Froment, 1994: 54); such local patronage, which launched the brilliant career of individuals like Jean Moulin, was eventually replaced by a competitive entry examination in 1935 and the creation of the ENA in 1945.

This brief historical overview shows how a curious mixture of political prestige, administrative power and vulnerability has always been a constant element in the prefectoral system; those who chose to govern or administer under Vichy likewise gained enhanced power but exposed themselves to greater risks of dismissal or retribution. Governments under Marshal Pétain were no more stable than the fragile alliances which were constantly made and unmade during the Third and Fourth Republics; thus there were five different ministers of the interior during the occupation. Although no prefect actually resigned when the armistice was signed in June 1940, thirty-five were immediately sacked by the new regime in July; by September 1940, only twenty-seven pre-war prefects remained in post, while by July 1941, there were eighty-two new prefects in the eighty-seven metropolitan departments. Laval replaced half of the eighteen regional prefects on his return to power in the spring of 1942 (removing those deemed too sympathetic to the retrograde ideology of National Revolution). Altogether, during the four years of German occupation, 220 prefects passed through the eighty-seven *départements*. Some seventy prefects and sub-prefects suffered dismissal and deportation, mainly in the closing months of the occupation; half of them survived. After the liberation, about twenty prefects were convicted of collaborationist crimes (six were sentenced to death); only twenty prefects who served under Vichy were reappointed by de Gaulle's provisional government.

As has been noted, the replacement of elected local councils by small administrative committees reinforced the power of prefects, as did the creation in April 1941 of the eighteen regional prefectures (which were replaced by the provisional government's *commissaires de la république* from 1944 to 1946). The constant purges of prefects had the advantage of offering chances of advancement to their less scrupulous rivals. One of the 166 prefects promoted from the corps was René Bousquet, appointed prefect of the Marne when aged only thirty-one in September 1940, prefect of the Champagne region in August 1941, and secretary general of police in April 1942. But for all that they were assisted by *intendants* of police and economic affairs in their efforts to maintain public order and the distribution of resources, the fragmentation of the territory, the demands of the occupying forces, the pressures of resistance groups and the growing belligerence of the population towards Vichy and its officials in the final eighteen months of occupation meant in practice that the prefects were far from omnipotent figures. As Mazey and Wright observe in 'Les Préfets', 'The prefect is often an isolated and exposed man: he is no longer a link in a solid and strictly hierarchical chain of command' (in Azéma and Bédarida, 1992: 279). Frequently they were reduced to negotiating compromises with one or other hostile group from a position of extreme vulnerability. For example, Rivalland, the regional prefect in Marseille, was sacked in January 1943 for refusing to provide the Germans with a list of hostages. Those who stayed in post, whether from genuine loyalty to the community or misplaced ambition, had to confront the same dilemmas. To study the moral and material consequences more fully, we need to look at particular cases.

Good and bad servants: case histories

The two most famous administrators in France from the occupation years are no doubt the prefects Jean Moulin and René Bousquet. Superficially at least, they seem to reveal the sharply contrasting moral nature of resistance and collaboration, of heroic self-sacrifice in the first case and unscrupulous self-promotion in the second. Thus while Moulin was dismissed from his post as prefect of Chartres a few months after the armistice, subsequently joined de Gaulle in London and over a period of eighteen months played a major role in unifying the external and internal resistance, until he was betrayed to the Gestapo and tortured to death, Bousquet remained a faithful servant of the Vichy regime and was one of the main organisers of anti-Semitic persecution and deportation. Although he was dismissed in December 1943, he was arrested by the Gestapo only in June 1944 and his 'deportation' took the form of detention with his family in a villa in Germany. After the High Court acquitted him in June 1949, he became a wealthy banker; fifty years after Moulin's martyrdom in 1943, the eighty-four-year-old Bousquet was gunned down by a publicity-seeking crank and spared the public humiliation of a trial for crimes against humanity, a trial which his influential allies in government had managed to delay for many years.

Yet even if they stand as opposing models of the heroic martyr and the base survivor, in many ways Moulin and Bousquet are curiously complementary figures who incarnate many of the ambiguities and complexities of resistance and collaboration. Moulin aroused the hatred of some of the leaders of resistance movements whom he brought to heel, and was almost certainly betrayed to the Germans by a senior member of Combat. Some of his rivals saw him as an agent of dissension rather than unity within the resistance. On the other hand, Bousquet's claim to resistance credentials, however dubious, was enough to gain him acquittal from charges of treason. Both these dynamic and personally courageous young men came from similar backgrounds, prosperous middle-class families rooted in centre-left politics in southern France, from which they were launched into highly successful careers. Neither left any very substantial testimony explaining their motivation and choices, and both in fact only emerged as historically significant figures several decades after the end of the war.

Jean Moulin did in fact keep a short journal for the period from 14 June to 14 November 1940, although it was largely written up in the spring of 1941 in Montpellier and published posthumously by his sister Laure in 1946 under the title *Premier combat* (and reprinted with some cuts restored in Cordier's biography). Laure presents her brother as 'a born artist and a man of action' (Cordier, 1989: I, 557); he was a commanding administrator and also a skilful caricaturist, running an art gallery in Nice after his dismissal by Vichy. His diary of the debacle offers a vivid account of his efforts to maintain order and the dignity of the state in Chartres as the German invaders approach and most of the inhabitants take flight, along with millions of other refugees from further north. In the days preceding the armistice, normal civil society effectively collapses; although hordes of refugees swarm into the town, only 800 out of its 23,000 citizens remain, while 'Now we no longer have gas, electricity, telephones or radio. Henceforth we are cut off from the rest of the world' (p. 559). Passages noting how most of the *notables* in the community behaved with cowardly selfishness were discreetly trimmed from the post-war version. Thus Moulin observes increasing panic among his staff: 'My secretary general, with his gas mask dangling from his shoulder, is running around in all directions, as though struck by madness' (p. 560). However, his aim is not to cast aspersions on others but rather to offer a record of how he as prefect, aided by a small band of helpers from all social classes and occupations, did his best to assist the wounded and homeless and to feed innumerable refugees.

Moulin notes the acts of pillage and atrocities committed by the German invaders (such as the summary execution of an eighty-three-year-old woman). The prefect himself was nearly the victim of such an act: in the incident which he recounts in some detail, since it famously marked his first act of resistance and explains the diary's title, he was ordered to sign a statement accusing Senegalese troops of committing atrocities against French civilians (the Germans needed a pretext to justify their execution of these colonial troops). His refusal earned him a severe beating from two German officers, protracted over several hours on 17 June; fearing that eventually he would give way if this brutal punishment continued, Moulin used a piece of broken glass he found in the room where he was imprisoned with an African soldier to cut his throat. His life was saved by the arrival of the guard (the African, whose subsequent fate is not recounted, apparently remained sound asleep while his cell mate was slowly bleeding to death), and Moulin made a complete recovery from this suicide attempt within a few months. The German authorities hushed up the affair and Moulin returned to his post until he was sacked by the government in November 1940, on account of his association with left-wing political figures (he declined an offer made after Laval's return to power to take up a new prefectoral position in May 1942).

Curiously, Moulin draws few explicit conclusions from this traumatic incident, whether personal or political. He offers no introspective reflections on what motivates resistance or political analysis of how such arbitrary acts of Nazi brutality can be equated with supposedly amicable cooperation between the French state and occupying forces. The journal is very much a report on practical action accomplished by a loyal functionary and patriot, who remained a servant of the new regime for several months until dismissed for ideological reasons. As Julian Jackson notes somewhat mischievously, Moulin was praised for his 'collaboration' as a conscientious administrator by the local German *Feldkommandant* in September 1940 (2001: 167). Yet Moulin was consistent in his physical courage, his rectitude and refusal to accept German domination, however enigmatic his personality. A recent biographer calls him 'a secretive man with the social habits of a libertine', whose 'secular canonisation' as 'the personification of the resistance' (Marnham, 2000: 62, 16, 17) actually occurred in December 1964, two decades after his death, when his remains were transferred to the Pantheon in an elaborate ceremony presided over by President de Gaulle and his Minister of Culture André Malraux.

The personality of René Bousquet is even more intractable for those who seek to penetrate his motives or to generalise from his career about the dilemmas and pitfalls of collaboration. One commentator claims that Bousquet 'had the misfortune at the age of twenty to be hailed as a hero, which knocked him off course' (Limagne, quoted by Baruch, 1997: 388), arguing unconvincingly that physical bravery cloaked or stimulated the reckless pursuit of glory. The reference is to Bousquet's active role as a junior official in Montauban in rescuing citizens trapped by floods in March 1930 (a colleague was drowned in this hazardous enterprise), for which he was awarded the Légion d'honneur the following year, aged only twenty-two. Thereafter, Bousquet's promotion was so rapid that it broke the normal rules of advancement through the grades at three-year intervals. His success in pleasing higher authority for most of the occupation continued after the war; although he was imprisoned in Fresnes from May 1945 until July 1948, his interrogation and trial were protracted over four years, little effort was made to investigate his role in anti-Semitic persecution, and he was eventually acquitted.

Bousquet had been attacked by the collaborationist press for supposed resistance sympathies in the months preceding his dismissal and replacement by the fanatical Darnand, and was able to incorporate this hostility into his defence, which consisted essentially of citing testimony from individuals whom he had assisted to escape persecution, while exploiting the vastness and complexity of the police system to claim ignorance or shift prime responsibility on to others, such as the infamous head of the Commissariat for Jewish Affairs Darquier de Pellepoix. At his interrogation on 1 October 1948, he stated:

> I was the constant defender and agent of a policy of protection regarding all the Jews. It was to me that the government ceaselessly turned when it sought to give this protection a specific and courageous form ... If words mean anything, that means that I adopted, both as a civil servant and a man, an attitude which can be called *resistance*. (Quoted in Froment, 1994: 252)

Since 59,000 Jews were deported in 1942 and 1943, most of them having been arrested by French policemen under Bousquet's command after his negotiations with SS leaders Oberg and Heydrich, this statement is an exact reversal of the truth. Hence his biographer Pascale Froment's observation that Bousquet was 'a man capable of reaching great heights in the art of lying' (1994: 292). Nonetheless the High Court believed this defence, although later researchers like Serge Klarsfeld had no difficulty in confounding his mendacity. Ironically, it was only when his venomous rival Darquier used a press interview from his exile in Spain in 1978 to accuse him of being the main organiser of the Vel d'Hiv arrests that 'l'affaire Bousquet' became a national controversy; charges of crimes against humanity were however laid against his subordinate Leguay in 1979, since Bousquet's acquittal in 1949 made him a harder target. Bousquet was charged formally only in 1991, and murdered two years later.

As has already been suggested, the Papon affair replicated the Bousquet case on a smaller scale, with the crucial difference that, despite his more junior status during the occupation, Papon achieved international notoriety as a war criminal by surviving long enough to be tried and convicted in 1997–98. His lower position as secretary general in the Bordeaux prefecture allowed Papon to make an uninterrupted transition from collaboration to resistance and from occupation to liberation. He transferred his allegiance from the regional prefect Sabatier to de Gaulle's *commissaire de la république* Gaston Cusin, who appointed him as his *directeur de cabinet* with the rank of prefect after Papon ensured the loyalty of the Bordeaux police to the new government. In his previous incarnation as a zealous agent of collaboration, Papon had been directly involved in organising ten deportation convoys of some 1690 Jews from Bordeaux. He had also crushed any efforts at resistance by subordinates: his biographer Gérard Boulanger cites the example of a junior member of police staff whom he had sacked and sent abroad on forced labour for expressing Gaullist sympathies. However, as Boulanger caustically observes, 'Papon's resistance record grew ever greater as the war years receded' (1997: 169). After several rejections, he was finally given a CVR card (that is, accreditation as a resistance combatant) after de Gaulle's return to power in 1958, at which time he was prefect of police in Paris.

Documents incriminating Papon were discovered by chance in the Bordeaux archives in February 1981, by three local researchers, Cavignac, Bergès and Slitinsky. These unclassified papers from the *Service des questions juives* for the Gironde were leaked to the satirical investigative newspaper *Le Canard enchaîné* by Michel Slitinsky (whose father Abraham had died in Auschwitz after being arrested in the region in October 1942). The article exposing Papon's contribution to Nazi genocide as an 'aide de camps' appeared on 6 May 1981, a few days before Mitterrand's presidential election victory over Giscard d'Estaing (Papon was now a minister in Giscard's government), and launched the campaign to prosecute and convict him, which was to last for nearly two decades. Gérard Boulanger, who was the lawyer for the *parties civiles* (civil plaintiffs) at Papon's trial, is a declared adversary of such self-serving bureaucrats and their political allies (though anyone who accepts the factual validity of the evidence incriminating Papon is likely to share his view of this evil and callous individual). This view is that Papon's conviction shows a belated success for individual citizens, human rights, and the independent investigators and media which aid them, over a state establishment which protects its servants at all costs. Noting that out of 13,533 functionaries employed in the Gironde during the occupation, only 167 (or 1.2 per cent) received any punishment at the liberation, Boulanger argues that the failure of the liberation purges to root out crimes of collaboration has nothing to do with public indifference or a general urge for reconciliation. On the contrary, it is

> the result of a political battle lost by the nation in resistance against state Gaullism, with the latter being strongly supported by the solidarity of state organisms charged with purging themselves, which is hardly a guarantee of impartiality, still less of severity. (1997: 157)

According to this analysis, with the liberation Gaullism ceased to embody resistance and indeed became its enemy. Boulanger quotes Raymond Aron's observation about the 'Gaullist clan' which embraced Papon, that 'Those who came over learned quickly that former Vichyists, once baptised in the Gaullist faith, were accepted more easily than those who had served the allied cause outside Gaullism' (1997: 106).

Far from expressing remorse or contrition, Papon, along with his defenders, presents himself as the misjudged victim of persecution. The journalist Daniel Schneidermann calls him 'an arrogant old man clinging rigidly to his convictions' (1998: 32), adding: 'Your hands are only stained with ink. You owed us above all a great story. You owed our curiosity a guided tour of the bowels of the French state, its nauseous dealings and mysteries' (p. 11). But the metaphor of the ink-stained bureaucrat understates both his responsibility and guilt: the active imposition of brutal repression remained a characteristic of Papon's use of

his authority, most notoriously in the massacres of unarmed demon-
strators perpetrated by the police in Paris which he sanctioned as police
chief in the final years of the Algerian crisis in 1961 and 1962.
Moreover, Papon actually produced several autobiographical books at
various stages of his career, although these were complacent works of
self-aggrandisement and self-exculpation rather than confessions.

For example, *Les Chevaux du pouvoir*, which Papon published in
1988, some years after his criminal wartime record had been exposed,
makes no reference either to the occupation or to the author's recent
problems. The dossiers which he claims he is releasing in the book's
subtitle do not incriminate him but reveal him as de Gaulle's right-
hand man, the iron-fisted prefect of police who, at the General's
behest, kept down agitators in Paris from 1958 to 1967. The photograph on the back cover shows Papon literally standing at the right
side of de Gaulle, both of them uniformed guardians of the state. The
accompanying blurb also traces his brilliant trajectory from its supposedly glorious origins in the resistance: 'Serving as secretary general
in the prefecture of the Gironde at the liberation, Maurice Papon was
promoted to prefect by General de Gaulle's government owing to his
actions in the resistance...' Eleven years later, facing a prison sentence, the disgraced Papon attempted to defend himself in a work
entitled *La Vérité n'intéressait personne* (1999), co-authored with the
local historian Michel Bergès.

Here his tactic is the customary one adopted by mendacious statesmen and governors of blaming current political adversaries for present
misfortunes (such as the regional prefect of Bordeaux Gabriel Delaunay,
not to mention François Mitterrand and Roland Dumas), denying personal guilt, and shifting responsibility on to other figures within the
administrative hierarchy. Thus he suggests that in wartime Bordeaux
real power lay with the regional prefecture and the police; his boss
Sabatier had sole responsibility for Jewish questions, while Papon was
in charge only of personnel and recording data. Hence his protest:
'That's all I did, record and inform! That was the main part of my job
as secretary general. I was not a decision maker!' (Papon, 1999: 76).
Extracts are cited from his unpublished occupation journal (although
it contains no references to Jews). Papon's philosophy of administration (to which he had devoted earlier works), however, reveals him as
a simple-minded authoritarian and does little to buttress his defence.
Thus he asserts that 'The administration is the guardian of France!'
against political instability and public disorder, offering the syllogism:
'The administration is the state. The state is the nation. The nation is

France', to which he adds 'the police is the state!' Far from enforcing repression, the police keep the peace; hence the term 'peace officer, a most fine title, one justified on a daily basis!' (pp. 288–92). The Vichy regime and Papon's subsequent career do not of course offer much evidence to support these assertions.[9] Papon concludes rather predictably that, as the victim of a 'lynching by the media', 'I am at peace with my conscience, in an affair that has been singularly lacking in any' (p. 312). It is more interesting that his interlocutor Bergès, who originally helped expose him, should have changed his mind about Papon's guilt, on the grounds that the documentary evidence presented at the trial did not prove his complicity. Otherwise, he has few important allies: Papon's appeals both to the European Court of Human Rights and the French president for release on compassionate grounds were rejected in 2001, although the European Court decreed in 2002 that he had the right to appeal against his conviction (which in fact led to his release).[10]

It is no doubt unsurprising that figures who sacrificed themselves in the cause of resistance like Moulin or who were so compromised as servants of collaboration like Bousquet and Papon were unable to produce substantial or veracious written records of their wartime activities. To find more persuasive and comprehensive first-hand accounts of how public servants dealt with the ethical and material problems of occupation, one needs to turn to individuals who both occupied more neutral positions and survived the occupation. Before looking at the journals and memoirs published by prefects like Lecornu and Trouillé or teachers like Guéhenno and Pannequin, it is interesting to note in passing that few novelists have managed successfully to fictionalise the dilemmas of the wartime bureaucrat. Yves Amiot's novel *La Onzième Heure* (1984) reveals some of the pitfalls which await authors who attempt to reconstruct the occupation at second-hand. His unnamed narrator recounts his misadventures as a *pétainiste* prefect, whose attempt to play a double game makes him a hostage pulled between the Germans and resistance. After saving the local German commander from an assassination attempt, he is himself shot by the resistance, survives and is imprisoned by a *cour de justice* in 1945. His sentence of forced labour involves de-mining a beach. His ex-wife (whose life he saved by protecting the German officer) attempts to get him released, but he is blown up by a mine in October 1945. However, the weakness of this novel is not so much its melodramatic plot (many such lurid incidents are described by first-hand witnesses), but rather the author's complete inability to recreate from his historical sources an engaging narrative and an imagined world peopled by believable characters. At best, we are given a series of wooden dialogues and sententious observations about the dilemmas of resistance and collaboration, which not only fail to ring true as fiction but also lack the intellectual rigour or analytical insight of an essay.

In comparison, the best autobiographical accounts written by firsthand witnesses and participants nearly always do convey the perils, humiliations, triumphs and betrayals of occupation life with an emotional intensity and immediacy that communicate a real sense of historical authenticity (even though they may contain a large element of retrospective reconstruction and self-justification). A documentary authenticity, that is, in convincingly evoking feelings, attitudes and experiences, as well as material details, which is not to be confused with the more dispassionate veracity or objectivity to be found in the research and interpretation of a historian chronicling events experienced by others. Whereas a novelist like Amiot patently has only the most superficial knowledge of what it was really like to be a local governor under Vichy (and therefore fails either to inform, edify or entertain his readers), diarists like Lecornu and Trouillé have the immense advantage of reconstructing a world which they experienced at first-hand, at a time when the prefect was a key figure in the violent struggle for power and survival between the rulers and citizens of the French state and their adversaries.

After serving as a *chef de cabinet* for five years, Bernard Lecornu was somewhat ingloriously invalided out of the wartime army with a severe attack of boils and returned with his family to his post as *sous-préfet* in Châteaubriant, where the Germans arrived on 17 June 1940, his thirty-fourth birthday. His memoirs, entitled *Un préfet sous l'occupation allemande*, recount the professional and personal crises which he had to confront for the next five years. The book documents some of the horrors inflicted on the civilian population, which he did his best to assuage, while at the same time offering a defence of his own role as a collaborator: 'as head of the local administration, is it not my duty to remain and intercede between the Germans and my compatriots?' (Lecornu, 1997: 22). An early example of his efforts to protect French citizens was his altercation with a German officer who refused to arrest a soldier accused of rape; this led to Lecornu himself being brought before a German military tribunal on 2 July, on the charge of insulting a German officer, a charge dismissed by the court, perhaps because the Germans at this stage wished to uphold the rule of law.

By the end of the following year, relations between the Germans and their reluctant hosts deteriorated severely, as resistance attacks brought violent reprisals in the form of mass executions of civilians. The internment camp of Choisel where political prisoners were detained (including the judge Didier, the only member of the judiciary who refused to swear the oath of loyalty to Pétain) was located near Châteaubriant. The camp soon became a reserve from which hostages were drawn for execution. When Lieutenant-Colonel Hotz, the *Feld-kommandant* of Nantes, was shot by communist resisters on 20 October 1941, the Germans threatened to shoot 100 hostages; 48 communist militants and war veterans were executed two days later, although the other executions were eventually not carried out. While attempts to prevent these large-scale killings were of little success (as a junior official, the author was a mere bystander, 'reduced to impotence', p. 62), the Vichy authorities did become involved in macabre discussions about which unfortunate victims were to be selected.[11] In particular, the Minister of the Interior Pucheu and his *directeur de cabinet* Paringaux were directly implicated in the designation of communist hostages; as a result, both of them subsequently met violent deaths. As further hostages are sacrificed, the author becomes aware that the initial appeal to patriotic duty now rings hollow; in practice he is safeguarding neither his fellow citizens nor his own authority. Hence the rueful observation: 'How much simpler my life would have been if I'd gone to London!' (p. 76). He points out, however, that 'Free French radio is advising Gaullist administrators to stay, so that they are not replaced by collaborators' (p. 137).[12]

In December 1941, he was transferred to Saint-Nazaire, a coastal town which was an important German submarine base and a key port in the battle of the Atlantic. On 28 March 1942, a British commando attack inflicted major damage on the naval installations, although over half of the 611 men in the attacking force were either killed or taken prisoner; in addition, German troops shot dead eighteen local citizens in random reprisals and arrested a large number of others. In February 1943, the town was largely destroyed by allied bombing. Lecornu himself was promoted in July 1943 to become prefect of the Corrèze, under the authority of the regional prefect of Limoges in the southern zone. In this more remote part of France, the conflict between Vichy or German forces and the resistance was particularly intense (128 attacks by the communist FTP were recorded in the single month of October 1943, for example). Lecornu notes that his predecessor was a marginalised figure who was not even informed of police operations against the maquis by the *intendant* in Limoges or the colonel commanding the Gardes Mobiles and Groupes Mobiles de

Réserve. The new prefect became a resistance agent and narrowly avoided being arrested. However, he was denounced by the Milice and summarily dismissed in February 1944, 'without salary or pension benefits' (p. 238). After returning to his parents' home in Caen, he was placed under house arrest by the Gaullist authorities and imprisoned in Fresnes after the liberation. Although press articles accused him of direct involvement in the Châteaubriant executions, a judicial investigation vindicated him and he was released in March 1945 after six months' detention. Decorated with the *médaille de la Résistance*, the following year he was appointed prefect of the Hautes-Alpes.

Ostensibly, then, Lecornu's story is one of triumph against adversity, both professionally, in terms of promotion and honours, and morally, insofar as his commitment to civic duty despite the hazards of war is vindicated. A cynical reader might interpret Lecornu's version of events as no more than the classic defence produced by many collaborators, from Pétain downwards: while retaining their privileges, they act as intermediaries with the Germans in order to save the citizens whom they govern from an even worse fate. In fact, Lecornu shows how flimsy this protective cover is: he can do virtually nothing to stop the suffering caused by mass executions or wide-scale bombing. He is probably most effective when betraying collaboration by acting as an intelligence agent for the resistance. One also wonders why he waited for several decades before publishing his account of the occupation (and how much he has embellished or distorted the record in the meantime).[13] He himself observes that simply by remaining in post, he is automatically an object of suspicion, even if he took far greater risks than the Gaullist émigrés who presume to judge him. In fact, it is his conflicts with authority in its successive, inhuman forms that make him a sympathetic and credible witness: prosecuted by the Germans, sacked by Vichy, imprisoned by the Gaullists, he does seem to be an honest man rather than the compliant, self-serving scoundrel one sees in Bousquet and Papon.[14]

Lecornu's successor as prefect of Corrèze was Pierre Trouillé, who also published his *Journal d'un préfet pendant l'occupation* in 1964, a gripping book which deserves to be far better known. Cast as a diary covering the final six months of occupation from 29 February to 23 August 1944, Trouillé's account is much more compressed and compelling, partly because it contains less retrospective, pious self-justification, and partly because of the escalating, tragic violence and incompetence that it recounts. The fragile peace brought by the armistice has long since collapsed, as the author remarks:

The present conflict differs from the previous one in that it has reached supposedly untouchable regions; in France in particular there is not a single human being who feels safe. What Cassandra would have dared predict, in 1939, that the Massif Central would become a combat zone where French and Germans would clash? (Trouillé, 1964: 33)

In fact, the conflict is considerably more complex than a straightforward clash between French and Germans; even the more customary, less manichean four-part division, involving a guerrilla war conducted by the resistance against the Germans and their Vichy paramilitary auxiliaries, with French civilians being terrorised and murdered by all three belligerents, does not adequately describe the various forces competing for dominance in the region. What Trouillé observes is an increasing fragmentation of order and authority, where loyalty and cohesion no longer stem from the state or national leaders, but are found much more locally, sometimes in armed groups that are more like marauding bands led by renegade figures than disciplined military units. In this chaotic situation, where summary and random acts of violence are common, the prefect retains only the dubious moral authority of the peace-broker.

Trouillé observes that the department is actually enduring two occupations: 'seventeen cantons are in the hands of the maquis, nine in the hands of the Germans' (p. 19), while the authority of the Vichy government is virtually non-existent ('I really wonder what a prefect can do who exists only through the tolerance of the maquis and the Germans', p. 24). The former may not be much preferable to the latter. The unification of resistance military groups as the Forces Françaises de l'Intérieur (FFIs) under General Kœnig is far from assured in practice. For instance, two resisters from the Armée secrète (AS) return voluntarily to prison after a break-out, when they discover it was organised by the rival FTP, leading Trouillé to note despairingly: 'This is unbelievable. If Philippe Henriot knew about it, it would certainly give him ammunition for his propaganda broadcasts' (p. 9). There is open conflict between AS and FTP units in Ussel on 15 June. In reprisal for FTP attacks, the Germans impose a reign of terror: by 7 April, 200 Jews have been shot from the 6000 banished to Corrèze, and 55 other civilians have been shot and 1500 arrested. The maquis, on the other hand, systematically steal supplies intended for the old and young (as a deterrent, FTP leaders have some looters shot in public).

On 28 March, the former gangster Henri Lafont, now an SS officer, arrives with his associate Pierre Bonny, the 'disgraced cop', and their band of 250 Arab *gestapistes*; they quit the region on 28 May after desultory attempts to track down resisters. Trouillé notes that many officers in German uniform are actually from Soviet states (in a further bewildering exchange of loyalties, some of the Georgian and Armenian mercenaries recruited by the renegade General Vlassov, and much feared for their atrocities, eventually joined the FFI in Toulouse). On the other hand, the *milicien* Antonietti proves to be an FTP company leader. (Lecornu had discovered to his cost that the regional NAP leader Aline was a Gestapo double agent.) Worse was yet to come. On 5 June, Tulle was invested by troops from the Francs-Tireurs et Partisans, who were forced to withdraw three days later on the arrival of the German armoured division Das Reich. The Germans retaliated with their customary ruthlessness: the author escaped summary execution only by appealing to Teutonic reverence for hierarchical authority and asserting his status as a superior officer akin to a general. His fellow citizens were less fortunate: 5000 men from Tulle were rounded up and 99 of them hanged on 9 June. The plan to destroy the town and kill all male inhabitants was abandoned, however, thanks to the humane treatment given to German wounded earlier in the week. Systematic killing was routine for the warriors of the SS: members of the division boasted of hanging thousands of civilians during the eastern campaign. The neighbouring village of Oradour-sur-Glane (in the Haute-Vienne) was destroyed and 700 villagers murdered on 10 June.

After a further nine weeks of terror, during which Trouillé witnessed three *miliciens* torturing a man with acid and others shooting an old woman, the resistance returned to Tulle on 16 August, whereupon the prefect was able to persuade the German garrison to capitulate the following day. However, the arrival of a retreating German column of 350 vehicles on the 19th caused panic and flight for a few hours, although the resistance now numbered 10,000 armed men; Trouillé concludes caustically that their leaders are 'a gang of incompetent jackasses' (p. 228). The Comité Départemental de Libération finally reinstalled itself on 23 August. The hostility which General de Gaulle displayed towards such maquis leaders, especially in the south-west, and his haste to replace them as soon as possible with experienced public officials, are often taken by resistance sympathisers as signs of base ingratitude or authoritarianism; Trouillé's account of the vainglorious incompetence of some local resistance leaders (and the appalling consequences of their tactical blunders for their own men and neighbouring civilians) suggests that de Gaulle's scepticism was largely justified.

While the journals of prefects like Lecornu and Trouillé doubtless reveal the most creditable aspects of senior administrators, who strove to temper the horrors suffered by local citizens in the violent transition from occupation to liberation, nevertheless such members of the governing elite inevitably remained remote from ordinary people and their retrospective self-justifications have to be viewed with considerable suspicion. The same objections do not apply to those who worked for the state in humbler occupations, such as schoolteachers, particularly if they became active supporters of resistance. One of the best-known diarists of the period is Jean Guéhenno, whose *Journal des années noires* was published in 1946, this author having no reason to delay publication for fear of being discredited by hostile witnesses. Indeed, the publisher's blurb for a paperback reprint (Guéhenno, 1973) insists on his typicality and universality: Guéhenno's account offers 'the best general account of the daily life and the intimate reactions of an average Frenchman during the occupation'.

By his initial social background, Guéhenno represented the common man, even if his subsequent educational and intellectual achievements gained him promotion to academic and cultural elite organisms as influential and prestigious as the prefectoral corps. He was born in a working class family in 1890 and became a factory worker at the age of fourteen, before serving in the army in the First World War. Success in the baccalaureate and the competitive examination for the École Normale Supérieure, however, marked the beginning of a career as a teacher of 'classes préparatoires' in Parisian *lycées* (which, though technically part of secondary education, are effectively equivalent to a post as a university professor); he ended his career in education as an *inspecteur général*. At the same time, he was active as a literary critic, autobiographer and social commentator, editing the journals *Europe* and *Vendredi*, contributing to the clandestine *Lettres françaises* during the occupation, and gaining election to the French Academy in 1961. Guéhenno was not a creative artist, as he admits in his wartime journal (which explains why his work is relatively unknown outside France); nevertheless, the trajectory of such a committed humanist exemplifies the most attractive features of the republican meritocracy.

David Boal is oddly dismissive of Guéhenno, in his study *Journaux intimes sous l'occupation*, arguing for instance that he overdoes his condemnation of Vichy and collaboration, at the expense of accurate observation, and complaining about 'his inability to reconstruct the smell, taste and atmosphere of a bygone period'. Hence 'one often has the impression that the author misses his target, that he is too right-thinking, well-intentioned and indignant to give an effective account of the events (which are themselves extremely interesting) he witnessed' (1993: 156). A more sympathetic reading, however, does not support these objections.[15] It is hardly surprising that a left-wing intellectual should be hostile to Vichy and ready to point out its hypocrisies and absurdities. As Guéhenno remarks, he is a 'Caliban unbound' (1973: 23), that is a member of the common people who has found his voice, and thus by definition a vocal adversary of those reactionary notables who seek to gag and repress the lower orders. The occupation, however, reduces him to silence (other than in the pages of a clandestine diary or in occasional asides in the classroom); after 'the invasion of the rats' in June 1940, Pétain's seizure of power is dismissed from the outset as 'an ignoble piece of political score-settling' (pp. 17, 19), the revenge of a conservative elite eager to disenfranchise the classes which had begun to receive more equitable treatment.

Guéhenno presents his account as an expression of solidarity from a citizen dispossessed by a brutal invader and a dishonourable government: 'This is no more than a journal of our common suffering. You will not find in it an account of any unknown event or an explanation of any secret intrigue...The average Frenchman will recognise himself here...he will rediscover his shame, that terrible sense of shame that devoured us' (pp. 9–10).

He observes that he has in fact censored the darkest pages of his manuscript and eliminated the names of collaborators whom he criticises (other than public figures). At the same time, however, he is aware that he is not really an average citizen, but rather a member of an alternative and opposing elite, which sees its mission as upholding and propagating the values of enlightened humanism. He recognises that the masses are all too prone to sink into torpid indifference: 'Already we are settling into servitude...Few men perhaps really need liberty' (p. 18). As for the defeatist dictator Pétain, this 'old man, who no longer even has a man's voice but talks like an old woman' (p. 15), his physical impotence does not merely give the lie to his pretension to act the role of heroic saviour but also betokens his future political impotence.

Guéhenno notes, for instance, on 1 January 1942, that in delivering a speech on the radio Pétain read the same paragraph twice in succession: 'How can one not feel an immense sense of pity. This old man, whose attention wanders at every instant, how can he be France? Naturally the Paris newspapers don't breathe a word this morning about the speech' (p. 230). Indeed, this failure of language exposes the speciousness and absurdity of his claims to authority; Hitler at least writes his own speeches and seduces the masses:

> Can one imagine Mirabeau, Danton or Robespierre reading out speeches written by their secretaries? The movement of a speech should be the movement of the man himself. There is nothing more carnal than true eloquence, which is violent and dominates the crowd as one might a woman. (p. 237)

Guéhenno observes how pretence and duplicity are at the heart of the political process. Like too many governments, Vichy is driven to sub-terfuge and mendacity in order to conceal its own failings: for in-stance, by suppressing the facts about the true extent of German requisitions or by mounting 'l'ignoble comédie de Riom', the show trial which unsuccessfully sought to blame Third Republic leaders rather than the military command for the debacle of 1940 (p. 241). Pétain, as the faltering leader of a phantom regime, is compared to the dramatist Alfred Jarry's parody of a monstrous tyrant, Ubu-Roi (though he obviously lacks Ubu's grotesque charisma and linguistic verve). He is more trenchantly summed up as a senile colonel elevated far beyond his competence: 'Ageing always means the hardening of one's main characteristics: in ageing, this former colonel has hardened in his au-thoritarian vanity' (p. 302).

Such examples show Guéhenno to be both an astute observer and a persuasive *moraliste*, in the sense that he attempts to abstract a general, ethical lesson from some specific incident. It seems odd to criticise him for lacking impartiality (unless one feels an urge to defend Nazi atrocities and Vichy propaganda). He is aware, however, of the moral and material ambiguities of his own position, as the citizen of a defeated nation, a public servant who enjoys certain privileges and influences, and an intellectual commentator reduced to virtual silence. Thus he remarks sarcastically in August 1940, as the new regime at-tempts to assert its authority, that 'France from now on is at work and ministers are taking in hand idle public employees like me' (p. 33). In practice, however, mass unemployment (with as many as two million people out of work) adds to the suffering and deprivation caused by warfare. While all the birds in the Parisian conurbation have already perished, asphyxiated by the burning of fuel dumps, the human inhab-itants are forced to adopt humiliating and selfish survival tactics: 'The main thing is not to die of hunger this winter. And each of us waits his turn, like a dumb animal, at the ration-card office, the trough' (p. 45).

A black market in ration tickets is thriving within a few months of the armistice; like many urban residents, Guéhenno's household is highly dependent on food parcels sent by friends and relatives in Brittany.

Guéhenno describes at length how shortages and restrictions circumscribe the daily life of most ordinary citizens like himself (obtaining a permit to travel to the south zone is practically impossible; he has to wait for two years to visit Montolieu). But he is also aware that, while some privileged groups bypass these problems, for others conditions are far worse. From curiosity, he attends the first meeting of Marcel Déat's fascist party, the Rassemblement National Populaire, in February 1941. Like Guéhenno, Déat was a *normalien*, but he abandoned his socialist beliefs and is cast as an embittered opportunist: 'He's not bothered about the cattle, provided he can be the herdsman. Only one true passion moved him yesterday: hatred for the Vichy government which has not made him a minister' (p. 107). The betrayals of this government (which Déat joined belatedly in 1944 as an out-and-out collaborator) preoccupy the diarist from an early stage. He observes of the statute of October 1940 which barred Jews from most key professions: 'the victor is inoculating us with his diseases . . . I feel full of shame' (p. 57). He has the same reaction when the government hands over the German Social Democrat leaders Breitscheid and Hilferding to Hitler (16 March 1941). Noting the increasing use of terror methods by the occupying forces, he argues that 'there is not a Frenchman who soon will not owe a debt towards the Jews and communists, imprisoned and shot for us, true sacrificial victims for the nation' (p. 197). Such moral obligations are rarely translated into expressions of solidarity or action, unfortunately. By February 1943, Guéhenno is deploring the population's docile acceptance of forced labour and the compliance of the administrative authorities which do the Germans' work for them, concluding that 'the whole of this country has become a fearful protoplasm' (p. 320). In a bizarre twist, we learn that even dogs are to be requisitioned from May 1944 (the author's dog is too short to be conscripted, however).

Such despairing accusations of cowardice and complicity are tempered by more measured reflections on the responsibility of intellectual and political elites:

What people lives other than through a minority, through the few who inspire and lead them. This minority is now forced to remain silent. Only traitors and cowards speak. Hence the impression of sluggishness given by opinion. But really there is no opinion and, if one thinks about it, the sort of inertia with which the masses, normally so malleable, oppose propaganda is a good sign of the instinctive dignity of the country. (p. 406)

Guéhenno's own position as a teacher of the most gifted students of their generation makes him a privileged observer of one such minority, the academic and intellectual community. For much of the occupation, he was teaching *khâgne* classes (which prepare students aspiring to enter the École Normale Supérieure) at the prestigious Parisian *lycées* Henri IV (where he replaced a colleague who was a prisoner of war) and Louis-le-Grand. His resistance sympathies, however, earned him a humiliating demotion to teaching junior classes from September 1943: henceforward, as he notes, instead of lecturing to brilliant students, 'My new job is to explain things to little children and hear them recite their lessons' (p. 361). His weekly schedule of six lectures was tripled to seventeen hours of classes, 'the workload of a novice teacher, everything my colleagues wanted to avoid' (p. 365), an exhausting burden, which causes him to exclaim in a rare moment of self-pity: 'I'm in prison and so tired that I cannot even write up this journal' (p. 376).

Until this point, Guéhenno had not been directly affected by the repressive measures inflicted on individuals who were suspected of dissent or resistance activities, although he had recorded the totalitarian tendencies of the state administration which increasingly limited the autonomy of the teacher and sought to make education little more than indoctrination. Even in the first year of occupation, he notes that literature readily degenerates into 'mere diversion and display of readily accepted servitude' (p. 75) and that universal education merely encourages docility: 'Never have so many men in Europe known how to read, and yet never have there been so many herd animals, so many sheep' (p. 95). A teacher at Janson de Sailly was arrested for subversive behaviour after being denounced by a pupil in February 1941 (although he was later released and his denouncer was left vulnerable to retaliation). Such incidents represent a progressive loss of innocence for Guéhenno, who is himself warned by an administrator in October 1941 to make his lecturing 'more technical and more practical'. In other words, 'From now on the history of ideas is suspect' (p. 193). While hitherto he has taught without fearing material or moral constraints, now he is aware that the need to earn money makes resignation impossible and dismissal perilous. By 1942, a minority of pupils openly support collaborationism and act as 'informers for Doriot and the PPF' (pp. 293–4), following in the footsteps of such members of the intellectual elite as Pucheu, Déat and Brasillach who have made themselves the 'ignoble servants of the powerful, whoever they may be' (p. 210).

Ultimately, however, the travails of occupation reinforce and justify Guéhenno's faith in humanity and in those who profess and propagate the value of liberal culture. His basic principles are stated from 1940: 'if nature undoes at each moment what we do, liberty, equality, fraternity, then all the more reason for us to rebuild them through our will, our laws, and to oppose natural disorder with human order' (p. 49). The Germans represent a denial of humanity: they are 'Robots of the enslavement machine, slaves themselves' (p. 150). As for teaching, it is 'The main thing in my life' (p. 101), 'a profession which allows one to live almost continually amid greatness. A profession which reveals marvels' (p. 418). Fortunately, his story has a happy ending which vindicates his optimism: in August 1944, 'Liberty and France are reborn' (p. 438). However, other more obscure members of Guéhenno's profession have left us bleaker and more cynical accounts, where hard-won liberation proves to be only a new form of oppression.

For Claude Jamet, a journalist and teacher who supported collaboration, August 1944 marked not merely a further stage in his personal suffering as one of the millions thrown into captivity in the course of the war (previously he was a prisoner of war in a POW camp for officers) but more particularly the beginning of his professional disgrace, as he notes in a series of embittered books such as *Fifi roi* (1947). On 24 August, he was held up at gunpoint by FFIs and detained overnight. Jamet was under suspicion for taking Guéhenno's place at the *lycée* Louis-le-Grand after the latter's demotion to the *lycée* Voltaire and, more significantly, for articles published in collaborationist journals such as *Germinal*. He was placed on the CNE black list and suspended from his teaching post on half-pay from October 1944; on 2 November 1944 he was arrested again and detained in Fresnes prison until 11 February 1945 (during which period the more notorious collaborationist journalists Georges Suarez and Robert Brasillach were executed for treason). In April 1945, he was acquitted by the *Chambre civique* but sacked from his teaching post. Jamet concludes dourly that liberation reveals how 'One militia has simply replaced the other. Only the badges have changed, really, and the songs' (1947: 64).

The reader may be unconvinced by this relativist lesson: apart from the very dubious equivalence between atrocities perpetrated by the occupying forces or their Vichy acolytes and the abuses committed under the liberation government, Jamet's refusal to accept any responsibility for his journalistic propaganda (or to concede that four months' detention seem fairly lenient) effectively subverts his credibility as a witness. The same cannot be said, however, of Roger Pannequin, whose memoir *Ami si tu tombes* (2000, first published in 1976) presents a scathing indictment of the betrayals and duplicities of administrators (be they Vichy bureaucrats or Communist Party apparatchiks), from the viewpoint of a low-ranking resistance militant. Alain Raybaud argues in his preface to the book that resistance is essentially 'a movement that starts at the bottom' and begins with 'thousands of minor acts of insubordination' (Pannequin, 2000: 10). Insubordination and contempt for state and party hierarchies may well be what distinguish the truly independent man of action from the organisation men whose pliability and subservience he scorns; yet no individual can operate effectively as a partisan without the support of a larger organisation which may ultimately need to sacrifice him (even as prestigious a figure as General de Gaulle was driven to resign as head of government eight months after the end of the war). Although Pannequin's career as a paramilitary activist clearly makes him a combatant (the subject of the next chapter), his observations on the problematic nature of administrative authority are highly relevant to the present discussion.

Pannequin was brought up in the mining communities of the Nord and Pas-de-Calais and chose as an alternative to becoming a miner to train as an *instituteur*. By 1940 he was a qualified primary school teacher and militant socialist. In May 1940 he was called up to join the army and rapidly captured during the debacle, narrowly escaping being shot by the Germans, who massacred 380 civilians and 94 French and British soldiers in the Pas-de-Calais during their victorious advance. Returning to work after the armistice, the author discovers that the local inspector of schools has reported him to the Germans as an escaped prisoner of war. This leads him to reflect on the loyalties of 'my senior administrators, capable of denouncing one of their own men to the enemy in order to cover themselves' (2000: 81). He concludes that they are radically opposed both psychologically and ideologically to the dissidents and have-nots who form the core of resistance. Self-preservation and respect for hierarchies predominate. The head teacher is derisively nicknamed 'Gutless', as 'a pure product of the petty regimentation of public education' (p. 92) (although some time later, he does in fact risk his own neck by defending the narrator from the Gestapo). Such acts of courage or defiance from those in authority are rare, however.

Although the Nord/Pas-de-Calais was incorporated into the German military government of Belgium, the Vichy government retained administrative control of the prefecture, police and education. According to Pannequin, the French police in the region were actively involved in repressing dissent and resistance (arresting over 300 striking miners for example in May/June 1941). His own involvement in sabotage of railways and mining installations led to his arrest by

> the special brigade of the mobile police in Lille, one of the essential components of the French Gestapo. German services rarely intervened directly. They had found more collaborators than they needed among French policemen and gave them their dirty work to do in the field. (p. 155)

Intimidation, beatings and torture were routinely used in the interrogation of 'terrorists'. Hence the author's observation: 'I made the acquaintance with the scum of humanity, those whom each and every society always entrusts with its worst repressive tasks' (p. 158). Brought before the special section of the *cour d'appel* created in July 1941 on the charge of 'Terrorist activity and communist propaganda', the author and his comrades receive heavy prison sentences and become hostages who may be shot in reprisals for a period of three months. He also learns that 'We had already been harshly dealt with by our courageous superiors.' The teachers arrested are dismissed by the local schools inspector in Arras, Faucheux. Nevertheless, 'Turning into a Gaullist resister at the last minute, this scoundrel ended his career as a senior inspector under a socialist government in the Fourth Republic' (p. 186).

After an initial escape attempt was foiled by a spy (who was liquidated), Pannequin escaped successfully in July 1943, although a comrade involved in the enterprise who was accused of black-marketeering and wearing German uniform was abandoned on Party orders and died in imprisonment. Later, Pannequin discovered that this man's only 'crime' had been to criticise the Nazi-Soviet pact; he himself would be expelled from the PCF for dissident behaviour in 1953, like many other resistance activists. The escapees were in fact aided by Belgian gendarmes; and Pannequin acknowledges that gendarmes outside the Brussels military government were less hostile to the resistance. The resistance police group under Achille Rassez in Boulogne is entirely exceptional, however. In any case, by the end of the occupation Pannequin is driven to conclude that all organisations that exert power and influence are contaminated and self-serving, whether their loyalty is ostensibly offered to Vichy, the resistance or communism. After returning to teaching, he observes how many erstwhile Vichyists have converted themselves to Gaullists fully armed with resistance credentials: 'They penetrated the administrative services' (p. 384). The Communist Party hierarchy is little different: in the final episode of his account, he attempts to have his membership officially recognised, only to discover that the individual now in charge of recruitment is someone who had refused to join the resistance. Ever the irate man of action, Pannequin throws this bullying bureaucrat out of his office window. But 'I should have realised I was wrong. He was right: his kind's time had come' (p. 392).

Once order is restored, there is no place for such impulsive and disobedient individuals, however distinguished their past record; on the other hand, the dutiful administrator able to transfer his loyalties in expedient fashion will always please the new masters. Such is the bitter lesson delivered by Pannequin, a lesson repeated by many other combatants, as we shall see. But without administrators, there would be no order, a paradox which Pannequin is reluctant to acknowledge. To conclude these case histories of public servants, it is therefore preferable to return to a more senior figure, the police superintendent Georges Ballyot, author of *Un flic dans la tourmente* (1992). This account encapsulates the dilemmas and ambiguities which confronted the well-intentioned functionary during the occupation. Ballyot was promoted to the rank of *commissaire de police* in 1937, at the unusually early age of thirty-four; despite his lack of experience (having moved up through the *police judiciaire*), he was put in charge of the uniformed branch in the XVe arrondissement of Paris, and transferred to the VIIIe in December 1940. He was suspended at the liberation, cleared by a purging committee on 28 March 1945, and then promoted.

Like the prefects discussed earlier, Ballyot did not compose his memoir until many years after the events depicted (his text is dated 1970). Such accounts thus mark the conclusion of a whole career, if not of a life; the gap between events and narration is doubtless due to the discretion expected of senior officials. Inevitably, the reader assumes the account will be fragmentary and sanitised in some areas. Ballyot is indeed a rather unreliable witness at times. For example, describing 'the great round-up of foreign Jews' of 16 July 1942 in which he and his officers participated (1992: 155), he informs us that 4500 foreign Jews were arrested, and only four or five of them from his district; in fact, nearly 13,000 people were arrested and detained in the

Vel d'Hiv stadium. By reducing the numbers arrested by over 60 per cent, whether intentionally or accidentally, the author clearly seeks to diminish the responsibility of the French police in anti-Semitic persecution. There is a different sort of diminution of responsibility when Ballyot criticises the execution of the ex-Vichy minister Pucheu. In his view, 'the Pucheu affair shows that people did not have the right to make a mistake at a given time and then repent, even quickly' (p. 216). But he omits to mention Pucheu's direct involvement in choosing communist hostages for execution, an error which is more than hasty (one of those shot was Charles Michels, the PCF deputy for the XVe, whom Ballyot knew personally). Elsewhere, Ballyot refers to Bousquet's role as Secretary General of Police in handing over full police powers to Darnand and the Milice in June and July 1944, forgetting that Bousquet had been dismissed six months earlier.

Such blunders remind us that personal memoirs have to be read sceptically; they do not invalidate the author's testimony in other areas, however. Ballyot casts himself in as sympathetic a light as possible, remarking for instance 'I feel very close to my men, almost like their father confessor' (p. 135), while showing how his hierarchical superiors unscrupulously try to shift blame for sensitive incidents on to him. Nevertheless, Ballyot's hostility to collaboration and indirect involvement in resistance seem genuine. He informs us that he was recognised officially as having been a member of the *réseau Kléber*, a resistance intelligence network, from January 1942; his associate Mme Pagniez was one of the eighty-five members of the movement Organisation civile et militaire arrested on 4 June 1944 (she escaped from Ravensbruck and miraculously survived to tell her story). As a senior policeman ostensibly serving authorities which he actually opposes, Ballyot is evidently in a delicate and ambiguous position. Indeed, in the closing weeks of the occupation, as the allied armies approach Paris, 'Our situation between the devil and the deep blue sea has become impossible' (p. 228). He cites several cases of officers from the *police judiciaire* and *police municipale* denounced and arrested for resistance activities, sometimes in particularly tragic circumstances. A senior colleague is shot by the Germans only a few days before the liberation, for protecting a group of impetuous junior officers who had been caught trying to arrest him.

Ballyot insists that the uniformed police were mainly concerned with maintaining public order, whereas pursuit of the resistance was the domain of the *Renseignements généraux* (RG), whose officers had no scruples in practising torture and arresting their own colleagues. He records a bizarre conversation at the beginning of 1944 with the head of the RG, Rottée, who knowing the author's double game asks if he too can change sides:

> The statement that he won't reach a courtroom alive astonishes him and leaves him stunned. The technical success of his services has left him unaware of the wider implications, unable to measure the extent of his treason, committed against his compatriots for the benefit of the occupier. No doubt like the chief superintendent in my sector he had retained his pre-war perspective, both of them forgetting the presence of the Germans? (p. 217)

He further notes that one of the latter's subordinates, involved despite himself in anti-communist operations, was sentenced to seven years in prison in 1945. As for the zealous chief superintendent, he received a sentence of fifteen years and died in prison, 'from grief and shame, for he was deeply sincere and had thought himself a patriot' (p. 219). Technical expertise divorced from ethical or political judgement can thus have disastrous consequences for the functionary who finally joins the victims of his zeal in a fate which some might view as a form of ironic justice. Not all those bureaucratic intermediaries between the warring forces of collaboration and resistance were able to exchange loyalties and escape relatively unscathed, in other words. But what of those who committed themselves openly to the causes of resistance and collaboration?

4

Combatants

Rebellion and sacrifice

Those who engaged in resistance against the Nazi invasion of Europe from within the territories occupied by the Germans became combatants in a struggle that overturned the conventional distinctions between soldiers and civilians and between geographically separated battlefields and the home front. Article ten of the armistice convention signed on 22 June 1940 by General Keitel and the French government's plenipotentiaries explicitly forbade French citizens from fighting against Germany or aiding countries at war with Germany. Continued resistance became illegal and resisters were liable to suffer summary justice as terrorists. In December 1941, Keitel, as head of the German armed forces, also promulgated the decree known as 'Nacht und Nebel', under the terms of which men and women guilty of committing hostile actions against the Reich in the occupied territories of France, Belgium, Holland and Norway could be either sentenced to death immediately or deported without any further contact with the outside world being permitted. Hitler is said personally to have chosen the Wagnerian expression 'night and fog' to evoke this disappearance into a living death which awaited at least 6000 French prisoners of the 65,000 deported for political offences including resistance (see La Martinière, 1989). While such brutal repression was to be expected from the Germans, it was harder for resisters to accept that their own government also considered them to be dissidents and terrorists; in practice, however, non-communist resistance activity was sometimes tolerated by the Vichy authorities in the south zone in the first two years of the occupation, just as espionage committed by German agents was liable to be repressed.[1]

117

Nevertheless, those who actively espoused collaboration did so with the material support of the Germans and the approval of a legally constituted government. French citizens were permitted to act as auxiliaries for German police and security agencies or to join paramilitary organisms which supported the Germans, such as the LVF (Legion of French Volunteers against Bolshevism), sent to the eastern front, or the notorious Milice which persecuted Jews and resistance groups in mainland France. In the event, relatively few chose to undertake such commitments, and those who did sometimes paid a heavy price after the liberation, becoming in turn victims of summary justice as the provisional government which replaced Vichy sought to establish its legitimacy by prosecuting its most blatant adversaries. As Roger Grenier remarked in a polemical essay entitled *Le Rôle d'accusé*, written a few years later, 'Through the punishment of collaborators, the country is washing away its shame and indeed pretending never to have known shame, since it is setting itself up as a deliverer of justice' (1948: 104). Questions of legality, trials and imprisonment, not to mention the violent abuses of human rights practised by the state against rebels and other political adversaries, feature in the accounts of resisters and collaborators, since both categories by their very existence opposed the authority of successive governments engaged in warfare. Grenier observed that authors of resistance literature, which was by then the dominant mode, usually elided such troubling parallels and sought to restore a simpler confrontational posture:

> Resisters are on one side, the Germans on the other. And generally they write about skirmishes or single combat between two enemies who appear from opposite points on the horizon. Few are the accounts which reconstruct that strange war where your adversary was not separated from you by a no man's land, but would be seated at the next table in a café, come into your shop, or on occasion, politely stand aside to let you past. (1948: 106)

As for those unfortunate individuals whom circumstances or divided loyalties turned into double agents, obliged to 'intrigue on both sides at the same time' (p. 107), such ambivalence is conceptually and morally repellent to the public and media, which much prefer the more straightforwardly appealing notion of treason.

While the cause of resistance was ultimately victorious, many resisters felt that the fruits of victory had been denied them; as resistance was retrospectively transformed from a dangerous minority activity into a sacred legend supposedly inspiring the majority who had largely ignored it, the material benefits, moral authority or even symbolic recognition through awards and decorations offered by the restored republic were misappropriated by individuals and groups whose contribution to the struggle against the occupying forces was perceived as at best minimal or at worst invented. (To repeat a telling statistical example: the vast majority of the 1061 Compagnons de la Libération were drawn from the Free French, the immediate allies of de Gaulle, whereas only 157 members of the internal resistance and six women were granted this prestigious award.)

What were the real risks incurred by those who sacrificed the relative material security and tranquillity of existence under occupation by committing themselves to active resistance (or collaboration)? What motivated such commitment, and what impact did it have on the course of the war? How did those who made the wrong choices (in the sense that their actions had highly negative consequences, with no apparent compensating positive material or moral benefits) attempt to justify their actions? How much do we learn about resistance and collaboration from the first-hand accounts produced by individuals whose behaviour was often exceptional? How reliable are such accounts as sources of information? These questions will be addressed in this chapter. In the first instance, it is interesting to look at the factors which motivated resistance, and what indeed resistance actually meant in practice, as a daily activity, for those who undertook it. The discussion will then turn to problems of veracity and fabulation, looking in detail at cases of individuals whose resistance commitment eventually led to charges of duplicity, fabrication or treason, before finally examining paramilitary collaboration.

Henry Rousso has noted how the controversy aroused by Marcel Ophuls's documentary film *Le Chagrin et la pitié* (to be considered more fully in a later chapter) in 1971 was due in large part to its revaluation of collaboration as a legitimate ideological option, entailing heroic commitment rather than venality and moral turpitude (the case of the Waffen SS volunteer Christian de La Mazière is a prime example, as we shall see). At the same time, the film downgrades resistance by presenting it in a very partial fashion. In his interview, the leader of Libération Sud, Emmanuel d'Astier de la Vigerie, caused offence and consternation by presenting resisters as drop-outs and marginal figures ('Nous étions des inadaptés'),[2] an interpretation which fitted the film's anti-Gaullist, *soixante-huitard* bias but which distorted historical fact: 'resistance groups ... recruited ... far more from the most integrated strata of society, notables, office and factory workers, than from among drop-outs' (Rousso, 1990: 127). D'Astier himself contradicts his own thesis: despite the reputation he carefully cultivated in the interwar years as a provocateur and opium-addicted 'anarchist in patent-leather shoes',[3] he was in fact the son of a baron, a former naval officer, and was appointed *commissaire à l'Intérieur* to the Comité Français de Liberation Nationale (CFLN) by de Gaulle in November 1943 (although he was dismissed from the provisional government in September 1944); his two brothers François and Henri were also important figures in the Free French, the first holding the rank of airforce general.

Nevertheless, while it is true that most of those who played a key role in the resistance came from socially integrated, successful backgrounds, at the same time their commitment to resistance demanded a strong element of rebelliousness and willingness to sacrifice personal security, qualities rarely found in their peers. Hence Claude Bourdet's observation that the majority of early resisters were 'men who had broken with their professional and social milieu. Such a breaking away was based, of course, on an accurate awareness of the historical perspective, but primarily on a great strength of inner feeling' (1998: 26). Bourdet was one of the leaders of Combat, whose founder Henri Frenay quit the armistice army, since 'Soldiering, like the novitiate, entails total submission' (Frenay, 1976: 40), and from spring 1941 adopted a clandestine existence as a resistance activist. His mother disapproved of what she perceived as his unpatriotic dissidence; when she threatened to denounce him, he ceased to see her until after the liberation, by which time he was a member of the provisional government. Resisters, in Frenay's words, were 'at once soldiers in mufti and citizens in revolt against the established authorities' (1976: xiv–xv).

Their aim was ultimately to help overthrow these authorities by assisting the allies in expelling the German occupying forces. Such an enterprise seemed to most people a practical impossibility during the first three years of the war. Those who had the courage and faith to undertake it, particularly in these initial stages, often had little useful prior experience of subversive actions. Thus Serge Ravanel, a *polytechnicien* who became the organiser of the *groupes francs* (armed action units of the Mouvements Unis de Résistance) and ultimately a colonel in the FFI in his early twenties, remarks that 'One of the tragedies of resistance was the slowness with which we learned to adapt to clandestine action, compared with the speed with which we recruited' (quoted by Benamou, 1999: 109). Resistance memoirs are indeed often dramatic accounts of how grossly inexperienced agents failed to learn or obey basic security procedures and fell into the clutches of French or German security police, sometimes however then escaping almost miraculously against overwhelming odds. The drama and danger lay more often in the risks of capture (with torture, deportation and execution as likely consequences) than the actual tasks undertaken. Contrary to popular belief, perpetuated by films and novels which derive their momentum and excitement from violent action and spectacle, most resistance activity did not involve sabotage of factories and railway communications, daring prison escapes, guerrilla attacks on German troops or assassination of Nazi leaders and collaborators.[4] Collecting and forwarding sensitive military information, acting as a courier, preparing and distributing propaganda, receiving and distributing messages, money and supplies from allied and Free French sources, finding safe accommodation and creating support and rescue networks: such activities were more common. They were often monotonous and carried out in conditions of personal discomfort and isolation. Resistance narratives are full of examples of ordinary individuals who by lending a hand in such rather mundane actions sometimes lost everything, including even posthumous recognition of their modest heroism. (Ravanel for instance records the typical case of a man who used his lorry to ferry munitions and was eventually deported, after his property had been confiscated.)

Jacques Baumel, who eventually became secretary general of the MUR (Mouvements Unis de la Résistance, the overarching movement created in January 1943 by the amalgamation of the three main resistance movements in the south zone, Combat, Libération and Franc-Tireur), estimates that resistance activity in its early stages involved 80 per cent intelligence-gathering and 20 per cent propaganda. Although resisters were engaged in covert warfare against the Germans and their supporters in Vichy, he argues that resistance action was essentially political rather than military or paramilitary (1999: 102). Baumel was one of the few senior resistance figures (apart from the communists) to spend three years clandestinely in mainland France and to escape arrest. By 1943–44, he claims that many agents were likely to survive at most for six months; had the allied landings of June 1944 been delayed, he suggests any further resistance action would have been crushed within six months (1999: 403). His own survival he attributes to his adherence to the security rules devised by Jean Gemahling, head of Combat's intelligence service (although Gemahling himself was arrested and escaped several times). These involved such precautions as avoiding meetings in popular places, fixed routines and unnecessary relationships, never trusting strangers, not sending uncoded messages or keeping compromising documents. Many resisters broke some or all such precautions quite regularly. Senior figures held meetings in easily accessible places where betrayal and arrest were quite probable. The most notorious example is the arrest of Jean Moulin by Klaus Barbie and a small force of German security police at Caluire on 21 June 1943 (to be discussed below), where the absence of any armed protection group has often been noted. Such lack of protection, despite the existence of *groupes francs* trained for such purposes, was common: when the Conseil National de la Résistance held its first meeting in Paris a month before, its seventeen members could have been caught by a few gendarmes. Hence Emmanuel d'Astier's comment that 'Resistance was a childish, deadly game' (quoted by Baumel, 1999: 307).

Luck and chance thus played a vital role in survival: 'The destiny of different people often hung on something minor, like a hesitation or a simple decision which would prove irrevocable' (Baumel, 1999: 99). A chance encounter with a dominant individual might determine the decision to offer one's loyalty to a particular organism. In some cases, the identity of the agency or the individual might remain unknown to the recruit: 'the period abounded in fantasists and agents provocateurs, police informers and double agents' (p. 64). Betrayal was therefore a regular, even predictable event; many agents revealed their contacts under torture or the threat of torture, sometimes triggering mass arrests and the destruction of an entire network (although we should recall that others, whose heroism deserves commemoration, such as Jacques Bingen, Pierre Brossolette, and probably Berty Albrecht, committed suicide after their arrest, or died under torture like Jean Moulin, without revealing anything). Some agents were deliberately betrayed to the Gestapo, so that they could unwittingly reveal false information. Anonymity and strict compartmentalisation of clandestine activities provided an important means of protection. In practice, this could mean abandoning entirely one's official identity and the professional and personal contacts that supported it. Claude Bourdet describes in detail the fascinating intricacies of manufacturing a false identity. He points out the distinction between a pseudonym, which is well known, easily changed and recognised as a disguise serving to conceal one's real identity, and a false identity known to as few people as possible and supported by official documentation, the purpose of which is to provide a shield against recognition of one's real identity. The creation of seemingly authentic false identity papers was an art that became increasingly refined as underground resistance became a professionalised activity. Since the totalitarian controls imposed on citizens by warfare and occupation meant that authorisations and *Ausweise* (travel passes) were required to fulfil many daily activities, no resistance agent could function without such documentation. Bourdet distinguishes with a certain humour between various categories of false and authentic forged identity papers, explaining that gross forgeries using stamps moulded from potatoes that would bear little scrutiny from a suspicious police or security official were rapidly replaced by genuine documents often stolen from official sources, with a false identity then being added.

Most active resisters used a whole range of pseudonyms and fake identities; some became better known under their assumed names and retained them after the liberation. Thus Raymond Samuel (whose parents perished in Auschwitz) replaced his Jewish patronym with the geographical place name Aubrac. Serge Ravanel adopted the name of the alpine guide Ravanel and kept it

> Because later on I felt that this period had been one of rebirth for me. The mountaineer's name evoked the effort which man can accomplish to attain disinterested objectives. Finally, because, by deciding to engage in resistance, I had accomplished an act of liberty, that of choosing my own life. (Ravanel, 1995: 123)

This act of self-baptism and naturalisation as a French adventurer was also due to his complex and perhaps distressing family circumstances: although his real father, whom he never knew, was the Czech painter Arnold Koblitz, his mother subsequently had two other husbands, the stepfather who raised him being Swiss. On the other hand, Jacques Baumel records his and others' attempts in late 1941 to persuade General Weygand to declare himself head of the resistance in North Africa, where he was on the point of being dismissed from his position as commander in chief. Weygand declined, not merely from misplaced loyalty towards Pétain (who did nothing to prevent his subsequent deportation) and hatred of the mutinous de Gaulle, but also because his foreign origins seemed to him a serious impediment to playing the part of patriotic dissident. Such misplaced and conventional reverence for origins, hierarchy and discipline explains why most professional soldiers remained *attentistes* for most of the occupation, when they were not actively obstructive towards resistance. Claude Bourdet observes sourly that 'However, these were the men (apart from those most compromised) who were called upon, after 1945, to reshape the new French army and navy' (1998: 163).

The Franco-Spanish writer Jorge Semprun has also analysed the reconstruction of his own identity as a political exile, member of the French resistance, deportee to Buchenwald and aspirant writer. Exiled after the Spanish civil war, Semprun was briefly a student in the prestigious *hypokhâgne* class (for those aspiring to enter the École Normale Superieure) at the *lycée* Henri IV in Paris, until he joined the resistance network 'Jean-Marie Action' run by the British officer Buckmaster's SOE French section. Semprun was still only nineteen when he was arrested by the Gestapo in Joigny in September 1943. His interrogation included being savaged by a dog and torture by partial drowning in a bathtub full of filthy water, an experience which he sums up with laconic, philosophical forcefulness: 'My body was suffocating, becoming mad, begging for mercy, ignobly. My body asserted its presence in a visceral revolt which strove to deny me as a moral being' (Semprun, 1996: 148).[5] In January 1944, he was one of many resistance prisoners deported to Buchenwald (Claude Bourdet was another). The camp was situated a few miles from Weimar (home of the illustrious poet Goethe) and named after the beech forest that surrounded it; a beech tree favoured by Goethe was piously kept as a memorial in the camp, a good example of sentimental Nazi didacticism, whose gestures towards civilised values rarely cloaked the most sadistic brutality. Another example was afforded by the infamous slogan 'Arbeit macht frei' posted above the camp gate: 'This is a fine paternalistic maxim: it's for our good that we are shut up here, it's through hard labour that we are taught liberty' (Semprun, 1989: 197). The real business of the camp was, of course, the enslavement, starvation and systematic killing of detainees. Semprun observed how Jews evacuated from Poland to Buchenwald were packed two hundred to a cattle wagon, without food or drink (eighty more per truck than the convoys sent from France). Most froze to death during the winter journey and arrived packed together 'like skittles' (p. 116); the few survivors were set upon by dogs and then shot. As the allied armies advanced, the SS was able to evacuate only half the 50,000 inmates. After the camp's liberation on 11 April 1945, heaps of twisted, emaciated corpses ten feet high remained awaiting disposal in the ovens of the crematorium, the chimney of which Semprun discovered was plainly visible from a house overlooking the camp. The KGB made use of the camp for its own detainees until 1950 and the creation of the German Democratic Republic.

Much of Semprun's writing deals soberly with the problem of restoring one's moral and physical integrity after such horrors. He himself survived partly through good fortune and political connections (he was part of the clandestine communist leadership in Buchenwald, and worked in the office registering the entries and deaths of prisoners), partly through physical and intellectual courageousness and resilience. While in prison, he sought distraction by recalling stories and previously memorised poetry, including Valéry's 'Le Cimetière marin' ('It was certainly the only time that distinguished imbecile Valéry was useful for something'; Semprun, 1989: 68). Recording experiences which for immediate survival and sanity had first to be forgotten proved to be a painful and protracted process: it took nearly twenty years to produce his first autobiographical novel *Le Grand Voyage* (1963). As he observes in *L'Écriture ou la vie*, 'writing made me vulnerable again to the agonies of memory' (1996: 303). In any case, after the war he resumed his career as a clandestine militant, juggling a variety of new false identities (as a Uruguayan or French business man) while running the Spanish Communist Party's underground organisation in Madrid. His expulsion from the Party allowed him to become a professional writer (in 1987 he joined Felipe González's government as Minister of Culture and subsequently was elected to the Académie Goncourt). Writing in French is for Semprun another means of reasserting his identity: 'I had chosen French, the language of exile, as another maternal language. I had chosen new origins for myself. I had made exile into a homeland' (p. 353). He also argues that the camp survivors have a moral obligation to bear witness to what they suffered, for as they die 'there will be no one left to tell, with words uttered by the memory of the flesh, rather than by a theoretical reconstruction, what hunger, sleep, anguish and the blinding presence of absolute Evil were like' (p. 374).

Semprun acknowledges his belated realisation of 'the murderous illusion of the communist adventure' (p. 332), noting too that his own writing in the early 1960s coincided not only with the tardy recognition of Primo Levi's now celebrated books on Auschwitz but also with the appearance of testimony denouncing the Gulag (Solzhenitsyn's *Ivan Denisovich* came out in 1963). A generation needed to pass, it seemed, before the worst experiences inflicted on their victims by totalitarian states could become accessible or acceptable to a wider public. He also states that 'the true fraternity of communist militants' was devalued by 'the false coin of our ideological discourse' (p. 330). The French Communist Party soon expelled its resistance militants deemed to be too intractable to Stalinist dogma, preferring to appoint a General Secretary, Georges Marchais, who had been a volunteer worker for Messerschmidt in Germany. Semprun recast himself as an independent intellectual, thereby partially illustrating Claude Bourdet's assertion that true resisters remain rebels, disrespectful and distrustful of authority and those who accept its uniforms and grades: 'the resistance made all of us into *contestataires*, in every sense of the term, against men and against the social system' (Bourdet, 1998: 384).

Bourdet's memoirs, first published in 1975, are marked by strong hostility towards de Gaulle's authoritarian rule as president and by the divisions of post-war colonial struggles. According to his account, the divorce between de Gaulle and the forces of resistance in the post-war settlement came about rapidly. While the resistance failed to launch itself as a viable political body, the General was eventually recalled to power as a monarchical president by a bankrupt Fourth Republic. However, de Gaulle's supposed liberalism in colonial policy, one of the defining features of his new Fifth Republic, is dismissed by Bourdet as mere pragmatism (although such pragmatism helped end the conflict in Algeria which hitherto had been intractable). A senior figure in Combat, Bourdet himself was arrested in March 1944 and sent to Fresnes prison (as he was in 1956 after writing anti-government articles), from where he was deported to Neuengamme, Oranienberg, and finally Buchenwald. Having survived these experiences, he has no hesitation in stating that the Germans' pretence of ignorance about what went on in concentration camps is to be equated with French citizens' ignorance and indifference about atrocities committed in Algeria during the 1950s.[6] The police too are cast as agents of repression: 'In all countries, but particularly in totalitarian regimes, the fundamental goal of all police forces is to degrade the human being... Nazism is the police in its purest form' (pp. 356–7).

Bourdet's credibility and moral stature as a first-hand witness should not deter us from pointing out that his analogies are crudely overstated (and therefore misrepresent the systematically evil nature of totalitarian regimes). The atrocities and excesses committed by both sides during the undeclared war for Algerian independence may appal civilised observers, but they were caused more by government failures to direct military forces coherently than by a deliberate policy of violent repression, pillage, enslavement and mass murder. As for the SS state, which in effect institutionalises lawlessness and criminality, it is really the obverse of a society where the police and judiciary exist to uphold legality and human rights, however imperfectly. Bourdet's criticisms of de Gaulle are less easily dismissed. His charges (echoed by many resistance leaders) are essentially that de Gaulle and London never really understood the nature and evolution of the maquis, and that de Gaulle's successful linking of resistance movements, political parties and trades unions under the umbrella of the CNR seemed to be an attempt to destroy (and therefore betray) the autonomy of the internal resistance. Jean Moulin was the prime mover in this process, as de Gaulle's delegate sent to France to take the pulse 'of this interior resistance that resisted him so much' (Baumel, 1999: 277).

The debate about the unification and subordination of the resistance hangs on understanding the political goals and military efficacy of resistance. Those who criticise de Gaulle for perceiving resistance as a means to an end (the restoration of an independent, republican French state) rather than simply as an end in itself (local struggle against the occupying forces, with national insurrection as the longer-term goal) rarely offer a more convincing strategy. Instead, they tend to concentrate, with considerable justification, on the smaller-scale injustices and betrayals occasioned by the Gaullist takeover. Jacques Baumel (one of the very few partisans from the internal resistance to become a close associate of de Gaulle in the post-war years) notes that, in the course of the Fourth Republic, 'Practically all those who genuinely fought in the resistance were eliminated or marginalised, whatever party they had joined, from the Communist Party to the right' (1999: 442). Ironically, this included both de Gaulle himself and the entire Communist Party (who left power in 1946 and 1947 respectively, despite accusations from their detractors of harbouring dictatorial ambitions).

Henri Frenay, the principal creator of the movement Combat, was flown out of France in June 1943 a few days before the arrest of Jean Moulin. He reluctantly agreed to join de Gaulle's embryonic government in exile as commissioner for prisoners, deportees and refugees and did not return to France until after the liberation in September 1944. He was well aware that this promotion to ministerial rank was a means of removing the disruptive effect he exercised on the internal resistance. His memoirs, published in 1973, are another vivid record of the adventure of early resistance, whose victory is overshadowed by a sense of having been deceived and thwarted by unworthy political adversaries. De Gaulle, whom he first met in September 1942, is characterised as 'a cold and calculating strategist. The Resistance, for him, was one pawn among others. The devotion and courage of its members, the dangers, the arrests, the executions were for him only the inevitable tithe paid to the god of war' (Frenay, 1976: 206). Frenay asserts that he mistook de Gaulle for the enemy of oligarchies and vested interests, for a revolutionary rather than an authoritarian statesman: 'We had thought he was Proudhon when he was simply Richelieu' (p. 389). Frenay's own political ambition was for resistance to 'give birth to a great revolutionary party based on a marriage of the Socialist tradition (stripped of its narrower Marxian side) and Christian humanism' (p. 367). In practice, the Mouvement de Libération Nationale (MLN), created in early 1944 by the fusion of the MUR with movements in the north zone, fell under communist control after the arrest of Frenay's deputy Bourdet.[7] It was eventually transformed into a fledgling political party, the Union Démocratique et Sociale de la Résistance (UDSR), outside communist influence (and remembered mainly because it served as a launch pad for François Mitterrand's political ambitions, after the latter advanced from serving as an official in Frenay's ministerial office), but from the municipal elections of April/May 1945, the non-communist resistance fared badly; when the UDSR won only 7 per cent of votes in the election for the Constituent Assembly in October 1945, this marked the 'demise of the Resistance as a political force' (p. 432).

Frenay admits that temperamentally he was unsuited for politics. What he perceived as idealism, de Gaulle brushed aside as political naivety (informing Frenay, for instance, that 'noble sentiments' don't make foreign policy, p. 420). Nevertheless, he defends his own record as minister responsible for the immense task of repatriating French prisoners and deportees (half a million of whom had returned to France by VE Day, although the railway infrastructure had been severely damaged and only 10 per cent of the pre-war stock of cars and trucks were available for transport), despite slanderous abuse from the Communist Party (he won a libel action against Marcel Cachin, director of *L'Humanité*, in June 1946). De Gaulle's own political aspirations did not survive for long after the liberation, as the old political parties reasserted themselves and together with the new centre-right Movement Républicain Populaire (MRP) sidelined the resistance and MLN. The Consultative Assembly subverted de Gaulle's government and worked against the public interest, in Frenay's view.

Though many of Frenay's complaints are justified, his overall vision of resistance is inevitably coloured by his own commitment as a clandestine activist, whose sacrifices he feels merit greater acknowledgement and the reward of genuine political authority. He is unable to accept that once the resistance had succeeded in its primary military goal of assisting the allies in expelling the Germans, its authority was more likely to be symbolic than real. Most notoriously, Frenay's particular resentment is reserved for Jean Moulin, sent by de Gaulle in 1942 to unify, finance and ultimately subordinate the independent resistance movements. Moulin's ignorance as a high-ranking functionary of basic resistance activities is noted: 'Our rank-and-file militants, their work, their inherent constraints and problems, were a complete mystery to him' (p. 255). When Moulin proved ungenerous with funds, in February 1943 Combat accepted the offer of US finances channelled through Switzerland and eventually received 37 million francs, until, to Frenay's fury and frustration, Moulin and London ordered the cessation of this American attempt to subsidise and thus to infiltrate the internal resistance. Frenay concludes, 'It seems Moulin had presented us with the same options as the Germans – to capitulate or to resist' (p. 256). Noting that the creation of the CNR in effect humbled the non-communist resistance movements by equating them with political parties and unions which had contributed far less to the struggle, he also observes how the communists progressively manoeuvred their way into the majority of key positions in the internal resistance. This leads Frenay to assert that by creating the CNR, Moulin 'was the Communists' man' and that de Gaulle thus 'chose as his agent a political partisan whom he had mistaken for a disinterested servant of the state' (pp. 445–6). Moulin's defenders and biographers have devoted the thirty years since Frenay's memoirs first appeared to rebutting these libellous accusations, for which there is no convincing evidence. Indeed, Moulin showed considerable hostility towards the Communist Party, despite or because of his left-wing sympathies. It is particularly regrettable that Frenay, whose achievement as the founder of a democratically inspired resistance movement deserves admiration, should have resorted to the same factionalism and smears against rivals which he regarded as the stock in trade of communist totalitarianism.

Nevertheless, Frenay's account is indicative of the ways in which the goals and achievement of resistance and its leaders have been contested both by resisters and historians. There is no real consensus about the efficacy of resistance, beyond the acknowledged fact that its initial protagonists were men and women of extraordinary courage. Although there is no accurate figure for loss of life among resistance agents, estimates of political deportees usually give a figure of 65,000, of whom two-thirds were active resisters; about 50 per cent survived deportation. A further 20,000 people were probably shot during the occupation by the Germans for resistance activities in mainland

France, and about 24,000 members of the FFI killed in combat in 1944. How useful and important was their sacrifice? The issues can be interpreted tactically and strategically, or politically and symbolically. Broader-scale approaches are rarely flattering towards the resistance. In other words, while resistance activists tend to record local successes (or more occasionally failures), in which they had some personal involvement (such as acts of sabotage, the rescue of comrades, the liberation of small towns, the routing of German units retreating from the allied armies), historians who assess the global military contribution of resistance to the allied defeat of Germany accord it minimal significance. By early 1944, there were approximately 35,000 urban resisters and 50,000 maquisards in remote rural areas, most of them poorly armed and trained. By the liberation, these numbers had expanded threefold to perhaps 250,000, although General Leclerc estimated that at most 10 per cent of the Forces Françaises de l'Intérieur (as the armed units of the resistance were then collectively known) were 'really combatants' (cited by Dreyfus, 1996: 508). The FFI eventually contributed 125,000 men to the French troops fighting with allied forces in 1945.

By 1944, most resistance movements were committed to the principle of direct action against German and Vichy forces before the expected allied landings (with the notable exception of the Organisation de Résistance de l'Armée, belatedly founded by army officers in 1943 after the dissolution of Vichy's small armistice army in November 1942). Communist groups were more willing to practise assassination and indiscriminate bombings than Gaullists, who were more scrupulous about the vicious and indiscriminate reprisals usually inflicted on civilian hostages after such attacks. Disruption to the rail network and to German supply lines by resistance sabotage certainly helped the allies' advance through France in the summer of 1944, although Dreyfus asserts controversially that bombing by aircraft was far more effective in disrupting communications than sabotage (1996: 453–4), albeit at a very high cost to civilians who had the misfortune to live within the target zones (as many as 100,000 French people were killed by allied bombs).[8] Julian Jackson points out that allied plans took little account of the French resistance before D-Day, priority being given to supplying the guerrilla war in Greece and Yugoslavia: whereas the resistance in Yugoslavia received 16,470 tons of supplies between 1943 and 1945, only 2878 tons of equipment were supplied to their French counterparts (Jackson, 2001: 557). Hence his conclusion that 'In the history of France, resistance is more important as a social and political phenomenon than a military one' (p. 387).

Veracity and fabulation

As Azéma and Bédarida suggest in their essay (which was discussed earlier) on 'L'Historisation de la Résistance', resistance has to be understood in symbolic as much as material terms, and related to moral, psychological and political aspirations: the recovery of national honour, the integrity of national identity, the restoration of republican government. The historiography of resistance, especially in its early stages and popular forms, has always shown what these authors call 'the hybridisation of science and myth' (*Esprit* 1994: 21). Factual evidence was not always easy to obtain. By virtue of its clandestine nature, resistance did not lend itself to record keeping; what archival material survived was not always readily made available to outsiders for several decades. In addition, since many early historians of resistance were themselves veterans of the struggle, their uncorroborated personal testimony, with its inevitable exaggerations and omissions, was often central to their accounts. Although some commentators and would-be revisionists react with revulsion to the myth-making process, it is more honest to accept that the propaganda value of resistance both to political parties and to individuals made its inflation to legendary proportions almost inevitable. In this sense, the sacrifices and suffering of thousands of resistance activists paid huge dividends, even if those who profited most had sometimes done least to deserve it.[9]

Tournier's thesis that the minority of authentic resisters was swept away at the liberation by a mob of seekers after position certainly finds favour with those disenchanted with the post-war settlement (even if it implies rather curiously that the resistance stood up better to the Germans during the occupation than to their self-seeking compatriots afterwards). It is summed up aphoristically by Hélie de Saint Marc: 'Some helped a lot and never helped themselves; other helped very little and helped themselves a lot' (quoted in Benamou, 1999: 183). Since the usurping opportunists are rarely named in such complaints, it is virtually impossible to determine how numerous they actually were. It is certainly true that genuine resistance activists were sometimes treated extremely shabbily: apart from the lengthy prison sentence inflicted on Hélie de Saint Marc in the aftermath of the Algerian crisis, and the jailing of hundreds of local communist activists discussed earlier, figures as distinguished as André Dewavrin, better known as Colonel Passy, head of the Gaullist intelligence service the BCRA, were imprisoned and subjected to violent abuse. Passy was incarcerated in May 1946 on charges of embezzlement, while Georges

Guingouin, head of the maquis in the Limousin, was subjected to similar treatment in 1953 on trumped-up murder charges (both were released eventually without trial).

This raises the question, however, of how one determines what qualifies as 'authentic' resistance, and what boundaries are set to separate acceptable and unacceptable actions. The suspicions that hung over Passy and Guingouin were not entirely unjustified. Passy admitted that money from secret funds had vanished, but blamed his successor Jacques Soustelle, who supplanted him as head of the Direction Générale des Services Spéciaux (DGSS) in November 1943 (after the fusion of the BCRA and the Giraudist secret service). Similarly, though Guingouin was not personally implicated in assassinations, his right-wing critics have always accused him of tolerating a reign of terror under his command (thus for Baumel, he was 'an efficient guerrilla leader, but also the most ferocious sort of gang leader'; 1999: 430). But scrupulousness and squeamishness are hardly qualifications for resistance leaders engaged in covert warfare. Illegal acts such as espionage, sabotage, assassination, theft and deception are evidently central to resistance. They are justified in theory at least because they are committed, not for personal gain or gratification, but in order to serve a cause, the aim of which is to restore liberty and legality by overthrowing a dictatorial political regime such as National Socialism or the Vichy French State which has already institutionalised lawlessness (by acts such as internment without trial, summary executions, racial persecution and mass deportations). However, weighing up how far one could go in the direction of criminality without becoming as bad as one's adversaries was in practice extremely difficult.

A further, related problem is how much credence one can lend to self-justifying accounts written by resisters whose exploits and misdemeanours or errors and distortions do little to serve the cause of either resistance or resistance historiography. Since what concerns us primarily in this study is the experiences of individuals and the ways in which they were recorded, the rest of this chapter will concentrate on a selection of controversial cases (involving both resisters and collaborators) which show how easily honourable intentions could become corrupted. The boundary between resistance and collaboration could be crossed almost inadvertently, with genuine patriots finding themselves placed in circumstances where treason seemed the only outcome. This was the situation of agents captured by the Germans and persuaded to change sides; frequently, they would be duped, blackmailed or compromised in some way before being released to serve as a spy or decoy. Some tried to minimise the damage by informing their resistance superiors of their dilemma; others changed loyalties apparently with few qualms and helped destroy entire networks; some went into hiding or escaped the country to join the Free French; others still denied that they had ever betrayed anyone. Which category these putative traitors belonged to was (and sometimes remains) often the subject of intense debate: a death sentence or acquittal at a post-liberation trial might hang on such issues.

A notorious example is afforded by Mathilde Carré, whose pseudonym 'la Chatte' aptly sums up her supposedly glamorous mystique as predatory double agent and seductive sex kitten. Arrested in November 1941 by the Abwehr agent Hugo Bleicher, she was rapidly persuaded to betray a large number of the members of the British-run Réseau Interallié. Henri Noguères describes her touring Paris in Bleicher's car, obligingly identifying the addresses of all her contacts (1969: II, 215), while Alain Guérin remarks that 'She betrayed her own with a light-heartedness which everyone remarked on' (2000: 678). She was condemned to death in January 1949 for intelligence with a foreign power but received a presidential pardon. After she was released from prison in 1954, she produced two versions of her autobiography and briefly became a minor celebrity as a result of books and films based somewhat approximately on her exploits. While her accusers denounced her as 'the inhuman, green-eyed spy', to quote the words of her defence lawyer Albert Naud (quoted in Carré, 1959: 8), he preferred to present her as the victim of Abwehr machinations rather than an instigator, arguing that 'she would have been absolved, if it could have been admitted that at certain times in the life of a spy, a double game is part of the "game"' (p. 10). Such an adversarial approach of course sets up a false dichotomy between total condemnation or absolution, since one is asked either to condemn acts which did irreparable damage to a resistance network while ignoring the dilemma and motives of the perpetrator, or alternatively to excuse her as the victim of circumstances beyond her control.

In her own accounts, Mathilde Carré (also known as Lily, although her maiden name was Mathilde-Lucie Bélard) tells us that she was recruited by British Intelligence through a Polish friend in the autumn of 1940, having previously worked as a teacher and nurse. The Réseau Interallié was established to spy on German military operations, and also maintained links with Vichy's Deuxième Bureau. She provides many documents and technical details suggesting the effectiveness of their activities, while nonetheless insisting how amateurish their procedures often were (thus she kept an uncoded list of contacts in her diary). On her arrest, Bleicher easily got the better of her, especially after having sex with her in a house belonging to the actor Harry Baur (how much compulsion he exerted is left unclear). Thereafter, she was used as bait for innumerable arrests: 'I understood Bleicher's game. He wished to compromise me, to tie me down morally, so as to prevent me from saving myself' (Carré, 1959: 163–4). She claims, however, that none of the Interallié agents arrested were tortured or shot and that many agreed readily to work for the Germans. Compromising and corrupting resistance activists thus sometimes proved more effective than merely brutalising them. Bleicher relaxed his control by allowing her to go to England in February 1942. She was taken across the Channel on a Royal Navy boat, but once in London, she confessed her situation to her superiors in the hope of escaping the Abwehr trap. Having being ordered to write a lengthy report in April 1942 attempting to justify herself, she was arrested on 1 July 1942, her report was confiscated, and her potential career as a triple agent cut short.

Having spent one year as a resistance agent, followed by a further three months as a reluctant double agent for the Abwehr, Mathilde Carré would spend the following twelve years in English and French prisons. Punishment preceded judgement, in that her trial actually took place in 1949, halfway through this lengthy period of detention, although she was handed over to the French authorities in June 1945. In the meantime, her husband, from whom she was separated, had been killed fighting with the allies at Monte-Cassino in January 1944. Though pardoned in April 1949, she had spent nearly four months in chains awaiting the execution of the death sentence. In 1957, she retrieved the written account of her misadventures and used it as the basis of her memoirs published in 1959. However, the second version of her autobiography (like so many others, published a generation after the war in 1975) provides a much fuller and better defence. Self-justification is reinforced by more carefully considered attacks on those who brought her down. In addition, the essential immorality of espionage agencies and the cynical expediency displayed by prosecuting authorities are highlighted. Thus she observes that destroying the credibility of captured resisters was a deliberate tactic used by counter-intelligence: 'It was a basic principle in the technique of secret services, once an agent had been "turned", to dirty his hands, so as to tie him down for good, by making him appear irredeemably guilty regarding his former companions' (Carré, 1975: 146). She notes too that her main tormentor Bleicher was neither tried nor summoned to her trial:

he had 'bartered his freedom by delivering testimony that damned me'
(p. 251). Similarly, Armand, the head of the Interallié network, who
also became an Abwehr agent and escaped to England, was allowed to
join the RAF and enjoy a successful career; neither he nor his associate
Lucas-Vomécourt were ever prosecuted or did anything in her defence
(perhaps unsurprisingly, since so much suspicion hung heavily over
them).

Mathilde Carré found herself the subject of books by French,
German and British writers, which brought unwanted publicity: 'I
have no part in the sort of legend which journalists, writers, film-
makers or so-called memorialists have built up around my name'
(pp. 312–13). While Gordon Young's book, *The Cat with Two Faces,*
contains so many errors as to be more fiction than fact, Henri Decoin's
films *La Chatte* and *La Chatte sort ses griffes* are entirely fictional,
borrowing little more than the celebrated pseudonym. The first film in
fact derives from a novel by Jacques Rémy published in 1958, which
recounts the arrest of a radio operator for an underground network,
whose wife Cora is blackmailed by a Wehrmacht officer and used to
decimate the network. Cora is eventually discredited and shot by the
resistance. The story is sentimental in tone and stereotyped in its characterisation, revealing none of the messy complexity of the case by
which it is distantly inspired. One can nevertheless discern a pattern
in Mathilde Carré's career in which literary representation plays an
important part, a pattern typical of many resistance activists (or indeed
collaborators) who chose to use the written text in order to reconstruct
their wartime record, either as a means of self-justification or as an
attempt to avoid passing into historical oblivion.

These autobiographers often cast themselves as wronged and tragic
survivors. The initial commitment to a cause, one which is shunned by
the majority of the population and which thus demonstrates a high
degree of courage and perhaps obstinacy on the part of the individual
volunteering his or her services, is followed by a period of apprenticeship where the risks to which the protagonist is exposed are compen-
sated by success and experience. Retribution soon follows, however,
usually in the form of capture, incarceration, interrogation, humiliation, prosecution and vilification. Survival and release are bought at a
high price, involving a tragic compromise which effectively depletes
the moral capital accrued by the idealistic engagement that set off the
chain. The whole sequence is then rehearsed again in a written act of
self-defence, which is more likely to bring notoriety than reconciliation or absolution. Mathilde Carré records her religious conversion in

the year before her release from prison, suggesting her overwhelming need for some consolatory external authority. Since there is little doubt, in her case, that she betrayed many fellow resisters, her guilt and incrimination are undeniable, however much credence one gives to the compensating factors which she stresses, such as her manipulation and humiliation by dominant males and long years of personal suffering.

While Mathilde Carré would have us believe that ultimately she was a passive victim of intolerable, sordid circumstances, other accounts by former resisters assert the triumph of willpower and faith over apparently insuperable odds, hubristic self-glorification replacing the dismal confessional. A much more recent and controversial example involving accusations of treason and retrospective falsification of the historical record involves the resistance activities and subsequent autobiographical writing of Lucie and Raymond Aubrac, who for many decades were generally regarded as uncontaminated exemplars of heroic commitment to resistance. Both were co-founders of Libération Sud; Lucie Aubrac became the first woman parliamentarian when appointed to represent the MUR in the Consultative Assembly set up under the aegis of the CFLN in Algiers in 1944. Raymond Aubrac became a senior figure on the staff of the Secret Army and was one of the resistance leaders arrested with Jean Moulin in Lyon on 21 June 1943 (he observes that this was not only the second anniversary of the invasion of the USSR but also the date on which he became a prisoner of war in 1940). Following his escape, he was appointed *commissaire de la République* for Marseille, although after five months in office, he was sacked by de Gaulle in January 1945, ostensibly for failure to maintain food supplies; his youth, inexperience, lack of allies, proximity to the Communist Party and requisitions of local industries were all more probable causes for his dismissal.

Lucie Aubrac published a book of memoirs entitled *Ils partiront dans l'ivresse* in 1984 (the title refers to the BBC coded message signalling the arrival of a plane to evacuate them from France). The American translation has the less cryptic and more boastful title *Outwitting the Gestapo* (1993). She recounts how, while expecting their second child, she engineered Raymond's escape from the Germans on 21 October 1943 by launching an attack on a prison truck transporting him, having already helped him escape from captivity on two previous occasions. As the introduction points out, 'By any standard her account is one of exceptional heroism and commitment as well as of intense love and devotion' (Aubrac, 1993: vii). Provided, of course, that one actually believes it: which means finding it plausible as a literary text and credible as a historical statement. Writing on the theme of memory and occupation narratives, Claire Gorrara describes *Ils partiront dans l'ivresse* as 'a fictional autobiography', a work 'where historical event is mediated through self-consciously fictional structures' (1997: 36, 44). Can factual veracity survive such mediation? Lucie Aubrac herself remarks that resistance action justified rejecting such conventional moral values as truthfulness: 'We all entered the universe of lies with the greatest serenity' (Aubrac, 1997: 77). She also admits (despite her training as a history teacher) her tendency to exaggerate and distort events; however, 'Raymond prevented me from fabulating. I tended to invent my life, to embellish it. He accustomed me not to embroider too much' (p. 206).

At the same time, however, the Aubracs clearly wish to be taken seriously as historical witnesses and to defend their reputation as resistance heroes. When accusations of treason are at stake, they take a less serene and less relativistic attitude towards mendacity and embroidering on the facts. They won a libel action against Jacques Vergès, the lawyer who defended the Gestapo officer Klaus Barbie (who arrested Moulin and his associates and subsequently tortured Moulin to death) for alleging that Raymond was a double agent who sold out Moulin. Barbie was tried (and convicted) of crimes against humanity after being extradited from Bolivia to stand trial in France in 1987. When the historian Gérard Chauvy repeated similar accusations in a book published ten years later, the Aubracs won further damages for libel against him. The Aubracs nonetheless admit that certain facts were distorted in their accounts of the events surrounding Raymond's capture and release in 1943. A crucial example concerns his arrest by the French police on 15 March 1943, under the pseudonym François Vallet. Raymond Aubrac asserts that his real identity as a resistance leader of Jewish origins was never discovered, either in March or June 1943; he was considered by his captors to be only a rank-and-file individual. However, in Lucie's account, Raymond was released in May 1943 after she visited Ducasse, the local prosecutor in Lyon, and threatened him with reprisals if Vallet, whom she identified as de Gaulle's envoy, was not released immediately. Ducasse was invited to listen to a coded message purportedly confirming her story to be broadcast on the BBC that evening; after hearing the message, he duly ordered Raymond's release the next day.

According to *Ils partiront dans l'ivresse*, Raymond was freed on 14 May; we are supposed to believe that the French authorities had no hesitation in releasing a man who was not the petty trafficker he claimed to be but actually de Gaulle's envoy. In fact, surviving legal documents prove that his conditional release occurred four days earlier, on 10 May, and was motivated by a request from the magistrate examining his case and his lawyer on medical grounds (see Chauvy, 1997, for details). Noting such discrepancies in the Aubracs' stories, Klaus Barbie and his legal team concocted a lengthy document which alleged that these puzzling errors were explained by the fact that, following his arrest, Raymond Aubrac agreed to work for the Gestapo. According to Barbie's denunciation, 'Freed at our request on the 10th, Aubrac was kept by us until the 14th for working meetings. Aubrac like Hardy was afraid of death and agreed to work for us' (quoted by Chauvy, 1997: 69). René Hardy (the man accused by the Aubracs and many others of betraying Jean Moulin) was therefore not the only traitor present at Caluire. The Aubracs' own explanation for the variation between the dates is a more romantic one: Lucie decided to modify the date to the 14th because this happened to be the anniversary of their first meeting on 14 May 1939.

Gérard Chauvy painstakingly (not to say laboriously) demonstrates a profusion of such errors and contradictions in accounts given by resistance activists associated with the Aubracs of arrests, escapes and suspected betrayals. His argument shows the limits of a purely empirical approach: 'From the historian's viewpoint, there are however so many variants, with protagonists who do not always play the same role, that it is practically impossible to re-establish a reliable history based only on personal testimony' (1997: 80). His conclusion is in effect to acquit the Aubracs of treason but to convict them of betraying the historical record: 'Today no archival document allows us to validate the accusation of treason made by Klaus Barbie against Raymond Aubrac, but at the end of this study, it must be noted that fanciful accounts have sometimes been put together' (p. 267).

For Chauvy, this proved somewhat self-defeating, since what were taken by many readers as unwarranted innuendoes earned him both opprobrium and a costly court case. His book's publication coincided with the appearance of Claude Berri's film *Lucie Aubrac*,[10] which eschewed all such complexities in favour of traditional stereotypes of heroic valour: in the opening sequence, Raymond Aubrac is seen blowing up a train, while Lucie is played by the implausibly glamorous former model Carole Bouquet. Having initially helped promote the film, Lucie Aubrac decided to distance herself from its simplifications.[11] However, the Aubracs' apparent willingness to perpetuate a distorted version of their resistance activities undoubtedly damaged their reputation.

In May 1997, they agreed to appear before a panel of eight historians organised by the newspaper *Libération*, which published the findings of this impromptu tribunal as a supplement. The panel members treated the Aubracs unsympathetically. While conceding that Barbie's accusation of Raymond Aubrac was made fifty years after the events purely in order to defame the resistance and to divert attention from his own atrocities, Daniel Cordier accepts that Chauvy's investigation of the documentary evidence certainly reveals the 'inaccuracies of Lucie's memories and especially Raymond's alternative versions' (*Libération*, 9 July 1997). As for Lucie's memoirs, *Ils partiront dans l'ivresse* is:

> A stimulating adventure novel which you had the imprudence to present as your memories... When you produce endless inaccuracies, when you don't give clear answers, when you contradict yourself, you are serving neither history nor the cause you claim to be defending. (ibid.)

The generic indeterminacy which appeals to certain academic literary critics thus looks dangerously like vainglorious falsification to more sceptical commentators who retain a belief that historical investigation is meant to distinguish fact and fiction. Summing up the debate, the director of *Libération* Serge July concluded that the Aubracs had 'set in motion the legend-making machine'. A few days later, the British historian Douglas Johnson published an article in *The Spectator* unflatteringly entitled 'Fabulist Wife, Mysterious Husband', in which he observed that 'A hero can be destroyed. Everything that made him appear heroic is shown to be false' (19 July 1997). In all fairness, a more measured conclusion is that *Ils partiront dans l'ivresse*, if read with the scepticism that should be applied to most memoirs, offers a fascinating insight into many aspects of the resistance struggle. Whatever Lucie Aubrac's tendency to blur fact and fiction, there is little doubt about the indomitable courage which both she and Raymond displayed when confronted with Klaus Barbie, 'the all-powerful master of the city of Lyon', whose physical insignificance belied or perhaps explained his sadistic temperament (Aubrac, 1995: 91). As she asserts, Barbie's calumnies should not trivialise 'the glorious and tragic history of the resistance' (p. 266).

The trials of René Hardy

While some journalists, historians and surviving resisters expressed disgust and indignation at what they saw as the unjustified vilification of the Aubracs, a former member of the resistance like Jacques Baumel chose to direct his revulsion at Lucie Aubrac's self-promoting antics, remarking that he found a largely forgotten figure like Berty Albrecht much more admirable: 'No big budget film has recalled her sacrifice. Probably she made the mistake of dying. Posterity rather likes major witnesses to be still alive, so they can be made into idols who visit schools and television studios' (1999: 161). Baumel notes too that René Hardy, 'that most sombre or most pitiful hero' (p. 331), would make a good subject for a feature film (although the films inspired by Mathilde Carré and Lucie Aubrac hardly offer promising models). Like Mathilde Carré, Hardy was an authentic resistance activist arrested by the Germans, released and thereafter accused of being a double agent. While 'la Chatte' certainly betrayed a large number of minor agents working for the British, Hardy was a senior figure holding the rank of lieutenant-colonel in the independent movement Combat. The crime for which he is remembered is the betrayal of Jean Moulin at Caluire, although Hardy persistently denied any guilt and was in fact acquitted of all charges at two trials, after spending several years in detention.

As Baumel remarks, Caluire has become one of the most notorious events in the history of the French resistance: 'Caluire is probably what will remain of the resistance when everything else has been "forgotten". Rightly no doubt, since it was a tragedy, a telling, capital moment, the consequences of which would disrupt the history of our struggle' (1999: 313). The events surrounding the betrayal and subsequent martyrdom of Jean Moulin encapsulate many of the elements which define resistance, not simply as a political and paramilitary activity but as a symbolic, dramatic struggle, which put most simply can be seen as a confrontation between good and evil, between the courageous endurance of patriotic freedom fighters and the cowardly brutality and duplicity of the Nazi oppressors and their traitorous henchmen. That some of these henchmen had originally been patriotic resisters gives a further tragic dimension to the story. Added to this is the mystery concerning the individuals who betrayed the meeting (there are at least three suspects) and the exact fate of Moulin himself. Although he certainly died after suffering appalling torture, he may have hastened his end by a suicide attempt. Whether the ashes eventually interred in the Pantheon twenty-one years later were actually Moulin's remains is also a matter of doubt. Barbie's denials of responsibility for Moulin's murder are generally seen as unconvincing attempts to exculpate himself for the astonishing blunder of liquidating the most important man in the resistance without obtaining any information at all from him.

Caluire thus shows the failure of heroic endeavour against overwhelming odds, although in the longer term Moulin's death and belated canonisation as a republican, Gaullist saint were to give the resistance immense symbolic capital. Nevertheless, the immediate tactical setback for the unification and coordination of resistance activity (which were essentially Moulin's mission) caused by his arrest once again exposes the vulnerability, limitations, uneasy rivalry and amateurish incompetence of those involved in the underground struggle. Baumel notes 'a stream of slips, errors and strange coincidences' (1999: 320) in the organisation of the meeting at Caluire on 21 June 1943. In order to understand the case of René Hardy, these facts and related issues merit some examination. Two months previously, on 28 April, the resistance agent Jean Multon (aka Lunel), who was secretary to the head of the Secret Army in Marseille, was arrested by the German security service. Readily agreeing to work for the Germans, he proceeded to betray both valuable information and personal contacts. This included a letter box used in Lyon by the head of staff of the Secret Army Henri Aubry to communicate with René Hardy (aka Didot), whose main responsibilty was organising the sabotage of railway networks. On 9 June 1943 the newly appointed head of the Secret Army (the clandestine paramilitary organisation set up by the MUR), General Delestraint, was arrested in Paris, following the interception of an uncoded message sent from Aubry to Hardy, summoning the latter to meet Delestraint. While travelling to Paris by train on 7 June, Hardy had the misfortune to encounter Lunel (who knew him) in the company of the French Abwehr agent Robert Moog;[12] they had him arrested, along with his travelling companion Cressol, and taken off the train at Chalon-sur-Saône. Unsurprisingly, Delestraint was convinced that Hardy had betrayed him, as he told his comrades in captivity (the unfortunate General himself was executed in Dachau in April 1945).

Hardy was interrogated by Klaus Barbie, taken back to Lyon, and released on the evening of 10 June. He concealed his arrest and release from his resistance associates, claiming that he had escaped the Germans by jumping from the train (he went so far as to publish an account in a newspaper of this imaginary exploit after the liberation).

The principal purpose of the meeting, organised at a house belonging to Dr Dugoujon situated in the suburbs of Lyon at Caluire, was to appoint a successor to General Delestraint. The meeting was organised by André Lassagne of Libération; Aubry, whose lax security had already triggered the arrests of Delestraint and Hardy, invited Hardy to attend. Apart from Dugoujon and Moulin, seven senior resistance figures were arrested when Klaus Barbie and a small group of armed German security men burst into the house before the meeting had actually started (namely, Aubrac, Aubry, Hardy, Lacaze, Larat, Lassagne and Schwarzfeld). Three of them escaped or were released: as we have seen, Aubrac was freed in October after a daring assault commanded by his wife Lucie; Aubry was interrogated brutally and eventually struck a deal with the Germans, who released him later in the year and let him retire to obscurity (despite his security blunders and the suspicious nature of this release, investigations against him after the war were dropped and he vanished from the historical record). Most notoriously, Hardy effected his second miraculous escape only a few minutes after the mass arrest, in the street outside the doctor's house: as the prisoners were being bundled into the waiting cars, he broke free of his escort and made a run for it. While the others had been handcuffed, Hardy had been restrained only by a loose wrist chain and had managed to keep a pistol concealed in his coat; his captors fired a few perfunctory pistol shots in his direction, but made no serious attempt to pursue him. Nevertheless, he suffered a flesh wound in the arm and was arrested shortly afterwards by the French police. He was taken to the Antiquaille hospital for treatment (those who consider him guilty of betraying the meeting sometimes allege this wound was self-inflicted) and then transferred to the German-run Croix-Rousse hospital. Despite having an arm in plaster, he escaped from this institution in August: this was his third miraculous escape in as many months.

It must be said that Hardy has had very few persuasive defenders (apart from his defence counsel, the celebrated academician Maître Maurice Garçon, who achieved the equally miraculous feat of getting Hardy acquitted at two trials, despite a mass of incriminating evidence and hostile testimony against him). Allies in Combat such as Frenay and Bénouville who loyally stood by him at first were soon repelled as his duplicity and mendacity were exposed. A recent British biographer of Jean Moulin, the journalist Patrick Marnham, notes the virulent campaign launched against Hardy by the communist press during his trials. Hardy had in fact briefly been a Party member and was thus a 'perfect traitor' (Marnham, 2000: 223), a renegade to be reviled, not to say a convenient scapegoat. Like other commentators, Marnham also remarks how certain resistance witnesses hostile to Hardy attempted to incriminate him in order to divert attention from their own role in the affair. The best example is provided by Edmée Deletraz, a Belgian agent in Colonel Groussard's Gilbert network, which was penetrated by Robert Moog in March 1943. She was arrested in April 1943, may have become Moog's mistress, and was used to help trap Berty Albrecht, who was arrested on 28 May. She was given access to Gestapo headquarters in Lyon and alleged that she saw Hardy there on the morning of 21 June, when she learned of the ambush being prepared. A warning which she sent through her own network failed to reach Moulin in time to save him.

But as we know, such attempts to damn Hardy legally failed, since he was acquitted at two trials. Whether he can be morally vindicated is another matter. In any case, what is interesting about Hardy is not so much the question of his guilt or innocence, but rather the fact of his double acquittal and the way in which he reconstructed his life after his release from prison. After escaping from hospital, he eventually made his way to North Africa and joined the Free French administration in Frenay's embryonic ministry. He was arrested in December 1944, brought to trial on 20 January 1947 on charges of intelligence with an enemy power before the *cour de justice de la Seine* and acquitted four days later, mainly because the most compelling evidence against him was not presented by the prosecution and the most hostile witnesses were not called or when called were discredited. Moog and Multon were already dead (the latter having been executed only a few months earlier in September 1946); as an avowed double agent, Mme Deletraz was disbelieved. In addition, Hardy's liaison agent Jean Bossé committed perjury by providing him with a false alibi for the time he was seen by Deletraz in Gestapo headquarters. Two months later, however, definite proof of his initial arrest on the train was discovered in the railway company archives. He was promptly rearrested and, after a further three years' detention, brought to trial before a military tribunal in April 1950 on different charges of betraying secrets to the enemy. Once again he was to be acquitted, on 8 May, this time on a technicality: although most members of the panel of judges actually found him guilty, the majority of four out of seven was not large enough to ensure a conviction.

Hardy's sorry odyssey has been rehearsed by many historians of the resistance, though usually in a piecemeal fashion which provides only a truncated and partial version of events (thus Marnham's attempt to

vindicate Hardy as a victim of communist vilification involves ignoring the much more compelling documentary evidence against him).
The most interesting narratives are the contrasting versions provided
by Hardy himself, by his defence counsel Maurice Garçon, and by
Daniel Cordier. These are revealing in rather different ways: Hardy
offers a demonstration in evasive self-justification and confirms his
role as outsider turned pariah; Garçon offers a forensic defence of mendacity as a survival tactic; Cordier returns to the documentary evidence. All three men were notably prolific and skilled authors, albeit
in different genres, since Hardy started a new career after the war as a
novelist and autobiographer, Garçon wrote extensively about legal and
literary matters, and Cordier (who was originally Jean Moulin's secretary) began publishing a monumental multi-volume biography of
Moulin from 1989. That a historian and biographer renowned for his
belief in empirically-based research provides a more objective account
than the accused turned autobiographer or his advocate is perhaps
predictable.

In his most recent volume, published in 2000, Cordier offers a clear
and comprehensive review of the evidence, concluding that three separate documents provided almost incontrovertible evidence of Hardy's
guilt. The first was the 'Rapport Flora', dated 19 July 1943 and discovered in September 1944 in the archives of the Marseille Gestapo.
This was written by the Gestapo agent Ernst Dunker using information
provided by Multon about the MUR and named Didot (Hardy's
pseudonym) as having become a double agent after his arrest on the
train. A separate earlier SD report written by Kaltenbrunner (the head
of the RHSA, that is, German security services) to Ribbentrop, dated 29
June 1943, was found in the Berlin archives of the Reich Foreign Ministry: this explicitly identified Didot as Hardy and as the betrayer of
the Caluire meeting. This report was sent to the French government in
October 1946. Finally, after Hardy's acquittal at his first trial and the
publication of his phoney memoirs in the newspaper *Ce matin* (where
he persisted in denying his arrest on the train), the *contrôleur* Morice
tracked down the record of his arrest, which led to the second trial. It
is also clear that the prosecution did not present a strong case against
Hardy at the first trial, refusing to call German witnesses, and allowing
the defence to discredit hostile French witnesses (such as Cressol, who
witnessed his arrest on the train), while Hardy's false alibis went unchallenged. In addition, since only the 'Flora' report was presented at
the 1947 trial, Hardy and Garçon were able to argue that it was a
forgery.

Maurice Garçon published his *Plaidoyer pour René Hardy* in 1950, shortly after the second acquittal. It makes for strange reading, since his reconstruction of the facts is not dissimilar to Cordier's half a century later: in the first instance, his defence paradoxically involves accumulating evidence of Hardy's certain duplicity and probable guilt. The defence won the first trial because insufficient evidence was presented to refute Hardy's denial of his initial arrest on 7 June. Once the sleeping car attendant Morice (who was not heard at the first trial) produced cast-iron proof of the arrest, Hardy admitted he had perjured himself when he was rearrested on 24 March 1947. He admitted too that Barbie had released him on 10 June and that he had failed to inform any of his resistance associates of these circumstances, but denied that he had been identified as 'Didot'. Garçon acknowledges too that Hardy was 'a man who had deceived justice and had led me, against my will, to betray the truth' (1950: 72). The defence was, then, no longer based on straightforward (albeit mendacious) denial of any association with Barbie before the Caluire meeting but on a more subtle argument: the necessary duplicity practised by Hardy, both in playing a double game with Barbie to ensure his release, and in concealing the double game from his resistance comrades for fear of being eliminated by them. In short, Hardy 'found himself obliged to lie in order not to appear the traitor which he was not' (p. 103). Garçon also argues once more that the accusations of traitors and war criminals like 'la femme Deletraz' and Klaus Barbie lack all credibility. The minority of judges who accepted this argument saved Hardy from a death sentence or further years in prison.

Hardy may have been freed, but for most members of the resistance he was a disgraced figure. The wider lesson of the trials was, in Daniel Cordier's judgement, that 'justice is not authorised to establish historical truth' (quoted in *Libération*, 9 July 1997). Edmée Deletraz, on the other hand, who suffered unpleasant abuse from Maître Garçon in her role as an avowed double agent, was strongly defended by her superiors in the Gilbert network (they included André Devigny) and legal proceedings against her were dropped. Hardy's mythomania and skill in fabricating stories were put to better use in his new career as a novelist, although by the end of his life he deteriorated to being a virtual 'clochard' (down-and-out), to quote Henri Noguères's words in a book entitled rather optimistically *La Vérité aura le dernier mot* (1985: 100). He died in 1987, aged seventy-five, one month before the trial and conviction of his nemesis Klaus Barbie for crimes against humanity. Barbie's accusations, reiterated in *France Soir* in 1972, forced Hardy to renew his defence in the last fifteen years of his life. His method was principally to shift the blame on to others. Interviewed with Barbie's lawyer Jacques Vergès for Claude Bal's documentary film *Que la vérité est amère* in 1984, Hardy accused Aubrac and Bénouville of complicity in the arrest of Jean Moulin, while also accusing Aubry of betraying General Delestraint and Moulin of being a crypto-communist. Following a successful libel action launched by the Aubracs, the film never received a public showing. In 1983, Hardy claimed that he had informed Bénouville of his arrest on the train on the day after his release, that is on 11 June 1943. In other words, he was alleging that Bénouville had always been an accomplice in his perjury, since Bénouville was aware from the outset that he had effectively become a double agent. This brought an indignant response from Bénouville: 'no proof of this betrayal has ever ultimately been produced by anyone. Now you have taken it upon yourself to produce proof of your ignominy and baseness... You are a liar and a coward!' (quoted by Noguères, 1985: 150–1). Noguères notes more coolly that it is in any case unlikely that Hardy could have encountered Bénouville in Lyon on 11 June to make this confession, as he set off for Nîmes on the morning of the same day. Noguères's conclusion is that Hardy was probably the victim of his own vanity and fabrications rather than a calculating traitor; the most likely hypothesis is that, having concealed his initial arrest and release by the Gestapo, he was effectively ensnared into betraying the Caluire meeting.[13]

Finally, what of Hardy's own writing? Between 1951 and 1984, he produced a dozen books, beginning and ending his career as an author with works of autobiography, but achieving popular success with nine novels as well as a study of Delacroix. His first book, *Le Livre de la colère* (1951), was begun during his detention in Fresnes prison in 1949. The unnamed first-person narrator (whom we assume to be Hardy) recounts his arrest by the Sûreté Nationale in 1947, after already spending two years in prison. He presents himself as the victim of authorities which shamelessly switch their ideological loyalties while callously exploiting and destroying individual citizens. Whereas his father 'had been broken by the war like so many others' (Hardy, 1951: 26), the narrator has become a more defiant outsider, 'a reprobate who can inspire only pity or distrust' (p. 30). He recalls that he had first been arrested in 1941 as a 'gaulliste' 'by cops who looked like former convicts' (p. 39). Hardy contrasts the suffering which he has endured for his own patriotic integrity with the opportunistic, unscrupulous self-promotion of such time-serving functionaries. He records the brutal, insanitary conditions and humiliations inflicted on prisoners: 'For ten years I have been spending my time stripping naked in front of policemen' (p. 72). By 1944, the *juge d'instruction* who got him imprisoned in 1941 for dissidence had become a Gaullist in Algiers. Like many other resistance activists, Hardy denounces such figures who have 'chosen institutions and governments instead of the defeated nation, comfort instead of sacrifice', and the way in which 'Medals grew like cancer on unworthy chests' (pp. 81–2).

Released after fifteen months' imprisonment in Toulon in 1942, he rejoined the resistance and enjoyed 'the richest period in my life' (p. 42); but his capture by the Germans in 1943 set off a nightmare that was to last seven years. He claims that he was rapidly freed after being arrested by the Germans, while admitting that he then concealed the fact of his arrest. What really happened after he was taken off the train is, however, not disclosed. The omission of such crucial details has the effect of invalidating Hardy's effort to defend his case. The fact that the book consists of a series of loosely connected memories, which eschew linear narrative, ostensibly allows the elision of such inconvenient episodes. However, his blustering denunciations of iniquitous acts committed by others ultimately look more like a desperate attempt to divert attention from the treachery of which he is suspected than justified anger and bitterness. Thirty-three years later, Hardy produced a longer and more conventional autobiography entitled *Derniers mots* (1984; with the editorial assistance of Claude Dubois). He maintains the defence of self-protective mendacity offered in the second trial, affirming that 'I never collaborated, Barbie never succeeded in turning me' (Hardy, 1984: 351); had he agreed to aid the Gestapo, he could have betrayed most of the major resistance figures in Lyon. Since, within eleven days of his release, one of the most important resistance meetings held by resistance leaders in Lyon was indeed betrayed, this is a rather weak line of defence.

Hardy admits nothing, in other words, other than that his own existence was ruined by the events of June 1943. In old age, he cuts a doleful figure, writing from an appropriately symbolic address, the rue Crève-Cœur in Melle, that:

> For nearly forty-five years, I have exchanged one form of solitude for another: combat, prison, attempts to survive, sad marriages, without communication, solitude again, hospital, solitude...I present the strange particularity of having been a victor who was vanquished (Hardy, 1984: 128, 154).

The younger Hardy was a more dynamic, resilient individual, who was able to adopt a whole variety of professional roles: primary school teacher, communist activist, railway manager, resistance organiser, army officer and writer. After his second acquittal in 1950, he received ten years' back pay from the SNCF and moved to Italy. A story, 'La Troisième Nuit', which he published in *Les Œuvres libres* in June 1952, is a naturalistic account of railway sabotage during the occupation. Otherwise, he did not make much direct use in fiction of his resistance background. Echoes of his own circumstances are more indirect, since his novels are frequently adventure stories about men of action, heroic outsiders betrayed either through tragic circumstances or by the malevolence of callous superiors. *Amère victoire* (1955) was the most successful; a film adaptation directed by Nicholas Ray starring Richard Burton and Curt Jürgens came out in 1957. The title aptly sums up Hardy's disenchanted experience of occupation, resistance and liberation, and that of many other resistance activists, although the novel itself is set in the Libyan desert and presents the rivalries between a set of stereotyped British officers, two of whom have been sent on a suicidal commando mission by an incompetent general (they are also rivals for the same woman). One is killed after massacring wounded German prisoners, while the other survives, but is exposed as a coward and disgraced. The book thus offers the cynical lesson that heroic sacrifice is utterly futile either tactically or morally: the mission has little purpose, while those who undertake it act like war criminals and poltroons. Since Hardy possesses none of the satirical verve, first-hand knowledge of the British army, ear for dialogue, ability to create memorable, eccentric and sinister characters, still less the tragi-comic sensitivity to human failings of a novelist like Evelyn Waugh who dealt with similar topics, his story is little more than a dull entertainment.

French collaborators in German uniform

Hardy tells us that he was fond of wearing his colonel's uniform during his time in Fresnes prison (he had been promoted to this rank by General Delestraint), in order to stand out as an authentic resister from most of the other inmates, who were avowed collaborators. Hardy thus presents the extreme case, if we believe he was guilty of betraying Jean Moulin, of a resister turned collaborator with the Germans masquerading in French uniform. Most collaborators took a less tortuous path towards treason; in some cases, their willingness to put on German uniform was enough to convict them. It is interesting, in conclusion, to compare their experiences and self-justifications with those of their erstwhile adversaries in the resistance. (The discussion covers only military or paramilitary collaboration undertaken voluntarily, rather than enforced by conscription.) That both collaborators and resisters who took on paramilitary roles in the occupation inevitably shared certain experiences (such as serving causes or carrying out violent or illegal tasks shunned by most people, or enjoying a degree of power and euphoric fulfilment often followed by disillusion and ostracism) does not however imply an equation between collaboration and resistance as moral, ideological and tactical choices. Nevertheless, Hardy's case does illustrate how resisters motivated by disinterested patriotism could ultimately have their moral and psychological integrity destroyed; in his own words, once his association with the Gestapo was exposed, 'I was a renegade, I was a dirty bastard' (Hardy, 1984: 359).

The three bodies most notoriously associated with uniformed collaboration were the Légion des volontaires français contre le bolchevisme (LVF), the Waffen SS, and the Milice. The LVF was created in July 1941 a few weeks after the German invasion of the Soviet Union as an anti-Bolshevist legion, at the instigation of the Paris-based leaders of collaborationist movements rather than the Vichy government (which banned French army officers on active service from joining). Abetz allowed the LVF to use the former Soviet Intourist offices on the rue Auber, and it was dependent on German finance. Most fascist intellectuals who supported the crusade against communism did their best to avoid volunteering for action (with the notable exceptions of Marc Augier and Jacques Doriot); their self-preserving scepticism was shared by the general population, since only about 6000 men were recruited to the force (with 7500 being rejected for medical or other reasons). Legionnaires were obliged to wear German uniform and swear allegiance to Hitler; two LVF battalions were constituted, forming the 638th regiment of the Wehrmacht, under the command of Colonel Labonne, a retired French officer. The LVF was sent into action on the eastern front in December 1941 and withdrawn after one week, when it failed to capture the village set as its objective: the men were poorly trained, its officers and equipment inadequate, and its commander incompetent. Labonne and half his men were dismissed in January 1942 (Labonne received the Iron Cross, and subsequently a life sentence for treason from the court of justice in Paris in November 1946).

For the next two years the LVF was confined to rear-line action against partisans in Belarus, whose numbers overall multiplied from

30,000 in 1941 to 250,000 in 1944. Destroying villages and harassing civilians suspected of supplying partisans were their most frequent functions; the Germans sometimes intervened to contain LVF excesses. Belated attempts by Vichy, inspired by the main theorist of collaboration Benoist-Méchin, to gain control of the LVF, rebaptised the 'Légion tricolore', and thus to institutionalise military collaboration with the Germans, were blocked by Hitler in September 1942. Apart from its military limitations, the LVF proved costly in administrative terms, probably because of large-scale embezzlement of funds; legionnaires acquired more unwelcome notoriety for drunken brawls when on leave (seventy-four policemen were injured in an incident in Paris on 27 August 1943). The LVF was eventually dissolved in November 1944, with about 1000 of its surviving members being incorporated into the French division of volunteers for the Waffen SS, established by the Germans the previous year, when failing manpower obliged them to recruit foreign volunteers into elite formations, and authorised by Laval in July 1943. The Division Charlemagne, as it was called, comprised four battalions of about 8000 men, half of whom came either from the LVF or the military units of the Milice, and fought in eastern Europe and Berlin until the closing days of the war in April 1945. Pierre Giolitto, whose book *Volontaires français sous l'uniforme allemand* (1999) should be consulted for more details, estimates that as many as 30,000 Frenchmen served in various German military units during the occupation (their numbers included for example about 5000 volunteers in less well-known organisations like the motor corps (NSKK) and Kriegsmarine). Survivors of the LVF and SS battalions generally received less severe treatment from post-war French courts than members of the Milice, since their misdeeds had been committed outside France rather than against French civilians and resisters. This point is certainly illustrated by the contrasting cases of Christian de La Mazière and Paul Touvier. The first was a forgotten though interesting figure in the world of military collaboration, whose return to fleeting notoriety in the early 1970s was almost entirely due to unabashed self-promotion; the second was a mid-ranking officer in the Milice, whose attempts to escape retribution were protracted over several decades and ultimately made him a public figure whose scandalous odyssey was held to encapsulate the evils of paramilitary collaboration and the failings of post-war justice.

Christian de La Mazière observes that the *miliciens* who joined the Division Charlemagne 'were pariahs and had no goal other than to fight' (La Mazière, 1972: 58). His book *Le Rêveur casqué* was published in 1972, following his appearance as an unrepentant defender of military collaboration in Ophuls's documentary film *Le Chagrin et la pitié*. La Mazière offers a somewhat romanticised account of his experiences in the Waffen SS, stressing the thirst for adventure and ideological naivety inherited from his family background. He was brought up on a diet of *L'Action française* and anti-Semitism by his father, a former cavalry officer who swore the oath of loyalty to Pétain (he was briefly a member of his cabinet) and who refused offers to join the resistance, while dissuading his son from joining the Free French. The latter finally joined the Waffen SS only a few days before the liberation in August 1944: 'I saw in them a quite separate race, an invincible race' (p. 44). The military virtues of the SS are described with an ingenuous (or disingenuous) enthusiasm: thus he asserts that his comrade Georges de La Buharaye learned more in a month of SS training than in two years at Saint-Cyr followed by ten years in the French army; that the fighting prowess of the Waffen SS allowed Germany to defer its military collapse for at least a year; and that the Waffen SS had no connection with the SS units which guarded concentration camps. On the other hand, the systematic atrocities committed by Waffen SS units in Nazi-occupied territories (such as the massacre of hundreds of civilians at Oradour-sur-Glane, a justly infamous event in France, but one which merely represented a barbaric norm in eastern Europe) do not merit his attention.

En route to the eastern front, La Mazière and his comrades paid a visit to Sigmaringen, whither the remnants of the Vichy government had been forcibly transplanted after the liberation, but were refused an audience with Pétain; 'As the disaster became clearer, these political refugees began to find us compromising' (p. 101). He was to witness the collapse of the Third Reich at first hand, fighting in medieval conditions when trapped in East Prussia behind the Russian advance, under the command of Bassompierre (who was to be executed in Fresnes). La Mazière says that one third of his fellow volunteers were workers, one third students, and one third 'aristocrates, grands bourgeois et aventuriers' (p. 145). Finally, he surrendered to the Poles, claiming to be a journalist in a propaganda *Kommando*; he was handed over to the Russians and then to the French. His name featured on a French wanted list, which invalidated his ploy of claiming to be an STO (forced labour) deportee. He was remanded in Fresnes, 'the political prison, in which a certain form of civilisation reigned' (p. 209), mixing with such luminaries of collaboration as René Bousquet. Tried by the Twelfth Chamber of the Court of Justice on the anniversary of

VE Day, he was sentenced to five years' imprisonment and ten years' national indignity for endangering the security of the state and intelligence with the enemy. Articles in favour of collaboration which he published in *Le Pays libre* counted against him more than his service in the SS. He was angered at his sister's suggestion that he plead insanity, though writing twenty-five years later doubted whether his commitment to defy democratic values had much use, beyond a juvenile urge to self-destruction: 'death belongs to the revolutionary act, which is an act of love whereby one commits oneself totally – and not a calculation where one weighs up the consequences of what one is doing' (p. 252). After some eighteen months' further imprisonment (during which he enjoyed relatively tolerable conditions, including fortnightly conjugal visits from his girlfriend), he was pardoned by President Auriol and released.

La Mazière thus casts himself as a misguided but sincere adventurer, whose heroic commitment to a lost cause demands a dubious respect. His case is helped by the lack of very incriminating evidence against him, even if the Waffen SS systematically committed wide-scale atrocities. The crimes committed inside occupied France by the Milice and its members, on the other hand, were too apparent and too numerous for a similar attempt at rehabilitation to have much chance of success. The Milice was established as an 'auxiliary police' on 31 January 1943, following a meeting between Hitler and Laval the previous month (Delperrié de Bayac, 1994: 153), nominally under the authority of Laval, with Joseph Darnand as its secretary general. The Milice inherited its mission and dark blue uniform from the Service d'Ordre Légionnaire (SOL), which had emerged from the Légion des combattants in mid-1941, though SOL members were not necessarily former combatants. By the end of the year 1943, it numbered about 29,000 members, both male and female, only half of whom were seriously committed fascist militants, drawn from the 'remnants of the right and the far right' (p. 176). In practice, most of the atrocities which made it the most infamous collaborationist organism in occupied France were committed by members of the elite paramilitary corps, the Franc-Garde, set up officially in June 1943, which numbered about 8000 men aged between eighteen and forty-five, and the security and intelligence branches (the *deuxième service*), whose cadres were styled 'inspecteur régional de la Milice'. Crimes committed by the Milice ranged from theft and extortion to torture, murder and mass executions. Seven Jews were machine-gunned by the *2ᵉ service* in the cemetery at Rillieux, near Lyon, on 29 June 1944. At least two hundred resisters were summarily executed by courts martial staffed by *miliciens*, while hundreds of bodies of other victims were found in mass graves after the liberation. The Jewish politicians Zay and Mandel were assassinated by the Milice in June and July 1944. Although the Milice preferred such small-scale 'police' operations to military engagement, some 800 *miliciens* were included in the force used to attack 465 maquisards on the plateau de Glières in March 1944, while 500 Francs-Gardes were deployed against the resistance bastion in the Vercors, though withdrew before the final onslaught in July 1944. When Darnand became Secretary General for order in January 1944, in effect the head of all Vichy police forces, his underlings were able to infiltrate important areas of administration and government and turn the dying regime into a police state.

One of these underlings was Paul Touvier, whose notoriety derives less from the crimes he committed as a member of the Milice than from the fact that he was the first Frenchman to be convicted of crimes against humanity and sentenced to life imprisonment, when he was belatedly brought to trial in March 1994 at the age of seventy-nine. While Darnand had been executed for treason in October 1945, along with other senior figures such as Gombert, Knipping and Bassompierre, Touvier managed to evade justice for half a century. He had been sentenced to death in absentia for treason in 1946 and 1947, sentences which however lapsed under the statute of limitations in 1967. In 1971, President Pompidou issued a pardon to lift the less serious charges not covered automatically by the lapse of the death sentence, namely the confiscation of Touvier's property and a residence banning order. Ironically, the publicity which this gesture attracted had the effect of turning Touvier from an obscure and forgotten collaborator into a war criminal whose atrocities were, apparently, being complacently forgiven by the French state. Defending his decision at a press conference held in September 1972, Pompidou asked: 'Has the moment not come to draw a veil over and forget those times when French people disliked and even killed one other?' (quoted by Flory, 1989: 166). This somewhat plaintive request, as we know, would be resoundingly dismissed, since the 1970s were to mark the beginning of a far more critical examination of the occupation and the crimes and compromises committed under the guise of collaboration.

In 1964, the French parliament exempted crimes against humanity from the *prescription* or limitation applying to war crimes. This allowed new charges of crimes against humanity to be brought against Touvier in March 1973. He was however to be arrested only sixteen years later (in May 1989) and convicted twenty-one years later after a tortuous legal process which allowed little understanding of the historical events to emerge. The case thus throws up three key questions: of what crime was Touvier actually guilty, as a member of the Milice? Why did it take fifty years to bring him to justice? Were the charges of crimes against humanity meaningful? The journalist Claude Flory carried out extensive interviews with Touvier, which he published in book form as *Touvier m'a avoué* in 1989. Until 1940, Touvier worked for the SNCF. He joined the Milice (having previously been a member of the SOL) in March 1943 and became 'chef du Deuxième Service pour le département de la Savoie', moving to Lyon in October 1943. His method of defence is principally repeated denial: of practising torture or extortion, of participating in the murder of Victor Basch and his wife in January 1944 (they were arrested by his service, though he denies this too, while also blaming his subordinate Gonnet). He does concede he played a minor role in the execution of seven Jewish hostages at Rillieux-la-Pape on 29 June 1944, claiming 'I prevented the worst' (Flory, 1989: 51). These murders formed the main basis of the charges against him in 1994. Contrition or admission of responsibility were foreign to Touvier, whose career in the Milice resembled that of the petty gangsters who were recruited by the Germans as their police auxiliaries. At the same time, he must have possessed a degree of seductive charm, since shortly after escaping from detention in the rue des Saussaies in August 1947, he married Monique Berthet, and for decades found refuge with Catholic priests and in religious institutions. During the first two decades spent in hiding, he raised two children, while finding the time to meet such show-business personalities as Pierre Fresnay and Jacques Brel. In other words, the prosecuting authorities showed little enthusiasm in actually pursuing him.

Even after he was finally detained, it seemed likely that the case against him would fail, when three judges in a chamber of the Paris Court of Appeal ruled in 1992 that charges of crimes against humanity could not be levelled against Touvier as a member of the Milice, since the Vichy government and its agents did not have a policy of systematic genocide. Only crimes committed on behalf of Nazi Germany apparently qualified as crimes against humanity. Unfortunately for Touvier, in an attempt to exculpate himself he had claimed that he had been acting in response to German intervention during the Rillieux killings (although there was little evidence to show such complicity); this helped to secure his conviction as an avowed agent of the Third Reich. Vichy's responsibility in setting up paramilitary collaboration and abetting the final solution were effectively sidelined, while those individuals foolish enough to commit themselves to violent acts of collaboration remained convenient and expendable scapegoats. This last case shows once again the painful contortions and evasions of a judicial system attempting to come to terms with the complexities of individual and collective guilt years or decades after the events in question. The lengthy deliberations of judges and lawyers and the pompous ritual of courts rarely reconstruct more than the grossest approximation of the truth, as Camus's novel *L'Étranger* (1942) famously shows. It must be admitted that the fictionalised version of Touvier's crime and punishment imagined by the Irish novelist Brian Moore in *The Statement* is too melodramatic to carry much conviction as a measured reflection on the pursuit of collaborators. But this brings us to our next topic: what exactly do novelists and literary writers have to offer us, when it comes to further understanding of the perils and dilemmas endured by those under occupation?

5
Writers

In her quantitative sociological study, *La Guerre des écrivains* (1999), Gisèle Sapiro notes that some 185 literary writers were active in France in 1940. In the decades following the occupation, hundreds of memoirs and novels were produced by individuals seeking either to bear witness to their wartime experiences or, for later generations, to reconstruct such experiences at second-hand. Any account of writing about the period is therefore bound to be highly selective, particularly if detailed attention is paid to specific texts. My aim in this chapter is to examine works by five writers, all of whom lived through the occupation but engaged in quite different activities (ranging from resistance activist, childhood witness of government circles, contributor to collaborationist journals, to petty gangster) and responded in varied though equally interesting ways in their writing. In the first instance, we will look at the resistance novel and Roger Vailland's contribution to the elaboration of this genre. Vailland's revolutionary idealism as a communist fellow traveller may evidently be ideologically opposed to authors like Pascal Jardin, René Barjavel and Marcel Aymé whose sympathy for Vichy and distrust of ideologues are all too apparent in much of their writing. All of them, however, observe the same collapse in the social order and conventional morality and flirt with utopian (or dystopian) solutions: Jardin re-enacting an idyll of Vichy as lost childhood paradise, Barjavel using science fiction to explore alternative ways of restoring French integrity, Aymé and José Giovanni examining the criminal and traitor as anti-heroic but authentic models of behaviour.

Roger Vailland and the resistance novel

What constitutes a resistance novel and how should we interpret it? To what extent did Roger Vailland contribute to the creation of a new fictional genre with the publication of *Drôle de jeu* in the autumn of 1945? The first classic examples of the genre are themselves acts of resistance and historical statements as much as works of literature, given that they were written by active participants during the struggle against the Germans (witness Vercors's *Le Silence de la mer*, 1942, and Kessel's *L'Armée des ombres*, 1943). On the other hand, most post-war novels about resistance are inevitably written from a second-hand perspective and tend to be derivative works of entertainment (not necessarily devoid of critical interest, but serving a different purpose): among countless recent examples, we can mention Michel Jeury's *Le Printemps viendra du ciel* (1995), or *Night Sky* (1983) and *Charlotte Gray* (1998) by the British novelists Clare Francis and Sebastian Faulks. This raises further questions regarding the historiographic, literary, ethical and ideological value of such writing. Vailland's own observations about *Drôle de jeu* likewise indicate the problematic nature of his text, particularly the relationship between historical reality and the fictional world of his novel. In a preface signed 'R.V.', he insists somewhat dubiously on the purely imaginary qualities of his book, denying that it is a 'historical novel' or a 'novel about resistance'. The reader is discouraged from seeking historical or political arguments in it, let alone the real identity of the protagonists.

What explains such odd denials (apart from a certain modesty, which deterred Vailland from ever talking directly about his personal experience in the resistance)? In fact, Vailland's biographers have shown that *Drôle de jeu* was very clearly linked to his resistance activities. As in all his later novels, first-hand, journalistic observation of a socio-historical milieu gives the text an authentic, documentary value, which is reinforced by the deliberate coincidence of the characters' pseudonyms with the noms de guerre adopted by Vailland and his associates during the occupation.[1] No doubt Vailland wished to emphasise the autonomous aspects of his novel as a literary creation, while discouraging otiose decoding of personal elements concealed by his fictionalisation. All the same, one wonders why he denies having portrayed the maquis when in fact several chapters are devoted to the exploits of maquisards in the area around Bourg-en-Bresse.

Contemporary novelists who wish to assert the authenticity of their texts cannot afford such coy denials; lacking the authority of the first-hand witness who has no need to lay out his credentials, they generally are driven to claim a sort of vicarious authority, by stressing for example the amount of historical research underpinning their texts. Thus Michel Jeury reverses Vailland's disclaimer by asserting in his preface to *Le Printemps viendra du ciel* that his imagined heroes 'often resemble real people. The events and circumstances [described] are most frequently transposed from authentic facts.' He even identifies three models for the main characters, and appends a bibliography of some twenty-five historical sources to his novel. Similarly, Clare Francis stresses the authenticity of the historical background in *Night Sky* by acknowledging expert advice received from naval and air force officers and adding a postscript which sketches in the factual details about radar and resistance escape networks underlying the plot of her novel.

Neither first-hand experience nor assiduous research necessarily mean that a novel will succeed either as fictional documentary (that is, in a didactic sense) or as literature (whether one takes this to mean effective storytelling, creation of memorable characters, aesthetic innovation or simply entertainment). In fact, it is a reasonable generalisation to state that most novels inspired by the Second World War tend to be either crude and violent adventure stories or wooden, sententious reconstructions (Faulks's rather disappointing *Charlotte Gray* falls into this latter category). As Jean-Pierre Azéma remarks, the popular image of the resistance fighter transmitted by most cultural representations does not extend far beyond recycled clichés and stereotypes: 'a mixture of the secret agent, the lawman or outlaw derived from actors in westerns, the fearless, dauntless knight, toting a sub-machine gun and blowing up endless factories and trains' (1979: 169).

Such recourse to stereotypes is perhaps inevitable. Any resistance story, be it film or novel, which is constructed as a linear account of actions presented as typical and which stresses the conflict between the agents of resistance and their opponents, is inevitably based on a number of highlights and key incidents. These can easily degenerate into implausible melodrama, an unending cycle of miraculous escapes, spectacular acts of sabotage and derring-do, heroic sacrifices, betrayals of double agents, torture sessions, liquidation of traitors, and so on. At the same time, the perception of the resistance as a legendary, sacred struggle is often combined with a crude manicheism in ideological or psychological terms which eschews any nuances or subtleties. Marcel Aymé satirised such reductive tendencies in his novel about the excesses of the liberation, *Uranus*, in 1948, where he has a former collaborator pick up a novel glorifying resistance and contrasting 'the nobility of heart and virile beauty of resisters' with 'the cowardice, cupidity, conceit and bottomless stupidity of Vichyist traitors' (Aymé, 1972: 185). Although this caricatural opposition between vice and virtue bears no resemblance to the complexity and ambiguity of historical reality, it has already taken a firm grip on the popular imagination. Aymé's revenge is to delete resistance as an authentic phenomenon from his own fictional portrayal of the period.

To discover how Vailland attempts to avoid the simplifications of popular or doctrinaire fiction, we need to turn to a more detailed analysis of the elements that make *Drôle de jeu* an original work. Re-reading *Drôle de jeu* in 1961 with a view to adapting it for the cinema, Vailland noted its weaknesses: 'Bad dialogue when read as dialogue; often one doesn't know who's talking, it's always me, as in Malraux's novels. It works all the same because it's hung on a thriller-type plot: Marat as private detective' (Vailland, 1968b: 646). This is an implicit admission that the novel owes its success to its autobiographical elements, rather than to its creation of varied characters with an existence independent of the narrator and main protagonist. If the characters' voices sound the same, this is because the author is using them as mouthpieces to communicate ideas and provide information, without attempting to give them any psychological depth beyond their pseudonyms and a few sketchy features and gestures (Marat evidently being an exception). At the same time, this didacticism is found rather curiously in a novel whose plot is cast as thriller or adventure story but which uses narrative forms remote from the usual conventions of popular literature (for example, frequent switches between present and past tenses, or first-person narration and Marat's italicised journal or monologues). The novel's originality owes much to this combination of philosophical reflections with the individual and collective drama that made up resistance life and action. While displaying his games of love and chance with a sceptical distance that prevents the fabrication of vainglorious legends, Vailland nonetheless insists on the crucial importance of resistance as a historical and symbolic phenomenon, as well as its potential for renewing committed literature.

Any serious writing about resistance, even in the form of fiction, imposes certain ethical constraints on its authors, assuming that their aspirations extend beyond simple entertainment. This takes us a long way from the perception of literature that was perhaps more fashionable in the 1960s and 1970s when the 'nouveau roman' retained some vitality, namely that literature's only object is ultimately itself. Vailland observed that 'The "new novel" is an attempt to escape from

History. A false solution, I think: the universal must be found in the singular, the concrete, that is what is dated and situated' (1968b: 644). In fact, most books written by former resisters set out to deliver a lesson on history and ethics, to link pedagogy, propaganda and persuasion, even if the degree of personal invention varies according to the specific genre chosen. Vailland is unusual in creating an ambiguous distance between fiction and historical reconstruction in his preface to *Drôle de jeu*. Despite its demystifying posture, Margaret Atack argues that the novel shares 'the characteristic features of persuasive fiction in its delimitation of the enemy, and its positive resolution of its conflicts and dilemmas' (1989: 147). To accept this argument, one evidently has to identify the traitress Mathilde as the main enemy of the group; she is liquidated, while Marat/Lamballe's virtuous double Frédéric is sacrificed. This leads to the objection that assassinating one's compatriots is an odd way either to fight the enemy or to achieve a positive resolution. Hence Michel Picard's more pessimistic interpretation, in 'Un objet littéraire: le mythe de la résistance chez Roger Vailland', that the quest for unity is doomed to failure, since resistance is perceived to contain a series of conflicting elements:

> Sociality/solitude, concrete/abstract, real/ludic, qualifying test/ mortal danger, excessive hope/ever-present disillusion...What basically characterises the evolution [of *Drôle de jeu*] is the flattening of this duality, the elimination of contradiction and consequently of any dialectical potential. (*La Littérature française sous l'occupation*, 1989: 118)

It is true that *Bon pied bon œil*, the sequel published five years later, shows the surviving characters to be in a sorry state: thus the sensualist philosopher/adventurer Marat has not only literally been emasculated, but reduced to breeding cattle. However, the progressive disillusionment of Vailland's characters does not alter the fact that the resistance allowed him to become a genuinely creative writer after his protracted apprenticeship in journalism.

As a reflection on the consequences of commitment and underground action, *Drôle de jeu* invites comparison with Simone de Beauvoir's novel *Le Sang des autres* (also published in 1945). Unlike de Beauvoir's retrospective narrative with its multiple points of view, Vailland's text retains a more conventional form, close to the thriller (as he observed), with its linear sequence of five key days covering some three weeks in March–April 1944 and its fairly predictable plot development. The main objectives are to set in action the dramatic events and character configurations surrounding Marat (allowing him to solve the enigma posed by Mathilde), and at the same time to present what is basically a chronicle of the daily routines and risks of resistance. Like Marcel Aymé (one of whose characters in *Uranus* blames the defeat of 1940 on the excessive reading of demoralising novels), Vailland inserts ironic references to literature, or rather literariness, throughout *Drôle de jeu*. One reason for this is because the characters are conscious of acting in a collective drama which is partly explained and validated by cultural references. Such references also add to the effect of ludic distance that characterises the novel (distinguishing it radically from a work like Kessel's *L'Armée des ombres*, which attempts to promote resistance in a much more straightforward fashion, sometimes approaching propaganda). Thus the tragic dilemmas and blood-letting entailed by action against the occupier mean that 'we have all become characters from Corneille' (Vailland, 1968a: 87–8). The narrator asserts his presence as social commentator and creator of fictions by informing us that the social geography of Bourg-en-Bresse 'would be a subject for a different novel' (p. 231). Jealously pursuing Marat, Frédéric describes him as a 'would-be Valmont' (p. 412), aping the hedonistic intriguer of Laclos's novel *Les Liaisons dangereuses* (1782). As for Frédéric, he shares both the name and ineptitude of the protagonist in Flaubert's *L'Éducation sentimentale* (1869) (from which his knowledge of Paris is supposedly drawn, p. 401); unsurprisingly, he is caught by the Germans in place of Marat, the libertine who has seduced his fiancée Annie.

Such examples show that the 'funny game' heralded in the novel's title does more than call into question the usefulness of resistance; it also embraces the creation of the text, which draws both on real experience of resistance and on the pre-existing conventions and references of literary culture. Commitment does not necessarily inhibit sceptical detachment, either as a resister or a novelist. The characters in the novel are willing to risk their lives, while sometimes doubting the usefulness of their acts. The narrator gives us, almost entirely through Marat's viewpoint, a full chronicle of the activities of a resistance militant, who also acts as a somewhat sententious pedagogue, ever ready to lecture his younger associates. At the end of the book, he establishes a link between resistance and the humanist values of classical culture, with Marat's parallel reading of Xenophon's *Anabasis* and Frédéric's sacrifice, although this belated expression of solidarity with a despised rival rings rather hollow. Normally, Marat displays a more cynical detachment of a less hypocritical nature; this corresponds to that 'separation of self from self' which Vailland considered typifies 'in the theatre, and in life... true heroes [and] expresses to the highest degree the real conflicts of their age' (1953: 179). The literary referentiality of the novel is further demonstrated by its division into five days, evidently matching the acts of a classical drama. Less frequently noticed is the fact that the plot hinges on meticulous topographic timing, for it essentially comprises a series of movements across Paris (with a brief detour to the provinces), with time and place always being precisely announced (from the opening words, 'Ten o'clock in the morning on the rue Lepic' (Vailland, 1968a: p. 11) to Marat's final retreat to a luxury hotel on the faubourg Saint-Honoré, at 'a quarter past eight' (p. 427)).

The resistance activist is very much a solitary traveller, whose existence is regulated by strict time-keeping. Hence Marat's observation that he has 'taken his interior monologue to every hotel in France, in both unoccupied and occupied zones, as a commercial traveller in terrorism' (p. 66). The conspirator's itinerary justifies the episodic form taken by the story, whose coherence derives from the focusing presence of this single character (his absence in a couple of scenes or the occasional intrusion of an external narrator strike a false tone, since we become habituated to this single voice). The conspirator has to achieve the difficult feat of compartmentalising his activities without breaking contact with his network, since resistance can only exist if communication is maintained. The action of the fifth day emphasises this theme, illustrated by the need to counteract Mathilde's conspiracy while simultaneously renewing contact with Caracalla before the fateful rendezvous. Given the authentic insistence on security precautions throughout the novel (with for example the abandonment of letter drops that are easily penetrated and Marat's reprimand of Rodrigue and Frédéric for gossiping indiscreetly with Mathilde), the writing or very existence of Marat's journal (containing enough autobiographical indiscretions to destroy the whole network) is hard to justify (whether in terms of security or plausibility).

Such flaws in thematic or narrative coherence are rare in Vailland's novel, however. One has only to compare *Drôle de jeu* with *L'Armée des ombres* to see how much more careful Vailland is than Kessel about the cohesiveness of his novel. Although both novels contain similar episodes, their tone is quite different. *L'Armée des ombres* contains two chapters written in the first person, yet these are not personal journals but rather diffuse and episodic accounts of exploits committed by various resisters. Intimacy is a trap for Kessel's characters, who have had to abandon any inner or past life (his Mathilde is destroyed by retaining her family ties). On the other hand, Kessel places much more stress on violence, whether suffered or inflicted on others; he presents resistance primarily as a dangerous business. Entire chapters are devoted to the execution of a traitor or the escape from the firing range in the prison. Vailland maintains a sort of classical decorum, in that he evokes such brutal acts much more discreetly. Thus Mathilde's liquidation or Frédéric's arrest take place off stage. Marat is supposedly willing to beat Mathilde to death, but we take this as a fantasy.[2] Marat describes at length how a woman organised her husband's escape from a prison van in Lyon (an adventure doubtless inspired by Lucie Aubrac's), but he himself did not take part in such events, just as he is only a distant witness of the sabotage of a train (a witness who literally is left in the dark). Whereas the resisters of *L'Armée des ombres* accomplish melodramatic exploits and suffer physically, Vailland's Marat remains an intellectual commentator who profits from his experience to lecture his associates about fidelity or eroticism.

No doubt the intellectual distance which Vailland adopts in *Drôle de jeu* is largely due to the fact that the novel was written during the liberation, while Kessel was writing earlier in the occupation, at a time when he needed to convey a simple, direct message: to depict 'pictures of a sacred struggle', to praise heroes who 'arouse almost mystical emotions' (Kessel, 1972: 6, 124). Unlike Vailland, Kessel uses his preface, not to erect an artificial barrier between fiction and historical reality, but to stress the authenticity of his enterprise (even claiming 'there is no fiction' in his novel) and to emphasise the moral and ideological obligations of the citizen confronted with the crisis of occupation: 'France no longer has bread, wine or fire. But above all she no longer has laws. Civil disobedience, individual or organised rebellion have become patriotic duties. The true national hero is the underground fighter, acting illegally' (pp. 5, 8). Marat, on the other hand, is struck by the paradoxical reversal of values caused by the collapse of the social and political order. Thus the French are 'amazed to see those whose professional business is patriotism going over to the enemy, the victor of Verdun organising the defeat, and anti-militarists taking over groups of partisans to carry on the struggle despite the armistice' (Vailland, 1968a: 83).

The ultimate goal of resistance, according to Marat, is neither the allied landings nor even the liberation of French territory but rather 'the Revolution and the building of socialism' (p. 164). However, such utopian idealism hardly fits his behaviour, which is that of a sceptical libertine. As his double name Marat/Lamballe suggests,[3] he is an 'artisan of the Revolution, but still an *ancien régime* character' (p. 162). In practice, Marat has not actually joined the Communist Party and never discovers whether his resistance activities have much useful effect. The title of the novel does indeed question rather provocatively the use of resistance and the motivation of its agents, issues taken up in a discussion between Marat and Annie when they are distant observers of a maquis attack. Annie offers a very disillusioned analysis, saying they are players in an absurd but 'bloody game, that is intolerably gratuitous' (p. 276), to which Marat responds with a rather woolly idealism: the 'deepest urge' of resistance is always revolution, that is 'total individual liberty' and the idea that 'happiness is possible, the most powerful explosive that will ever be invented' (pp. 270, 284). Practical reality is both more mundane and more brutal. Marat's activities involve following a bureaucratic routine, 'sending London information that no doubt will never serve any purpose' (p. 33). Moreover, the rather hackneyed slogans which this communist fellow traveller utters (for example, 'the revolutionary is someone who is not resigned to the misfortune of humanity', p. 432) are contradicted by the more egotistical (and persuasive) moral which he draws from the conclusion of the story, namely that 'destiny has no morality' (p. 422).

The main character in *Drôle de jeu* is thus a sort of seductive pedagogue, unconvinced of the value of his lessons but observing the inexperienced young people who surround him in a paternalistic manner. The youthfulness of the other resistance activists may well match historical reality, but is emphasised to the point of caricature at times. For instance, Caracalla is the 'boss', although he is 'almost an adolescent' who 'hasn't outgrown the age when you still like cakes' (p. 94); Rodrigue, whom Marat has known since childhood, amuses himself by stealing a bicycle, further evidence he has yet to reach adulthood or 'the age of reason' (p. 324); Annie, who 'has always lived with her mummy and daddy' (p. 369), needs Marat to be initiated into sexual pleasure, for her boyfriend Frédéric is a puritanical virgin whose only ambition is to become a teacher, 'a profession which allows you to escape the real world...and remain irresponsible, like a child' (p. 172). In a long monologue, Marat finally realises that such infantilism typifies most of his compatriots enduring occupation; they are 'not old enough for their age, not measuring up to their century' (p. 370).

Marat is not merely a privileged commentator but also at times a superman endowed with improbable advantages over others. We are told that he is even able to direct his dreams and remove unpleasant events from his unconscious (p. 208). The characterisation of others tends to be equally schematic, albeit in a reductive form. Vailland sometimes uses summary physiognomic stereotypes to encapsulate physical and moral traits. Thus Mathilde's facial deterioration hints at the frustrated passion and despair behind her treason, whereas Annie, as a more malleable object of desire, is 'a rare and precious success of nature' (p. 239). This reifying vision of others can be motivated within the text. Marat criticises himself for the 'racism' which arouses his immediate hostility at the sight of Frédéric's naked, fleshy body; the latter's over-enthusiastic tooth-brushing also reveals a 'hygiene psychosis' (pp. 12–13). The interplay of human relations within the underground struggle might well resemble a waking dream, where all Marat's desires are realised and the resistance of the real and the other is abolished, were it not for the solid anchoring of the novel in a documented vision of the occupation. The unstable, arbitrary identities adopted by characters (symbolised by pseudonyms that transform them into mythical or historical figures) derive both from oneiric wish fulfilment and the practical needs of clandestine action. Some choices lead to annihilation. While Marat is a chameleon who can mingle with the worlds of collaboration and trafficking as easily as resistance and who keeps 'several new identities ever ready' should he be found out (p. 389), the unfortunate Frédéric, equally inexperienced as a resister and a lover, had considered surrendering to the police or even joining the collaborationist LVF in order to 'undertake an irremediable commitment' (p. 176).[4]

Marat's voluntarism and egotism (shared with his creator) might well have made him a fascist or collaborator, as he implicitly acknowledges in remarking that 'revolt, if not integrated into class consciousness, can lead equally well to fascism as to communism' (p. 29). Yves Courrière also points out in his biography that Vailland was indeed briefly a 'partisan of Vichy's new order', of a government which 'is restoring order and tracking down all sorts of hooligans and dealers', as he himself put it. If he finally joined the resistance, the reasons were 'much more patriotic than political. With a pronounced taste for adventure'. Towards the end of his life, Vailland observed: 'I like war…Everything's allowed, you can escape reality' (quoted in Courrière, 1991: 251, 269, 294). This allows us to sum up, by way of conclusion, the utility of resistance and the resistance novel. Resistance is neither unproblematically 'real' nor a purely gratuitous game, in that its agents literally gamble with their lives and the destiny of their country. It is defined by an initial act of revolt, which overturns the rules of the established order and obliges its protagonists to sacrifice everything, including their personal identity, in a heroic (but possibly futile) quest for liberty (which is constantly postponed). No doubt the author of *Drôle de jeu* can be criticised for a degree of psychological and ideological over-simplification. Nevertheless, he succeeded in creating a more original fictional form for these paradoxes of liberty than most other novelists inspired by resistance, who tend to produce much narrower reconstructions (such as Vercors's allegory of passive resistance, largely detached from the material constraints of occupation; Kessel's work of Gaullist propaganda, moving and credible at times, but using quasi-anonymous figures and melodramatic action; or the second-hand pot-boilers churned out by innumerable post-war writers). Vailland used his personal experience to bear witness through fiction (thereby avoiding the pitfalls of facile identifications of invented and real characters, or of accusations of fabulation). His novel works both as historical documentary and fictional reflection on the joys and suffering of the combatant engaged in the struggle for collective liberation and individual conscience.

Pascal Jardin's Vichy idyll

Although Pascal Jardin shared Vailland's dandyistic scorn for bourgeois conventions and his awareness of the wretched conditions endured by less favoured social classes, the options of commitment to resistance, a left-wing political party or the production of novels documenting social and political abuses were completely alien to him. Jardin was a prolific writer (in his short career, he produced nearly one hundred film scripts, two plays, and six works of fictionalised autobiography), but two decades after his premature death from cancer in July 1980, he is remembered mainly for one book: *La Guerre à neuf ans* (1971). For eighteen crucial months, from 20 April 1942 to 30 October 1943, his father Jean Jardin (1904–76) was the *directeur de cabinet* of Pierre Laval, the prime minister who at this time had effectively supplanted Pétain as head of the Vichy government. Pascal Jardin was born on 14 May 1934 and in his ninth year found himself a juvenile but privileged witness of the inner workings of Marshal Pétain's puppet regime; hence the title of his book, which is a reflection on his own identity, his relationship with his father, and the political responsibilities and moral ambiguities of the *État français*.

La Guerre à neuf ans was the first volume of an autobiographical tetralogy, continued with *Guerre après guerre* (1973), *Le Nain jaune*

(1978), and *La Bête à bon Dieu* (1980). Death and loss, of people and places, remain central, obsessive themes in all four books, exemplified by the quest for the father (who died halfway through the cycle) and by the return to Vichy. Jardin himself died a few weeks after the publication of the final volume, after fighting leukaemia for several years. That said, his writing is far from being lugubriously morbid; he recaptures childlike ingenuousness and insight with a mischievous sense of fun and provocation. Typically, Jardin offers us revealing and unexpected snapshots of the famous as they cross the path of his juvenile protagonist. Thus in the days following Laval's notorious speech of 22 June 1942 expressing his wish for German victory, the Jardin household becomes a 'buzzing, crazy hive' (Jardin, 1989: 107). The narrator emerges from his refuge in a tent in the garden at midnight to discover his father and Jacques Bousquet (better known to us as René) discussing Laval's likely fate, absorbed in 'that passionate dream which is political madness'. While the Minister of Supply and Agriculture Jacques Leroy-Ladurie occupies Pascal's bedroom to bemoan the Germans' duplicity (he eventually resigned in September 1942 in protest at the forced labour law), Yvonne Printemps entertains the company in the salon with a song recital and acrobatics.

All Jardin's texts are disrupted narratives, which dissolve the rigid boundaries between fiction, biography and autobiography. They replace linear chronology with anecdotal snapshots and reminiscences which move in apparently random, staccato cycles between the present and a succession of different past times. In fact, they are shaped not by a predictable sequence of events but by the recurrence of certain key dates and by the interaction or substitution of the different generations of the Jardin family. Thus Jardin notes, at the end of *Guerre après guerre*: '1944. I will always return to this year, for as far as I'm concerned, it was the end of a world' (1995: 192). This remark indicates too how the private and public domains constantly overlap, since the world that ended was not just that of the Jardins. In *La Bête à bon Dieu*, the writer recalls that as a child he found his father a distant, albeit dominating figure: 'I never saw him, in any case never alone... Personal relations with this being were impossible for me' (Jardin, 1980: 103–4). He was partly brought up by his maternal grandparents, who were known Napoleonically as 'Monsieur Père' and 'Madame Mère'; subsequently, he realised that his own daughter Nathalie had achieved an intimacy with her grandfather, Jean Jardin, which again bypassed a generation.

Chapter 4 of *La Bête à bon Dieu* is entitled 'Who writes what and to whom?' Writing allows the author to assert his own identity, to resuscitate a lost childhood, and to mythify the departed father; how-ever, it is also a public act, especially in the form of autobiography, which exposes all those depicted to possibly unwanted scrutiny. The controversial historical setting – collaboration with the Nazis – evidently adds to the fascination and potential offensiveness of the subject matter. Jardin's preoccupations are in many respects those of an entire age. As he observes, Vichy in 1942 marked 'the beginning of the tearing asunder of a whole generation' (1995: 78). His books con-tributed to and helped define that collective neurosis about the occu-pation which the historian Henry Rousso subsequently diagnosed in *Le Syndrome de Vichy* as the phase of the syndrome which in the 1970s signalled the 'return of the repressed'.

Jean Jardin escaped the liberation purges of collaborators by exiling himself to Switzerland and retreating from the public arena (his master Laval was of course executed for treason in October 1945). The older Jardin's discreet silence about the occupation is as typical of the behav-iour of his generation as is his son's prolixity twenty-five years after; the former *directeur de cabinet* consistently refused to write his memoirs or to communicate information about his activities in Vichy and Berne. Pascal remarks that his father 'is not one of those men who bear witness, but one of those who act' (Jardin, 1995: 179). Although Jean Jardin had purportedly 'been steeped in the most important secret affairs of his time', under both Vichy and the Fourth Republic, this grey eminence left no traces; a trunk laden with incriminating docu-ments proved, when finally opened after his death, to contain only family ephemera. The secretiveness was quite intentional; his biog-rapher Pierre Assouline (1988) reminds us that Jardin senior had been an accomplished writer in his day, contributing to the right-wing polit-ical review *L'Ordre nouveau* and ghosting books for his superiors in the 1920s and 1930s.

While Jean Jardin's literary activities were deliberately short-lived or anonymous, his son's writing represents a different sort of triumph of the will, for he tells us on several occasions that as a chronic victim of dyslexia and maladjustment he was barely able to read or write until the age of fifteen, concealing his deficiency thanks to a prodigious memory. The reticent father did not welcome the public attention on his former career awakened by his son's books or the fact that he was eclipsed by Pascal's literary celebrity.[5] In the 1970s, however, Pascal Jardin's books coincided with and formed part of a literary and cultural fashion, the so-called 'mode rétro', that is, the re-examination of the occupation years by writers and cineastes whose experience of

the period was either purely second-hand or vicarious (through paren-
tal involvement, for example), or at best limited to the role of infantile
or adolescent observers of a world beyond their immediate control
and comprehension. Alan Morris (1992) observes that the somewhat
disparaging expression 'mode rétro' suggests that heresy soon becomes mere fashionable nostalgia. Since the mode has now lasted over
twenty-five years, it seems more of an obsession than a passing
fashion.

Pascal Jardin is a stylish and persuasive chronicler, although Henry
Rousso sees him as a somewhat frivolous author, arguing that the
memorialist turns Vichy into 'an amusement park full of delightful
encounters' and enjoys 'a bourgeois life barely troubled by events'
(1990: 150). I think this is a serious underestimation of the expressive
and moral range of *La Guerre à neuf ans* and its sequels. For all his
childhood privileges, the younger Jardin is an emotional orphan; moreover, the older, retrospective narrator constantly asserts the threat of
disgrace, deportation or destruction which hangs over so many of the
adult players in his tragi-comic drama. Morris embraces the personal
impact of the book more judiciously by calling it 'an urgent, compul-
sive filial exorcism' (1992: 126). Jardin's fondness for light-hearted
anecdotes and eccentric antics should not blind us to the personal
loss and desperation, intimately linked to the national humiliation of
defeat and collaboration, that he records throughout the cycle. In the
closing chapters of *La Bête à bon Dieu*, he notes bluntly that while he
'never recovered from the death of my father' (1980: 149), Jardin
senior never recovered from his elimination from public affairs: 'My
father was one of those men who saved many people, but who destroyed themselves by failing to grasp the truth of history. Men find it
easier to survive unhappy love affairs than losing power' (1980: 127).

One reviewer described Pascal Jardin's writing as 'Chateaubriand re-
written by Walt Disney' (Garcin, 1980: 52). We might gloss this back-
handed compliment to mean that Jardin combines romantic nostalgia
and a shrewd awareness of public affairs with the stylised simplifications of the cartoon; in other words, he unites the emotional depth of
literature with the sensual immediacy of the cinema in which he had
made his career. He does in fact offer guidelines for reading his works.
Significantly, we are told that the protagonist of the faltering novel
Toupie la rage is unable to invent stories, hates works of fiction and
finds Balzac an immense bore. The solution is to vary the proportion
of the ingredients: not to distil an insipid blend of fiction from
barely disguised personal experience, but to produce autobiography

enhanced by a zest of fiction. Jardin explains his urge to 'reject reality wherever possible in favour of organised dream. Gradually, my dreaming became a practical option, until finally I succeeded in becoming a complete spectator of my own life, a voyeur, an author' (1989: 55). Yet if the self and its world become other, however much they are reshaped, 'Nothing which I write about is invented' (p. 78).

Appropriately, Jardin was offered a half-share of the 'Grand prix du roman de l'Académie française' in 1978 for *Le Nain jaune*, as though the judges were uncertain how to categorise this 'legendary transfiguration' of the writer's father. Such generic quandaries were further complicated by the resurgence at this time of another of Laval's more poisonous underlings, the former Commissioner for Jewish Affairs, Darquier de Pellepoix, who emerged from his hiding place in Spain to offer an impenitent interview to *L'Express* on 28 October 1978. Jardin's golden legend thus coincided with a more noxious version of the Vichy story: Darquier was particularly keen to recall how his own rabid anti-Semitism had been fully shared by many influential figures in the regime. There were grumblings from the right-wing press that Jardin's half-prize was a belated chastisement for his father's ideologically incorrect role in the *État français*.

How, then, does Jardin recall the world of Vichy and its effect on father and son? Does he attribute blame or responsibility for the regime's moral and political failings? Jean Jardin himself categorised his son as a fantasist, who insolently used real people's names when his account was actually a provocative fabrication. No doubt to discover himself a premature subject of an exercise in literary exhumation was an unnerving experience; after his demise, Jean Jardin was subjected to an even more exaggerated process of comic mythification. He was the eponymous *Nain jaune* and *Bête à bon Dieu* (yellow dwarf and ladybird) of the last two books. These nicknames encapsulate the almost magical survival skills which Jean Jardin displayed not only in his professional life but also, according to his filial chronicler, in everyday existence: leaping through windows, physically matching bullies and rivals, despite his diminutive stature, outwitting and escaping the spies and assassins of the Gestapo.

Much of the appeal of *La Guerre à neuf ans* derives from the author's ability to link family rituals and personal obsessions to wider social and historical topics. Even the scatological references have a wider application. The debacle of 1940 was the reverse of Verdun. 'This time, there will not be one million five hundred thousand dead, but at what a price: forty million Frenchmen simultaneously shitting in their pants. My memory is filled with the shameful sound of colic' (1989: 49). As this example shows, Jardin approaches the business of defeat, occupation and collaboration with caustic cynicism. Nevertheless, Jardin's aim is to rehabilitate at least those servants of the regime with whom he had a personal connection. Colin Nettelbeck has noted the parallels that Jardin draws between his own and the nation's troubles, but maintains that the picture is highly tendentious, revealing in the writer a blinkered egoism verging on the pathological; this commentator thus concludes that 'Despite himself, Pascal Jardin himself appears as the emotionally crippled victim of the overweening paternalism that Jean Jardin shared with the Vichy regime' (in Hirschfeld and Marsh, 1989: 279).

In Jardin's defence, one can make the obvious point that autobiographers, especially those of childhood, are by definition egocentric, and that the child's perspective is inevitably partial. However, those determined to damn Vichy and collaboration will be undeterred by Jardin's anecdotal apologia and will find in certain factual distortions further reason to dismiss his chronicle. Yet, however objectionable one finds the implicit ideological stance, it would be perverse to ignore the writer's skilful evocation both of the child's private sensual and emotional universe and of the political universe of which he was a spectator. Ostensibly, of course, the adult narrator who adopts the child's perspective is an observer rather an analyst; hence his remark that 'My memory is that of a photographer, not a historian' (Jardin, 1989: 78). Consequently, an outline of the complexities of Vichy is attributed to his mother:

> In Paris, administrative power belongs to the Germans. In Vichy, you can meet Japanese, supporters of Pétain, supporters of Laval, and resisters who support de Gaulle, Giraud or the communists. You can also meet *miliciens*, Germans in mufti, Jews indistinguishable physically from other French people, and anti-Semites, the worst of whom are Romanians and who could easily be mistaken for Jews. (p. 80)

Most of the time, however, Jardin's comments on Vichy are obviously retrospective. The English translation of *La Guerre à neuf ans* is subtitled 'An Insider's View of the Pétain Regime', although the Marshal himself barely figures at all in the book and the child narrator is a dispossessed figure ('a being who possesses nothing: no car, no house, no love, no liberty'; Jardin, 1989: 56), whose uneasy neutrality invites comparisons with the occupied nation to which he belongs. While the mother's version of a fivefold power struggle between Pétain, Laval and the tripartite forces of resistance may suggest a knot of vipers, other metaphors are more neutral. Thus he sums up the political scene as 'a tissue culture swarming with future victims of firing squads, historians and Gaullist ministers' (p. 82). Vichy as police state dominated by collaborationist ultras imposed by the Nazis on the vacillating Pétain is not an image he proposes, but it should be recalled that he is describing the middle years of the regime in 1942–43, when some illusions remained to be shed.[6] Nevertheless, he is aware of the persecution of the Jews, and consequently anxious to stress his father's eagerness to assist these and other potential victims of the government he served. Jean Jardin paradoxically offers safe haven in his house to those officially perceived as enemies of the state. Thus in a striking scene the Jewish writer, resister and future historian of Vichy, Robert Aron, inadvertently blunders into the drawing room at Charmeil while the German consul Krug von Nidda is holding forth (the latter discreetly avoids enquiring after the former's identity).

Aron survived such adventures and in the books which he subsequently wrote about the occupation and liberation offered what Rousso calls a minimalist interpretation of Vichy. In other words, he minimised its excesses, while emphasising the dubious notion that Pétain did his best to protect the nation by providing a buffer between occupiers and occupied. Aron also denounced atrocities committed in the name of resistance, particularly as regards the summary executions of collaborators carried out at the liberation, the number of which he notoriously exaggerated. Jardin is happy to follow this historian's lead, since it suits his own purposes. Thus he writes at the end of *Guerre après guerre*: 'With liberty, the purging begins, and the peace will cause as many French deaths in six months as the war did in four years' (1995: 197). This statement is factually untrue, and also very characteristic of the propaganda put out by supporters of collaboration.

Should we conclude, then, by condemning Pascal Jardin for defending the indefensible or at least by censuring his wilful myopia? Only, perhaps, if we are thereby willing to condemn a whole generation who shared his perspective. Jardin's perception of the compromises of the period and its legacy of collective guilt and cowardly complicity seems to me at best to achieve genuine pathos and empathy, evoking the sorrow and the pity which some critics failed to find in Ophuls' film. Jardin recalls how his grandparents and their neighbours studiously ignored a nearby house used by the Gestapo for torturing prisoners: 'Insidiously, schoooled by adults, I learn silence and cowardice' (1989: 162). Such observations suggest that guilt and complicity can be acknowledged rather than denied or shifted on to others. In this respect, Jardin's presentation of Laval can serve as a final illustration.

While Marshal Pétain, the senescent head of the *État français*, has always benefited from a 'double legend, at once illustrious and criminal, as the hero of Verdun and the traitor of Vichy' (Garcin, 1995: 63), his prime minister Laval has long been perceived as an ignoble traitor, whose physical ugliness betokened his moral ignominy. Jardin prefers a more personal parallel to such stereotypes. In the first instance, the head of the Vichy government is equated with his Free French rival in London, since both gamble desperately on future events: 'For Laval was no more trusted by the Germans than de Gaulle was by the English. Reduced to the role of spectators unable to set events in motion, both of them could only await the outcome of the conflict' (1989: 86). And second, the analogy places them in the same position of vulnerable, impotent curiosity which characterises the child in the adult world. The writer recognises, however, that the politician has rather more opportunity to exercise choice. Once he had returned to power and made his notorious broadcast of 22 June 1942 declaring his desire for German victory, Laval had sealed his fate and made himself 'a man to be gunned down', as Jardin's father realised (hence no doubt his own departure from Vichy, as the archetypal survivor) (1989: 107, 163). De Gaulle (described by Jean Jardin as 'The only general in the world who won the war by deserting') duly achieved his own political legitimacy by sacrificing Laval to a firing squad (Jardin, 1980: 125).

Typically, within a few years of the liberation, Jean Jardin had found it convenient to become a Gaullist himself. And equally typically, his son offers a personal rather than ideological explanation of the vicarious sympathy which he shows in his writing for Laval. Though as a child he encountered him only once:

> his overhanging shadow dominated and conditioned more than half my life. Because my father was his collaborator, later on they spat in my face in public at school in Évreux. They beat me up too. I can still hear my schoolmates asking: 'How many Jews did you denounce?' (Jardin, 1989: 165).

Hence Pascal Jardin's rather startling conclusion: 'It was no easier for me to ignore my childhood than it was for a Jew to forget during the war that he was a Jew' (1989: 166). Later he adds that, having spent his early adult years as an unskilled labourer in the paper industry, he knows at first hand 'the concentration-camp existence that working-class life often still is in France' (p. 179).

In such ways does the writer strive to give a wider historical dimension to his personal suffering. The rhetoric is provocative and consequently memorable, even if it is unlikely to win the reader's sympathy: however unpleasant, an insult, beating or dull job are hardly equivalent to exclusion, arrest or mass extermination. One disenchanted reviewer pointed out that both Jardins, senior and junior, for all their insouciant humanism, actually display extremely objectionable political tendencies; what for Jean Jardin was a Maurrassian faith in the privileged position of the ruling class to which he had gained promotion, degenerates in his son into 'elitism bordering on snobbishness' (Poirot-Delpech, *Le Monde*, 29 September 1978, p. 15). The cultivation of politicians and captains of industry is replaced by somewhat toadying portraits of showbiz personalities like Alain Delon or Jean Gabin. No doubt Pascal Jardin was a flawed and partial chronicler; but he never claimed otherwise. The authenticity and impact of his childhood 'rêve organisé', his reconstruction of a ruined world and a broken idyll, remain undiminished.

René Barjavel's utopian science fiction

Although René Barjavel (1911–85) remains little known outside France, he was a prolific and popular novelist, journalist and screenwriter from the 1940s to the 1980s. His novels belong to the genre of utopian or dystopian science fiction and fantasy, with an ecological and philosophical spin. In the context of our discussion of writing inspired by the dilemmas of occupation and divided loyalties, we will concentrate on his first two novels, *Ravage* (1943; 1996b) and *Le Voyageur imprudent* (1944; 1996c). Both these works merit detailed attention: they shed a fascinating sidelight on the occupation of France; they are imaginative, innovative and compulsively readable as SF adventure stories, making an impressive contribution to this nascent genre in France; and they pursue in an original fashion the debate about utopias and technology raised in the late nineteenth century by thinkers such as Morris and Wells and developed in the mid-twentieth century by Aldous Huxley, Orwell and other more famous contemporaries of Barjavel. In both novels, the national catastrophe of defeat and occupation is the starting point.

It is worth recalling that the debacle was more than an embarrassing historical interlude which made France briefly part of Hitler's new Europe. Had the Third Reich survived, France was planned eventually to become a sort of national holiday camp, a tourists' utopia for victorious Teuton warriors; moreover, military defeat in 1940 also created a crisis of social and national identity whose repercussions have continued till the present day. From the defeat of the Third Republic, both novels move to posit ideal societies which might be considered better replacements, but treat them rather differently: *Ravage* operates on a spatial dimension and might be called 'Vichy pastoral', were it not too bloodthirsty; whereas *Le Voyageur imprudent* alternates between successive disasters and utopian (or pseudo-utopian) resolutions, using the devices of time travel, memory and the paradoxes which are generated by infringement of the temporal dimension.

One could in fact argue that *Ravage* and *Le Voyageur imprudent* do for the 1940s what H.G. Wells's *The Time Machine* does for the scientific and political issues of the 1890s: that is, they project a future from a world riven by totalitarian ideologies, industrialised warfare and mass extermination. Unsurprisingly, Barjavel's prognosis is pessimistic. The near future heralds the total collapse of (post-)industrial civilisation, to be followed by various utopias which no twentieth-century person would find tolerable. As Yves Ansel says, '1942 casts a shadow over 2052' (Barjavel, 1996b: 322). *Ravage* is divided into four unequal parts, whose titles sum up the action of the novel: 'Les temps nouveaux', 'La chute des villes', 'Le chemin des cendres', 'Le patriarche' (the new age, the fall of the cities, the way of ashes, the patriarch). The second part, which describes the collapse of civilisation in the year 2052 following the disappearance of electricity, occupies over half the text, whereas the last part, describing the twenty-second century utopia that arises from the ruins takes up only twenty pages. Barjavel's main interest is in building up and then destroying his twenty-first century technological dystopia, and in recounting the survivalist tactics of his hero François Deschamps through his journey from the ruins of Paris to south-east Provence (the author's birthplace), where a pre-industrial agricultural community survives and thrives under his direction.

At the beginning of *Ravage*, François is a brilliant but impoverished student of agricultural science, reluctantly living in Paris, along with his chaste childhood sweetheart Blanche Rouget, herself a student at the 'National school for women, offering physical, moral and intellectual training for mothers of the élite' (Barjavel, 1996b p. 44). (The novel is, incidentally, full of fascistic echoes of this sort; these might be seen as obeisance to the counter-revolutionary, elitist dogmas of Vichy's National Revolution or arguably as mild ridicule of such notions.) In any case, Blanche has been seduced from her future maternal goal by the media tycoon Jérôme Seita, who offers to promote her as an international pop star to be called Regina Vox, and who does his best to eliminate François by wrecking his career. Although the symbolism of names like Deschamps, Blanche and Regina Vox is generally transparent, on the other hand, Rouget means 'mullet' and Seita is an acronym for 'société nationale d'exploitation industrielle des tabacs et allumettes' (national tobacco and match company): such ambiguity indicates that Barjavel does not commit himself to a simple message. In the event, Regina Vox's debut performance is halted by the power cut that marks the disappearance of electricity (as well as the failure of mechanical weapons and products made from iron) and of the civilisation dependent on electricity; subsequently, water supplies fail, cities are destroyed by fires which rage uncontrollably, and their populations are wiped out by violence, starvation and contagious diseases. François rescues Blanche and Seita from the skyscraper where they are trapped. Without his technological resources and social prestige, Seita is an impotent figure and is rapidly killed off in a street brawl. On the other hand, François becomes a warrior leader of infinite resource and ruthlessness, leading Blanche and a band of survivors to Provence, where he founds a dynasty and lives to be 129.

As this account suggests, *Ravage* is inventive, comic and disturbing. The characters are largely schematic, partly allegorical, partly comic-book simplifications. The central figure, François, is more appealing in his initial guise as a sceptical misfit looking critically at twenty-first century civilisation than as the patriarchal superman which he eventually becomes, slaughtering those who oppose his will to survive and dominate. For the reader on the threshold of the twenty-first century, much of the novel's interest derives less from such dubious heroics than from its predictive success (or failure) about the world of 2052. Technological progress appears to have outstripped political and economic reforms. The French government rapidly perishes in the inferno, having been briefly satirised as it attempts to confront the catastrophe very much in the terms of the ideological quarrels of the Third Republic (capital versus labour, Catholics versus secularists, militarists versus defeatists: see pp. 114ff.). In fact, Barjavel shows little sustained interest in matters of either technology or governance, since his main focus is on the survival strategies of François and his group (who eventually form a clan based on kinship and land ownership of a pre-industrial or even protohistoric kind). This cursory treatment of political issues may be partly due to the constraints of censorship; more obviously it corresponds to Barjavel's preference for what could be called a pantheistic and ecological perspective. The community that survives the holocaust of industrial civilisation is a rougher version of William Morris's 'garden world'.

All these examples demonstrate how richly entertaining *Ravage* is, both as a speculative satire and as an adventure story. Nevertheless, when the author chooses to emphasise his message (rather than leave it implicit), his tone at times comes uncomfortably close to the mealy-mouthed propaganda of Vichy's 'National Revolution' (which can be summed up as the nostalgic urge to return to pseudo-feudal social hierarchies and supposedly natural activities).[7] Hence for example the dedication of the novel to 'the memory of my peasant grandfathers', and the rural, ancestral values which they embody. Unsurprisingly, the city is Babylon, while technology offers men unlimited scope for evil-doing. As in George Orwell's *1984*, other continents are ravaged by war. The South American emperor 'Noir Robinson', descendant of transported slaves, announces an all-out missile attack on the white races of North America (though probably annihilates his own people as well when the power fails). The loss of electricity works literally and allegorically to show the abject dependency of civilised man on technology, as well as the benefits for those who are able to escape this dependency and re-establish a more authentic rapport with nature. Culture which does not involve agriculture or breeding is seen as corrupting. The narrator describes with sarcastic or even sadistic relish the impotent panic of the crowds confronted with the failure of their machines: 'Everyday reality had disappeared, giving way to the absurd' (p. 89). Actually, it was their previous world that was absurd; according to François, whose perspective largely dominates the narrative, 'Nature is putting everything back in order' (p. 92). The consequence is that 'each individual would rediscover his place in a universe matching the sharpness of his senses, the length of his limbs, the strength of his muscles' (p. 92). A little earlier, François has offered a fuller analysis of the enticing perils of progress:

> Men have unleashed terrible forces which nature had carefully held in check. Men thought they could master such forces: this is what they called Progress. This was just progress rushing towards death. For a time men used these forces constructively, but one fine day, men being men, that is creatures in whom evil dominates good,

because their moral progress lags far behind the progress of their science, they turned science to destructive ends. (p. 83)

Barjavel (insofar as he espouses the sententious observations of his protagonist) thus aligns himself with the common anti-technological line of utopian thinkers from Morris to Huxley, with the pessimistic Wells of *The Time Machine* and *The Island of Dr Moreau* rather than with the more optimistic but imaginatively duller essayist of *A Modern Utopia*. There are however two problems in elaborating Barjavel's stance: one is whether we are meant to take the outcome of *Ravage* either seriously or literally, which only the most ingenuous reader is likely to do; the other is that François in practice rejects not only technological but also moral progress in favour of a more primal, minimalist survivalism, which seems a poor basis for any amelioration of human society. Thus we learn that 'He was determined to rid himself of all useless objects, of all the habits and scruples which events had made irrelevant' (p. 147). Eventually, after a century has passed, he becomes the ruler of a small community based on agriculture, barter and polygamy (he has one wife for every day of the week, including an ugly one to set an example of connubial good practice, these spouses successively producing 228 children). Bronze has replaced iron, and books have been destroyed as 'the very spirit of evil' (p. 294). The novel ends with François ordering the destruction of a steam engine and its inventor; the latter kills him, however, before being crushed by his machine. Mechanical progress, it seems, destroys those who support it or those who oppose it; at the same time it is unavoidable. While the politicians who appear earlier in *Ravage* are sanctimonious, impotent figures of fun (a view the modern reader might have of governments under Vichy as much as the Third Republic), François himself in his final incarnation as supreme leader is at best a caricatural patriarch. There is little doubt that the community which he has founded does match Vichy mythologising and has unpleasant fascistic qualities; yet Barjavel ultimately shows both the technological utopia of 2052 and its rustic replacement to be flawed and vulnerable. In the end, we are left without any positive model, as the title of the novel implies.

Le Voyageur imprudent is dedicated to Robert Denoël, the publisher who employed Barjavel as a production manager from 1935 to 1945 and launched his literary career. Denoël enthusiastically leapt on to the bandwagon of anti-Semitic collaborationism by launching a series with German backing on 'Les Juifs en France', as well as publishing collaborationist pamphlets by Céline and Rebatet. In December 1945, five months after personal charges against him for collaboration had been dropped, he was killed in a Paris street by an unknown assassin. (The prosecution of his surviving business associates finally led to their acquittal in April 1948; cf. Fouché, 1987: II, 202–5.) The *pétainiste* or fascistic undertones of *Ravage* are, however, no longer discernible in *Le Voyageur imprudent*, whose time-travelling heroes are scientific entrepreneurs motivated by personal curiosity and self-interest rather than ideology (very much in the fashion of Wells's protagonists in *The Time Machine* and *The First Men in the Moon*).

Le Voyageur imprudent was written during 1942 and 1943, the middle years of the occupation, which form the starting and closing points of the novel. The military misadventures of the hero Corporal Pierre Saint-Menoux (a mathematical researcher in civilian life) are paralleled by Barjavel's own experiences as a supply corps corporal in 1940. *Le Voyageur imprudent* combines a documentary account of the rigours of defeat and occupation with science-fiction adventure and moral fable. The opening sentence, 'Il faisait un froid de guerre' ('it was as cold as war'; Barjavel, 1996c: 7), replaces the consuming inferno of *Ravage* with an arctic hell; a soldier freezes to death in the latrines and his ears snap off when his corpse is removed. The destruction wrought on humanity by man-made and natural catastrophes combined thus remains a central theme. Like the protagonists of *Ravage*, Saint-Menoux is at first a wretched nomad amid the disasters of phoney war and debacle. But ten pages into the naturalistic description of his tribulations, he stumbles (literally) through a doorway into the world of the golden-bearded physicist and time-traveller Noël Essaillon (who is disabled after losing his feet in an accident) and his daughter Annette, 'belle comme une apparition' (p. 14). Thanks in part to Saint-Menoux's mathematical researches, Essaillon has 'manufactured a substance which allows me to make use of time as I want!' (p. 19). The substance is called 'noëlite' – surely a deliberate echo of the inventor Cavor's anti-gravitational material 'Cavorite' in *The First Men in the Moon*.[8] In practice, the crippled Essaillon prefers to travel vicariously through the adventures of the neophyte Saint-Menoux, whose voyages form the substance of the book. The titles of the three parts, 'L'apprentissage', 'Le voyage entomologique' and 'L'imprudence' (apprenticeship, the entomological voyage, imprudence), once again offer a programmatic indication of his development.

The conquest of time might well be seen as the ultimate utopian aspiration. Saint-Menoux is allowed to fast-forward through two disagreeable years of the occupation in order to reach 1942, thus experiencing a new version of 'la guerre-éclair' (p. 30), a mocking gallicisation of 'Blitzkrieg' (literally, lightning war). Negative elements rapidly intrude, however. While Saint-Menoux and Essaillon are ostensibly motivated by a philanthropic urge to benefit mankind, in reality they live in total isolation from society, while their intrusions into other times, past or future, are disturbing and disruptive. Moreover, the massive destructive power of 'noëlite' was demonstrated in an atrocious experiment carried out by the military at Essaillon's instigation; we soon discover that Essaillon's ethics are those of the irresponsible scientist driven by obsession (for example, pp. 49, 52, 55). His use of Saint-Menoux is due to fear of his invention, although it is also a convenient narrative device for initiating the reader and the protagonist simultaneously.

Barjavel's inventions and play with the paradoxical regulations of time travel are enticing and thought-provoking. For example, Essaillon and his daughter use time travel for practical convenience, supplying themselves with provisions acquired in the past and stored in chambers which contain a timeless, non-perishable present; or resuscitating their old nurse Philomène by bypassing the events which originally caused her death (despite her protests). Saint-Menoux's first venture leaves him trapped between the present and the future in the 'conditional' (a hint of the perils to come). Subsequently, he encounters himself in the near future (although why characters who travel to the near past do not experience the same duplication remains unclear). After a visit to 2052, the year of the disaster recounted in *Ravage*, he pursues mankind's ultimate destiny by reaching the year 100,000. Following Wells's time-traveller, he discovers that humans have evolved not merely into the bovine Eloi and predatory Morlocks but into a vast range of highly specialised sub-species capable of performing only one function (such as cowherd, warrior, miner, reproducer or even digester of food). These Bosch-like, unindividuated monstrosities perform 'a nightmarish dance' (p. 125) before the horrified traveller. Nonetheless, their mutation represents perfect adaptation. It seems that electricity did not actually disappear in 2052, but rather changed form, being replaced by 'mental energy', which has caused the loss of individuality and therefore allowed complete social harmony: the individual has become 'a cell in a perfect social body' (p. 130), and 'the law of the species is henceforth the same as the law of the city' (p. 164). The result is a utopia totally alien to twentieth-century man.[9]

After performing a gratuitous and repellent experiment on a breeding queen, Essaillon (whose morbid curiosity has driven him to accompany Saint-Menoux) is killed in another accident as they return to the present. Once again, his companions retrieve him by returning to the past to forestall his death. Finally, however, Essaillon and Philo-mène opt to return voluntarily to their original deaths and forego further transgression of the natural order. Following his mentor's demise, on the other hand, Saint-Menoux finds little scope in the present and decides in the concluding part of the novel to subsist by criminal forays into the past. These incursions, recounted with amusing gusto, have the effect of causing unpredictable consequences in the present (thus a character whose parents' wedding is disrupted by Saint-Menoux vanishes, since as a result he is no longer born). Mas-querading as 'le Diable vert', Saint-Menoux is captured during a bungled robbery he commits in 1890; the faithful Annette comes to his rescue. Increasingly obsessed by the possibility of changing human destiny, he travels to 1793, with the intention of assassinating Bona-parte. By accident, he kills his own ancestor instead; as a consequence, Saint-Menoux vanishes on his own wedding night, since he too has no longer been born. As a further consequence of Saint-Menoux's annihi-lation, Essaillon fails to make his crucial discovery allowing time travel and all memory of the imprudent traveller is lost.

For all its whimsical inventiveness, *Le Voyageur imprudent* probes social catastrophe and individual destiny with considerable subtlety and ingenuity. Like Kurt Vonnegut's hero Billy Pilgrim in *Slaughterhouse-Five* (1969), who survives not only the fire-bombing of Dresden in 1945 but also intergalactic kidnapping, Barjavel's protagon-ist discovers that travel along the fourth dimension offers the best means of escape from the horrors of three-dimensional reality. But the problem is that one often arrives in a place as bad as or worse than one's point of departure. The ideal may be to remain suspended out-side time or space, since even time-travellers are still confined within the tunnel of their own existence (Barjavel, 1996c: 28–9). Indeed this is the fate that ultimately befalls Saint-Menoux, as Barjavel points out in an ironic 'Post-Scriptum' added in 1958, since the character is trapped in an ontological paradox, caught between existence and non-existence (he kills his ancestor and therefore cancels out his own birth; but if he's not born, how can he kill his ancestor?) The demands of individual identity thus seem to render any utopian solution based on modification of the social or evolutionary order unattainable. Barjavel observed that writing was a safer and more fruitful form of time travel: 'The writer can give himself the illusion of such voyages back in time. When he pins down memories on paper, they seem to return to life, unlike butterflies' (1996a: 9). And again: 'Each moment is eternity. If the world around me is perfect, I have no reason to feel contingent. It is through memory that the moment becomes eternity' (1995: i–v). In other words, René Barjavel lives on as a beguiling fabulist, a destroyer of civilisations and creator of marvels, whose awareness of men's moral flaws renders the realisation of utopian visions impossible, even in the purely imaginary context of literary fictions.

Crime and traitors: Marcel Aymé and José Giovanni

Unlike the fantastic reveries and idylls of Jardin and Barjavel, Aymé and Giovanni set out in their fiction to document the sordid reality of occupation. While Vailland's resistance activists and aspiring revolutionaries retain an ambiguous faith in heroic endeavour and sacrifice for the collective good, the protagonists of Aymé's and Giovanni's novels tend to adopt more cynical and egotistical behaviour, as suffering, injustice and adjustment of values are shown to be the conditions which determine most people's choices. Criminality and betrayal become almost inevitable options in novels like Aymé's *Le Chemin des écoliers* (1946) and Giovanni's *Mon ami le traître* (1977; 1988), assuming that one defines crime broadly as any act which transgresses public order, legality and conventional morality. Although Aymé's pre-war novels such as *La Jument verte* (1933) gained him a reputation as a light-hearted satirist of peasant mores, his tone in the works written in reaction to the occupation became far more acerbic and his fictional landscape far bleaker. For all that *Le Chemin des écoliers* is in some ways an amusing chronicle of Parisian life under the occupation, the novel also presents petty infractions and the most horrific crimes, seen not as exceptions but rather as a prevailing norm. In the private domain, we have black-marketeering, prostitution, murder, torture and cannibalism; and in a wider dimension exceeding individual dramas, the war crimes and atrocities (torture, denunciations, deportations, massacres, genocide) committed by all the forces engaged in the conflict. This latter dimension is mainly evoked in a series of footnotes which complement the main narrative.

Aymé shows how war and occupation (which amounts to a state of virtual war) act as a catalyst for violent reactions and deviant behaviour which would remain repressed in peacetime. Thus the character Malinier volunteers for the collaborationist LVF and is executed for treason at the liberation; the retired Colonel de Monboquin dies of grief after being accused of intellectual collaboration; and the adolescent

brothers Antoine and Frédéric Michaud are drawn respectively into trafficking and resistance. Although Lolivier claims that his psychopathic
family's misdeeds leave him indifferent to patriotic matters, in fact the
collapse of this family (the son becomes a sadistic killer, the daughter a
whore) and the domestic warfare between its members correspond fairly
obviously to the crisis of values and social relations gripping the entire
nation after its capitulation to the murderous folly of Nazism.

The novel's title, *Le Chemin des écoliers* (deriving from the saying that
schoolboys take the longest route), clearly suggests that deviation and
generational conflict are to be important themes. Whereas mature
adults cling somewhat hypocritically to manifestly outdated humane
values, which have little relevance to the brutal mercenary reality of
occupation, younger characters adapt more spontaneously to the
demands of an existence transformed by defeat. The usual balance of
power is consequently modified: the sons of Michaud, Tiercelin and
Lolivier refuse to be led by their fathers, sometimes initiating new de-
partures. Antoine Michaud gives up black-market dealing just when his
father and his associate Lolivier finally decide to venture into this area;
while Antoine's sexual initiation by Yvette triggers the more burlesque
seduction of his father by Olga. While Tiercelin remains a cynical, selfish
profiteer, his son abandons trafficking in goods and women to look for
more patriotic commitments (though it matters little to him whether
they lead to resistance or collaboration). Tony Lolivier falls entirely out-
with conventional morality, with his grotesque indulgence in murder,
homosexual prostitution and cannibalism. No doubt his taste for torture
and abasement would make him an excellent auxiliary for the Gestapo;
the narrator however remains silent about his ultimate fate.

Criminality in this novel thus embraces the emotional, political and
economic spheres. Every character seems to encounter the possibility
of crime, either by having recourse to it or by becoming a victim of it.
For some, crime is a form of provisional liberation, while for others it
is a force destroying their autonomy. The most widespread illegal
activity in *Le Chemin des écoliers* is no doubt the black market. Its
ubiquitous presence reflects Aymé's faithful chronicling of daily life
under the occupation. Problems of obtaining supplies, the collapse of
normal social and economic relations, the disappearance of the state as
a lawful entity, time-serving and opportunism: these are all crucial,
connected factors. At the same time, trafficking and its networks easily
act as metaphors for the sexual and alimentary relationships which
unite or separate individuals, for the exchange of goods, love and cultural products on which collective existence is based. Although the

author is more interested in the comic and psychological possibilities of the black market than in its more technical aspects, the veracity of his portrait is confirmed by the historians of the period. For example, juvenile delinquency tripled during the early years of the occupation. Later on, pupils at the *lycée* Condorcet took advantage of the Americans' arrival to take up dealing in chewing gum (see Beevor and Cooper, 1995, and Halls, 1981, for further details). A celebrated comic play by the former English teacher Roger-Ferdinand (1944), *Les J3 ou la nouvelle école*, was performed in September 1943, on the subject of schoolboys enterprisingly practising black-marketeering. Its immediate success (like that of satirical cabaret singers such as Georgius who made dealing and bartering a stock theme in their performances) shows that, far from being a taboo, the black market was always an easy target for licensed satirists who celebrated the ingenuity of dealers without paying much attention to the moral ambiguities and economic connivance implied by their activities. Despite its illegality, the black market was indeed seen as a necessity by most citizens. The extent of the phenomenon is indicated by the growing number of convictions in lower courts for offences related to rationing and supplies (at least 80,000 in 1942 and 1943, though in most cases only fines were imposed: see Aubusson de Cavarlay, 1993). The law of 15 March 1942 defining the black market sought mainly to deter gross profiteering, even excluding 'personal or family needs' (Amouroux, 1982: 144).

In *Le Chemin des écoliers*, Marcel Aymé certainly goes beyond the boulevard frivolities of *Les J3*, even if he repeats the theme of the relative independence of adolescents from parents and teachers themselves inhibited by outmoded scruples. The father Pierre Michaud, who erroneously considers himself to be the uncontested head of his clan, is forced to endure a ridiculous and humiliating apprenticeship engineered by his children, instructing him in the new political, financial and sexual realities. The black market is a key example. At the beginning of the novel, Michaud refuses naively to be associated with it, either professionally, at the property management company he directs, or in his private domestic arrangements. But he insists in vain that 'this management company will never be an agency for the black market' (Aymé, 1972a: 24), for its position as an intermediary between owners, tenants and suppliers places it of necessity in the chain of supply and demand created by the shortage of goods and exploited by clandestine dealing, as his more pragmatic partner Lolivier observes. Furthermore, Michaud happily consumes the butter and chocolate provided by Antoine without enquiring further about the implausible exchange mentioned by his son to justify this bounty. Antoine, on the other hand, is calmly earning 30,000 francs a month on the black market and thriving on the influence brought by his position in a network which he entered thanks more to the friendship of Paul Tiercelin than to any real talent as a trafficker. Eventually Antoine donates his profits from a deal involving the sale of coffins to his parents (the staggering sum of 750,000 francs) and returns to his life as a studious schoolboy, while Michaud senior abandons his scruples and takes up dealing in turn.

Various justifications of the black market are inserted in the novel as characters' trajectories change direction. Michaud's wife observes that 'you really have to accept the living conditions of your age', although Michaud retorts that 'with that argument, theft pure and simple and even crime might be called normal living conditions' (pp. 231–2). Apart from its immorality, the black market debases the value of objects and work, insofar as the enormous sums of money involved have little intrinsic relation to the value of the commodities being supplied, still less with the work undertaken by the dealers. However, the material scarcities confronting the family no longer allow them to govern 'their behaviour according to sentimental reasons or a certain idea of humanity which was only likely to come about in the future' (p. 232). Michaud eventually accepts Lolivier's more cynical opinion that money 'which you put in your own pocket is money taken off someone else to stop them abusing and humiliating you' (p. 247). The last footnote (on p. 252) describes the Michauds' future prosperity, as they abandon disinterested idealism for bourgeois comfort (anticipating the embittered conclusion of the disgraced resistance hero at the end of Jean Dutourd's satirical novel *Au bon beurre*, which shows how pious virtue is always outwitted by unscrupulous commercialism: 'My son will be a grocer'; 1989: 376).

The black market thus represents a semi-respectable form of illegality, a short-cut giving access to material liberty without the need to become an out-and-out criminal. Ultimately, the black market only harms those who remain excluded from such new economic circuits. Like the Michauds, M. Coutelier, a retired primary-school inspector, deprived of his former authority as a pedagogue and official, and obliged to take on humiliating tasks in order to support his grandchildren, is nonetheless ready to defend dealing:

> In his eyes, the black market was a phenomenon governed by the law of supply and demand, almost a heroic survival of the liberal

economy blocking fascist oppression, and its illegality was not a matter for serious objection at a time when most restrictions bore the mark of the occupying authorities. (Aymé, 1972a: 41)

To reject the laws of the occupier is therefore to express one's individuality and independence. It is interesting to note that historians' interpretations of this justification vary noticeably. Some do accredit Coutelier's thesis, however ingenuous it may seem. R. Sédillot (1985) goes so far as to claim that the black market was 'a form of resistance' (in that dealers were precisely subverting the economic controls imposed by the occupation authorities). Yet for most commentators, it was really nearer collaboration. The phenomenon of wholesale purchasing bureaux analysed by Henri Amouroux (1982) and Jacques Delarue (1968) shows that the clandestine economy was frequently manipulated by profiteers working for the Germans. Otto Abetz, the German ambassador in Paris, saw in such large-scale German trafficking (to be distinguished from smaller-scale local dealing between French people) a legitimate revenge for the economic oppression exercised by France over Germany after the Treaty of Versailles.

In mocking Michaud, Aymé's novel also derides some of the basic concepts of *pétainisme* (as Müller, 1993, has observed), summed up by the slogan borrowed from the pre-war far right, 'travail, famille, patrie'. The black market devalues honest work, the family is divided by conflicts among its members, and patriotism is overthrown by universal egotism. The few patriots who attempt to counter such abuses, by committing themselves for or against Vichy and the Germans, usually make matters worse; far from reducing the pernicious effects of war, they exacerbate them at the cost of pointless personal sacrifice. Hence the provocative equivalence between collaborationism and resistance established by Paul Tiercelin's hesitation about whether to join the LVF or the maquis (Aymé, 1972a: 194). Both activities are equally illegal (the choice is between treason and terrorism), and neither more evidently useful than the gangsterism from which he wishes to escape. In another similar case, Malinier's perverse sense of patriotism leads him to abandon his family obligations and to join the LVF. By such examples, the author emphasises the futility and criminality of both resistance and collaboration, the dangers of unthinking commitments, although he never offers a deeper analysis of the political positions underlying his equation of apparently opposed ideological choices. In fact, Aymé criticises resistance by removing it from his books about the occupation, showing resistance to be at best a marginal phenomenon taken over by a few braggarts. On the other hand, he does not seek to defend collaborationism, even if he refuses to condemn it automatically. A character like Malinier (or the fascist collaborator Maxime Loin in the later novel *Uranus*) is sympathetic only in his sincerity; he is a man for whom 'the misfortunes of France were always present' (p. 97). Such patriotic awareness does not however justify his right-wing authoritarianism and absurd logic, which turn him into a rabid anti-Semite and fervent admirer of Nazi discipline, although Nazi imperialism is the main cause of his misfortunes (and the objects of his hatred, such as cubist painters and Racine, have little obvious connection with his country's predicament). It is never explained why joining the LVF to fight on the eastern front will do anything to remedy the ills of France. A laconic footnote informs us that at the liberation, Malinier is taken prisoner, tortured in a French gaol and sentenced to death by a court infuriated by his protestations of patriotism (p. 177).

In other words, Aymé does not conceal the stupidity and futility of collaborators like Malinier, even if he does not share the opinion of jurors who dismiss him as a traitorous criminal. The author eschews such simplistic moralising and notes its violent and unjust consequences. Malinier's ideological adversary, the retired school inspector Coutelier, is not spared either. The latter's outdated and rigid views about humanism and French civilisation make him equally ridiculous. Malinier promises Coutelier that he intends to restore to him 'liberty which he no longer merits' (p. 176), by ridding the country of its Jewish and communist vermin (in fact, Coutelier's Jewish son-in-law has already been interned in Drancy). But events justify neither of these antagonists. While the liberty proclaimed by Malinier is purely illusory, Coutelier betrays his own patriotic and pedagogic ideals by selling ready-made essays to schoolboys (including one on 'the idea of the nation').

The indifference of younger characters towards such debates at least prevents them from showing the absurd contradictions of their elders. Antoine Michaud and Paul Tiercelin should be distinguished from all the other characters, in that they are not encumbered with the tedious illusions of older people and nevertheless retain a degree of honesty in their dealings with others. Other members of the younger generation, however, enjoy very little autonomy. Thus circumstances drive Yvette towards high-class prostitution and horizontal collaboration, while Tony Lolivier is an even more extreme case. His 'degenerate face' (p. 72), inherited from his vicious, idle mother, his schooling in crime, as he graduates from prostitution and theft to torturing animals and homicide, mark him as someone whose behaviour is driven by bestial appetites, like a figure from a novel by Zola. This character is an aberration in Aymé's imaginary universe, intended to show the true monstrosity of the age. The occupation creates a society which fractures into isolated units of selfishness or misery, where solidarity and responsibility become increasingly rare. By dissuading Colonel de Monboquin from attending a lecture at the *Institut allemand*, Michaud attempts to give weight to such actions, on the grounds that a notable like the Colonel is endowed with 'a certain propaganda value, which will act in favour of the Nazi cause' if he attends. (This argument recalls the criticisms directed at Aymé himself after the occupation for publishing articles and stories in collaborationist journals like *Je suis partout* and *La Gerbe*. Aymé's texts were studiously neutral and humane in tone, but the context in which they appeared was fervently pro-Nazi.) Though he manages to convince Monboquin (who actually dies of grief after being humiliated in this argument), Michaud eventually rejects his appeal to patriotic duty as fatuous and decides that to define liberty and responsibility, 'one would do better to stick with an intuitive feeling for things' (pp. 57–8).

Liberty in *Le Chemin des écoliers* proves to be at worst just managing to survive; at best it is a provisional space or precarious sanctuary from which each individual risks expulsion, according to his or her temperament and choice of commitment, or merely as determined by accident and circumstances. Everyone is a potential criminal (cheat, dealer, traitor or killer), if not a victim of other people's criminal intentions. Thus the Polish Jewess Mme Lina Lebon is an exile virtually imprisoned in her apartment and abused by her own kind ('in the Jewish milieu of Paris', she is 'more displaced than among Christians', p. 62). Moreover, she is aware of the 'business of extermination' launched by the Germans in Poland and reminds Michaud (who typically refuses to believe in the reality of genocide) that hatred and vengeance are the guiding forces in existence. She also despises assimilated French Jews who think themselves invulnerable and turn their backs on their coreligionists from the east. Before seeking refuge in Algeria, Lina Lebon offers a harsh judgement on the existence endured by French citizens during the occupation: 'Here, you are sad dogs who've just stolen a thing off their masters' (p. 244). The twenty footnotes inserted throughout the different chapters of the novel offer an even bleaker vision of the upheavals caused by occupation, since they demonstrate how violence and chance combine to destroy lives in an instant. Although a few individuals escape catastrophe, most of these notes present atrocious crimes showing human nature at its most vile (Aymé apparently insisted that the incidents cited were based on fact: see Lécureur, 1985: 144). Twelve out of twenty notes deal with atrocities directly linked to the occupation and liberation, committed by both French and Germans (murders, cannibalism, delation, rapes, deportations, torture, executions), whereas only four provide extra information about the main characters. The arbitrariness of most of these footnotes thus opens a wider perspective which emphasises the disorder and violence that define the period. Only at the very end of the novel does Aymé gesture briefly towards a less grim future by showing us Antoine and Chou taking refuge at the circus and offering a fragile rampart against the 'inexhaustible reserves of cruelty and sadism' which Aymé observed in everyone (Aymé, 1946).

José Giovanni's novel *Mon ami le traître* (1977; 1988) is written in the laconic style of a hard-boiled thriller and offers an even bleaker and more cynical account of the betrayals and double-dealing necessitated by occupation and its aftermath, unredeemed by Aymé's fondness for comic touches and ability to treat rather unappealing characters with sympathetic comprehension. But Giovanni also provides a sardonic commentary on the historical circumstances which determine his characters' fate. Thus chapter 8 begins with the following observation:

> Within every Frenchman there is a sleeping gendarme. And the Liberation had awoken those gendarmes.
> Schools, town halls, village halls were turned into concentration camps. As Marcel Aymé wrote later: '...In 1944 I looked like a collaborator...' During the preceding years it had not been good either to have a nose that was too long or slightly hooked. (p. 97)

The parallel implied here between pursuing suspected collaborators and Jews on the basis of physiognomic prejudice alerts us to Giovanni's sceptical, relativistic attitude towards the operation of justice and its purifying mission. In fact, Giovanni's hero, or anti-hero, is a former gangster and Gestapo agent, Georges Galtieri, who is taken on as an informer against his former associates by the head of an intelligence agency, Major Adrien Rove. Rove hopes that Galtieri's contacts may lead him to a German master spy, one Dr Goetz, who was behind the disappearance of the Major's wife on a resistance mission. Together they forestall a plan by German agents to blow up the Paris metro, a devastating act of sabotage timed to coincide with the German counter-attack in the Ardennes in the winter of 1944. But for all his skill and courage as a double agent, Galtieri remains a wanted man. One incident in particular anticipates his own fate and shows how commitment to betrayal ultimately destroys the betrayer. While briefly detained by another branch of the French security service, he recognises that a bearded captain posing as a maquis veteran and interrogating alleged collaborators is in fact a former Milice leader responsible for instigating a massacre of civilians in the Luberon in April 1944 (at which Galtieri and his brother François, a malevolent hunchback and sadistic torturer, were present). The captain is tricked into shaving off his beard and returning to the scene of his crimes; identified by the surviving villagers, he is arrested and later executed.

This incident leads the narrator to reflect that:

> The French dirty washing needed a lot of rinsing. As the water would never flow clearly any more, you might wonder whether it had been really beneficial for the country to take on this washing. (p. 137)

As for the security services in charge of the purification, you might also ask 'who would check those who were supposed to check others, since traitors were sneaking in everywhere' (p. 138). In other words, the purges are driven by the same sort of opportunism that governed the behaviour of those in authority under the occupation. Authority itself is by definition repressive and wielded unscrupulously; those who enjoy power may suddenly find themselves victims in turn, as changing circumstances reveal the fragility of their influence. Georges Galtieri himself is presented as a victim of circumstances, who joined the Gestapo to escape a prison sentence and who did not share his malformed brother's delight in inflicting suffering (this latter character was a 'whipping boy who had done a lot of harm in order to try to exist more fully' (p. 15) and who commits suicide when he sees he is beyond redemption). Georges, on the other hand, is clearly redeemable (both through channelling his talents as a man of violence into more patriotic acts and through love for Jacqueline and friendship with Adrien). But society, or rather the sinister elites which impose their authority on everyone else, prefers expediency to redemption. Having accomplished several dangerous missions, Georges is finally ensnared into a shoot-out with rival agents from the DST (French counter-intelligence) and tried for treason before the court of justice in Marseille. Major Rove having been ordered to deny all knowledge of him, Galtieri is duly convicted under article seventy-five and executed (Rove's belated attempt to vindicate Georges is easily blocked by his merciless superiors).

That Galtieri proves expendable is hardly surprising, given the narrator's disillusioned (and historically valid) reflections about power and loyalty. Thus the magistrate investigating Galtieri's case is called Lost; inappropriately for an English reader, since 'He had perhaps sent resisters to firing squads, but it was one of the privileges of the police and the magistracy to stay in place through different regimes' (p. 181) (this point was often made by victims of judicial repression, as René Hardy's case reminds us). The fact that Georges had previously received a ten-year sentence for beating with an iron bar a prosecutor who vilified his deformed brother does not endear him to the court, which consists of three professional judges and a prosecuting lawyer acting without a jury, although the reader may interpret such outlaw's revenge on a conceited and dishonest judicial office-holder as a type of rough justice no worse than that meted out by the state. Major Rove also discovers that his wife (a genuine resistance agent) has been tortured, liquidated and her body dumped in a lake; the mysterious Dr Goetz, who was behind her disappearance, escapes unscathed. However, even the more powerful can fall victim to violent retribution. Rove's retired boss is a sinister figure known as 'L'Inhumain': 'It was said of L'Inhumain that he had as many wrinkles on his face as dead men on his conscience. And you couldn't count his wrinkles' (p. 46). He lives in isolation, guarded by a pack of dogs ('No human being could match up to their unconditional fidelity', p. 190). In the penultimate chapter, however, Adrien discovers that his former mentor and his faithful hounds have been murdered by unknown assassins; at which point, the Major decides that his loyalty to Georges and Jacqueline counts for more than obedience to a service that cannot defend its own.

Giovanni's writing shows the strengths and weaknesses of the thriller genre, where dramatic immediacy, violent action, sardonic humour and punchy dialogue tend to degenerate into formulaic plotting, stereotyped characterisation and tritely predictable cynicism. Despite the two-dimensional nature of his characters, his narrative offers a historically persuasive commentary on abuses of power and double-dealing at the liberation. Like Aymé, he uses paratextual devices to authenticate his narrative, telling us in a preliminary note that his story is based on a death-row confession, using a footnote (p. 53) to point out he has used a pseudonym to refer to a real person, or inserting references to historical characters like Bonny and Lafont (whose parties combined 'Champagne, caviar and treason', p. 54). But in fact it is Giovanni's own biography that gives him most authority as a witness to the murky underworld of gangsters and double agents. The blurb to the Folio edition of *Mon ami le traître* notes coyly that having been born in 1923, in the course of the occupation he experienced 'the maquis, prison, escapes, violence' (p. 7). Giovanni's memoirs, *Mes grandes gueules* (2002), recount his transition from jailbird to writer and film director, or to becoming a 'tragédien de la truanderie' (tragedian of gangsterdom; Giovanni, 2002: 515).

Giovanni argues that the theme of the film version of *Mon ami le traître*, which he directed in 1987, is 'the possibility, even the right, for a human being, to change, to evolve from good to evil' (p. 531). The problem is that Georges Galtieri consistently remains a brutal man of violence and that the agency of the French state to which he offers his services seems almost as evil as the Gestapo. Giovanni's account of how he reconstructed his own life offers a much more persuasive model of redemption, even if he remains disappointingly reticent about the crimes that earned him a death sentence after the liberation. He claims that in September 1944, he was engaged by *commissaire* Antonini, head of the *Renseignements généraux* in Nantes, to infiltrate the German pocket of Saint-Nazaire as a resistance spy. After being arrested and escaping from detention in La Baule, he returned to Paris and joined his brother in Pigalle. This was a move from bad to worse, for his brother was shot dead by a gangster and José spent forty weeks in chains on death row, until his father persuaded President Auriol to commute his sentence to life imprisonment. He was finally released from prison after eleven years in December 1956. With the encouragement of his lawyer Stephen Hecquet and the support of the writers Roger Nimier and Albert Camus at Gallimard, he wrote three thrillers in the ten months after his release and was signed up for Marcel Duhamel's celebrated collection, the *Série noire*.

Like the protagonists of the previous chapter, Giovanni thus sought salvation through writing, with considerably more success. To conclude this discussion, it is worth noting that authors like Barjavel and Giovanni who might be perceived somewhat dismissively as 'genre writers', in that they espouse popular forms like science fiction and the thriller, have no difficulty in linking entertainment with more serious reflections on the historical context supporting their fiction. (The subject matter of *Mon ami le traître* invites comparison, which space does not allow us, with more obviously literary writers like Patrick Modiano, whose novel about a double agent, *La Ronde de nuit*

(1969; 1991), itself duplicates themes from Roger Nimier's *Les Épées* (1948; 1967).) All the writers considered in this chapter subscribe to a realist imperative, in the sense that their imagined world is patently intended to inform the reader about the socio-historical reality of occupied France, however varied their ideological stance or textual inventions may be. Apart from the credibility gained from having been first-hand witnesses, they share such authenticating traits as an eye for concrete and telling details, a fondness for clearly delineated characters who engage in actions which have objectively recognisable consequences, and a sense of moral rightness (which partly explains their sensitivity to the gross injustices perpetrated during and after occupation). As Vailland himself implied in his sceptical comments on the 'new novel', more experimental forms of fiction are rarely so clearly underwritten by the urge to comment on history. From fiction, we now turn to an equally popular form of cultural representation: films.

6
Films

The illusory immediacy created by motion pictures is so familiar and so beguiling that we tend to forget that our knowledge and comprehension of major historical events like the Second World War have been shaped far more by the mediated images of cinema and television than by personal experience or historical study. The seductive distortions of film are absorbed so painlessly that it requires a conscious effort to recognise them as glorious simplifications of real events and people; and even if one is well aware that Field Marshal Rommel or General Patton bore only passing resemblance to James Mason and George C. Scott, in practice the fictional version of heroic leaders embodied by such movie stars remains indelibly printed on our minds and supplants the much hazier notions we have of the historical figures themselves. Film feeds on history and reconstructs it, shaping and reinterpreting the facts of history for the purposes of fictionalised entertainment, mythification of national obsessions or, occasionally, more disinterested documentary enquiry. But even accounts which strive for a degree of objectivity are filtered through the imagination of producers, directors and screenwriters, whose perceptions are in turn affected by the wider attitudes and preconceptions of their age.

Thus whereas collaboration and resistance during the German occupation of France from 1940 to 1944 are undeniable facts which belong to a historical past, the way in which they are represented and judged is determined equally by the circumstances of the person observing them. Hence the observation offered by the film historians Andrault and Bertin-Maghit that 'the historical film is more informative about the period of its production...than about the history which it supposedly reconstructs' (1982: 73). Historical films in effect offer a parallel commentary on a past age as seen through their own. Evidently, we need to evaluate the degree of mediation or distortion involved, rather than interpret them as unproblematic reconstructions. Nevertheless, ethical and ideological criteria such as veracity and authenticity remain important (by which one means making judgements about the film-makers' intentions, credibility, reliability as witnesses), apart from more formal aesthetic aspects (where recourse to stereotyped conventions and myth-making may be the most typical pattern of films that aspire to be no more than entertaining spectacles).

For sixty years, film makers have drawn on the Second World War and in France more specifically on the occupation. Unsurprisingly, films made in France about the occupation have evolved in stages which correspond to wider shifts among producers, audiences and the political establishment in the perception and historiography of the occupation. Generalising widely, one can identify four overlapping phases in the evolution of French cinema, from the time of the occupation to the present: the allegorical, the heroic, the nostalgic and the satiric. Films made during the occupation rarely if ever were able to refer directly to the events of the war and therefore the more memorable movies that have survived invite interpretation on a symbolic rather than purely literal level; on the other hand, films made in the aftermath of the liberation tended unequivocally to glorify the resistance and suggest its universality. By the 1950s, a less reverential attitude was permissible, with treatment of such taboo subjects as the horrors of deportation or of the widespread acceptance of black-marketeering. On the whole, however, the cinema offered a relatively restrained view of the occupation until the 1970s, due in large part to the material conditions of production, censorship and distribution, which imposed much greater constraints on films than books. Thus while collaborators and their sympathisers were able to publish self-justifying memoirs from the 1940s, films which suggested that collaboration was a comprehensible and widespread phenomenon appeared only after the disappearance of de Gaulle in 1970. Not untypically, Marcel Aymé's caustic novel *Uranus* about the excesses and hypocrisies of the liberation was published in 1948 without creating a great stir, whereas a film version appeared only in 1990, and even then Claude Berri's adaptation toned down much of the novel's acerbic black comedy in favour of a gentler exercise in nostalgic reconstruction. As a consequence, few French films have offered a radical reinterpretation of the occupation; those that have done so have invariably stirred up great controversy.

Compared with the immense output from the USA or even the UK, the number of French films dealing with World War Two may seem relatively small. Roger Manvell (1974), for instance, indexes over 900 British and American films related to the war produced in the thirty-five years between 1939 and 1974 (that is, twenty-six films a year). On the other hand, according to Andrault and Bertin-Maghit (1982), 107 films dealing with some aspect of the war and occupation were produced in France between 1944 and 1969 and another 64 films came out in the following decade. While the cinema during the occupation has been studied in considerable detail by a large number of historians, rather curiously the post-war period has attracted far less attention. The only full-length book to deal with the period 1944 to 1969 in detail is Sylvie Lindeperg's *Les Écrans de l'ombre* (1997), which lists some 132 items in the filmography.[1] (The increased number of films is explained by her use of a wider definition of relevant subject matter.) Henry Rousso's celebrated study *Le Syndrome de Vichy* (1990) lists a further 98 feature and documentary films for the period from 1970 to 1989, which gives a total of 230 films produced altogether during the forty-five years between 1944 and 1989. This average of five films a year has probably been matched by similar numbers for production over the last decade. Even a long book cannot really encompass such a large corpus of material; a shorter discussion can only offer a meaningful analysis by focusing on a small selection of films, chosen because they exemplify the most interesting controversies in the battleground of historical representation. As far as the discussion here is concerned, we will concentrate firstly on the representation of French society produced during the occupation itself, and then examine in the post-liberation years the glorification and debunking of the resistance and in contrast the evolution away from crude stereotypes of collaboration.

The occupation has been perceived somewhat paradoxically as a 'golden age' of French cinema, insofar as the Germans allowed commercial interests to predominate over propaganda by promoting a successful, high-quality French film industry. The economic chaos that had led to the bankruptcy of both Pathé and Gaumont in the 1930s was replaced by tighter controls over production and distribution, the Vichy government establishing a corporatist regulatory body, the Comité d'organisation de l'industrie cinématographique (COIC), for the unoccupied zone. Cinema audiences increased by 30 per cent between 1938 and 1943 and box-office takings doubled (for more details, see F. Garçon in Rioux, 1990: 308–9). However, the production costs of films more than doubled during the early 1940s and there was an overall deficit in production of 500 million francs. The eventual banning of British, American and pre-war French films greatly benefited those producers and directors who were able to have their films made and shown, as did the exclusion of Jews from any role in the cinema industry (the fascist journalist Rebatet claimed that 80 per cent of producers in 1938 were Jews; in fact, about 9000 Jews lost their jobs out of the 60,000 people employed). Some 400 short documentaries (a few of which were overt propaganda for the Nazi cause) and 220 feature films were made between 1941 and 1944;[2] although these figures represent less than half the annual average production before 1939, the lack of competition for distribution greatly benefited the 82 directors of *longs métrages*, some of whom effectively launched their careers during the occupation. A striking example is Henri-Georges Clouzot.

Clouzot, *Le Corbeau* and Continental

Henri-Georges Clouzot (1907–77) directed ten feature films, from *L'Assassin habite au 21* (1942) and *Le Corbeau* (1943) to *La Prisonnière* (1968). Despite this relatively modest corpus, he is recognised as combining a distinctive personal style (due in large part to a blend of technical skill and sardonic pessimism) with popular appeal. His best films frequently add an unexpected and memorable twist to genres which at first sight look like superficial entertainments: for instance, *Le Salaire de la peur* (1952) turns an adventure story into an agonising odyssey, while *Les Diaboliques* (1954) and *La Vérité* (1960) subvert the normal plot and resolution of the thriller and the courtroom drama. Commercial success allowed him to use the major stars and actors of the day, from Pierre Fresnay, Paul Meurisse, Charles Vanel and Yves Montand, to Simone Signoret and Brigitte Bardot. When *Le Corbeau* was released in Paris on 28 September 1943 at the Normandie cinema, it was seen by some 240,000 people in the first two months of its showing.[3]

It is unnecessary to insist at greater length on the solidity of Clouzot's reputation, even if he is not among the handful of French directors who are easily identified by film buffs outside France. *Le Corbeau* and other major films such as *Les Diaboliques* or the documentary *Le Mystère Picasso* were shown regularly on French television throughout the 1990s, while in 1997 the Parisian cinema Le Champo had a retrospective of seven Clouzot films. That said, *Le Corbeau* has not had an airing on British television or in a UK cinema for a very long time; this is a great pity, since it is the director's most notorious film and takes us to the heart of how French cinema dealt with the social and moral crisis of occupation. *Le Corbeau* demands further investigation for three main reasons: firstly, because it was made during the occupation for the German production company based in Paris and known as La Continental; secondly, because despite its popularity with audiences, it was subsequently denounced as anti-French propaganda by the resistance organ *L'Écran français* in 1944 and banned after the liberation; and finally, because in both its subject and form it is a controversial and compelling film whose caustic message about the failure of authority and justice probably encapsulates the bleaker aspects of the moral climate of the occupation better than any other film of its period.

The film is essentially a satirical and allegorical melodrama which sets out to expose hypocrisy and double standards in a provincial community seen as emblematic of French society in the mid-twentieth century. Its view of human behaviour is tragi-comic; its characters are memorably embodied by the actors, while tending towards the schematic and overstated. (One should note in passing that the exigencies or limitations of feature films which attempt to offer a social panorama within ninety minutes invariably demand a certain curtailing of characters, a need for rapid positioning to reveal behaviour and establish relationships which tend to seem elliptical and over-determined if subjected to undue analysis.) The action takes place in Saint-Robin, 'A small town, here or elsewhere', apparently in the present. The ambulance which removes Laura at the end is from the *Département de Seine-et-Oise* (that is, the outskirts of Paris); the exterior scenes were in fact filmed in Montfort-l'Amaury (Yvelines). It is important to stress that, as is the case with all French feature films made under the restricted conditions imposed by occupation, there is no *overt* reference in the film to the war, the occupation or related political issues.[4] The plot recounts the nefarious effects on the community created by a writer (or writers) of anonymous letters which denounce the misdemeanours committed by local worthies, and the atmosphere of suspicion, hysteria and persecution which is created as the culprit is sought out. 'Le corbeau' (meaning literally crow or raven) is the pen name adopted by the anonymous accuser (and has gone into the French language as a familiar expression for a writer of poison-pen letters). Despite their gravity, the truth of the writer's allegations is perceived as less important than establishing his or her identity and stopping his or her malevolent efforts (which lead to suicide, murder, and the arrest of at least one innocent person). These events last about two or three months.

Delation (that is, denouncing one's neighbours to the authorities for mercenary or malevolent reasons) is a favourite French pastime. (The self-righteous whistle-blower would appear to be a more virtuous counterpart favoured by the British and Americans.) This custom reached a peak during World War Two, when as many as three million letters were sent to the occupation authorities;[5] at the liberation, supposed collaborators fell prey in turn to anonymous accusations which put them in prison or courtrooms. Denunciation and the invasion of personal privacy are among the defining features of totalitarian and dictatorial regimes. As the film historian Susan Hayward remarks (1993: 126), the encouragement of such nefarious activities exposes the lying paradoxes of Vichy moralising, 'a regime that decreed the constitutional legality of the logic of persecution, made a virtue out of spying and informing and yet, simultaneously, upheld the principles of moral regeneration and the triumvirate of the National Revolution' (the triumvirate being the values of work, family and patriotism). Films made a generation after *Le Corbeau* which attempt a more dispassionate appraisal of the most discreditable aspects of occupation inevitably return to this disturbing subject, which reveals not merely the uncharitable vindictiveness of ordinary French people but also a sort of civic and psychic derangement. In Marcel Ophuls's documentary *Le Chagrin et la pitié* (1971), one of the most disturbing interviewees (and the only woman to be interviewed at length) is the hairdresser Mme Solange, who gives a rambling account of being tortured and imprisoned at the liberation for denouncing a friend's husband (though she herself is the victim of a denunciation, and her actual guilt or innocence are left unresolved). In a more comical variant, the ingenuous and thuggish hero of Louis Malle's *Lacombe Lucien* (1974) is put to work by the local French Gestapo and assists the prim secretary in opening the hundreds of letters of denunciation which they receive every week (including one individual who regularly denounces himself). Both these films, with their relentless focus on such discreditable behaviour and their insistence on its banal normality, aroused furious protests from establishment figures of all political persuasions when first released in the early 1970s, as we shall see. Such controversies, which arose a generation after the event in the liberal climate of the post-Gaullist years, are a further demonstration of the extraordinary paradox that Clouzot was able to produce and release his film during the occupation – when conformity and censorship were rigorously imposed by both German and French authorities.

There are three probable explanations why *Le Corbeau* was not stifled at birth. These are the fact that the subject predated the Second World War (and indeed post-dates it too), the unusual status and independence of Continental as a film company, and Clouzot's own position of influence within the company. It has often been noted that Louis Chavance's script had been written by 1937 and was inspired by Dr Locard's account in 1933 of a vendetta conducted in Tulle between 1917 and 1923 by an anonymous letter writer who signed himself 'l'œil du tigre' (the eye of the tiger). After more than a thousand letters were sent, the culprit was exposed, after an enforced dictation exercise and a failed suicide attempt, as one Angèle Laval, abetted by her mother and aunt; she was sentenced to five years in prison. Defending himself after the liberation, when the film belatedly became the target of self-appointed moral regenerators, Chavance (see Chavance and Clouzot, 1948) somewhat disingenuously noted the irony of a film about the evil of anonymous denunciations itself falling victim to anonymous denunciations (though the resistance journalists who attacked *Le Corbeau* in 1944 perforce had to operate clandestinely). He also wondered how a plot dating from the 1920s and 1930s could allegedly serve German propaganda ends in the 1940s (with no great difficulty, one might retort, given that social conditions and attitudes were not so different). Finally, Chavance denied that the film had been released in Germany under the title *Une petite ville française*, as an object lesson in the decadence and corruption of French society. His denial was correct, although *Le Corbeau* was shown in Belgium, Switzerland, Czechoslovakia and Romania; and the *typicality* of Saint-Robin is deliberately established from the opening sequences. Indeed, the Laval affair has inspired a host of imitators, up to the present day. Thus an article 'Deux corbeaux dans la nasse', in *Le Figaro* dated 25 May 1995, reported the arrest of two sisters Jeannine and Ginette Assouline, who had terrorised the village of Cox, near Toulouse, with 150 anonymous letters. That the 'corbeau' may however have a positive, purgative function is indicated by Yves Boisset's film *Radio Corbeau* (1988), about a pirate radio station in the Jura which denounces local misdemeanours, or the unusual resistance comic book, *Le Corbeau déchaîné*.

Before discussing the film in more detail, we need to examine the case of La Continental, insofar as this is possible, for its existence is central to any understanding of collaboration and independence in the wartime cinema industry. The historian René Chateau (1995: 465) suggests that up to three-quarters of those engaged in French film production in the occupation period had some connection with Continental. The disappearance of the company's archives during the liberation of Paris in August 1944 (along with those of the COIC) thus spared many individuals from embarrassment or worse, however frustrating it may be for historians of the cinema. As a consequence, documented facts about Continental and Clouzot's links with it are relatively scarce and can be summarised briefly.[6] Between 1931 and 1941, Clouzot mainly wrote dialogue and scripts, including those for two Continental film productions in 1941, *Le Dernier des six* and *Les Inconnus dans la maison*. He also directed French versions of some German films made by Neubabelsberg studios in Berlin in 1933 for the Tobis production company. Tobis was subsequently absorbed by UFA (the Nazi-dominated German production and distribution company), of which Continental was effectively a French branch. This German connection was not publicly well known in France; and post-war copies of films produced by Continental delete all references to Continental and Tobis from the credits. The head of Continental was a German, Alfred Greven (*c*.1898–1970), who had been a director of production at UFA in the 1930s, when he first met Clouzot. Clouzot was put in charge of the script department at Continental in January 1941, a post from which he resigned in October 1943. UFA itself was taken over by the German government just before the outbreak of war and therefore was directly dependent on Goebbels's Propaganda Ministry. Continental Films opened its offices in Paris on 3 October 1940 (moving to its famous address at 104 Avenue des Champs-Élysée from 28 March 1941). Though legally registered as a French company, it was financed by German capital (which actually derived in large part from the extortionate 'frais d'occupation' levied from the French government under the armistice agreement). Its aim was to exert economic hegemony over the French cinema industry (although as early as 1933, 15 per cent of French film production was German-financed; cf. Chateau, 1995: 15). In addition to producing thirty feature films between 1941 and 1944 (out of a total of 220 films produced altogether during the period), the company bought up Jewish-owned cinemas and obtained exclusive use of some studios (such as the largest in the country at Billancourt).

Whereas French-produced films were subject to both German and French censorship (at the point of production and distribution), Continental films were subject to scrutiny only by the *Propaganda Abteilung*. The motivation behind Continental was economic rather than ideological: in other words to revive and then dominate French film production. Hence Evelyn Ehrlich's comment that 'Continental was the MGM of French studios during the occupation' (1985: 50), that is that its films aimed generally to be star-studded and uncontroversial entertainments. Nonetheless, three Continental films were attacked and banned after the liberation: Decoin's *Les Inconnus dans la maison* (1942), which supposedly contains anti-Semitic elements; Valentin's *La Vie de plaisir* (1944), a light satire of establishment hypocrisy; and the much darker *Le Corbeau*. The exact nature of Clouzot's relations with Greven remains unknown, as does the reason why he was allowed to make such a provocative film. This short-term independence soon exposed Clouzot and his associates to ferocious criticism from a variety of quarters, however: notably, the church, the resistance, and jealous rivals. As a result, he was interrogated by a cinema purging committee and banned from working between 1944 and 1946.[7] At the same time, critical reactions to *Le Corbeau* in the 1940s (and ever since) nearly always acknowledge its effectiveness and impact as a piece of filmmaking (even if few commentators actually pay much detailed attention to the intriguing intricacies of its plot, characters and *mise en scène*). What divides critics is their moral (or moralising) position; as is usual with scandalous films, some take an authoritarian and others a libertarian stance. In this sense, François Vinneuil (the alias used by the notorious fascist journalist Rebatet) was unusual, and wrong, in observing in *Je suis partout* on 8 October 1943: 'this film will not make a very lasting impact on our memory, and this we regret' (quoted by Chavance and Clouzot, 1948: 206). The majority of film critics and the public have always treated the film with respect, as a technical success and an independent-minded social critique.

Since Continental was effectively a German company masquerading as a French one, there is no doubt that anyone who worked for it voluntarily, as did Clouzot, was engaged in a form of economic collaboration. (Certain well-known figures claimed in self-justification that they had been compelled to work for Continental, like the director Marcel Carné and the actor Paul Meurisse.)[8] On the other hand, with few exceptions, the content of films produced by Continental is innocuous; they are never pro-German propaganda vehicles. However, quite exceptionally, Clouzot and his team were accused both of economic collaboration and either of moral depravity (usually by right-wing critics) or of anti-patriotic betrayal (usually by left-wing critics). The first attack, entitled 'Le Corbeau est déplumé', appeared anonymously (the authors were Georges Adam and Pierre Blanchar) in number fourteen of the clandestine magazine *L'Écran français*, the 'organe du Front National du cinéma' (a section of the CNE *Lettres françaises*) in March 1944. They stated that the film was 'produced and encouraged by camouflaged Boches' and 'fed anti-French propaganda' (quoted by Barrot, 1979: 15). A second article published in April 1944 by the communist Georges Sadoul reaffirmed the opinion that the film's merit 'does not excuse those who sell themselves to the enemy to make films for them' (quoted by Chavance and Clouzot, 1948: 219). In 1947, when the three-year ban on *Le Corbeau* was finally lifted, with the film being released in three Parisian cinemas in September, the Gaullist Joseph Kessel reiterated the complaint that it offered 'the most perfect illustration of the German thesis that France was rotten'. What was at issue was not the film's truthfulness but its appropriateness in the circumstances: 'In time of war, to choose to show the worst side of one's country, with the support of the enemy, is to aid and abet the intentions of the enemy in the domain of psychological conflict' (quoted by Chateau, 1995: 486).

Unsurprisingly, the Centrale catholique du cinéma was equally keen to attack and suppress *Le Corbeau*, categorising the film as a 'six', the most negative classification: 'To be rejected: a deeply pernicious film, from the social, moral and religious point of view' (quoted by Siclier, 1990: 447). Valentin's *La Vie de plaisir* received the same grade, doubtless for its 'Deliberate and strongly emphasised anti-clerical tone' (p. 456). Before we turn to closer analysis of the film, the validity of such criticisms merits brief investigation, together with the legal and professional consequences which they had for Clouzot and his associates; such issues are central to the notion of artistic collaboration, the social and moral responsibility of the artist or entertainer, and the sanctions which those who betray such a responsibility deserve.

As has already been suggested, the basis of such criticisms is moralising and authoritarian: the Communist Party, the Gaullists, the Catholic Church all represent conflicting forces of ideological and social order (just as did the Germans and Vichy regime). *Le Corbeau*, on the other hand, deliberately satirises the incoherence and double standards of authority (be it legal, political, medical or religious); its two most sympathetic characters (Dr Germain and Denise) are eccentric, if not deviant, individualists. Significantly, both Pierre Fresnay and Ginette Leclerc, the actors who played these roles, were imprisoned after the liberation; in fact Ginette Leclerc spent nine months in detention before being released without charge and her career never recovered.[9] The film's satirical programme does not of course justify banning it and penalising those who made it. Nevertheless, Kessel's objections carry considerable weight, in the circumstances of occupation (when the freedoms of liberal democracy were in abeyance). *Le Corbeau* does offer a bleak portrait of a mendacious, divided community; its makers were unequivocally opportunistic in using their association with Continental to further their careers. The attribution of blame and retribution after the liberation has always been controversial, allowing ample scope for special pleading, partiality or downright duplicity on the part of supposed collaborators or their would-be 'purifiers'. Most entertainers escaped fairly lightly in practice, in comparison with the death sentences or long terms of imprisonment handed out to political collaborators.[10] It is also worth recalling that the cinema industry was policed in a draconian fashion under the Third Republic, as well as under the occupation, and indeed the Fourth Republic (when the realities of the Algerian war rarely reached the cinema). For example, the scriptwriter Henri Jeanson was sentenced to five years' imprisonment in December 1939 for insulting Prime Minister Daladier in the press (he eventually served eight months).[11] Supposedly demoralising films like *Quai des brumes*, *Hôtel du Nord* and *La Bête humaine* were banned in October 1939 (whereas curiously the Germans allowed the showing of films like *La Belle Équipe* and *Le Crime de M. Lange* which promoted the socialist ideals of the Popular Front).

The legality, severity and inconsistency of post-liberation sanctions are further problematic areas, apart from the protagonists' actual responsibility and veracity. Three directors of films for Continental were banned from working (Decoin, Valentin, Clouzot), as was Clouzot's scriptwriter Chavance; Clouzot and Chavance were originally banned in perpetuity in September 1944 and then for two years; others associated with *Le Corbeau* were banned for a few months (Francey, Roquevert and Brochard), while some were imprisoned (Fresnay, Balpêtré, Leclerc). Although imprisonment on suspicion of collaboration followed a ponderous legal process, of accusation, investigation and trial or dismissal of the case, professional sanctions were generally imposed by 'épuration' or purging committees composed of self-appointed members of the profession in question, which raised evident questions as to their legality and partiality. Hence the film historian Evelyn Ehrlich's conclusion that such committees were 'little more than platforms for personal vendettas' (1985: 175). The serious cases of collaboration which came before the courts of justice constituted for the purpose rarely involved people working in the cinema and entertainment industry; those who were prosecuted were generally avowed ideological collaborators, like the actor and PPF member Robert Le Vigan, who was sentenced to ten years in November 1946 for propaganda broadcasts made on Radio Paris (he was released in 1949 and went into exile abroad). The death sentence was imposed as late as March 1949 on Jean Mamy, the director of the propaganda short *Forces occultes*; the main charge against him was, however, betraying resisters to the Gestapo. In Clouzot's case, he was effectively unable to work for three years and was still technically banned when making *Quai des Orfèvres* in February 1947. Pierre Fresnay, on the other hand, was released after six weeks' detention and returned to the stage in 1945 (the charges against him were that he had starred in four Continental-produced films, had been awarded the Francisque by Pétain, and was a 'staunch *pétainiste*'; see Chateau, 1995: 187).

Le Corbeau: characters and configurations

Putting aside these wider historical factors, we can return to the film itself. A trenchant evaluation is given by the report of the Centrale catholique du cinéma in 1945, which is worth quoting at length:

> A painful, hard film, constantly morbid in its complexity. Free love provoked cynically and with crude insistence by the woman. Doctor who behaves equivocally by his attitude to childbirth. Poisonous atmosphere to arouse suspicion against the authors of anonymous letters, which includes a young girl of fourteen and a half with an equivocal, painful attitude. Atheistic profession of faith from the most sympathetic character. Suicide, murder, bad language, oaths. (quoted by Siclier, 1990: 453)

Beneath the ideologically motivated disapproval of a film which derides so many of the reactionary values dear to the Catholic church, one senses at the same time the curious fascination exerted by *Le Corbeau*. Its complexity is acknowledged, as are its equivocal and painful dissection of emotional and physical disturbance, its provocative exploration of taboo subjects (such as abortion, disease, religious faith and female sexuality).

Ostensibly, the plot of the film hinges on the initial appearance of the 'Corbeau', then on the revelations and turmoil caused by the anonymous and seemingly ubiquitous letters despatched by the writer, and finally on the identification and liquidation of the 'Corbeau', after suspicion has fallen on all the major characters apart from the actual perpetrator. I must apologise at this point to any readers unfamiliar with the dénouement for giving away the culprit's identity, since it is impossible to discuss the film meaningfully without doing so. In fact, *Le Corbeau* does not really depend on suspense or surprise for its effects: were it intended to be a standard psychological thriller, one would have to complain that Clouzot brazenly overturns convention and practises narrative duplicity by belatedly revealing the 'Corbeau' to be the chief investigator of the crimes, who is also an apparent source of world-weary wisdom. The Tulle affair (with its guilty female trio) and the characters' emotional and physical configurations lead us to suspect that the 'Corbeau' must be one (or more) of the women who surround Dr Germain, the chief object of the writer's vituperation. In fact, the 'Corbeau' is finally revealed to be his colleague and quasi-mentor, the psychiatrist Dr Vorzet (who has played the part of a world-weary Merlin). The film seemingly confirms the trite adage that psychiatrists are madder than their patients, except for the fact that Vorzet's mental state is barely explored; the sanity or malice of the 'Corbeau' are less important than his ability to expose unpleasant truths and his apparent omniscience about the community. Chavance's original script did not in fact identify Vorzet as the culprit.[12]

This opacity is compounded by further complexities of plot, particularly in the relationships between major characters. One consequence is that critics who take the trouble to examine the film in detail sometimes conflate characters or misattribute their functions, in an unwitting urge to simplify or clarify. For instance, the original Tobis publicity erroneously says that Liliane Maigné plays Ginette Leclerc's sister, when in fact the character Rolande is Denise's niece (the daughter of her brother) (compare Chirat, 1983: 101; Siclier, 1990: 63). Again, Ehrlich says that Laura Vorzet is Denise's sister, when Laura (played by Micheline Francey) is actually the sister of the nurse Marie Corbin (played by Héléna Manson); and Marie Corbin was the original fiancée of Laura's husband Dr Vorzet. These group dynamics may be better explained by a simple diagram indicating characters' and actors' names and relationships:

CORBEAU(X) = ???

Dr Vorzet [Pierre Larquey] *husband of*   Laura Vorzet [Micheline Francey] *sister of*

Marie Corbin [Héléna Manson] *nurse of*

Cancéreux [Roger Blin]
His mother [Sylvie]
Dr Germain [Pierre Fresnay]
Saillens [Noël Roquevert] *father of*   Rolande Saillens [Liliane Maigné] *niece of*

Denise Saillens [Ginette Leclerc]

To return to the question of motivation, while the cancer patient and Dr Germain are among the principal victims of the poison-pen missives, and the male characters Vorzet and Saillens are given no obvious motive for sending anonymous letters, the four women in the right-hand column are all foregrounded as possible suspects. Admittedly, one could argue, somewhat perversely, that by making Vorzet the culprit Clouzot is merely following (and/or deriding) the hackneyed convention of detective stories whereby the least probable character turns out to be the real villain. (Vorzet does in fact teasingly hint at an early stage that he could be the culprit.) But given the film's creation of genuinely plausible and intriguing characters whose behaviour exceeds lazy stereotyping, one is left wondering why the conclusion is so strangely cursory, leaving as many questions unanswered as resolved. For example, Denise and Laura both admit to writing letters signed by the 'Corbeau', even though in reality they are innocent; on the other hand, Vorzet is murdered in the act of writing a final letter, which presumably would have confirmed his guilt. In fact, Laura first accuses Denise, before being herself accused by Vorzet and counter-accusing him, as a consequence of which Germain is duped into having Laura interned. Laura also admits to penning the first letter, whereas it is left unclear whether subsequent letters were produced by one or both Vorzets acting in complicity and why, in an act of self-directed hostility, they feature in the accusations contained in their own letters (since hundreds of letters are eventually sent, it is indeed possible they have several imitators).

Dr Vorzet's explanation for his own behaviour is curiously reductive: 'A very young wife...A very old husband...There's the whole drama!' (p. 76).[13] Sexual frustration explains all, or nothing. His younger rival Dr Germain blunders his way towards the truth, wrongly suspecting everyone but Vorzet. While Vorzet's unexplored despair and mischievous penmanship lead to him having his throat cut, the jaundiced Germain (whose brusqueness hides a cynical humanitarianism, it seems) is reconciled by these troubling events to accept human weakness and his union with the sluttish Denise (who is pregnant by his works). He is surrounded by four women who compete for his attention in the enclosed surroundings of the local hospital and school, where spying, rivalry and dishonest complicity are the norm. Thus in the opening sequences of the film, Germain catches the spinsterly, brutal nurse Marie Corbin reading his correspondence and accuses her of stealing morphine meant for the cancer patient. He appears to encourage the advances of her more respectable but 'hysterical' sister Laura, but repels the seduction attempt of the vampish Denise. While reading the letter from the 'Corbeau' which accuses him of being Laura's lover, he is spied on through a gigantic keyhole by Denise's adolescent niece Rolande (who engages in occasional petty theft from her post office job). Rolande is later seen sobbing outside Denise's bedroom when Germain finally succumbs to her charms.

To these configurations drawn by frustrated, destructive passions can be added the film's insistence on the physical or psychological mutilation of many characters. Denise is lame, following a car crash in which her brother Saillens lost an arm; Vorzet admits to being a drug addict, abetted by Marie; Germain has changed his identity after an incompetent surgeon killed his wife and unborn child, while his own deliveries suggest infanticide, since three infants have died in six weeks (hence the accusations of abortion made by the 'Corbeau'). Denise is accused of nymphomania by her brother, and attempts to induce an abortion by throwing herself downstairs. Outside the circle of principal figures, the atmosphere is equally deleterious: Dr Delorme regales his colleagues with an 'amusing' case of gangrene, while most of the accusations of corruption made against the town's leaders seem well-founded. Expressionistic camera effects which suggest the dominance of certain characters or the distortion of their perspective further heighten this claustrophobic, oppressive atmosphere. A shot of Vorzet's gigantic shadow on a staircase prefigures his eventual exposure as the arch-manipulator. Falsely suspected and imprisoned, Marie Corbin (whose surname is an archaic form of the word 'corbeau') is pursued by a mob across town, down streets which are slanted at crazy angles; seeking refuge in her vandalised apartment, she catches her reflection deformed by a broken mirror, but her panic-stricken terror and distorted perspective reveal her as victim rather than perpetrator; whereas her sister Laura feigns a submissive but seductive posture before Germain, seemingly a meek victim when she is actually another manipulator.

All these details tend to create the impression that *Le Corbeau* is a dourly misanthropic and misogynistic film which sets out to deride the hysterical indiscretions and disloyalties of the bourgeoisie. When Germain first refuses to continue his relationship with her, Denise's chosen insult is 'bourgeois'. Significantly perhaps, the main victim in the film is the working-class cancer patient hospitalised in bed number thirteen, who is identified only by the illness consuming him and offered little pity or treatment. He is first seen being brutalised by Marie and is finally driven to suicide by an anonymous letter revealing he is incurable. He is avenged by his mother (the school cleaning lady), who cuts Vorzet's throat with the razor which her son used to kill himself. 'Malade no 13' thus seems to be innocent of any misdemeanour (unlike most of those accused by the 'Corbeau') and to be betrayed by all those whose mission is supposedly to assist him. Retrospectively, the spectator looks for some commentary, whether explicit or implicit, on the compromises and betrayals wrought by occupation in a film which confronts social and personal divisions so caustically. For example, the sick patient might be taken as a symbol of France, betrayed and neglected by all those whose weaknesses and quarrels lead them to fail in their civic duty. But the film cannot be read very convincingly as an allegory directly about the occupation, since for all its bickering and unappealing *attentistes*, it contains no very obvious equivalents to the main active participants (the invading Germans, the competing forces of collaboration and resistance). In fact, the film does strive towards a more positive resolution, albeit of a somewhat sentimental and melodramatic variety, by placing the personal and private before the professional and social domains. Thus while professional males invariably fall down on the job in scenes sometimes played as farce (the investigating judge or *substitut* fails to identify the 'Corbeau'; the sub-prefect is transferred to another town; and Germain is bamboozled by his patron Vorzet, who instigates a marathon dictation exercise to conceal his own culpability), women who are shown to be frustrated and hysterical nevertheless are able to discover the truth intuitively and act with far more humanity than male authorities. Laura and Marie support Vorzet (though their motives are never explained); in the final scenes, Denise persuades Germain of Laura's relative innocence by personal entreaty, having earlier exculpated herself by a similar appeal to emotional authenticity: 'Be quiet and look at me...I'm not intelligent like you, but I can feel things' (p. 74).

In a scene like this, the film is clearly offering a positive message. Ultimately, the misanthropic Germain (whose refusal of human contact was triggered by the surgeon who killed his family) is humanised by Laura and Denise. Whereas the opening scenes show him washing his hands like a vet in a farmyard vat, after failing to deliver a baby alive but saving the mother, and shutting out the noise of children playing outside Denise's bedroom ('These screeching brats get on my nerves', p. 12), at the end he concedes that 'You can't sacrifice the future to the present' (p. 78) and re-opens Denise's window to let the noise of children back in. In a similar way, Germain's interaction with the 'Corbeau' (that is, the real culprit Vorzet, but also his imitators

Laura and Denise) forces him to adopt a less rigorous and more humane posture. At the beginning, Vorzet reproaches him, 'You have no indulgence for life, my dear fellow' (p. 14), and in a famous scene mocks Germain's 'Cornelian' severity, observing: 'Where is the boundary of evil? Do you know if you're on the right or wrong side? . . . Ever since this whirlwind of hatred and denunciation blew over the town, all moral values have been more or less corrupted' (p. 72).

Most critics of *Le Corbeau* comment favourably on the chiaroscuro symbolism created in this scene by the swaying electric bulb alternately casting light and shadow over Vorzet and Germain, and over a globe in the room as well, although Chirat remarks sarcastically: 'This conversation, with its facile philosophising about good and evil held between Fresnay, Larquey and a lightbulb swaying in front of the protagonists' noses, really labours the obvious' (1983: 117). Germain's conversion and acceptance of the necessity of evil may well seem facile, and in the context of occupation to imply an insidious moral relativism, implicitly dismissing all sides and choices as equally ambiguous. In fact, at this point Germain has still not realised that the real source of evil stems from Vorzet rather than the supposedly 'insane' Laura; indeed, Germain is duped by the 'Corbeau' throughout the film, even if in personal terms his reconciliation with Denise and future role as a paterfamilias restore him to humanity. This bird of ill omen remains highly mysterious and ambiguous. Retrospectively, at least, Vorzet has to be seen as a Mephistophelian, ironising figure, who subverts his claims to knowledge, authority and truth by hinting at his true destructive role. Thus he characterises himself as a 'Graphologist and hoaxer' (p. 14), an 'expert in cases of anonymous letters' (p. 16), and diagnoses anonymous letter writers as sick rather than culpable, 'always repressed, more or less sexually perverted' (p. 68). While all these statements prove to be true, Vorzet's lessons are intended not merely to curb Germain's rigidity (which could be seen as proposing a form of liberation from the hypocritical boundaries imposed by Vichy and by fascist attacks on supposed cultural and moral deviance) but also, more sinisterly, to propagate evil by making everyone seem more or less guilty or perverted. Hence his remark to Germain: 'You are infected like the others. You'll fall like them!' (p. 72). Moreover, the personality revealed in the anonymous letters shows the 'Corbeau' to be driven largely by petty envy and sexual malice. Vorzet's last act as the 'Corbeau' is to write a letter stating that 'The guilty woman Laura is punished. The curse is lifted' (p. 79), although by accusing Laura *after* she has been interned, the 'Corbeau' is to all intents and purposes vindicating her, since she is no longer in a position to write anonymous letters. To the very end, we are left uncertain as to what motivated Vorzet and how many imitators the 'Corbeau' has spawned.

The current critical consensus about *Le Corbeau* is that a sometime 'film maudit' has now attained the status of a classic. In other words, 'la malédiction est levée' for the contemporary spectator, who is doubtless able to set aside the issues of collaboration and anti-French propaganda which troubled earlier commentators, and to judge the film on its cinematic and aesthetic virtues, without direct reference to the socio-historical context of occupation cinema. This approach implies that contemporaneous prejudices and preconceptions somehow temporarily block true understanding of artistic works, especially provocative and disturbing ones. An alternative reaction for later generations is occasionally one of disappointment or bemusement, when the object of critical adoration ceases to speak to a modern audience. In the case of films, this can simply be due to technical reasons which impair their quality irrevocably (damaged film stock, poor video copies, inaudible dialogue, unexplained cuts and so on).[14] A minor example in the case of *Le Corbeau* is that the scenarios of the film held by the Bibliothèque du film and the text published in 1948 refer to an opening shot of flocks of crows which are invisible either in the transcript provided in *L'Avant-scène cinéma* or the versions shown on French television. My argument has been that we need both to undertake an archaeological reconstruction of occupation cinema and to interrogate the film as image and text in order to understand fully its value as a historical and artistic document. *Le Corbeau* succeeds as filmic drama and as a potent period piece full of satirical insights into the vices and virtues of Vichy France. In this sense, Claude Mauriac's equation of *Le Corbeau* with Renoir's celebrated *La Règle du jeu* as a satire of universal historical significance is entirely justified. The remainder of this discussion will focus on how certain films made after the end of the war have pursued the attempt to demystify and demythify or remythify the lies and truths engendered by occupation.

Resisters and collaborators: from stereotypes to revisionism

The resistance makes only a brief appearance in Clouzot's films. His film *Manon*, released in 1949, updates the Abbé Prévost's famous novel to liberation France. Des Grieux is a maquisard who rescues Manon from a mob planning to shave her head for horizontal collaboration; he rapidly abandons his comrades to abscond with her to Paris, where she becomes a high-class prostitute and des Grieux is persuaded by her unscrupulous brother (played by Serge Reggiani) to become a trafficker, for 'Liberated France had a queen who was called dealing' (Clouzot, 1949: 56). Roger Vailland saw a tendentious cynicism in this skilful adaptation, observing in a review:

> ϯ In Clouzot's work there is a deliberate intention to show that in 1944 all French people without exception were spineless rogues. To draw the conclusion that those who are considered heroes now-adays achieved this merely by chance or by mistake takes only one more step. (Quoted in Vailland and Ballet, 1973: 115)

What is interesting about this judgement is that it could be applied equally well to two films which were made more than two decades later and created far more controversy: Ophuls's *Le Chagrin et la pitié* establishes self-interest and *attentisme* as the norm for most French people during the occupation, while Louis Malle's *Lacombe Lucien* em-ϯ phasises the role played by chance and error in the choices which turn a would-be resister into a collaborator. In other words, one does not have to wait until the 1970s to find revisionist tendencies in French films which portray resistance and collaboration.

Sylvie Lindeperg relates Clouzot's *Manon* to André Cayatte's *Nous sommes tous des assassins*, which came out three years later in 1952. Recalling the often overlooked fact that members of the communist FTP sometimes were prosecuted in the post-war years for alleged crimes committed under the guise of resistance, she notes how both directors 'portrayed dubious resisters, potential delinquents or assas-sins linked to the world of organised crime' (1994: 110). Cayatte's film evokes the urban squalor of the *zone*, the no-man's-land outside Paris, where his illiterate, alcoholic protagonist Le Guen (played by Mouloudji) accidentally joins a resistance network after disposing of the body of a German murdered by his sister, a prostitute. For reasons that remain obscure, he then kills or betrays several members of his group, is arrested in a shoot-out with the police and condemned to death. As the title of the film suggests, Cayatte and his fellow script-writer Charles Spaak use the turbulent events of the occupation to elaborate a deterministic thesis which accuses society as much as the individual: social deprivation added to the violence engendered by war-time inevitably lead to crime. Much of the film focuses in unusually harrowing detail on the inhumane brutality of the death sentence, while the protagonist's resistance actions are more incidental. But the supposed glory of resistance is viewed with considerable scepticism. In a curious scene, Le Guen finds that the authorities refuse to accept that he liquidated the leader of his network, for the victim's wife insists, falsely, that her husband was killed by the Gestapo: the fact that the real murderer (and possibly the victim too) was a traitor from within the resistance is deemed inconceivable.

While such films should make one wary of sweeping generalisations about what was considered acceptable in French cinema in the decade immediately following the liberation, it is nevertheless perfectly true that, as has already been said, the epic and heroic mode was the most favoured by directors who portrayed the struggle of resistance, and conversely that collaborators are shown in stereotyped fashion as a minority of base traitors. The most celebrated example of the first category is René Clément's *La Bataille du rail*, released in February 1946 and sponsored by the Conseil National de la Résistance. The film celebrates the heroic struggle of French railway workers against their stupid and brutal German adversaries and is cast in a deliberately documentary style (with the use of unknown actors, many scenes shot on location, a fragmentary plot line). According to J.-P. Bertin-Maghit: 'Whatever its use of authenticity ... the film achieves a codification of resistance, creating a genuine heroic epic whose influence would mark all subsequent post-war productions' (1986: 283–4).

In a purifying act of national union, all members of the nation, including those in the audience, are drawn into the resistance, while the more unsavoury aspects of the occupation are left aside; hence the film's success on its first appearance. Such 'authenticity' has not aged well: the film's simplifications generally reduce it to the level of a propaganda piece today, particularly if one watches it in its entirety. Certain episodes, however, are justly celebrated, such as the scene portraying the execution of an anonymous group of hostages, who are brutally shot down without false heroics, with only the wailing of the railway engines to mark their passing in a pathetic and moving gesture of solidarity. And the documentary reconstruction of certain scenes is so convincing that they are sometimes cited or copied as though they were authoritative, first-hand documents by subsequent film-makers: thus a BBC documentary on the maquis uses a clip of a train being derailed as though it were a piece of newsreel, without bothering to point out its fictional source.[15] The derailment of the train has in any case become a convenient shorthand for resistance activity, especially for directors who prefer spectacle to controversy and complexity: typically, Claude Berri's *Lucie Aubrac* (1997), which returns to the simplified model of heroism and reaffirms many of the stereotypes and clichés of the genre, opens with such an episode.

Even in 1946, however, a degree of complexity was possible. René Clément also directed *Le Père tranquille*, which was released in October and offers an interesting contrast eight months after *La Bataille du rail*. The film was largely the inspiration of the comic singer and actor Noël-Noël, who both wrote the script and starred in the main role. The anonymous cast and vast spaces of urban railway lines are replaced by the more intimate environment of a provincial family, whose members eventually prove to be equally heroic, for all their mundane preoccupations. The drama turns indeed on the disparity between appearance and reality: the middle-aged protagonist M. Martin seems to be a harmless, self-centred bourgeois whose main occupation is cultivating orchids, much to the scorn of his rebellious son, when in fact he is the head of the local resistance; the noisy braggart who arrives in the village claiming to be an envoy from London proves to be a double agent and traitor. Despite the comic capital which such ambiguities generate, ultimately the moral can be seen as profoundly comforting and conventional: for all his apparent cowardice and egotism, the average Frenchman (Martin is one of the most common surnames in France) has the heart of a lion. The fact that many French people ignored or feared the resistance, while accepting the authority of Marshal Pétain, remains a forbidden subject. Marcel Carné's *Les Portes de la nuit*, which came out a few weeks later, was far less of a popular and critical success, probably because it is an unusual blend of documentary melodrama and sentimental allegory. Two central characters are the profiteer Sénéchal (Saturnin Fabre) and his son Guy, who passes himself off as a hero of the resistance when in fact he has betrayed his network to the Gestapo; the treacherous double-dealer is played once again by Serge Reggiani and finally receives his just punishment. Despite their recourse to stereotypes and implausible retribution, however, such films do begin to suggest that the boundaries between resistance and collaboration are highly permeable and not always distinguishable.

Feature films set out to entertain rather than inform their audience, of course, and can rarely risk deterring potential spectators by shocking or boring them with unpleasant truths. But thanks to a few more adventurous film-makers, the margins of acceptability are gradually widened. From the 1950s onwards, comedy is usually used as a pretext for presenting a more irreverent view of the occupation, as we shall see. However, the films that set out to offer more serious historical analysis are usually documentaries, Alain Resnais's short film *Nuit et brouillard* (1955) being a justly celebrated early example; its subject is deportation, shown unflinchingly in a series of harrowing images of the death camps, and accompanied by a poetic, philosophical commentary written by Jean Cayrol, himself a former deportee. The political establishment's reaction to the film revealed how sensitive this material still was (particularly at a time when torture, mass murder and internment were being increasingly used in the conflict in Algeria). The French censors demanded the removal of a still photograph showing a gendarme guarding the camp at Pithiviers (in effect suppressing the direct association of the French state in deportation), while at the German ambassador's request the film was withdrawn from the Cannes film festival, on the grounds that it might incite anti-German feelings (see Lindeperg, 1997, for details). Another thirty years would pass before a film would appear that sought to encompass the monstrous legacy of the Holocaust, Claude Lanzmann's nine-hour testimony *Shoah* (1985).

The scandal aroused in some quarters by *Nuit et brouillard* is a sort of rehearsal for the much noisier controversy created sixteen years later by the lengthy documentary film *Le Chagrin et la pitié*, which sets out to present a demythifying account of French attitudes and behaviour during the occupation. Since this film unquestionably changed perceptions of collaboration and resistance, not only within the cinema but also across a much broader spectrum of public opinion, it is a key reference in any discussion. While *Le Chagrin et la pitié* is certainly a famous landmark for historians and students of World War Two or of documentary films, in my experience few other people inside or outside France have seen it (in an amusing running gag, the obsessive hero of Woody Allen's *Annie Hall* tries to remedy this ignorance by forcing all his successive girlfriends to watch *The Sorrow and the Pity*, although a four-hour documentary on French collaborators is an unlikely method for sealing a relationship). The film was produced for German and Swiss television in 1969 by André Harris and Alain de Sedouy and directed by Marcel Ophuls (who co-wrote the script and conducted the interviews with Harris). All three were employed by French television to produce history programmes until they were removed from the ORTF (French state television and radio) in the aftermath of May '68. The ORTF refused to buy *Le Chagrin et la pitié* or even to view the completed film, which was therefore released in a Parisian cinema in April 1971 where it attracted 600,000 spectators (but only 30,000 when shown again in 1979, according to Ophuls). Finally, it was shown on French television a decade later in October 1981 (the first year of Mitterrand's presidency) and seen by 15 million viewers. This inordinate delay was effectively 'censorship through inertia', in Ophuls' words (1980: 20), caused according to his producers by the fact that 'They were afraid to show French people, particularly in the mirror which is television, an image of themselves that was less glorious than the one they wanted to perpetuate' (p. 11).[16] The controversy aroused by the film, in other words, was as much political and social as historical: by whose authority are history and national identity reassessed in a popular medium like film and television? Marcel Ophuls himself enjoys the role of the provocative outsider: he was born in Frankfurt in 1927, the son of the celebrated Jewish film director Max Ophuls, who moved his family to France in 1933 and to the USA in 1941. Marcel Ophuls returned to France in 1950 and acquired French nationality. He chose to film much of *Le Chagrin et la pitié* in Clermont-Ferrand, perceived as a typical provincial city in the south zone and conveniently close to Vichy.

Rereading the reactions aroused by the film thirty years after its appearance, one is struck either by their hysterical fury or their extraordinary condescension. For once it is not an exaggeration to see an authoritarian establishment struggling to prevent a revisionist view of its dearly held myths from being disseminated to a wider public; this applies equally to critics from the left as from the right, from the ranks of former resisters as from collaborators, from de Gaulle's supporters as from his adversaries. The essential objection was precisely, to cite J.J. de Bresson, the President of the ORTF and a former resister, that the film 'destroys myths which the French still need', myths most easily summed up in the word 'résistancialisme', that is of overwhelming and universal support for a rather nebulous notion of resistance which carefully elides all the ambiguities and contradictions of the occupation. The convenient notions of national solidarity in a historic struggle are replaced in *Le Chagrin et la pitié* by a less agreeable insistence on cowardice, self-preservation and indifference as the norm, with resisters being seen as bizarre and dangerous eccentrics. This revised judgement was not particularly new; we have already seen that even feature films sympathetic to the resistance touch on its ambiguities and that deportation, collaboration, trafficking and revenge all feature in earlier films (just as the satirical films of later decades also have predecessors in the 1950s). The key difference, however, is that *Le Chagrin et la pitié* is not a fictional entertainment but a systematic, didactic documentary based on careful research and above all on the use of authoritative witnesses willing to spell out, for example, the complicity of the French government and people in anti-Semitic persecution. At the same time, authentic resisters are set against former collaborators, as both seek to justify their choices and examine the ensuing consequences; the very idea of comparing such choices seemed a further provocation, particularly when they may appear to be arbitrary and the choice of resistance may not lead to a happy ending.

One criticism of a more subtle variety frequently directed against the film has been that it replaced the myth of glorious resistance with another myth that was no less false but much less glorious: universal cowardice. Hence the complaint made by Germaine Tillion, a former resister and deportee: 'From this compilation there emerges the profile of a hideous country. This profile is not accurate' (p. 79). An objection matched by that of the collaborationist writer Alfred Fabre-Luce, who was imprisoned at the liberation: 'M. Ophuls shows us an ignoble France, apart from a few heroes. This is to go to the opposite extreme. His film is often accurate in details, but the proportions are out of place' (p. 79). The portrait which fails to capture a true likeness becomes a grotesque caricature, at least in the eyes of those whose view of the occupation is already firmly determined. A more open-minded commentator (P. Mazara, p. 73) was impressed by the film's innovative use of authoritative witnesses:

> It is quite possible that this form of cinema could completely renew the methods of historians. What books or teams of researchers could ever equal the authenticity of these witnesses' statements, collect such a large number of them, and refrain from any sweeping judgement?

In fact, the use of oral testimony by historians was hardly an invention of *Le Chagrin et la pitié*: many early histories of the resistance drew heavily, sometimes almost exclusively, on the first-hand narratives of resisters (the massive five-volume *Histoire de la Résistance en France* produced by Henri Noguères being the most striking example). The novelty was for a film, particularly a film made for French television, to aspire to the status of radical historical investigation. Nor is it true that the film refrains from making judgements; for many critics indeed it offered a pitiless condemnation: 'As for sorrow and pity, one can say that they are most lacking in the film. A spirit of resentment and vengeance is manifested throughout its four hours. It does not accuse the regime of Marshal Pétain, but France itself' (M. Mohrt, p. 73).

Such provocative ruthlessness is far from apparent to the viewer thirty years later, for whom the film seems at first sight to be a relatively objective documentary about the occupation. In the first place, a certain effort is required simply to identify the characters and the positions they represent (such as Mendès-France, Anthony Eden, René de Chambrun). It is worth spelling out that the informative nature of *Le Chagrin et la pitié* can easily obscure the subversive, not to say tendentious technique which often lies behind its editing and *mise en scène*. The effect created is not mere crude propaganda, but the addition of a subtle extra dimension (often contradictory or satirical) to the words of the interviewees or the newsreel footage which form its subject matter.

The film, then, offers a chronological account extending from the defeat in 1940 to the liberation in 1944, frequently returning to the present when it was filmed in 1969: present and past intertwine and explain each other. It lasts 260 minutes (setting off a fashion for long documentary films, most famously followed by *Shoah* lasting twice as long) and comprises interviews with thirty-six witnesses interspersed with newsreel extracts (these lasting forty-five minutes, 17 per cent of the total running time). The choice of witnesses hardly reveals an unpatriotic bias, for the most important figures are all drawn either from the resistance or the allies: Emmanuel d'Astier de la Vigerie (Libération Sud), Georges Bidault (President of the CNR), Colonel Gaspar (aka Émile Coulaudon, a leader in the Mont Mouchet maquis in Auvergne), Jacques Duclos (head of the clandestine Communist Party), Pierre Mendès-France (imprisoned for 'desertion' by Vichy, he joined the Free French and was prime minister in 1954–55), not forgetting ordinary citizens like the Grave brothers and the British SOE agent Denis Rake. All these commentators drawn from the ranks of the victors are faced by fairly minor personalities such as Georges Lamirand (Vichy's Minister of Youth in 1941–43), René de Chambrun (Laval's son-in-law), Christian de La Mazière (a French Waffen SS officer), and the only woman interviewed at length, the hairdresser Mme Solange, imprisoned for alleged collaboration at the liberation. Not only does the balance lean heavily towards the resistance in this line-up, but also none of the collaborators manage to convince us of the correctness of their views and choices.[17] To explain the hostile reactions of so many critics in 1971, one has to examine some episodes in rather more detail.

One significant factor is the film's insistence on the mundane and unheroic as the guiding norm for people's behaviour, especially in the interviews with ordinary citizens. (Ophuls himself observed that the film was about 'courage and cowardice at a time of crisis'; 1980: 20.) The pharmacist Marcel Verdier (who, perhaps recollecting Aristotle's definition of tragedy, evokes the sorrow and pity which give the film its title) is asked to recall the material problems of the occupation. Ophuls suggests that Verdier's self-disparaging frankness is a form of courage (1980: 240). However, surrounded by his large family (who are not invited to offer their views) in relatively comfortable surroundings, this interviewee exudes a degree of self-satisfaction somewhat reminiscent of his notorious literary ancestor, Flaubert's M. Homais. The historian Stanley Hoffmann (in Ophuls, 1975) characterises Verdier as the anti-hero of the film, in that he displays a disturbing self-centred complacency (although at one point he claims that he assisted Jewish girls in finding work). To my mind, 'anti-hero' is an inappropriate term (better applied to the former SS officer Christian de La Mazière, an impenitent fascist). Verdier surely embodies a more banal norm, with his account of how he overcame shortages of food and tobacco and how his children did not suffer in their development (his son grew up to be a colossus, he adds proudly). A question about persecutions curiously leads him to describe the restoration of hunting in September 1942, hunting game rather than Jews. Such details about daily life clearly form part of the film's documentary function; but they also show, in the wider context, how deliberately limited the vision of the typical Frenchman was, and remains.

The contrast is all the more blatant when the film deals with anti-Semitism, or rather Vichy's deliberate complicity in the Nazis' persecution and murder of the Jews, confronting a painful topic that had been mostly avoided in films in the previous twenty-five years. Pierre Mendès-France is a primordial witness in this respect, not merely as a statesman and resister but also as a victim of the repressive measures inflicted by the Vichy regime on its opponents. It is made clear that anti-Semitism is part of a long-standing French tradition predating Hitler's conquest of France and that it was a central part of Vichy's programme for national renewal. Interviews with individuals from Clermont-Ferrand emphasise that they were well aware of the practical effects on Jewish colleagues, but felt impotent to assist them. When Ophuls suggests to two former members of staff at the *Lycée* Pascal that all the teachers could have resigned collectively to protest against the dismissal of a Jewish teacher, they laugh sheepishly and retort that such a gesture was outside people's mentality. Ophuls tracks down another citizen who decided to advertise publicly that he was not

Jewish, despite being called Klein (such onomastic confusions are the subject of Joseph Losey's 1977 feature film *Monsieur Klein*).

Such witnesses are inevitably shown in a humiliating light, as they are forced to admit to dishonourable acts. As Ophuls has noted, 'For most of our contemporaries, the ritual of the interview has replaced that of Catholic confession', the difference being that 'If taken far enough, any documentary work is a form of pornography' (1980: 220, 237). The accusing gaze levelled by the film is on occasion somewhat unjust, not to say arbitrary, insofar as we are often led to judge and condemn interviewees by their lack of frankness in front of the camera. Conversely, a self-confident witness able to defend his actions with a certain vigour, like La Mazière, comes across far more sympathetically than individuals like Mme Solange or Maurice Chevalier, whose stumbling exculpations create an impression of shifty mendacity. Yet such implied judgements are invidious: by any sort of objective scale used to measure collaboration, an impenitent SS officer who fought with the Nazis on the eastern front, whatever the courage of his convictions, is guiltier than a singer or a hairdresser who offered their support to Marshal Pétain. This particular irony probably escaped the producers and directors of *Le Chagrin et la pitié*, although ironic counterpointing is one of their favourite techniques (indeed the film critic A.P. Colombat (1993) has discovered no fewer than nine types of disjunction in witnesses' testimony).[18] Thus La Mazière is interviewed at length by André Harris in the castle of Sigmaringen – the final refuge of Pétain's government in 1945 (a government in effect kidnapped by the Germans and which abandoned even its last defenders like La Mazière). The choice of this location subverts La Mazière's pro-German sentiments and recalls Vichy's political bankruptcy; on the other hand, his evocation of the chivalrous spirit of SS warriors and denial of knowledge about the extermination of the Jews are allowed to pass unchallenged. The French Waffen SS may well have called Hitler 'le grand Jules', but they still defended him up to the final days in his Berlin bunker in April 1945; this perverse sacrifice is left unexplored, and we are left with the impression that La Mazière possesses considerable physical and moral courage.

By comparison, the only woman to be interrogated at length in the film is shown in a fashion that is both cruel and unrevealing (thereby giving a rather misleading and very limited sense of women's activities in the occupation, as Siân Reynolds has observed, 1990). Mme Solange's body language (nervous gestures and tics, evasive and incoherent replies) conveys a sense of guilt and dishonesty, although she presents herself as a victim of the excesses of the liberation, falsely accused of denunciation, arrested, tortured, and sentenced to fifteen years' imprisonment after a summary trial. The director interrogates her with apparent hostility, interrupting her account of torture to confirm that she was a *maréchaliste* (hardly sufficient cause to merit the punishment she received), and makes no attempt to elucidate her garbled story by producing corroborating evidence. Ophuls later pointed out in a long article reviewing the film that this episode was shot in great haste and therefore badly prepared; what looks like guilt on the interviewee's part or hostility on the interviewer's is more likely to be due to nervousness and clumsy editing. All they knew about Mme Solange was 'C'en est une!' (that is, a convicted local collaborator) (Ophuls, 1980: 258), whose willingness to be interviewed was untypical. Nevertheless, such episodes show how the film shifts from being an apparently objective documentary to a more partial *réquisitoire* which does not always home in on the right targets. Needless to say, Ophuls' picture of the resistance also brought accusations of bias and undue cynicism (Emmanuel d'Astier's statement that resisters were by definition misfits or 'inadaptés', Louis Grave's conclusion that most people thought he was a fool to join the resistance). *Le Chagrin et la pitié* is certainly an anti-conformist polemic that commits injustices, whether by distortion or omission, but its central thesis that passive collaboration characterised most French people's behaviour during the occupation and that their government actively colluded with genocide was a necessary statement of a truth previously thought unmentionable in French cinema.

To conclude this discussion, we need to return to feature films and consider the noticeable effects created by Ophuls' documentary on films produced from the 1970s. As was suggested earlier, the heroic mode has been supplanted by more questioning approaches, ranging from the mildly satirical to the more burlesque; in some cases, the large budget enjoyed by certain films can lead to a painstaking historical reconstruction of surface detail, even a sort of wallowing in nostalgia, which effectively overwhelms any sort of critical element. Chronological generalisations about such trends are rather dangerous; for instance, it is probably true that *Le Chagrin et la pitié* put paid to the unduly reverential approach found in most films which predate it, but nonetheless it is possible to cite films made in the 1950s that are far more challenging than others made in the 1990s. Claude Berri's watered-down adaptation of Marcel Aymé's debunking satire *Uranus* has already been cited; this expensive production compares very unfavourably with Claude Autant-Lara's adaptation of another story by Aymé, *La Traversée de Paris*, released thirty-four years earlier in 1956, which is both much livelier in its comic moments and more virulent in its derision (the black market is shown to be rather more popular than the resistance and most of the population to be envious poltroons and losers). Similarly, Berri's adaptation of Lucie Aubrac's self-glorifying memoirs makes resistance into a violent spectacle of good confronting evil (the heroine is played by a perfectly coiffured supermodel). Leaving aside the fact that Berri carefully ignores all the doubts cast on the Aubracs' exact role in the arrest of Jean Moulin, simply as a dramatic adventure about a miraculous escape, *Lucie Aubrac* again compares unfavourably with another film released in 1956, Robert Bresson's *Un condamné à mort s'est échappé* (also based on the memoirs of a celebrated resister, Andre Devigny), a brilliant illustration of how to do far more with much less. No doubt few if any commercial film makers could be expected to match Bresson's sublime minimalism.

Rather than end by enumerating further brief references to contrasting films and trends, it is preferable to look in more detail at two important films dealing with resistance and with collaboration, particularly as there is no clear critical consensus about their intentions and success. Like *Le Chagrin et la pitié*, Jean-Pierre Melville's *L'Armée des ombres* was made in 1969 (though it was released immediately in the same year). It derives from a novel proselytising on behalf of the resistance, published in 1943 by Joseph Kessel, who had joined the Free French the previous year. While Kessel's novel, as we have seen, can be read as an upbeat attempt at patriotic propaganda, the film is a more sombre celebration of the heroism and sacrifice of a small resistance network. In tone, it alternates between documentary reconstruction and the stylised menace and violence of the thriller. The main characters are played by Lino Ventura, Paul Meurisse and Simone Signoret, all of whom were familiar to French spectators from appearances in *films noirs* (a genre in which Melville himself was an accomplished practitioner). Thus the opening sequences show the detention of the main character Gerbier in a Vichy-run concentration camp and skilfully suggest the grim world of oppression and deprivation which its inmates inhabit. Having later escaped from detention in German headquarters, Gerbier journeys with his chief Luc Jardie to London where they encounter Colonel Passy (played by himself), and Jardie is decorated by de Gaulle (played by a convincing double).

The most memorable episodes of the film do indeed deal with miraculous escapes from situations of extreme peril: while detained by the Germans, Gerbier stabs a guard and flees across city streets until he takes refuge with a barber, who offers him a coat to disguise his appearance. (Somewhat ironically, the barber who shows the modest but courageous solidarity of the average French citizen with resistance activists is played by Serge Reggiani, better known in previous films for his roles as a treacherous turncoat.) Later, the group rescues another member detained in hospital by posing as a medical team, and liberates Gerbier once again as he is about to be gunned down by a firing squad. But for all the melodramatic excitement engendered by such scenes, the group is shown to be highly expendable. They are forced to assassinate two members who have been turned by the Germans, while another takes cyanide, and the rest are executed or die under torture. While Kessel left most of the main characters alive in the novel (since killing them off in a book published in 1943 was hardly much incentive to potential recruits for the resistance), Melville's film ends with a tragic affirmation that all its heroes have died for their cause in the bleakest circumstances.

Despite the considerable gap between book and film, it is often seen as a conventional and belated celebration of resistance glories which were increasingly under threat. Hence Jean-Pierre Jeancolas's conclusion that this is 'the last film from the Gaullist establishment' (1975: 57), 'Gaullist' here referring as much to the president of the Fifth Republic as the eventual leader of the provisional government in Algiers; the General had of course retired a few months before the film appeared and died in 1970. Intellectuals and critics did not recall his authoritarian ways with fondness in the years following his disappearance, and tended to apply equally harsh judgements to his epigones. Perhaps this is why René Prédal, recalling the general jingoism and particular toadying towards Chaban-Delmas to be found in Clément's *Paris brûle-t-il?* (1966), goes on to dismiss its successor *L'Armée des ombres* as compiling:

All the commonplaces of the genre: Germans parading down the Champs-Élysées in the opening scene, the harsh necessity [for resisters] to behave like assassins as ruthless as the Nazis themselves in order to save the network, and the little man of no importance amid his books and records who soon turns out to be the great leader of the resistance. (1972: 278)

This list could in fact be extended, in that the film deliberately sets out to be a wide-ranging chronicle of resistance centred on the activities of one particular network. But revisiting familiar themes does not necessarily mean automatically lapsing into clichés. Whether one reacts with hostility or sympathy to what is certainly a celebration of resistance also depends as much on one's ideological stance as the film's inherent merits. Prédal underestimates the troubling ambiguities of *L'Armée des ombres*, whose image of a 'gangsterised resistance' offers 'reflections on legalities, the law, official and subversive power, the military and the State', as well as the suicidal 'codes of honour and loyalty' of resisters whose 'only end is death', as Margaret Atack remarks in a more sympathetic appraisal (in Peitsch et al., 1999: 164–5, 171). Thirty years on, Melville has the advantage of having attained quasi-classic status. Moreover, the discredit thrown on such films in the 1970s by their association with Gaullism has long gone; the *soixante-huitard* mentality which usually inspires such animosity has itself long since passed out of favour.

It is certainly true that the mood of sombre and solemn celebration which characterises *L'Armée des ombres* was out of phase with an age which had heard enough about past glories. The most popular films in the 1960s and 1970s about the occupation were neither sober reconstructions of heroic sacrifice nor scathing deconstructions of establishment mystifications but farcical comedies, such as Gérard Oury's *La Grande Vadrouille* (1966), which reportedly drew seventeen million spectators into French cinemas to watch the combined antics of Bourvil, Louis de Funès and Terry-Thomas as an imbecilic Anglo-French trio who outwit their even more imbecilic German adversaries in an odyssey across France. A few years later, Robert Lamoureux's *Mais où est donc passée la 7e compagnie?* was the first of three more movies to make light work and heavy-footed comedy of the defeat and its consequences. While audiences clearly revelled in these distractions, critics usually deplore them, seeing them as evasive and dishonest. As Sylvie Lindeperg remarks, 'A zest of irreverence added to two fingers of sycophancy, a trace of audacity to a good dose of conformity: this was the recipe for these new cocktails served up to the younger generation' (1997: 364). One may accept that such films have no didactic or historical intentions worth criticising, but their humour is so laboured and puerile that they barely survive viewing even as purely frivolous entertainments.

To my mind, one of the better examples of the comic genre is Jean-Marie Poiré's *Papy fait de la Résistance* (1983), not simply because its gags are less desperately feeble but more particularly because it clearly sets out to parody the stereotypes and clichés of many of its predecessors. Thus the invincible, masked hero known as 'Super-résistant', who leaps into action in the fashion of Batman or Zorro, clad in the opera cloak and top hat associated with the more Gallic outlaw figure of Arsène Lupin, in order to rescue hostages from execution or to kidnap a Reich Marshal who is supposedly Hitler's half-brother, turns out to be a camp hairdresser posing as a collaborator. Such a farcical amalgamation offers us a very interesting encapsulation of how the resistance has been mediated in a more sceptical age by films and television. This ironic self-reflexivity is well illustrated by the end of the film, for instance, when the protagonists (or rather their supposed real-life equivalents, played by the same actors), assemble for a raucous studio debate in which they denounce both the film's burlesque exaggerations and the self-aggrandising claims of their rivals.

Louis Malle's *Lacombe Lucien* (1974) and its successor *Au revoir les enfants* (1987) eschew such frivolities and now count as the best feature films to deal with collaboration and anti-Semitism since *Le Chagrin et la pitié* brought these painful subjects back into the forum of topics available to the cinema. Like Ophuls, Malle became the target of some harsh criticism when *Lacombe Lucien* first appeared. The resistance heroine Lucie Aubrac saw no difference between Malle's sensitive account of a youthful collaborator and his relationship with a Jewish girl and Liliana Cavani's excruciating *Portier de nuit*, which came out at the same time and recounts the sado-masochistic bonding of an SS guard and a seductive inmate in his concentration camp: Mme Aubrac called for the withdrawal of both films.[19] Other critics accused Malle of inaugurating a trend that was not pornographic but rather a denial of historical choices, the so-called 'mode rétro', which was defined trenchantly by Michel Foucault in *Cahiers du cinéma* as a 'snobbish fetishism for antique effects (clothes and décor) and derision towards history' (see Bonitzer 1974a: 5).[20] It is perfectly true that *Lacombe Lucien* meticulously recreates the look and physical world of 1940s France (which includes the use of popular music on the soundtrack), and undoubtedly owes much of its nostalgic charm to such naturalistic authenticity. Unlike Claude Berri, however, Malle goes beyond the pleasure of surface details, or rather invests such details with more than superficial interest. Lucien's acquisition of a suit, for instance, marks his promotion from rustic hospital porter to pistol-toting Gestapo agent; to a modern audience, however, the supposedly fashionable *pantalon-golf* which he sports as part of this accoutrement suggests that he remains a misfit and outsider. Foucault notes that the film does show the mass appeal of fascism, how it offers power and the fulfilment of desire to its smallest minions. But the director 'treats his hero like a simpleton' (Bonitzer 1974a: 13), explaining away fascism on psychological grounds.

Such at least is the complaint made by another contributor to the debate in *Cahiers du cinéma*, Pascal Bonitzer, who takes the scene where Lucien gags a prisoner with a piece of plaster on which he then daubs a false mouth as exemplary of the film's equivocal urge to 'disguise meaning', to 'Strip of meaning all commitment, or at least to conflate Nazism, collaboration and resistance...as showing the imbecility of any historical choice' (Bonitzer 1974b: 44, 46).[21] He also objects to the presence of a Black in the Gestapo gang as an obfuscation of racial or racist issues. For all the neo-Marxist rhetoric in which this hostile interpretation is garbed, it now seems curiously conservative, in that what really shocks such commentators is Malle's attempt to show his hero's motivation sympathetically, as comprehensible and perhaps unavoidable. The director himself observed that he saw Lacombe as illustrating the 'banality of evil'; in other words, the character is ordinary rather than monstrous. Nonetheless, he still commits himself to a cause manifestly shown to be criminal and evil (he is an accomplice if not an active agent in torture, blackmail, denunciation and treason). He gags the resistance prisoner because he is offended by the latter's patronising manner and aggressive criticism of him as a collaborator (in a crucial earlier scene, the village schoolteacher brusquely rejects Lucien's bid to join the maquis, on the pretext that he is too immature; Lucien's first act of treachery and revenge is to gain admittance to the local Gestapo by denouncing the teacher).

An obvious point missed by Malle's detractors is that the spectator is not supposed to approve of Lucien's behaviour or see it as some sort of apology for collaborationism, simply because chance and petty spite play a large part in his engagement. Writing twenty years after the film's appearance, Sylvie Lindeperg notes Lacombe's passivity in the face of historical events. Certainly, he is not a thinking being, beyond his rather brutish urges for immediate gratification, although on a purely physical level he is extremely active (violence defines a large part of his character). She then draws a very similar message from the film:

✗ Against the conception of a just war, with sound ideological foundations, valuing commitment as a driving historical principle, Louis Malle set up a philosophy of chance, expressed by an ambivalent

morality, and supported by a deep sense of the vanity of commitment... Louis Malle and Patrick Modiano vigorously denounced all
the ideological mystifications which give a meaning to history despite its confused and disorderly nature. (1994: 119)

For all that Malle and his fellow scriptwriter Modiano suggest the arbi- ⅄
trary nature of certain key choices, specifically that between resistance
and collaboration, and their protagonist's inability to foresee the likely
consequences of making the wrong choice, it seems to me a perverse
misreading of the film to infer from this that commitment and moral
decisions are simply rejected or seen as meaningless. Admittedly, one
might be tempted to see this rather nihilistic equation of both sides in
some of Modiano's early novels (the protagonist of *La Ronde de nuit*
(1969), for instance, is simultaneously a member of the Gestapo and a
resistance network). However, the insistence on the arbitrary and alea-
tory is not an invention of provocative fiction-makers thirty years after
the event, but in fact a stock theme of much writing on the occupation, whether fictional or historical: to recall an infamous example, the
leader of the Milice, Joseph Darnand, who was executed for treason in
October 1945, might well have joined the Free French had circumstances been marginally different.

In any case, as far as *Lacombe Lucien* is concerned, for all the provocative insistence on social determinism in the depiction of the central character, Malle nonetheless adopts a fairly traditional moral
position, since right and virtue are shown to belong to the side of the
resistance throughout the film, even if the protagonist is a pawn in a
game whose rules he barely grasps. This can be demonstrated by
recalling the basic configurations of the main characters and one or
two illustrative scenes. The characters fall into three groups: most visible are the Gestapo agents and their leader Tonin based in the Hôtel-
Restaurant des Grottes; the refugee family comprising the Jewish tailor
Albert Horn, his mother and daughter, who lead a semi-clandestine,
precarious existence; and finally, much less noticeably, the resistance,
whose members do not form a coherent group but rather a rarely seen
background presence. At first sight, the role of the resistance may seem
minimal: a farmer dismisses his son as a 'feignant' for joining the
maquis, suggesting this is an activity for layabouts rather than genuine
patriots. Nevertheless, Peyssac rejects Lucien, as a result of which the
teacher is arrested and tortured (the fate of both men is effectively
sealed by Peyssac's rebuff and Lucien's subsequent drunken act of
betrayal). In a similar, dramatic scene, Lucien's mentor Jean-Bernard

de Voisins tricks a doctor by pretending to be a wounded maquisard; while the doctor is arrested, Lucien amuses himself by vandalising a model boat belonging to his son. Voisins's betrayal of human decency and Lucien's spiteful destructiveness are silently contrasted with the doctor's prosperous, happy family, and their patriotic integrity. The Gestapo may ruin the lives of those individual resistance members who fall into their hands, but historically and morally it is obvious that collaboration is a spent force. The Gestapo and Milice seem to come off worse in a skirmish with maquisards; after Lucien refuses to help the prisoner escape, the hotel is stormed by the resistance and most of the gang are killed.

Only someone of Lucien's stubborn obtuseness would chose to join the Gestapo in the final weeks of the occupation, when, as the servant Marie points out to him, it is obvious the Americans will win the war. The opening sequences of the film show Lucien washing down the floor of a hospital ward to the accompaniment of Philippe Henriot's daily propaganda broadcast on the radio; he distracts himself by killing a small bird outside the window with a catapult. This act of gratuitous violence shows the brutal, sadistic personality that seems to qualify him all too well as a trainee *gestapiste* (perhaps Peyssac's rejection is based on an accurate assessment of Lucien's character). But the cause he does join is finished: Henriot will be assassinated by the resistance within a few weeks, just as finally we learn that Lucien is executed by a 'tribunal militaire de la Résistance' in October 1944. In the Gestapo group, he finds a sort of substitute family (it includes women, children and a dog), but a family whose members and values are unpleasantly perverted (the children play and a party goes on while people are being tortured in another part of the building). Most of the agents whose characters are delineated are rejects and failures who have gained a short-lived power by serving the Germans. The leader Tonin is a former police inspector dismissed in 1936 (the parallel with the notorious Gestapo agent Inspector Bonny is obvious); Aubert a cyclist whose career came to nothing; Jean-Bernard a sacked schoolmaster and his girlfriend Betty a failed actress. Only Faure seems to be a genuinely committed fascist; Tonin refers to Marshal Pétain as 'le vieux cul' (the old bum), while Aubert and Lucien use a poster of him for target practice.

The West Indian Hippolyte is an extreme case of marginality, his presence justified by historical fact, in the director's opinion: Malle discovered that two torturers in the Bordeaux Gestapo were Martiniquais who were stranded in France after leaving the army. One might also note that Bonny's chief, the even more infamous Henri Lafont, was sent to south-west France in the final weeks of the occupation at the head of a Gestapo group consisting of two hundred north Africans.[22] The forces of collaboration were more diverse than is commonly realised. Apart from Hippolyte and Lucien, no members of the group have any qualities to attract the audience's sympathy, and even if we are persuaded to see the main character as a victim of circumstances, his brutish bullying makes him singularly unappealing. This is illustrated by his relationship with the Horns, for whom he is part menacing intruder and part inept protector: he manages to seduce the daughter, named with ironic symbolism France, after inviting her to a party at Gestapo headquarters, an unlikely place for a Jewish girl to regain social insertion. He boasts drunkenly to her father of having killed someone and offers him a stolen watch; Lucien's obtrusive presence is perhaps one reason why M. Horn surrenders himself to the Gestapo. But the only person we see Lucien kill on screen is the SS NCO who arrives to arrest France and her grandmother; Lucien's final violent act is thus to save the lives of two Jewish women, even if personal resentment against the German for confiscating the watch may be the immediate motivating factor.

It is hard to see an apologia for collaboration or denigration of the resistance in a film whose main characters are depicted with unusual sensitivity and subtlety. The director argued his aim was to present 'a reflection on the nature of evil' (quoted in French, 1993: 129) and the world of collaboration which he evokes, for all its relative complexity, is shown as decadent and perverted. The lesson implicit in *Lacombe Lucien* is actually rather uncontroversial: by joining the wrong side and denouncing his teacher, Lacombe deserves his fate, even if he is misguided and partly redeems himself. In comparison, other films which evoke collaboration in subsequent decades seem much more cynical and schematic: for example, in José Giovanni's *Mon ami le traître* (1988) and Laurent Heynemann's *Stella* (1984), minor collaborators suffer the full retribution of victors' justice, whereas their leaders change sides with impunity. Whereas Malle allows for psychological complexity and error in human behaviour, he also makes it quite clear where good and evil are to be found: his second film on the occupation, *Au revoir les enfants* (1987), a moving testimony about the deportation of Jewish school children, draws the line much more explicitly than *Lacombe Lucien* and as a result was widely acclaimed.

Some of the most interesting films about the occupation produced over the last fifteen years, on the other hand, are far more subversive, in that despite carefully reconstructing period detail and decor, they cast far more doubt on historical certainties, particularly the authenticity of resistance: betrayal and duplicity seem almost to be defining characteristics of clandestine activity. Christian de Chalonge's *Dr Petiot* (1990), for instance, takes the real case of Marcel Petiot, a doctor executed in 1946 for murdering and robbing at least thirty people during the occupation, most of them refugees who misguidedly hoped he would help them escape from Paris to the south zone. Not only did Petiot masquerade as a humanitarian resister, but eventually he stole the identity of an FFI officer and was given responsibility for hunting down collaborators after the liberation. The director makes these macabre events into a sinister black comedy, a grotesque phantasmagoria, where fictional and formal invention and historical fact blur together disturbingly. In the opening scenes, the demonic doctor, brilliantly played by Michel Serrault, enters a cinema to watch a newsreel, which reports on the notorious anti-Semitic exhibition held in Paris in September 1941. The feature which follows is a German horror film, whose monstrosities seem ridiculous in comparison with the more clinical horror dispassionately presented in the newsreel; the protagonist quits his seat in disgust but exits via the screen, passing through the horror film before reappearing in a Parisian passageway. In other words, the conventional boundary between historical outer world, cinema, and the character's hallucinatory derangement is dissolved.

In Jacques Audiard's *Un héros très discret* (1996), based on a novel by J.-F. Deniau (1991), the central character painstakingly constructs by prolonged historical research a fraudulent past for himself as an important figure in the Free French, though he spent the occupation as a travelling salesman, ignorant of the genuine resistance activities of his wife's relatives. By a combination of persistence, luck and help from a mysterious mentor, he is finally accepted as an authentic resister and promoted to a senior position in military intelligence in the French occupation zone in Germany, where he proves highly successful in tracking down Nazis and double agents. Heroes manufacture their own glory, it seems, or rather their glory depends on large part on a mixture of credibility and credulity. If fantasy is pursued with enough vigour, it can become an acceptable reality. Compared with the simplistic and dishonest commonplaces enacted by Claude Berri, such films offer a seductive originality which shows at least how the guilty memory of catastrophe continues to haunt and stimulate the imagination of French film-makers.

Conclusion

In his stimulating study *In Defence of History*, Richard J. Evans sets out
to rebut 'the postmodernist treatment of history as a form of literature', arguing for example that 'Auschwitz was not a discourse. It trivi-
alizes mass murder to see it as a text' (Evans, 2000: 244, 124). My
argument in this book has essentially been the reverse: that literary
and cultural representations of past events are a form of history. While
there is no need to cast doubt on the factual reality of past events, our
attempts in the present to recapture and interpret the traces of the past
can only be expressed in some type of partial, mediated discourse.
What is most striking about such reconstructions of events as cata-
strophic as the Second World War is not so much their triviality as
their persistence and multiplicity. As Evans himself remarks, 'Public
knowledge of the past – public memory, in other words – has always
been structured by influences other than historians, from folksong,
myth and tradition to pulp fiction, broadsheets and the popular press'
(2000: 207). Although all interpretations of the past are by definition
retrospective, this does not mean they are purely arbitrary or equally
valid: we need to distinguish the trivialising and tendentious from the
more complex and persuasive.

How then does the cultural legacy of the Second World War subsist,
and what does its enduring survival tell us? How does the French experience of the conflict differ from that of other Western nations? So
many images and representations deriving from the heroic age of war
surround us that one might conclude that national identity continues
to be in large part determined by a nostalgic and defensive dependency on the memory of former conflicts. To do so, however, risks over-
estimating the influence and importance of the entertainment
industry, which perpetuates so many of these images in debased and

endlessly recycled forms, or, for that matter, taking unduly seriously the tendentious metaphorical language used by politicians who (say) compare Saddam Hussein to Hitler, as a means of avoiding a more dispassionate and informed debate about the West's relationship with the Middle East. The fact that every week, for example, British terrestrial television stations aimed at general audiences devote several hours to programmes about World War Two, does not necessarily reveal the endurance of a national obsession but rather the economic factors that drive schedules, since such ready-made material can no doubt be broadcast much more cheaply than more original productions.

Nevertheless, such a phenomenon is worth noting if only because of its repetitive frequency, which habit and familiarity tend to make one overlook. At certain times, such as nominally Christian festivals which are effectively national holidays, the steady trickle of television pro-grammes about the war becomes a surging torrent, as if such mediated reflections formed an essential part of our collective leisure-time diet. In the week of 21 to 27 December 2002, for instance, the five British terrestrial television stations devoted no less than forty-three hours and thirty-five minutes to broadcasting programmes related to World War Two, with a peak on 24 December of fourteen hours and fifteen minutes. The great majority of these programmes comprised feature films and documentaries produced between the 1940s and 1970s: from such classic films as *Mrs Miniver* (1942), *Casablanca* (1942), *The Caine Mutiny* (1954) and *The Great Escape* (1963), to the excellent documen-tary series *The World at War*, originally produced for Thames Television in the late 1970s and shown on BBC2. Much of this material is of good quality, particularly when judged by the impoverished standards of present-day television: in such films we generally discover high pro-duction values and compelling star performances, linked to dramatic-ally plausible narratives and a patriotic ethic, as well as a laudable effort to couple entertainment with a didactic urge to inform younger generations. That such concepts of quality and cultural transmission are tacitly being abandoned by most broadcasters, or themselves per-ceived as outmoded, historical phenomena, is suggested by the fact that only one of the programmes shown during this week had actually been recently produced for British television: this was a homely docu-mentary called *Christmas under Fire*, lasting ninety minutes, narrated by Alan Bennett and shown on BBC2.

Such exercises in cut-price nostalgia clearly do serve a positive pur-pose of informing, even if the information given tends to perpetuate a simplified, legendary image of triumphant, heroic sacrifice (witness titles such as *Britain's War Heroes*, on Douglas Bader, *Glenn Miller's Last Flight, They Were Expendable, Gladiators of World War Two*). The perspective adopted is exclusively British and American, when not purely Hollywood's. It rarely seeks to disturb what may seem a somewhat complacent consensus about Anglo-American virtue and valour. This may explain why French television draws far less on such material, for it is linguistically, culturally and historically alien to the French experience of defeat, occupation and eventual renewal. Not that French television fails to produce more appropriate models for its own public, which again generally prefer to recycle very similar material and eschew controversy. Thus the two main television channels France 2 and TF1 recently found themselves in competition to finish production of drama-documentaries about Jean Moulin, with Yves Boisset's somewhat pious and wooden version being shown on France 2 in July 2002, six months before TF1 finally broadcast Pierre Aknine's *Jean Moulin, une affaire française*. While both films include episodes about Moulin's love affairs of dubious relevance to his resistance activities (such banal diversions are intended no doubt to personalise the drama but actually dilute its effect), the second film comes closer to controversy by suggesting that Pierre de Bénouville, René Hardy's superior in Combat, knew that Hardy had been turned by the Gestapo before the Caluire meeting and was thus complicit in Moulin's arrest and death. Both Jacques Baumel and Daniel Cordier appeared on a rival channel in January 2003 to point out that no evidence exists to convict Bénouville (who died in 2001) of such an accusation (see *Le Monde télévision*, 4 and 11 January 2003, for fuller details).

Such films stimulate and respond to the public's appetite for heroic drama about the occupation and war, with sacrifice and betrayal remaining staple themes. What most obviously distinguishes the French cultural legacy, in other words, is this re-enactment of dramas of betrayal. Each generation, it seems, seeks out new (or old) culprits to carry the blame and shame of defeat and collaboration. In this instance, it is alleged that even the leaders of the resistance were prepared to sell out a troublesome competitor. The nation virtuously united in resistance has become the nation motivated by perfidious and cynical self-preservation. Yet the endless, parasitical recycling of familiar stories and familiar controversies as stereotyped narratives inevitably suffers from a law of diminishing returns, so that this hunger for vicarious excitement and historical novelty remains unsatisfied.

The same objection could be made against many of the novels which continue to be produced, even as the war recedes into the past century, by authors whose experience of the event is inevitably second-hand. Few achieve a plausible or persuasive imaginative construction, probably because most of these writers have only a very limited engagement with their subject, either emotionally or intellectually (in other words, they have neither the need to bear witness of the first-hand participant nor the dedication and insight of the seasoned researcher). To give two brief, similar examples from both sides of the Channel. Guy Walters's *The Traitor* (2002) is inspired by the handful of renegades who joined the British Free Corps (BFC) in 1943 and were incorporated into the Waffen SS the following year (and by reputable studies on this obscure group of traitors by the historian Adrian Weale). On to this interesting factual background, Walters grafts a rather ponderous espionage novel, centred on an SOE agent who is duped into joining the BFC and seeks to redeem himself by destroying the Nazis' secret weapon. The book was sold with a guarantee from Headline's marketing department that readers disappointed with this concoction of sex, violence and exchangeable loyalties could request a refund of the purchase price by writing to 'The Traitor Refund Offer' and justifying their dissatisfaction.

While *The Traitor* thus aspires to be no more than an adventure story, to be consumed or rejected as entertainment, with the reader offered commercial redress if the product fails to please, Hervé Bentégeat's *Un traître* (2000) is ostensibly a more subtle, reflective enterprise about a family (and by extension perhaps a nation) riven and destroyed by divided loyalties. The novel consists of an account written in April 1945 by Jean Sauveterre to his son, explaining why he is in a prison cell under sentence of death for collaboration. We discover that Sauveterre was a Parisian bookseller of Jewish origins blackmailed by a policeman into betraying a resistance agent who occasionally visited his shop, in return for not being arrested and deported with his family. The story thus reveals how an ordinary man is driven to commit treason by the forces of 'History' (or his own lack of political and social awareness). A prologue further informs us that Sauveterre's son (who had become an assassin for Mossad) was found shot dead in a Paris apartment in 1993. A letter from Sauveterre's wife to their son serves as an epilogue: she admits that she was in fact a communist resistance agent who denounced her husband on discovering the evidence of his betrayal.

This exercise in fictional self-justification carries little conviction, however, whether in terms of the individual characters or the historical background. Sauveterre and his wife are curiously insipid figures, whose behaviour is motivated in a perfunctory fashion (witness Sauveterre's belated discovery of his Jewish identity or the ultimate revelation of his wife's clandestine activities). A much more interesting novel about the dilemmas of commitment and treason is Paul Nothomb's *Le Délire logique* (1999). While the authors of *The Traitor* and *Un traître* are journalists writing from second-hand knowledge, Nothomb was a Belgian resistance agent convicted by a military court and imprisoned for treason after the war (though eventually released and rehabilitated). His fictionalised account of his experiences was originally published by Gallimard in 1948 under the pseudonym Julien Segnaire, but passed largely unnoticed. This gives his book certain obvious advantages, irrespective of the quality of his writing: notably, the authority and authenticity of the first-hand witness now addressing a late twentieth-century audience far more sympathetic to his denunciation of the evils of totalitarianism than most readers in the 1940s. Paratextual additions (prefatory biographical material, a concluding essay by the author, now aged eighty-five, and three letters from André Malraux written to support him) further authenticate the historical interest of this novel.

This additional material tells us that the author joined the Belgian Communist Party in the 1930s and fought in Spain as a navigator on a bomber (he first encountered Malraux in Madrid). He was interned in a French camp at the beginning of World War Two, along with fascist sympathisers, this proximity giving him his first experience of fascist-communist collaboration and the 'délire logique' of his title, that is the mental contortions needed to subscribe to totalitarian belief systems. Having subsequently joined the resistance, he was betrayed to the Germans by an associate, was interrogated and tortured, and finally agreed to collaborate with the SD. On 24 January 1944 he succeeded in escaping from Gestapo headquarters in Brussels (thanks to a revolver smuggled in to him by his companion Margot). He joined the Belgian Secret Army and British post-liberation army, but was denounced by the Communist Party as a traitorous renegade and sentenced to eight years' imprisonment. He also learned after the war that several communist leaders had made similar deals with the Germans, which were kept secret. Although his case seems implausible, as he notes, it was thus not entirely untypical.

Although Malraux advised him to suppress the scene in the novel which describes the experience of torture ('Why attempt to recount what cannot be shared?'; Nothomb, 1999: 174), in fact the physical and psychological damage caused by torture is central to Nothomb's account, even if it is recalled in retrospect. The fictional hero, called Hubert, was captured carrying the keys to his house, which he fears will lead the Germans to his pregnant wife:

> For hours and hours pain that was more and more intense, more and more unbearable had shaken, twisted and torn him in spasms of agony, without however crushing him into unconsciousness. And once more he saw the torture room where, suddenly, on the table, not he but his wife was spread-eagled, beseeching her torturers, as they raised their clubs, to spare her stomach... while chained up and powerless in the corner he was forced to watch. (p. 44)

Realising that the idea that prolonged torture is bearable is romantic nonsense, Hubert decides to collaborate with his interrogators by claiming he has been converted to their cause (a claim which is a further sign of his 'delirium' and deluded state, given the increasing likelihood of German defeat). He soon discovers that much of his resistance organisation is already known to the SD, thanks to the betrayals of previous informants. Hubert duly betrays key resistance leaders in return for saving hostages; these leaders themselves need little persuasion to betray further secrets. Persuaded by his wife of the folly of his collaboration, Hubert attempts to escape from prison, but is shot down by the Germans and denounced by the communist press as a Gestapo informer.

The somewhat bleak moral of this fictionalised autobiography is summed up by a doctor who observes that 'apart from a few groups with clearly defined objectives, all these people playing at resistance do more harm than good' (p. 138). The only escape possible for the hero caught in the alienating cycle of betrayal (where resistance is reductively perceived as the first step on the path to collaboration) is a suicidal act of self-sacrifice. It is no doubt unsurprising that a renegade communist should produce such a nihilistic account of resistance, seen as little more than a tool manipulated by totalitarian forces. Such a dismal, pragmatic interpretation, however, underestimates the moral and symbolic power that can be attained by resistance. As Daniel Cordier writes: 'Because the sacrifice of resisters was excessive in terms of the slender results achieved, they have joined in a justified legend all the martyrs of liberty, whose nobility is measured not by results but by sacrifices' (1999: 25).

Such a legend is of course largely a cultural product, which derives from and in some ways supersedes a real historical phenomenon. The endurance of the legend, the urge to recapture the complexity of the phenomenon, do not merely reveal a neurotic obsession with past national disasters but our need to find heroic models to guide us in an age when the threat of catastrophe is ever present. In this sense, every book or film (however modest or flawed) about the humiliating abasement of collaboration or the redemptive potential of resistance is an acknowledgement of the debt we owe to those who gave their lives in the struggle for liberty and human dignity.

Notes

Preface

1. Nancy Wood observes that Daniel Goldhagen's controversial book *Hitler's Willing Executioners* was especially criticised by historians for the fundamental flaw of resorting 'to acts of psychological projection that have no place in historiographical discourse' (Wood, 1999: 93). Such traits more characteristic of fiction are in fact found in many popular history books, such as Martin Blumenson's *The Vildé Affair* (Robert Hale, 1978).
2. Innumerable examples of less well-known figures caught between heroic and treasonable sacrifice could be cited. The future novelist Pierre Boulle, for instance, joined the Free French in Singapore in July 1941; captured by the Vichy authorities in Indochina, he was given a life sentence for treason and stripped of French nationality by a court martial in Hanoi in October 1942. After his escape from detention in late 1944, he was awarded the Légion d'honneur, Croix de Guerre and medal of the resistance. Many of the novels he subsequently wrote explore the shifting boundary between heroism and betrayal (the most famous being the source of the film *The Bridge on the River Kwai*).
3. Of the 75,500 Jews deported from France, 42,000 were deported in 1942 and 17,000 in 1943, while 80 per cent of those deported were originally arrested by the French police (see Froment, 1994, for further details on Bousquet).
4. The Vichy minister Pierre Pucheu was less successful in his attempt to transfer his allegiance from collaboration to resistance halfway through the occupation, since he was one of only four senior government figures to be executed for treason (in his case in March 1944; the others were Laval, de Brinon and Darnand, condemned after the liberation).
5. A chapter originally planned on songs has been omitted for space reasons. The material has been published elsewhere (Lloyd, 2001, 2003 – in press).

1. Understanding and representing the occupation

1. Pierre Daninos in *La Composition d'Histoire* has produced an amusing analysis of the caricatural, jingoistic simplifications of historical subjects to be found in most school textbooks across the world, and he enumerates at length the howlers produced by pupils who have been instructed by such material (thus Hitler for one German teenager was 'the first man to land on the moon', 1979: 134). He concludes rather bleakly that 'it is better to be ignorant than to be wrong' (p. 92). However, Sellar and Yeatman, despite their amusing reduction of historical study to good things, top nations and waves, do offer a more persuasive and optimistic defence of the business: 'The object of this History is to console the reader... History is not what you thought. *It is what you can remember.* All other history defeats itself.' And half a century

before Francis Fukuyama, they note: 'History is now at an end' (1930: vii–viii).

2. Thus Robert A. Rosenstone argues that 'The notion of postmodern history seems like a contradiction in terms. The heart of postmodernism, all theorists agree, is a struggle against History. With a capital *H*. A denial of its narratives, findings, and truth claims' (1995: 200).

3. Unlike historians, novelists are generally not obliged to draw on archival and documentary sources, though in practice many historical novelists do refer explicitly or implicitly to sources which lend authority and credibility to their fictions. A fascinating and at times acrimonious debate has been pursued in France about the accessibility, or rather the inaccessibility, of state archives concerning the occupation and what may, or may not, be concealed from public view. The most substantial discussion is found in Sonia Combes's book, *Archives interdites* (1994). While professional historians claim that she sometimes overstates her case (see, for example, Conan and Rousso, 1994; or Baruch, 1997), she confirms by a whole range of persuasive examples the virtual impossibility of writing properly documented history about certain shameful episodes, such as French collaboration with the Gestapo, apart from reminding us that the amnesty laws of the early 1950s make it legally difficult even to name collaborators in print. Fiction attempts to fill such gaps by imaginative insight and speculation.

4. Popular genres however often contain a strong didactic element; in other words, they offer more than simple entertainment, however confused or misleading their message may be in some cases. If, for instance, one looks at a sample of French comic books dealing with World War Two, one finds pedagogic propaganda is often a prime concern. Thus Philippe Chapelle's *Armée secrète* (1997) is a somewhat pious, but informative, pseudo-documentary, offering 'a moving lesson in courage and fraternity', as Lucie Aubrac puts it in her preface. Similarly, Marie-Laureche Boucheron's *Lo* [sic] *Grand Guingouin* (1984) suffers from information overload, turning its protagonist into an heroic cipher. Alain Bouton et al. in *Vercors: le combat des résistants* (1994) omit all reference to the strategic failings behind the disaster or to the role of French auxiliaries on the German side, but at least offer a more readable, visually appealing narrative by centring their account on a fictional maquisard, uncontaminated by controversy and platitudes.

5. For a debunking account, see Gitta Sereny, *Albert Speer: His Battle with Truth* (Picador, 1996). Guitry and Jamet were briefly imprisoned for collaborationist activities after the liberation, though never formally charged and convicted, and wrote indignant memoirs protesting their good intentions. Heller was an SS officer responsible for censoring book publications in occupied Paris who was on close terms with many collaborationist intellectuals; he casts himself in the role of liberal-minded francophile in his memoirs, published after many of those who might have contradicted him had died.

6. The novelist G.M. Fraser amusingly contrasts his own recollections of the campaign in Burma with the austere and ordered account given in the official history of his unit in his book *Quartered Safe Out Here* (Harvill, 1992).

7. As far as Great Britain is concerned, Calder suggests that 'The greatest single fact suppressed by the Myth of the Blitz is this: in 1940, because Churchill refused to give in, world power passed decisively away from Britain to the USA' (1991: 52).

8. See Tudor (1972).

9. In fact, the French National Assembly officially recognised in January 2001 the genocide of over one million Armenians perpetrated by the Turks in 1915 (unlike the US Congress which remains reluctant to offend Turkey).

10. Cf. François Bédarida's contrast of history and memory: 'Whereas history is situated outside events and generates a critical approach from without, memory is placed within events, working back as it were in them, inside the subject. Memory makes itself contemporaneous with what it seeks to transmit, whereas history maintains a distance' (1993: 7). Prefacing the English translation of Pierre Nora's celebrated multi-volume collective study, *Les Lieux de mémoire*, L.D. Kritzmann similarly glosses memory as the 'variety of forms through which cultural communities imagine themselves in diverse representational modes', as opposed to history 'regarded as an intellectual practice more deeply rooted in the evidence derived from the study of empirical reality' (in Nora, 1996: ix). He further notes that memory can be contradictory and divisive rather than universalist. Given that anyone studying the occupation of France and its consequences is effectively obliged to account for the changing history of memories of the period, it seems to me more appropriate to include memory and myth within the process of historical enquiry, along with all the imaginary cultural productions which are their vehicles.

11. Davies praises the attempts of Major Denis Hills to save Ukrainians from the Waffen SS Galicia Division from repatriation to the USSR. Most were allowed to settle in the UK in 1947, although it is now clearly established that the division had engaged in systematic atrocities against civilians in Poland and the Ukraine (a point reiterated most recently by a documentary film broadcast on ITV in January 2001). Regarding the British officers and officials who did not oppose repatriation, Professor Davies concludes sententiously: 'the moral principle is unequivocal. If "obeying orders" could be no defence for Adolf Eichmann, it can be no defence for Allied officers' (1996: 1047). For further discussion of such moral issues, see later in this chapter.

12. See Henry Rousso, *Le Syndrome de Vichy de 1944 à nos jours*. Rousso defines the syndrome as the multitude of symptoms in French political, social and cultural life which reveal the deep-seated national trauma caused by the occupation, a trauma whose damaging effects continued to appear long after the initial divisions and disruption caused by defeat in 1940 (1990: 18–19).

13. Gisèle Sapiro's monumental *La Guerre des écrivains 1940–1953* (1999) does not conform to this generalisation about the narrowness of material sampled, since it is a quantitative study of 185 French writers who were active in 1940. Her interest lies however not in their writing and texts, whether perceived as historically informative or aesthetically innovative, but rather in the sociological status of the writer and related professional groups and associations, following Bourdieu's exploration of the ideo-

logical and economic factors which determine power and influence within the 'literary field'.

14. This figure is a rough estimate, deriving mainly from published bibliographies and the selective card index established by the BDIC (Bibliothèque de documentation internationale contemporaine) of several hundred works of fiction and autobiography about the occupation published in the post-war period. Henri Michel's *Bibliographie critique de la Résistance* (1964) lists 500 books categorised as memoirs. By way of comparison, Michael Paris in his bibliographical study of *The Novels of World War Two* (1990) lists over 2000 novels published in English (including translations) between 1939 and 1988.

15. Michael Burleigh (2001: 5, 17) notes the absence of a moral dimension from much 'modern historical writing, with its social science notions of freedom from value judgements, as if morality is related to moralising, rather than intrinsic to the human condition and philosophical reflection about it'. The Second World War demonstrates the brutal clash of two equally immoral totalitarian systems: 'Both Communism, the systemisation of bourgeois guilt or self-loathing and working-class resentment cloaked in universal benignity, and fascism or Nazism, the solipsistic, quasi-tribal veneration of one race or nation, shared this antipathy towards the world of civility, decency, prudence, law and order, and explicitly glorified violence.'

16. The same objection applies to Norman Davies's bizarre equation of allied officers with Eichmann, quoted above (note 11): minor complicity in acts whose consequences were unpredictable is hardly comparable to being a major agent of genocide, especially if the supposed 'victims' may themselves be war criminals.

17. Hence Alan Bullock's observation that Hitler's 'most original achievement was to create a movement which was deliberately designed to highlight by every manipulative device – symbols, language, ritual, hierarchy, parades, rallies culminating in the Führer myth – the supremacy of the dynamic, irrational factors in politics: struggle, will, force, the sinking of individual identity in the collective emotions of the group, sacrifice, discipline' (1993: 237–8).

18. As A. Postel-Vinany and J. Prévotat note in 'La Déportation' (in Azéma and Bédarida, 1993: 445).

19. For a fuller discussion, see Robert Zaretsky's chapter òn Todorov in Fishman et al. (2000).

20. 'Denouncing the weaknesses of a man during the Vichy regime makes me appear like a valiant fighter for memory and justice, without exposing me to any danger or obliging me to accept any responsibility for present-day suffering' (Todorov, 1995: 54).

21. Literally, 'white terror, pink library, black market'. The 'white terror' refers to counter-revolutionary reprisals exacted by royalists in southern France in 1795–96 and 1815, while the 'bibliothèque rose' is a series of edifying books for children.

22. Foreigners who refer to French national guilt about the occupation run the risk of lapsing into a facile francophobia. There is in any case an equally persistent obsession with the Second World War in Britain, which reflects a

different sort of defensiveness: harking back to former glories and moral righteousness (often to compensate for present failures and appeasements); the revisionist version insists on the ingloriousness and moral ambiguities of the war.

23. These figures are probably overestimates. Most historians suggest that at most 90,000 people were actually convicted of crimes related to collaboration by post-liberation courts in France.

24. Beevor and Cooper cannot resist noting, in their informative study of post-war France, that 'The very appearance of the squat Laval, with his toad-like features, decaying teeth and greasy hair, made hatred easy' (1995: 8), perhaps forgetting that in an age not yet dominated by mass media and the facile equation of healthy good looks and virtue, it was still possible for government leaders like Laval, Churchill and Roosevelt to be ugly chain-smokers, drunkards or even confined to a wheelchair. A congress of French psychiatrists held in 1947 addressed the topic of the psychopathology of treason, noting for instance that 'les rapports de la trahison avec l'homosexualité sont fort intéressants' (Daumézon, 1948: 286), but concluding that submission and dominance were more appropriate criteria than sexual attraction. Philip Watts has noted in his recent study of the post-war trials of French intellectuals, *Allegories of the Purge* (1998), that sexual deviation was often used by their adversaries as an abusive synonym for political betrayal. Roger Casement, whose conviction for treason in 1916 was discussed above, lost many supporters campaigning for a reprieve when private diaries recounting his promiscuous homosexual exploits were leaked. Forensic tests have recently shown the diaries to be genuine (see for example the *Guardian*, 13 March 2002).

25. From June 1942, control of German police services in France passed from the Wehrmacht to the SS, or more specifically the RHSA (Reich Security Head Office), which had seven sections in Paris. Section IV, the Gestapo (Secret State Police) was specifically responsible for repressing resistance and recruiting French auxiliaries. This role was also undertaken by the Abwehr (German military counter-intelligence), which was subsumed into the RHSA in 1944. The term Gestapo tends to be applied loosely to all branches of the German security police and their associates. The Vichy government itself controlled at least fifteen different police organisations. For a fuller discussion, see the lengthy section on the RHSA in Guérin (2000: 1245ff).

26. Famous examples include high-ranking resistance figures like Jacques Soustelle and Georges Bidault, who were both opposed to Algerian independence and supported the last-ditch terrorist campaign mounted by the Organisation Armée Secrète, whose members deliberately echoed the rhetoric of resistance.

27. The case against Sartre, Malraux and Simone de Beauvoir is made with particular virulence by Gilbert Joseph (1991).

28. In a fascinating article on 'Les Musées de la Résistance', for example, Marie-Hélène Joly notes that most of the sixty museums in France are really places of worship rather than historical understanding, their exhibits being displayed like religious relics (in Boursier, 1997).

29. See A. Guérin's exhaustive *Chronique de la Résistance* (2000) for an extensive list of over 300 officially accredited networks and movements. The post-

war struggle for acknowledgement by resistance movements is illustrated by the case of François Mitterrand's Mouvement national des prisonniers de guerre et des déportés, which achieved official recognition as an 'unité combattante de la Résistance' as late as May 1992 (eleven years after Mitterrand's election as president and after previous refusals). Legend has it that when Mitterrand offered the services of this POWs' movement to de Gaulle on their first encounter in Algiers in December 1943, the General sarcastically suggested that a movement of hairdressers might be as useful, thereby inspiring the enmity which was to divide the two future presidents for the rest of their careers.

30. Gilles Vergnon remarks in 'L'Évolution des représentations du maquis du Vercors' (in Boursier, 1997) that the Vercors remains the most famous symbol of the heroism, martyrdom and betrayal of resistance fighters; over thirty books have been written about it, including six novels.

31. It is generally accepted that the punishments of collaborators inflicted by courts tended to be most severe in cases where small-scale personal responsibility was clearly demonstrable (for example, journalists writing propaganda, low-ranking *miliciens* who had pursued resisters) and sometimes absurdly lenient in cases where industrialists or administrators in senior positions were able to shift blame on to subordinates or claim compensatory acts of resistance. See Rioux (1980, 57–9) for more details.

32. The European Court of Human Rights ruled in July 2002 that Papon was entitled to appeal against his ten-year prison sentence for complicity in crimes against humanity, overturning the refusal by the French Court of Cassation to allow his appeal. He was released two months later, pending this appeal.

2.   Leaders and the people

1. Some historians claim to avoid judgements altogether. Thus Marc Ferro prefaces his biography of Pétain with the dictum: 'The historian must conserve, explain, analyse and diagnose. He must never judge' (1987: vii). Similarly, Richard Griffiths, prefacing a re-edition of his earlier book *Marshal Pétain*, maintains that 'It is not the duty of historian or biographer to accuse or to justify, but to describe and to attempt to explain' (1994: xii). While tendentious polemics and denunciations may not serve the cause of historical enquiry, surely its ultimate purpose is precisely to arrive at balanced judgements of the achievements and responsibilities of individuals and institutions located within an acceptable ethical framework. In practice, both of these admirable accounts of Pétain constantly pass judgement on their subject, whether implicitly or explicitly: Griffiths, for instance, sums up Pétain as 'a symbol rather than a man' within a few pages of his initial caveat (p. xvi), and Ferro encapsulates the failings of the Marshal and his regime as 'impotence and glory' (p. 726).

2. For more 'bottom-up' accounts of warfare as legitimised violence, see Joanna Bourke, *An Intimate History of Killing* (Granta Books, 2000) and John Keegan, *The Face of Battle* (Penguin, 1978).

3. The pitfalls of this genre are well illustrated by Hervé Le Boterf's *La Vie parisienne sous l'occupation* (1997), an exhaustive and informative chronicle of cultural activities which is largely devoid of any linking, analytical commentary.

4. 'The chain running from suppliers to purchasing bureaux, via endless intermediaries, was continuous and by definition binding. They all took part (admittedly with varying degrees of cynicism and awareness) in the same gigantic operation of pillaging the country during the occupation, an operation which could not have succeeded as much as it did without the venality of industrialists, the zeal of their intermediaries, the organisational skill of the Germans who were really behind running the purchasing bureaux, and the lack of scruples of their French accomplices. All of them took part in the German war effort, albeit indirectly' (de Rochebrune and Hazera, 1997: I, 326).

5. For a more succinct recent comparison, see also Christopher Flood, 'Pétain and de Gaulle: Making the Meanings of the Occupation', in Holman and Kelly (2000).

6. It is interesting to note in passing how Pétain's defenders are invariably forced to argue from such a weak, negative position that there was always someone worse than the Marshal: other First World War generals were more callous in wasting lives, other collaborators were more fanatically pro-German or anti-Semitic, other academicians were even more intellectually dishonest and self-serving.

7. In an interesting article in *The Spectator* (21 October 2000), entitled 'A True Ghost Story', D.J. Taylor suggests that as many as half of the books by celebrities which feature in the UK bestseller lists have actually been written by other people.

8. Prefacing an edition of Pétain's speeches, Antoine Prost writes that 'the Marshal's political persona was constructed and presented with the utmost vigilance and attention' (Pétain, 1989: 10), while his biographer Marc Ferro adds that 'In Vichy, Pétain's speeches were the object of a cult, of an obsessive adoration: his speech-writers scrutinised them, two or three at a time, as though watching over the cradle of a new-born child' (1987: xii).

9. Christopher Flood elaborates these notions interestingly: 'In the course of their speeches both Pétain and de Gaulle used the assumption of narratorial omniscience to represent France's situation in terms which presupposed a form of ideological essentialism, a characteristic feature of political myth-making. That is to say, each assumed he knew the fundamental nature, the trans-historical essence, of the French nation ... Each of the two men told a story of decline and fall, a story of betrayal, a story of salvation through struggle and sacrifice, a story of national rebirth, and a story of the redemptive leader who guides the nation towards unity in renewal' (in Holman and Kelly, 2000: 109–10).

10. Pétain's jealous preservation of his moustache as a heroic trademark is shown by an anecdote from the Great War reported by Tournoux. Confronted by a junior officer sporting an unimpressive moustache, the General allegedly remarked: 'My mother used to blow my nose if I looked like that' (1964: 61).

11. According to an IFOP poll undertaken on 16 October 1944, 58 per cent of French people were opposed to punishing Pétain, with 32 per cent in

favour and 10 per cent undecided; only 3 per cent favoured the death sentence. The return of political and racial deportees the following year hardened opinion against him, however.

12. Hence Sartre's triumphalist assertion, in 'Qu'est-ce qu'un collaborateur?', published at the time of Pétain's trial in August 1945, that 'the leader of a small maquis unit had more initiative, more prestige and more real authority than Laval ever had' (1949: 51).

13. See Benamou (1999: 135). Passy adds that the General did in fact take note of this lesson, but not very successfully: the next day at Carlton Gardens, he deigned to speak to a black soldier, who was dumbstruck with terror at this uncustomary solicitude.

14. De Gaulle (like Pétain) was a 'head of state, with no constitution, electors or capital, who spoke in the name of France' (1980: 309). Thus 'I was nothing at the beginning... But this very destitution showed me the line of action to follow. It was by espousing uncompromisingly the cause of national salvation that I would find authority... At the age of forty-nine, I was embarking on an adventure as a man whom destiny had driven from all predictable paths' (1999: 88–9).

15. Tournoux says that both de Gaulle and Giraud (whose daughter died after being deported with her family) were unwilling to bargain with the Germans for the release of their relatives in exchange for high-ranking German prisoners, thereby practising de Gaulle's principle that 'feeling cannot count when faced with reasons of state' (de Gaulle, 1980: 374).

16. A situation which invites comparison with Céline's fictionalised account in *D'un château l'autre* of the last days of the remnants of the Vichy government in the castle of Sigmaringen.

17. Blum was eventually moved to Niederdorf, and was saved when a Wehrmacht company disarmed the SS guards in April 1945. He wrote of his experience: 'I was in the hands of the Nazis. I represented for them something more than a French [politician]; I embodied in addition what they hated most in the world, since I was a democratic Socialist and a Jew. But the same reasons that made me a particularly detested adversary made me a precious hostage, since I had an exchange value, not only for the French state, but also for socialism and international democracy' (quoted by Lacouture, 1982: 458).

18. The Croix de Feu originated as an association founded in 1927 for World War One veterans decorated with the Croix de Guerre for valour under fire (there were over a million holders of this medal), and became a mass political movement in the 1930s. 'Froides queues' translates less flatteringly as 'limp dicks'.

19. The immediate effect of the law was a significant increase in women's unemployment. By September 1942, however, labour shortages forced the government to suspend all such restrictions, a further example of the practical failure of the reactionary policies of the National Revolution. See Diamond (1999).

20. Witness Galtier-Boissière's observation, dated 8 September 1944: 'It is obvious that most of our stars are more or less compromised. In the bar at Maxim's, Sacha's trilby was the only civilian's hat amid a row of Germans' caps' (1992: 235–6).

3.   Servants of the state

1. Although Vichy's programme of social and political reforms amounted to little more than authoritarian, hypocritical moralising and its technocrats served the needs of the German war economy as much as their own country, one should however note from the outset that the regime did at least offer most of its citizens minimal levels of subsistence and security. This relative stability might be compared with occupied Greece, where the collapse of the state bureaucracy and national economy led to widespread famine, with 40,000 people dying of starvation in the first year of occupation. See Mazower (2001) for details.

2. Vichy's efforts to abolish local democracy met with varied success. The elected *conseils généraux*, numbering 30 to 50 councillors, became administrative commissions of up to nine appointees (usually the most influential members of the defunct *conseil général*). These were in turn expanded and renamed departmental councils, which convened from spring 1943. Elected mayors were likewise replaced with appointees, except in towns with fewer than 2000 inhabitants. In practice, left-wing mayors survived, provided they endorsed the regime and kept their population under control. As Robert Gildea observes, 'At the end of the day, the Vichy government was never as authoritarian as it pretended to be, both because it had to come to terms with vested interests, and because it was riddled by coruption' (2002: 132). Local notables sometimes proved a more effective 'shield' than Pétain in withstanding German demands.

3. 'Broadly understood, experts and professionals in various fields made up eighteen of the thirty-five ministers of the Vichy regime as against eleven parliamentarians, and seven of the eighteen secretaries of state as against four parliamentarians' (Paxton, 1982: 266).

4. The resistance also generated its own bureaucracy, as it grew in size and importance. Jacques Baumel, for example, became secretary general of Combat, that is 'a sort of high-ranking civil servant in the resistance, responsible for handling information for its leaders and transmitting decisions to regional cadres' (Baumel, 1999: 137). Claude Bourdet, who played a major part in the infiltration of public services, described his activities similarly, as a 'bureaucrat writing circulars and sitting on committees' (Bourdet, 1998: 118). Bourdet was arrested on 24 March 1944 and survived deportation. Since the risks run by such administrators and organisers were just as great as those faced by paramilitary combatants in resistance, they are considered in more detail in the next chapter.

5. As Arendt reminds us, much of the actual killing in the extermination centres was undertaken by commandos of other Jewish inmates acting under compulsion. Most moral or legal judgements would condemn those who imposed such appalling constraints on others rather than the perpetrators themselves. However, more controversially, she also draws attention to 'the darkest chapter of the whole dark story': the complicity of Jewish leaders in the destruction of their own people. Jewish police and administrators played an active role in arresting Jews for the Nazis. Without such connivance, Arendt estimates that perhaps 50 per cent more Jews might have survived the Holocaust (1994: 117, 125).

6. This political link was hardly a guarantee of independence; as she remarks, 'Set up shortly after the war, this committee directly linked to and appointed by the government was a strange phenomenon in the scholarly world' (Combes, 1994: 305).
7. The BCRA, SOE and other resistance agencies sometimes knowingly used Gestapo and Abwehr agents, ostensibly to catch larger prey or to dupe the Germans in a complicated game of double or triple bluff; betrayal and masquerade are an integral part of espionage.
8. For fuller details, see *Les Préfets en France* (1978) and Siwek-Pouydesseau (1969).
9. Mark Mazower remarks that Wehrmacht authorities in occupied Europe used similar euphemisms to convey a pretence of legality when in reality they used untrammelled violence to crush opposition: 'by portraying themselves as the restorers of order, they were able to justify a regime of extraordinary brutality to their own satisfaction' (2001: 160). It is worth recalling that the number of fatalities caused by police action ordered by Maurice Papon against a peaceful demonstration of Arabs in Paris on 17 October 1961 may have amounted to several hundred; this act of unprecedented brutality, committed in a western European capital city in peacetime, remained curiously absent from public consciousness until recently.
10. A legal controversy continues, however, as to whether the present-day French state should accept civil and/or legal responsibility for acts committed by Papon as a civil servant under Vichy.
11. Edmond Duméril, who worked as an interpreter in the prefecture at Nantes, offers a parallel acount of these grim events in his *Journal d'un honnête homme pendant l'occupation* (1990). He notes that the *mairie* was obliged to establish a list of 300 local hostages (on which he figured himself) from the arrival of the Germans in June 1940, even if those actually shot were habitually communists.
12. Hannah Arendt notes sceptically that many German civil servants claimed that they too remained in post to 'mitigate' Nazi excesses (1994: 128).
13. Robert Gildea shows Lecornu in a less sympathetic light by citing a letter which he composed to his superiors advising that complaints about the arrest of French Jews in his area should be raised with the Germans and not representatives of Vichy like himself (2002: 276). The same question about delayed publication applies to Pierre-Marcel Wiltzer's *Sous les feux croisés: parole de préfet*, published in 1999, the year of the author's death, more than half a century after his wartime service as a *sous-préfet* in the departments of Ain and Vienne. Wiltzer helped hide the Jewish children who took refuge in Izieu (Ain); tragically they were arrested and deported in the final weeks of the occupation.
14. Papon also recalls the perils of occupation: 'Death prowled around our administration. And everything else: deportations of Jews, and also resisters, summonses for forced labour and to the German military court, fines for traffic offences, requisitions of buildings, evacuation of children from schools during bombing...Destruction, risks, denunciations, fear, the deaths of those in our charge...' (1999: 80).
15. See for example the essay on Guéhenno contributed by his former student André Séailles to the collective volume *La Littérature française sous*

l'occupation (1989). Extracts from Guéhenno's journal were published clandestinely as *Dans la prison* by the Éditions de Minuit in 1944; this was his main contribution to the intellectual resistance.

4. Combatants

1. For example, Devillers, the courier for Combat, proved to be a Gestapo agent who had betrayed large numbers of his comrades to the French authorities. He was eventually arrested by Vichy's Service de Renseignements directed by Colonel Paillole and executed at Montluc in the summer of 1942, just before Laval sought his release.

2. It is worth quoting d'Astier's observations in full: 'I am going to say something that sounds very bad about my friends and myself: I think you could only become a resister if you were maladjusted . . . You can't imagine a true resister who was a plenipotentiary minister, a colonel or a business leader. They had succeeded in life . . . But we [*he emphasises the "we"*] were failures – I was one myself – well, we had the sort of quixotic feelings you expect from failures.' D'Astier's interview is intercut with that of Marcel Degliame-Fouché, a member of the Conseil National de la Résistance (CNR) and subsequently co-author of a major history of the resistance. He too asserts that 'People who respected order generally considered us to be extremely dangerous individuals who were likely to lay waste to France through actions which they judged to be foolhardy' (quoted in Ophuls, 1980: 143–7).

3. Quoted by Pierre Viansson-Ponté in Tuquoi (1987: 15).

4. Such events are of course what make resistance literature memorable and command our respect for its protagonists. To give one striking example: André Devigny's escape from the military prison of Montluc in Lyon inspired Robert Bresson's sublime film, *Un condamné à mort s'est échappé* (1956). Arrested in April 1943 after assassinating the Italian chief of police in Nice, Devigny was sentenced to death. Using an iron soup spoon as an improvised saw, he gradually cut through the panels and frame of his cell door to make an exit hole, and escaped from the prison using ropes made from blankets and the wires in his mattress, after strangling a sentry. Devigny writes in his own account that 'Dignity is a weapon, courage is another', and that 'The art of the prisoner is to make something from nothing' (1956: 77–8, 207). Although the film version ends with the triumphant achievement of liberty, in reality the escape had more troubling repercussions and complications. Devigny and his cellmate Gimenez (a volunteer for the LVF arrested for shooting a French policeman) were rapidly recaptured by a German patrol in a café. Devigny escaped again, but five other prisoners were shot as a reprisal, as well as the surviving German sentry, and several other people who aided Devigny were arrested. Devigny makes it clear, in other words, that resistance activists and their helpers pay a far higher price than most of their adversaries.

5. Semprun recommends Henri Alleg's book *La Question* (1958) as a first-hand account of torture. Alleg was a French journalist and member of the Algerian Communist Party detained in Algeria in June 1957 by French military authorities and subjected to violent physical abuse.

6. It is worth recalling that some former resisters sided with the European colonialists during the Algerian conflict. The name chosen by the terrorist Organisation Armée Secrète deliberately echoes the Secret Army of the wartime resistance, and attracted senior resistance figures like Jacques Soustelle and Georges Bidault, the latter entitling his memoirs *D'une résistance à l'autre* (1965). Despite their reactionary political views, some of its sympathisers had honourable motives and sacrificed a great deal in both conflicts. For example, Hélie Denoix de Saint Marc was a monarchist but joined the British-run Jade-Amicol network in the south zone, was arrested in July 1943, and deported to Buchenwald and Langenstein. As an officer in the Foreign Legion, he was involved in the abortive generals' putsch against de Gaulle's government in April 1961 and sentenced to ten years' imprisonment (he was released in December 1966) (see Benamou, 1999, for more details).

7. According to Philippe Buton, 'out of the 38 most senior military posts in the internal resistance, the communists in 1944 held 22, whether temporarily or not'. See 'La France atomisée' (in Azéma and Bédarida, 1993: 387).

8. A point vehemently contested by most resisters and their sympathisers, as H.R. Kedward notes: 'In one account after another in the *zone sud*, the ill-informed and futile Allied bombing across the South of France from June to August 1944 which resulted in hundreds of random and incomprehensible civilian deaths, is compared to the frustrated capacity of Resistance groups whose access to military targets was informed and direct' (1993: 288).

9. The term 'résistancialisme' is sometimes used to describe this (mis)appropriation of resistance. A negative interpretation, shared by many, is offered by the novelist Michel Tournier: 'In truth the resistance only became a phenomenon of national importance after the departure of the Germans. During the occupation, resistance was undertaken by a tiny minority of heroes whose courage doomed them to be massacred and whose disinterestedness would make them step aside from the rush for places after the liberation... Authentic resisters were often submerged, drowned and nauseated by the explosion of the myth of resistance after the liberation' (Tournier, 1977: 79–80).

10. An earlier low-budget adaptation of *Ils partiront dans l'ivresse* as *Boulevard des Hirondelles* was directed by Josée Yanne in 1993 and shown in French cinemas for only a few days after receiving a panning from the critics. See Langlois (1996) for details.

11. For example, she was interviewed along with a fawning Carole Bouquet by Anne Sinclair on the TV news magazine *Sept sur sept*, but admitted to *Le Figaro Magazine* (12 April 1997) that few scenes in the film corresponded to reality.

12. Moog had been an Abwehr agent and fifth-columnist in France since 1939. He was transferred to the SS security service, the SD, under Barbie and killed in a plane crash in 1944. Multon managed to escape from the Gestapo and joined the Free French army. After the war, he was arrested, convicted of treason, and executed.

13. Hardy's fiancée Lydie Bastien, whom he first met in Lyon in January 1943, may have been an Abwehr agent. Her career as a *femme fatale* has been

recounted by the investigative journalist Pierre Péan in *La Diabolique de Caluire* (1999), although he admits somewhat belatedly that the evidence against her is purely circumstantial (p. 253).

5. Writers

1. Vailland's biographer Yves Courrière (1991) has identified Rodrigue with Jacques-Francis Rolland, Caracalla with Daniel Cordier, Frédéric with Claude Dreyfus (who died in Buchenwald), and Chloé with Simone Mabille, for example.

2. Is it merely coincidence that both Kessel and Vailland call their traitresses Mathilde, or are they recalling the notorious exploits of Mathilde Carré in 1941–42 (discussed in the previous chapter)?

3. Marat's real name is François Lamballe. He derives his pseudonym from the revolutionary Jacobin politician Jean-Paul Marat, famously assassinated in his bath in 1793. The Prince de Lamballe was reputedly a descendant of Louis XIV through an illegitimate son.

4. This suicidal renunciation of individual autonomy is also the solution adopted in Jacques Laurent's novel, *Le Petit Canard* (1954), by a similar character, who does indeed join the LVF (not having the patience to discover a resistance network), in order to take revenge on his girlfriend for deceiving him with a Pole. The protagonist is not motivated by political or personal choice of a rational nature, but prefers to reject adulthood and its disappointments. Unlike *Drôle de jeu*, the passionate drama of this misguided adolescent (who shows no interest in the war or political options, but who is nonetheless executed at the liberation) is the main subject of Laurent's novel, which in turn reveals little interest in the wider issues of occupation.

5. Ironically, nowadays Pascal Jardin has himself been eclipsed by his own son Alexandre, born in 1965 and the precocious author of whimsical novels which find great favour with the French reading public, although these works have been accurately characterised by one unimpressed critic as 'bourgeois fairy tales for lady readers of *Le Figaro*'s women's magazine' (Françoise Verny, quoted in A. Fillon, *Alexandre Jardin* (Éditions du Rocher, 1993: 41)). In 1997, Alexandre Jardin published *Le Zubial* with Gallimard, a celebratory memoir of his father which pastiches the latter's mock heroic manner. There is however a brief reference to Pascal's pain and unending shame at being 'un fils de collabo', although he assures Alexandre that his grandfather had in reality undertaken 'a double commitment, to Vichy and in favour of the underground army' (p. 125).

6. Jardin's defence of Vichy is summed up in the following statement: 'At that time, there was something tragi-comic about the Hôtel du Parc, that little luxury hotel modelled on Marienbad. Courage, cowardice, ridiculousness and folly were all closely intermingled. If the collaboration practised there was indispensable to the economic survival of France, it proved however, after the event, to be intolerable in the eyes of history. However, in an occupied country, submerged by the fantastic military and police infra-

structure of the Third Reich, collaboration was reason. Resistance was hope. In any case, Vichy lost' (1989: 87).

7. Marshal Pétain notoriously used references to the earth and labours of peasants as a means of expressing the core of French identity. Thus in a speech of 25 June 1940 justifying the armistices with Germany and Italy, he stated: 'I hate the lies which have done you so much harm. But the earth never lies. The earth is your salvation, your very motherland. A field left uncultivated is a piece of France dying. A fallow field resown is a piece of France reborn' (Pétain, 1989: 66).

8. Marcel Aymé's well-known collection of stories *Le Passe-Muraille*, published in 1943, which combines observation of the hardships of occupation with allegorical and fantastic inventions, seems a still more immediate influence on Barjavel than Wells. For an earlier possible source of inspiration, see also André Rigaud, *L'Étrange Voyage de Teddy Hubbarth* (Albin Michel, 1926).

9. Barjavel's debt to Wells not only for certain concepts but also for specific descriptive passages in 'Le voyage entomologique' is worth spelling out. His source was clearly *The First Men in the Moon*: specifically chapter 23, entitled 'The natural history of the Selenites', which contains for instance a description of the physiological specialisation of bodily organs virtually identical to Barjavel's.

6. Films

1. There is also a documentary film about the treatment of the occupation in French cinema, *Cinéma de l'ombre*, made by P. Beuchot and J.-P. Bertin-Maghit in 1984, which offers an interesting selection of film clips and a few interviews with directors, but is sadly lacking in historical background and critical analysis.

2. Given the difficulty there is in obtaining many of these feature films, it is worth noting that Jacques Siclier provides a useful brief descriptive analysis of all of them in his book *La France de Pétain et son cinéma* (1990).

3. *Le Corbeau* was remade in the USA as *The Thirteenth Letter*, directed by Otto Preminger (1950).

4. Certain films of a more elevating nature were sometimes hailed by the resistance as embodying authentic patriotic values, such as Jean Grémillon's *Le Ciel est à vous* (1943), although as René Chateau notes (1995: 356), its producer Raoul Ploquin was an 'out-and-out *pétainiste*' and its star Charles Vanel was awarded the Francisque by Pétain. And François Garçon (in Ferro, 1984) discerns a 'fascist temptation' in a small number of films which celebrate heroic leaders, though the evidence adduced is not very convincing.

5. See Halimi (1983) for a large selection of examples; regrettably, the author leaves his sources unclear.

6. For a full account, see Courtade (1991).

7. Clouzot's case was dealt with by a Comité de libération du cinéma français (CLCF) committee on 17 October 1944, the main charge being his employment by Continental and supposed Nazi sympathies. 'Clouzot replies that

he is struck by the social side of national socialism because he is above all else anti-capitalist, and sees in it a possible solution to the struggle against capitalism.' The committee concluded: 'The general view that emerges is that Clouzot was a key employee of Continental and very much the firm's man; he carefully defended their interests and it is difficult to see how a man who did not harbour pro-German feelings could have continued to enjoy such close and intimate relations with a woman like Mlle Delair, who displayed her own feelings so clearly and ostentatiously' (quoted from J.-P. Bertin-Maghit, '1945, l'épuration du cinéma français: mythe ou réalité', in Ferro, 1984: 137). The singer and actress Suzy Delair was Clouzot's girlfriend and starred in *L'Assassin habite au 21*; she also joined the group of French actors who notoriously made a self-promoting visit to Berlin in March 1942.

8. By all accounts, Greven had no scruples about blackmailing his collaborators. Pierre Fresnay, the star of *Le Corbeau*, similarly claimed in his memoirs, co-written with F. Possot, that his work for Continental had been part of a 'deal' in return for which film stock was released to other French producers (1975: 73). Bertrand Tavernier's recent film *Laissez-passer* (2001) offers an interesting, semi-fictionalised account of film-making during the occupation and Greven's manipulative intrigues.

9. The sluttish Denise first appears in *Le Corbeau* smoking in bed and painting her toenails, signs of depravity that are more likely to amuse than shock modern audiences. However, Ginette Leclerc was typecast in such roles and suffered the misfortune of being confused in real life with her acting persona. For instance, the historian Pierre Darmon (1997: 346) refers casually to the actresses Ginette Leclerc and Mary Marquet as 'collaboratrices charnelles', without adducing a shred of evidence for this libel. Ginette Leclerc claimed in her memoirs (1963) that she paid the price for her association with the actor Lucien Gallas, with whom she ran a Parisian cabaret; Gallas was not detained, though she was only 'an unremunerated partner' in the business (p. 193). Mary Marquet was a stage actress at the Comédie-Française, whose son François was deported and died in Buchenwald (according to one account, which unsurprisingly she omits, she herself had denounced him). She recounts her arrest in August 1944 and subsequent two months' imprisonment in *Cellule 209* (1949). Both these actresses are much less well known than Arletty, who was also arrested in August 1944 for three months and banned from performing for three years, after associating much more ostentatiously with Colonel Serring, an officer in the Luftwaffe.

10. The CLCF examined about 1000 dossiers and inflicted minor sanctions in 50 per cent of cases, often in an arbitrary fashion. Many members of the purging committees could themselves have been accused of collaboration (see Chateau, 1995, and Darmon, 1997, for details).

11. Henri Jeanson's acerbic wit is illustrated by his later remark about the rather convoluted spy thriller *Les Espions*, which Clouzot made in 1957: 'Clouzot a fait Kafka dans sa culotte' (quoted by Bocquet and Godin, 1993: 113).

12. The 'archives scénaristiques' of *Le Corbeau* held in the Bibliothèque du film reveal that the characters' relationships went through various mutations: at

an initial stage, Laura alone was guilty and was also Vorzet's daughter, while Dr Monatte (Germain) was married to Denise.

13. Quotations from the film refer to the transcript published in *L'Avant-scène cinéma*, 186 (1977).

14. Marcel Ophuls illustrates this point about uncontrollable technical failure when recalling the first showing of *Le Chagrin et la pitié* at the Studio Saint-Séverin in April 1971: 'As usual, and as was to be expected, the "wide screen" beloved by cinema managers cut off the skulls, necks and chins of my unfortunate "talking heads", while half the sub-titles disappeared without trace from the bottom of this arbitrarily stretched out rectangle' (Ophuls, 1980: 12).

15. Bryan Haworth notes that 'Eisenstein's *October* has appeared many times, uncredited, as apparently authentic footage of the 1917 revolution, and the history of "faked" newsreel is as old as the cinema itself'. See 'Film in the Classroom', in Smith (1976: 162). Marcel Ophuls makes the same point about most documentaries on the resistance (1980: 209).

16. References to the film and its critics are to the version printed in *L'Avant-scène cinéma*, 127–8 (1972), unless otherwise indicated.

17. Hence Margaret Atack's observation that the film 'is generally seen as settling accounts, not with the Resistance, but with the Gaullist myth of the Resistance. The distinction is very important, because the film is undoubtedly pro-Resistance. That the notion of France as a nation of collaborators might stem from this film is an extraordinary misreading, no doubt sometimes a wilful one, but more often, I suspect, one which reveals a generational divide in its reception.' '*L'Armée des ombres* and *Le Chagrin et la pitié*: Reconfigurations of Law, Legalities and the State in Post-1968 France' (in Peitsch et al., 1999: 167).

18. Namely: inconsistencies and self-contradiction; slips of the tongue; betrayal by facial expression; betrayal by body language; ironic montage; contradiction between testimony and newsreels; or between newsreels and historical facts as perceived nowadays; in Ophuls' questioning; in the *mise en scène* of the interview. Hence his observation that Ophuls' main technique is 'to distort the distortions of the witnesses through the art of cinema' (Colombat, 1993: 57).

19. Interview with Lucie Aubrac in *Cinéma de l'ombre* (1984).

20. Jacques Siclier offers an overlapping definition of the 'courant rétro', which again he sees *Lacombe Lucien* as initiating: 'Ideological choices are due to chance, the war and occupation years are painted in the colours of modern uncertainties: there are no longer innocent and guilty people, but characters who arouse dubious curiosity, whatever camp they belong to' (1990: 252).

21. Lynn A. Higgins offers an alternative interpretation of the resister's taped mouth 'as emblematic of the censorship still in place in 1974 with regard to representations of the Occupation'. *New Novel, New Wave, New Politics* (London and Lincoln, University of Nebraska Press, 1996), p. 189.

22. For further details on the Brigade nord-africaine and the French Gestapo, see Aziz (1970). Aziz estimates that as many as 32,000 French agents were working for the German security services (SD and Abwehr) in 1943–44, although his source for this is unclear. In fact, this aspect of collaboration

has not received a great deal of attention from historians. Critics of *Lacombe Lucien* often confuse membership of the 'police allemande' with membership of the Milice (a paramilitary organisation run by Vichy), thereby revealing that they are considerably less well informed about the period than Malle and Modiano.

Bibliography and Filmography

Unless otherwise indicated, works in English are published in London and works in French in Paris.

Primary sources (novels, journals, memoirs)

Amiot, Y. (1984), *La Onzième Heure*, Corti
Andreu, P. (1977), *Le Rouge et le Blanc 1928–44*, La Table Ronde
Aubrac, L. (1995), *Ils partiront dans l'ivresse*, Seuil (trans. as *Outwitting the Gestapo* (1993), by K. Bieber and B. Wing, intro. M. Collins Weitz, Lincoln and London, University of Nebraska Press)
Aubrac, L. (1997), *Cette exigeante liberté*, Entretiens avec Corinne Bouchoux, L'Archipel
Aubrac, R. (1996), *Où la mémoire s'attarde*, Éditions Odile Jacob
Augiéras, F. (1980), *Une adolescence au temps du Maréchal et de multiples aventures*, Fata Morgana/Plein Chant
Aymé, M. (1946), *Le Trou de la serrure*, Éditions du Palimugre
Aymé, M. (1950), *Le Vin de Paris*, Gallimard
Aymé, M. (1958), *Le Passe-Muraille*, Le Livre de poche
Aymé, M. (1972a), *Le Chemin des écoliers*, Gallimard, Folio
Aymé, M. (1972b), *Uranus*, Gallimard, Folio
Ballyot, G.-J. (1992), *Un flic dans la tourmente*, Saint-Brieuc, Les Presses Bretonnes
Barjavel, R. (1995), *Romans extraordinaires*, Omnibus
Barjavel, R. (1996a), *Journal d'un homme simple*, Maxi-Livres/Profrance
Barjavel, R. (1996b), *Ravage*, ed. Y. Ansel, Gallimard, Folio
Barjavel, R. (1996c), *Le Voyageur imprudent*, Gallimard, Folio
Baumel, J. (1999), *Résister*, Albin Michel
Bénouville, G. de (1983), *Le Sacrifice du matin*, Laffont
Bentégeat, H. (2000), *Un traître*, Anne Carrière
Bood, M. (1974), *Les Années doubles: journal d'une lycéenne*, Laffont
Boulle, P. (1996), *Romans héroïques*, Omnibus
Bourdet, C. (1998), *L'Aventure incertaine*, Éditions du Félin
Carré, L. (1975), *On m'appelait la chatte*, Albin Michel
Carré, M.-L. (1959), *J'ai été 'La Chatte'*, Morgan
Le Chagrin et la pitié (1972), *L'Avant-scène cinéma*, 127–8
Chaix, M. (1985), *Les Lauriers du lac de Constance*, Seuil
Chavance, L. and H.-G. Clouzot (1948), *Le Corbeau*, La Nouvelle Édition
Clouzot, H.-G. (1949), *Manon 49*, Bibliothèque France Soir
Le Corbeau (1977), *L'Avant-scène cinéma*, 186
Curtis, J.-L. (1947), *Les Forêts de la nuit*, Le Livre de poche
Daeninckx, D. (1997), *Meurtres pour mémoire*, Gallimard, Folio
Daeninckx, D. (1998), *La Mort n'oublie personne*, Gallimard, Folio
Deniau, J.-F. (1991), *Un héros très discret*, Pocket

Devigny, A. (1956), *Un condamné à mort s'est échappé*, Gallimard

Devigny, A. (1978), *Je fus ce condamné*, Presses de la Cité

Duméril, E. (1990), *Journal d'un honnête homme pendant l'occupation*, ed. J. Borgeon, Thonon-les-Bains, L'Albaraon

Du Moulin de Labarthète, H. (1946), *Le Temps des illusions: souvenirs juillet 1940 – avril 1942*, Geneva, Éditions du cheval ailé

Dutourd, J. (1989), *Au bon beurre*, Gallimard, Folio

La France Nouvelle: chansons de la Résistance (1945), Éditions Salabert

Frenay, H. (1976), *The Night Will End*, trans. D. Hofstadter, Abelard

Fresnay, P. and F. Possot (1975), *Pierre Fresnay*, La Table ronde

Galtier-Boissière, J. (1992), *Journal 1940–1950*, Quai Voltaire

Gaulle, C. de (1973), *Le fil de l'épée*, Le Livre de Poche

Gaulle, C. de (1980), *Memoires de guerre*, vol. 2, *L'Unité*, Pocket

Gaulle, C. de (1999), *Memoires de Guerre*, vol. 1, *L'Appel*, Pocket

Gaultier, L. (1991), *Siegfried et le Berrichon: parcours d'un collabo*, Perrin

Giovanni, J. (1988), *Mon ami le traître*, Gallimard, Folio

Giovanni, J. (2002), *Mes grandes gueules: mémoires*, Fayard

Groult, B. and F. Groult (1974), *Journal à quatre mains*, Gallimard, Folio

Guéhenno, J. (1973), *Journal des années noires*, Gallimard, Folio

Guingouin, G. (1974), *Quatre ans de lutte sur le sol limousin*, Hachette

Guingouin, G. and G. Monédaire (1982), *Georges Guingouin: premier maquisard de France*, Limoges, Éditions Souny-Ponty

Guitry, S. (1947), *Quatre ans d'occupations*, Éditions de l'Élan

Hardy, R. (1951), *Le Livre de la colère*, Laffont

Hardy, R. (1952), 'La Troisième Nuit', *Les Œuvres libres*, June, 109–30

Hardy, R. (1971), *Amère victoire*, Geneva, Éditions de Crémille

Hardy, R. (1984), *Derniers mots*, Fayard

Heller, G. (1981), *Un Allemand à Paris*, Seuil

Jamet, C. (1947), *Fifi roi*, Éditions de l'Élan

Jardin, P. (1978), *Le Nain jaune*, Julliard

Jardin, P. (1980), *La Bête à bon Dieu*, Le Livre de poche

Jardin, P. (1989), *La Guerre à neuf ans*, Grasset

Jardin, P. (1995), *Guerre après guerre*, Grasset

Jeury, M. (1999), *Le Printemps viendra du ciel*, Pocket

Jeux interdits (1962), *L'Avant-scène cinéma*, 15

Kessel, J. (1972), *L'Armée des ombres*, Presses Pocket

La Mazière, C. de (1972), *Le Rêveur casqué*, Laffont

Laurent, J. (1985), *Le Petit Canard*, Grasset

Leclerc, G. (1963), *Ma vie privée*, La Table ronde

Lecornu, B. (1997), *Un préfet sous l'occupation allemande*, France-Empire

Malle, L. and P. Modiano (1974), *Lacombe Lucien scénario*, Gallimard

Marijac (1978), *Souvenirs de Marijac*, Grenoble, Éditions Jacques Glénat

Marquet, M. (1949), *Cellule 209*, Fayard

Merle, R. (1972), *Week-end à Zuydcoote*, Gallimard, Folio

Modiano, P. (1991), *La Ronde de nuit*, Gallimard, Folio

Nimier, R. (1967), *Les Épées*, Le Livre de poche

Nothomb, P. (1999), *Le Délire logique*, Phébus

Ophuls, M. (1975), *The Sorrow and the Pity*, trans. M. Johnson, Paladin

Ophuls, M. (1980), *Le Chagrin et la pitié*, Alain Moreau

Pannequin, R. (2000), *Ami si tu tombes*, Babel
Papon, M. (1988), *Les Chevaux du pouvoir*, Plon
Papon, M. (1999), *La Vérité n'intéressait personne*, entretiens avec Michel Bergès, François-Xavier de Guibert
Perrault, G. (1995), *Les Jardins de l'Observatoire*, Fayard
Perrin, J.-P. (1999), *Chiens et louves*, Gallimard, Série noire
Pétain, P. (1949), *Quatre ans au pouvoir*, La Couronne littéraire
Pétain, P. (1974), *Actes et écrits*, Flammarion
Pétain, P. (1989), *Discours aux Français*, ed. J.-C. Barbas, Albin Michel
Rémy, J. (1958), *La Chatte*, Éditions de Paris
Reynaud, P. (1997), *Carnets de captivité 1941–45*, Fayard
Roger-Ferdinand (1944), *Les J3 ou la nouvelle école*, Librairie théâtrale
Saint-Exupéry, A. de (1957), *Pilote de guerre*, Le Livre de poche
Saint-Loup (1965), *Les Hérétiques*, Presses de la Cité
Semprun, J. (1989), *Le Grand Voyage*, Gallimard, Folio
Semprun, J. (1996), *L'Écriture ou la vie*, Gallimard, Folio
Sledge, E. (1990), *With the Old Breed*, New York, OUP
Tournier, M. (1978), *Le Roi des aulnes*, Gallimard, Folio
Trouillé, P. (1964), *Journal d'un préfet pendant l'Occupation*, Gallimard
Vailland, R. (1953), *Expérience du drame*, Corrêa
Vailland, R. (1968a), *Drôle de jeu*, Le Livre de poche
Vailand, R. (1968b), *Écrits intimes*, Gallimard
Vailland, R. (1973), *Bon pied bon œil*, Le Livre de poche
Vailland, R. (1976), *Un jeune homme seul*, Le Livre de poche
Vercors (1951), *Le Silence de la mer et autres récits*, Le Livre de poche
Vidal-Naquet, P. (1995), *Mémoires I: la brisure et l'attente 1930–1956*, Seuil
Walters, G. (2002), *The Traitor*, Headline
Werth, L. (1992), *Déposition: journal 1940–44*, Viviane Hamy

Secondary sources

Amouroux, H. (1982), *La Vie des Français sous l'Occupation*, France Loisirs
Andrault, J.-M. and J.-P. Bertin-Maghit (1982), 'La Seconde Guerre Mondiale à travers neuf films', *Revue du cinéma*, 378, December, 72–99
Arendt, H. (1994), *Eichmann in Jerusalem: a Report on the Banality of Evil*, Penguin
Aron, Raymond (1990), *Memoirs: Fifty Years of Political Reflection*, trans. G. Holoch, New York/London, Holmes and Meier
Aron, Robert (1967), *Histoire de l'épuration*, vol. 1, Fayard
Aron, Robert (1977), *Histoire des années 40*, vol. 10: *Histoire de l'épuration. Le Monde de la presse, des arts et des lettres*, Tallandier
Assouline, P. (1988), *Une éminence grise: Jean Jardin (1904–1976)*, Gallimard, Folio
Assouline, P. (1990), *1944–1945: l'épuration des intellectuels*, Brussels, Éditions Complexe
Atack, M. (1989), *Literature and the French Resistance: Cultural Politics and Narrative Forms, 1940–1950*, Manchester, Manchester University Press
Atkin, N. (1998), *Pétain*, Longman
Aubusson de Cavarlay, B. et al. (1993), 'La Justice pénale en France: résultats statistiques 1934–54', *Cahiers de l'IHTP*, 23, April

Austin, R. (1990), 'The Conservative Right and the Far Right in France: the Search for Power, 1934–44', in M. Blinkhorn, ed., *Fascists and Conservatives*, Unwin Hyman, 176–99

Azéma, J.-P. (1979), *De Munich à la Libération 1938–1944*, Seuil

Azéma, J.-P., ed. (2000), *Jean Moulin face à l'Histoire*, Flammarion

Azéma, J.-P. and F. Bédarida, eds (1992), *Le Régime de Vichy et les Français*, Fayard

Azéma, J.-P. and F. Bédarida, eds (1993), *La France des années noires*, 2 vols, Seuil

Aziz, P. (1970), *Tu trahiras sans vergogne: histoire de deux 'collabos' Bonny et Lafont*, Fayard

Bardèche, M. (1948), *Nuremberg ou la terre promise*, Les Sept Couleurs

Barrot, O. (1979), *L'Écran français 1943–1953: histoire d'un journal et d'une époque*, Les Éditeurs français réunis

Baruch, M.-O (1997), *Servir l'État français*, Fayard

Baudot, M. (1960), *L'Opinion publique sous l'Occupation*, PUF

Bazin, A. (1975), *Le Cinéma de l'occupation et de la résistance*, 10/18, UGE

Bédarida, F. (1993), 'La Mémoire contre l'histoire', *Esprit*, (July), 7–13

Beevor, A. and A. Cooper (1995), *Paris after the Liberation 1944–1949*, Penguin

Bellanger, C. et al. (1975), *Histoire générale de la presse française*, vol. 4: *De 1940 à 1950*, PUF

Benamou, G.-M. (1999), *C'était un temps déraisonnable: les premiers résistants racontent*, Laffont

Benfredj, C. (1990), *L'Affaire Jean Moulin*, Albin Michel

Benjamin, R. (1941), *Le Maréchal et son peuple*, Plon

Bertin, C. (1993), *Femmes sous l'Occupation*, Stock

Bertin-Maghit, J.-P. (1986), 'Bataille du rail', *Revue d'histoire moderne et contemporaine*, April–June, 280–300

Bertin-Maghit, J.-P. (1989), *Le Cinéma sous l'Occupation*, Olivier Orban

Bidault, G. (1965), *D'une résistance à l'autre*, Les Presses du Siècle

Bieber, K. R. (1954), *L'Allemagne vue par les écrivains de la Résistance française*, Genève, Droz/Lille, Giard

Bloch, M. (1957), *L'Étrange Défaite*, Armand Colin

Bloch-Lainé, F. and C. Gruson (1996), *Hauts Fonctionnaires sous l'Occupation*, Odile Jacob

Boal, D. (1993), *Journaux intimes sous l'Occupation*, Armand Colin

Bocquet, J.-L. and M. Godin (1993), *Henri-Georges Clouzot cinéaste*, La Sirène

Bonitzer, P. (1974a), 'Anti-Retro', *Cahiers du cinéma*, 251–52, July–August, 5–36

Bonitzer, P. (1974b), 'Histoire de sparadrap (*Lacombe Lucien*)', *Cahiers du cinéma*, 250, May, 42–7

Booker, C. (1997), *A Looking-Glass Tragedy*, Duckworth

Boucheron, M.-L. (1984), *Lo Grand Guingouin*, Limoges, Éditions Lucien Souny

Boulanger, G. (1994), *Maurice Papon: un technocrate français dans la collaboration*, Seuil

Boulanger, G. (1997), *Papon: un intrus dans la République*, Seuil

Boursier, J.-Y. (1992), *La Guerre des partisans dans le Sud-Ouest de la France*, L'Harmattan

Boursier, J.-Y., ed. (1997), *Résistants et Résistance*, L'Harmattan

Bouton, A. (1994), *Le Vercors*, Bayard Éditions/Okapi

Bullock, A. (1993), *Hitler and Stalin: Parallel Lives*, Fontana Press

Burleigh, M. (2001), *The Third Reich: a New History*, Pan Books

Burrin, P. (1995), *La France à l'heure allemande*, Seuil

Calder, A. (1991), *The Myth of the Blitz*, Jonathan Cape

Calvocoressi, P. and G. Wint (1979), *Total War: Causes and Courses of the Second World War*, Penguin

Cassels, A. (1975), *Fascism*, Arlington Heights, Harlan Davidson

Catalogue des périodiques clandestins 1939–45 (1954), Bibliothèque Nationale

Cathelin, J. and G. Gray (1972), *Crimes et trafics de la Gestapo française*, 2 vols, Historama

Chateau, R. (1995), *Le Cinéma français sous l'Occupation 1940–1944*, Éditions René Chateau et la Mémoire du cinéma français

Chauvy, G. (1997), *Aubrac Lyon 1943*, Albin Michel

Chirat, R. (1983), *Le Cinéma français des années de guerre*, Hatier

Chollet, J.-J. (1997), *Georgius l'amuseur public no 1*, Christian Pirot

Colombat, A. P. (1993), *The Holocaust in French Film*, Metuchen and London, Scarecrow Press

Combats (Journal de la Milice) (1943–44), 8 May–10 August

Combes, S. (1994), *Archives interdites: les peurs françaises face à l'histoire contemporaine*, Albin Michel

Conan, E. (1993), 'Dossier Jean Moulin', *L'Express*, 27 May, 23–34

Conan, E. and H. Rousso (1994), *Vichy: un passé qui ne passe pas*, Fayard

Cordier, D. (1989–93), *Jean Moulin: l'inconnu du Panthéon*, 3 vols, Lattès

Cordier, D. (1999), *Jean Moulin: la République des catacombes*, Gallimard

Courrière, Y. (1991), *Roger Vailland*, Plon

Courtade, F. (1991), 'La Continental' in H. Hurst and H. Gassen, eds, *Tendres ennemis: cent ans de cinéma entre la France et l'Allemagne*, L'Harmattan, 216–30

Cru, J. N. (1967), *Du témoignage*, Pauvert

Daniel, J. (1972), *Guerre et cinéma*, Armand Colin

Daninos, P. (1979), *La Composition d'Histoire*, Julliard

Darmon, P. (1997), *Le Monde du cinéma sous l'Occupation*, Stock

Daumézon, G. (1948), 'Psychopathologie de la trahison', *Congrès des médecins et neurologistes de France*, Masson

Davies, N. (1996), *Europe: a History*, Oxford, Oxford University Press

Defrasne, J. (1982), *Histoire de la collaboration*, PUF

Delarue, J. (1968), *Trafics et crimes sous l'Occupation*, Fayard

Delperrié de Bayac, J. (1994), *Histoire de la Milice 1918–1945*, Fayard

Delporte, C. (1993), *Les Crayons de la propagande*, CNRS Éditions

Diamond, H. (1999), *Women and the Second World War in France*, Longman

Djilas, M. (1977), *Wartime*, trans. M. B. Petrovich, Secker and Warburg

Dompnier, N. (1996), *Vichy à travers chants*, Nathan

Drake, H. and J. Gaffney (1996), *The Language of Leadership in Contemporary France*, Aldershot, Dartmouth

Dransart, S. (1994), 'La Chanson de variété en France sous l'Occupation (1941–43)', mémoire de maîtrise, Université Paris I

Dreyfus, F.-G. (1996), *Histoire de la Résistance*, Éditions de Fallois

Durand, Y. (1972), *Vichy 1940–1944*, Bordas

Durand, Y. (2001), *La France dans la deuxième guerre mondiale*, 3rd edn, Armand Colin

Eck, H., ed. (1985), *La Guerre des ondes*, Paris, Armand Colin/Lausanne, Payot

Edinger, L. J., ed. (1967), *Political Leadership in Industrialized Societies*, New York, Wiley

Ehrlich, E. (1985), *Cinema of Paradox: French Film-Making under the German Occupation*, New York, Columbia University Press

Ellis, J. (1982), *The Sharp End of War*, Corgi

Esprit (1994), 'Que reste-t-il de la Résistance?', special edition, January

Evans, R. J. (2000), *In Defence of History*, Granta Books

Evleth, D. (1991), *France under the German Occupation 1940–1944: an Annotated Bibliography*, Greenwood Press

Faligot, R. and R. Kauffer (1989), *Les Résistants*, Fayard

Farcy, J.-C. and H. Rousso (1993), 'Justice, répression et persécution en France', *Les Cahiers de l'IHTP*, 24, June

Farwagi, A. (1967), *René Clément*, Seghers

Faulkner, C. (1992), 'Theory and Practice of Film Reviewing in France in the 1930s', *French Cultural Studies*, 3, 8, 133–55

Ferro, M., ed. (1984), *Film et histoire*, Éditions de l'École des hautes études en sciences sociales

Ferro, M. (1985), *L'Histoire sous surveillance*, Calmann-Lévy

Ferro, M. (1987), *Pétain*, Fayard

Fishman, S. F. et al., eds (2000), *France at War: Vichy and the Historians*, Oxford/ New York, Berg

Flory, C. (1989), *Touvier m'a avoué*, Éditions Michel Lafon

Footit, H. and J. Simmonds (1988), *France 1943–1945*, Leicester, Leicester University Press

Fouché, P. (1987), *L'Édition française sous l'occupation*, 2 vols, Bibliothèque de littérature française de l'Université Paris 7

French, P. (1993), *Conversations avec Louis Malle*, trans. M. Leroy-Battistelli, Denoël

Fresco, N. (1989), 'Parcours du ressentiment: pseudo-histoire et théorie sur mesure dans le "révisionnisme" français', *History and Theory*, 28, 173–97

Friedlander, S., ed. (1992), *Probing the Limits of Representation: Nazism and the Final Solution*, Cambridge, MA and London, Harvard University Press

Froment, P. (1994), *René Bousquet*, Stock

Fussell, P. (1979), *The Great War and Modern Memory*, Oxford University Press

Fussell, P. (1989), *Wartime: Understanding and Behaviour in the Second World War*, New York, Oxford University Press

Garcin, J. (1980), 'Dernière rencontre avec Pascal Jardin', *Les Nouvelles littéraires*, 7–21 August, 52

Garcin, J. (1995), 'Le Vieil Homme et la mort', *L'Express*, 8 June, 63

Garçon, F. (1984), *De Blum à Pétain: cinéma et société française (1936–1944)*, Les Éditions du Cerf

Garçon, M. (1950), *Plaidoyer pour René Hardy*, Fayard

Gervereau, L. and D. Peschanski (1990), *La Propagande sous Vichy*, BDIC

Gildea, R. (1997), *France since 1945*, Oxford University Press

Gildea, R. (2002), *Marianne in Chains*, Macmillan

Giolitto, P. (1999), *Volontaires français sous l'uniforme allemand*, Perrin

Girardet, R. (1990), *Mythes et mythologies politiques*, Seuil

Gofman, P. (1994), *Jean Dutourd*, Éditions du Rocher

Gorrara, C. (1997), 'Writing and Memory: the Occupation and the Construction of the Self in 1980s French literature', *Modern and Contemporary France*, 5, 1, 35–45

Gorrara, G. (1998), *Women's Representations of the Occupation*, Basingstoke, Macmillan Press – now Palgrave Macmillan

Gough, H. and J. Horne, eds (1994), *De Gaulle and Twentieth-Century France*, Edward Arnold

Grenier, R. (1948), *Le Rôle d'accusé*, Gallimard

Griffiths, R. (1994), *Marshal Pétain*, Constable

Guérin, A. (2000), *Chronique de la Résistance*, Omnibus

Guilleminault, G., ed. (1967), *Les Années difficiles*, Le Livre de poche

Guilleminault, G., ed. (1970a), *La France de Vincent Auriol*, Le Livre de poche

Guilleminault, G., ed. (1970b), *Les Lendemains qui ne chantaient pas*, Le Livre de poche

Guillois, A. and M. Guillois (1969), *Le Rire en guerre 1939–45*, Éditions de la pensée moderne

Guillon, J.-M. and P. Laborie, eds (1995), *Mémoire et Histoire: la Résistance*, Toulouse, Éditions Privat

Halimi, A. (1976), *Chantons sous l'Occupation*, Olivier Orban

Halimi, A. (1983), *La Délation sous l'Occupation*, Éditions Alain Moreau

Halls, W. D. (1981), *The Youth of Vichy France*, Oxford, Clarendon Press

Harris, F. J. (1983), *Encounters with Darkness: French and German Writers on World War II*, New York/Oxford, Oxford University Press

Hastings, M. (1983), *Das Reich*, Pan Books

Hastings, M. (1993), *Overlord*, Papermac

Hayward, S. (1993), *French National Cinema*, Routledge

Hirschfeld, G. and P. Marsh, eds (1989), *Collaboration in France: Politics and Culture during the Nazi Occupation 1940–1944*, Oxford, Berg

Holman, V. and D. Kelly, eds (2000), *France at War in the Twentieth Century*, New York/Oxford, Berghahn

Horne, A. (1990), *To Lose a Battle: France 1940*, Macmillan

Hyde, H. Montgomery (1964), *Famous Trials 9: Roger Casement*, Penguin

Irvine, W. D. (1991), 'Fascism in France and the Strange Case of the Croix de Feu', *Journal of Modern History*, 63, 271–95

Jackson, J. (2001), *France: the Dark Years 1940–1944*, Oxford University Press

Jaffré, Y.-F. (1953), *Les Derniers Propos de Pierre Laval*, Éditions André Bonne

Jaffré, Y.-F. (1962), *Les Tribunaux d'exception 1940–62*, Nouvelles Éditions Latines

Jankowski, P. (1991), 'In Defense of Fiction: Resistance, Collaboration, and *Lacombe Lucien*', *Journal of Modern History*, 63, 457–82

Jeancolas, J.-P. (1975), 'Fonction du témoignage (les années 1939–1945 dans le cinéma de l'après-guerre)', *Positif*, 170, June, 45–60

Joseph, G. (1991), *Une si douce Occupation: Simone de Beauvoir et Jean-Paul Sartre 1940–1944*, Albin Michel

Kedward, H. R. (1978), *Resistance in Vichy France*, Oxford University Press

Kedward, H. R. (1985), *Occupied France: Collaboration and Resistance 1940–1944*, Blackwell

Kedward, H. R. (1993), *In Search of the Maquis*, Oxford, Clarendon Press

Kedward, H. R. and R. Austin, eds (1985), *Vichy France and the Resistance: Culture and Ideology*, Croom Helm

Kedward, H. R. and N. Wood, eds (1995), *The Liberation of France: Image and Event*, Berg

Keegan, J. (1997), *The Battle for History: Re-Fighting World War II*, Pimlico

Kohut, K. (1982–84), *Literatur der Resistance und Kollaboration in Frankreich*, 3 vols, Wiesbaden, Athenaion/Tübingen, Gunter Narr Verlag

Koreman, M. (1997), 'The Collaborator's Penance: the local purge, 1944–5', *Contemporary European History*, 6, 2, 177–92

Kramer, R. (1995), *Flames in the Field: the Story of Four SOE Agents in Occupied France*, Michael Joseph

Kupferman, F. (1988), *Laval*, Flammarion

Laborie, P. (1990), *L'Opinion française sous Vichy*, Seuil

Lacassin, F. and R. Bellour (1964), *Le Procès Clouzot*, Le Terrain vague

Lacouture, J. (1982), *Léon Blum*, trans. G. Holoch, New York/London, Holmes and Meier

Lacouture, J. (1990), *De Gaulle: the Rebel 1890–1944*, trans. P. O'Brian, Collins Harvill

Lagrou, P. (2000), *The Legacy of Nazi Occupation*, Cambridge, Cambridge University Press

Langlois, S. (1996), 'La Résistance dans le cinéma français de fiction (1944–1994)', PhD thesis, University of McGill, Montreal

La Martinière, J. de (1989), *Les NN: le décret et la procédure Nacht und Nebel*, 2nd edn, Fédération nationale des déportés et internés résistants et patriotes

Le Boterf, H. (1997), *La Vie parisienne sous l'Occupation*, Éditions France-Empire

Lécureur, M. (1985), *La Comédie humaine de Marcel Aymé*, Lyon, La Manufacture

Lefébure, A. (1993), *Les Conversations secrètes des Français sous l'Occupation*, Plon

Lejeune, P. (1971), *L'Autobiographie en France*, Armand Colin

Lepape, P. (2000), 'L'Écrivain et le général', *Le Monde*, 21 April, II

Lévy-Klein, S. (1973), 'France 1940–1944: le cinéma de Vichy', *Positif*, 148, March, 51–6

Lévy-Klein, S. (1975a), 'Sur le cinéma français des années 1940–1944. I: l'organisation', *Positif*, 168, April, 21–30

Lévy-Klein, S. (1975b), 'II: les réalisations', *Positif*, 170, June, 35–44

Libération (1997), 'Les Aubrac et les historiens', 9 July

Lindenberg, D. (1990), *Les Années souterraines 1937–47*, Éditions La Découverte

Lindeperg, S. (1994), 'Les Ailes du temps: l'Histoire filmée', *L'Inactuel*, 2, 107–23

Lindeperg, S. (1997), *Les Écrans de l'ombre 1944–69*, CNRS

Littérature française sous l'Occupation, La (1989), P. U. de Reims

Lloyd, C. (1994), *Uranus/La Tête des autres*, Glasgow University, French and German Publications

Lloyd, C. (2001), 'Comic Songs in the Occupation', *Journal of European Studies*, 31, 370–93

Lloyd, C. (2003, in press), 'Divided Loyalties: Singing in the Occupation', in *Popular Music in France*, ed. S. Cannon and H. Dauncey, Aldershot, Ashgate

Lottman, H. R. (1982), *The Left Bank: Writers, Artists and Politics from the Popular Front to the Cold War*, Heinemann

Lottman, H. R. (1985), *Pétain: Hero or Traitor*, Viking

Lottman, H. R. (1986), *L'Épuration 1943–1953*, trans. B. Vierne, Fayard

Manvell, R. (1974), *Films and the Second World War*, New York, Barnes/London, Dent

Marnham, P. (2000), *The Death of Jean Moulin*, John Murray

Marrus, M.R. and R.O. Paxton (1995), *Vichy France and the Jews*, Stanford University Press

Marsh, P. (1981), 'Le Théâtre à Paris sous l'occupation allemande', *Revue d'histoire du théâtre*, 3, 197–369

Martinoir, F. de (1995), *La Littérature occupée: les années de guerre 1939–1945*, Hatier

Mazower, M. (2001), *Inside Hitler's Greece*, New Haven and London, Yale Nota Bene

Mertens, P. (1974), *L'Imprescriptibilité des crimes de guerre et contre l'humanité*, Brussels

Michel, H. (1964), *Bibliographie critique de la Résistance*, Institut pédagogique national

Michel, H. (1970), 'The Psychology of the French Resister', *Journal of Contemporary History*, 5, 159–75

Michel, H. (1972), *Histoire de la Résistance en France*, PUF

Miller, G. (1988), *Les Pousse-au-jouir du Maréchal Pétain*, Le Livre de poche

Morgan, T. (1990), *An Uncertain Hour: Lyon 1940–45*, New York, Arbor House/London, William Morrow

Morris, A. (1992), *Collaboration and Resistance Reviewed: Writers and the Mode rétro in Post-Gaullist France*, New York, Berg

Müller, D. (1993), *Discours réaliste et discours satirique: l'écriture dans les romans politiques de Marcel Aymé*, Paris, Champion/Geneva, Slatkine

Namer, G. (1987), *Mémoire et société*, Méridiens-Klincksieck

Naour, I. and M. Rajsfus (1995), *L'Humour des Français sous l'Occupation*, Le Cherche Midi

Nettelbeck, C., ed. (1987), *War and Identity: the French and the Second World War*, Methuen

Nobécourt, J. (1996), *Le Colonel de La Rocque (1885–1946)*, Fayard

Nogueira, R. (1971), *Melville on Melville*, trans. T. Milne, Secker and Warburg

Noguères, H. (1984), *La Vie quotidienne des résistants de l'armistice à la libération*, Hachette

Noguères, H. (1985), *La Vérité aura le dernier mot*, Seuil

Noguères, H. and M. Degliame-Fouche (1967–81), *Histoire de la Résistance en France*, 5 vols, Laffont

Nora, P., ed. (1996 and 1998), *Realms of Memory*, vol. 1: *Conflicts and Divisions*; vol. 2: *Symbols*, ed. L. D. Kritzmann, trans. A. Goldhammer, New York, Columbia University Press

Novick, P. (1968), *The Resistance versus Vichy: the Purge of Collaborators in Liberated France*, Chatto and Windus

Obuchowski, C. W. (1978), *Mars on Trial: War as Seen by French Writers of the Twentieth Century*, Madrid, Ediciones J. P. Turanzas

Ory, P. (1980), *Les Collaborateurs 1940–1945*, Seuil

Ousby, I. (1999), *Occupation*, Pimlico

Overy, R. (1996), *The Penguin Historical Atlas of the Third Reich*, Penguin

Paris, M. (1990), *The Novels of World War Two*, The Library Association

Paris Match (1990), 'Le Choc de 1940', May–June

Paxton, R. O. (1982), *Vichy France*, New York, Columbia

Péan, P. (1994), *Une jeunesse française: François Mitterrand 1934–1947*, Fayard

Péan, P. (1999), *La Diabolique de Caluire*, Fayard

Pearson, M. (1978), *Tears of Glory: the Betrayal of Vercors 1944*, Macmillan
Peitsch, H., C. Burdett and C. Gorrara, eds (1999), *European Memories of the Second World War*, New York/Oxford, Berghahn
Péret, B. (1986), *Le Déshonneur des poètes*, Corti
Perrault, G. and J.-P. Azéma (1987), *Paris sous l'Occupation*, Belfond
Pilard, P. (1969), *Henri-Georges Clouzot*, Seghers
Ponting, C. (1990), *1940: Myth and Reality*, Hamish Hamilton
Ponting, C. (1995), *Churchill*, Sinclair-Stevenson
Prédal, R. (1972), *La Société française (1914–1945) à travers le cinéma*, Armand Colin
Prédal, R. (1991), *Le Cinéma français depuis 1945*, Nathan
Les Préfets en France 1800–1940 (1978), Geneva, Droz/Paris, Champion
Les Procès de la radio (1947), Albin Michel
Procès René Hardy (1947 and 1950), sténographies, BDIC
Prost, A., ed. (1997), *La Résistance: une histoire sociale*, Les Éditions de l'Atelier/ Éditions Ouvrières
Proud, J. (1995), *Children and Propaganda: Fiction and Fairy Tale in Vichy France*, Oxford, Intellect
Pryce-Jones, D. (1981), *Paris in the Third Reich*, Collins
Quadruppani, S. (1981), *Les Infortunes de la vérité*, Olivier Orban
Ragache, G. (1997), *Les Enfants de la guerre*, Perrin
Ragache, G. and J.-R. Ragache (1988), *La Vie quotidienne des écrivains et des artistes sous l'Occupation 1940–1944*, Hachette
Ravanel, S. (1995), *L'Esprit de résistance*, Seuil
Revue du cinéma (1982), 'Le Cinéma français et la seconde guerre mondiale', 378, December
Rey-Herme, Y. (1978), *Mémoires de guerre: de Gaulle écrivain*, Hatier
Reynolds, S. (1990), 'The Sorrow and the Pity Revisited', *French Cultural Studies*, June, 149–59
Rigoulot, P. (1993), *Les Enfants de l'épuration*, Plon
Rioux, J.-P. (1980), *La France de la Quatrième République, I: l'ardeur et la nécessité 1944–1952*, Seuil
Rioux, J.-P., ed. (1990), *La Vie culturelle sous Vichy*, Éditions Complexe
Rochebrune, R. de and J.-C. Hazera (1997), *Les Patrons sous l'Occupation*, 2 vols, Odile Jacob
Rosenstone, R. A. (1995), *Visions of the Past: the Challenge of Film to Our Idea of History*, Cambridge, MA, Harvard University Press
Rouquet, F. (1992), 'L'Épuration administrative en France après la Libération: une analyse statistique et géographique', *Vingtième siècle*, 33, Jan–March, 106–17
Rouquet, F. (1993), *L'Épuration dans l'administration française*, CNRS Éditions
Rousso, H. (1985), 'Où en est l'histoire de la Résistance?', *Études sur la France de 1939 à nos jours*, Seuil
Rousso, H. (1990), *Le Syndrome de Vichy de 1944 à nos jours*, Seuil
Rousso, H. (1992a), *Les Années noires: vivre sous l'Occupation*, Gallimard
Rousso, H. (1992b), 'L'Épuration en France: une histoire inachevée', *Vingtième siècle*, 33, Jan–March, 78–105
Ruffin, R. (1980), *Ces chefs de maquis qui gênaient*, Presses de la Cité
Ruthven, K. K. (1976), *Myth*, Methuen

Sapiro, G. (1999), *La Guerre des écrivains 1940–1953*, Fayard

Sartre, J.-P. (1949), *Situations III*, Gallimard

Schneidermann, D. (1998), *L'Étrange Procès*, Fayard

Sédillot, R. (1985), *Histoire des marchés noirs*, Tallandier

Sellar, W. C. and R. Y. Yeatman (1930), *1066 and All That*, Methuen

Sergg, H. (1986), *Joinovici*, Le Carrousel-FN

Siclier, J. (1990), *La France de Pétain et son cinéma*, Ramsay Poche

Siwek-Pouydesseau, J. (1969), *Le Corps préfectoral sous la IIIe et la IVe République*, Armand Colin

Smith, P., ed. (1976), *The Historian and Film*, Cambridge, Cambridge University Press

Smithies, E. (1982), *Crime in Wartime: a Social History of Crime in World War Two*, Allen and Unwin,

Steel, J. (1991), *Littératures de l'ombre: récits et nouvelles de la Résistance 1940– 1944*, Presses de la Fondation nationale des sciences politiques

Stern, J. P. (1975), *Hitler: the Führer and the People*, Fontana/Collins

Sweets, J. F. (1976), *The Politics of Resistance in France 1940–1944*, Northern Illinois University Press

Taubmann, M. (1994), *L'Affaire Guingouin*, Éditions Lucien Souny

Taylor, L. (1997), 'The Black Market in Occupied Northern France 1940–44', *Contemporary European History*, 6, 2, July, 153–76

Thalmann, R. (1991), *La Mise au pas*, Fayard

Théolleyre, J.-M. (1985), *Procès d'après-guerre: Je suis partout, Hardy, Oradour...*, Éditions La Découverte/Le Monde

Thérive, A. (1951), *Essai sur les trahisons*, Calmann-Lévy

Todorov, T. (1994a), *Face à l'extrême*, Seuil

Todorov, T. (1994b), *Une tragédie française*, Seuil

Todorov, T. (1995), *Les Abus de la mémoire*, Arléa

Tournier, M. (1977), *Le Vent Paraclet*, Gallimard, Folio

Tournoux, J. R. (1964), *Pétain et de Gaulle*, Plon

Tudor, H. (1972), *Political Myth*, Pall Mall Press

Tuquoi, J.-P. (1987), *Emmanuel d'Astier*, Arléa

Vailland, E. and R. Ballet (1973), *Roger Vailland*, Seghers

Veillon, D., ed. (1984), *La Collaboration: textes et débats*, Le Livre de poche

Veillon, D. (1995), *Vivre et survivre en France 1939–1947*, Payot

Vidal-Naquet, P. (1993), *Le Trait empoisonné: réflexions sur l'affaire Jean Moulin*, Éditions La Découverte

Vincent, G. (1982), 'Le Cinéma français des années 70 regarde la guerre', *Revue du cinéma*, 378, December, 99–106

Watts, P. (1998), *Allegories of the Purge*, Stanford University Press

Weber, E. (1994), *The Hollow Years: France in the 1930s*, New York/London, W. W. Norton

West, R. (1982), *The Meaning of Treason*, Virago

Weygand, M. (1955), *En lisant les mémoires de guerre du général de Gaulle*, Flammarion

White, H. (1999), *Figural Realism*, Baltimore/London, Johns Hopkins University Press

Williams, A. (1992), *Republic of Images: a History of French Film-Making*, Boston, MA, Harvard University Press

Wiltzer, P. M., ed. (1983), *Nazi Propaganda*, Croom Helm
Wood, N. (1999), *Vectors of Memory*, Oxford/New York, Berg
Zdatny, S. (1996), 'Coiffeurs in Vichy France: artisans and the "National Revolution"', *Contemporary European History*, 5, 3, 371–99

Films

This is a highly selective list of the films found most useful in this study, indicating directors and year of release in France.

Le Corbeau, H.-G. Clouzot, 1943
La Vie de plaisir, A. Valentin, 1944
La Bataille du rail, R. Clément, 1946
Le Père tranquille, R. Clément, 1946
Les Portes de la nuit, M. Carné, 1946
Manon, H.-G. Clouzot, 1949
Le Silence de la mer, J.-P. Melville, 1949
Jeux interdits, R. Clément, 1952
Nous sommes tous des assassins, A. Cayatte, 1952
Nuit et brouillard, A. Resnais, 1956
La Traversée de Paris, C. Autant-Lara, 1956
Un condamné à mort s'est échappé, R. Bresson, 1956
Paris brûle-t-il?, R. Clément, 1966
La Grande Vadrouille, G. Oury, 1966
L'Armée des ombres, J.-P. Melville, 1969
Le Chagrin et la pitié, M. Ophuls, 1971
Lacombe Lucien, L. Malle, 1974
Mais où est donc passée la 7e compagnie?, R. Lamoureux, 1974
Chantons sous l'Occupation, A. Halimi, 1976
Monsieur Klein, J. Losey, 1977
Papy fait de la Résistance, J.-M. Poiré, 1983
Cinéma de l'ombre, P. Beuchot and J.-P. Bertin-Maghit, 1984
Shoah, C. Lanzmann, 1986
Au revoir les enfants, L. Malle, 1987
Mon ami le traître, J. Giovanni, 1988
Hôtel Terminus, M. Ophuls, 1989
Dr Petiot, C. de Chalonge, 1990
Uranus, C. Berri, 1990
Un héros très discret, J. Audiard, 1996
Lucie Aubrac, C. Berri, 1997
Laissez-passer, B. Tavernier, 2001

Index